THE ROAD TO SANTA FE

The Road

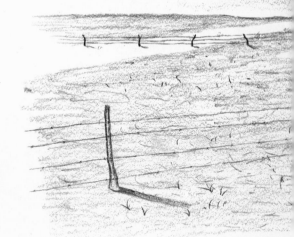

to Santa Fe

by HOBART E. STOCKING

Illustrations and Maps by the Author

HASTINGS HOUSE · PUBLISHERS

NEW YORK

To
Sarah Ward Stocking
(1864 - 1948)
whose courage and character I greatly admire
and to
Helen, Sarah and Martha
with love

Published simultaneously in Canada by
Saunders, of Toronto, Ltd., Don Mills, Ontario

ISBN: 8038-6314-4
Library of Congress Catalog Card Number: 75-150017
Printed in the United States of America

CONTENTS

Acknowledgments   *vii*

List of Maps   *viii*

List of Illustrations   *ix*

CHAPTER

     I The East End   1

    II Before and After Fort Osage   22

  III To the Rendezvous and Beyond   39

  IV Independence and Westward   56

    V Windwagons and Camels   65

  VI From the Narrows Southwest to Council Grove   72

 VII Beyond the Neosho and the Turkey Creeks   92

VIII Between the Little Arkansas and North Bend   105

  IX The Arkansas   121

    X La Jornada   139

  XI Springs Along the Cimarron   163

 XII To a Crossing on Stones   190

XIII The Mountain Branch   229

XIV The Road from Fort Leavenworth   255

 XV From Bent's Fort to the Mora   262

XVI The Road to Santa Fe   294

Chronology   354

Sources   360

Index   365

v

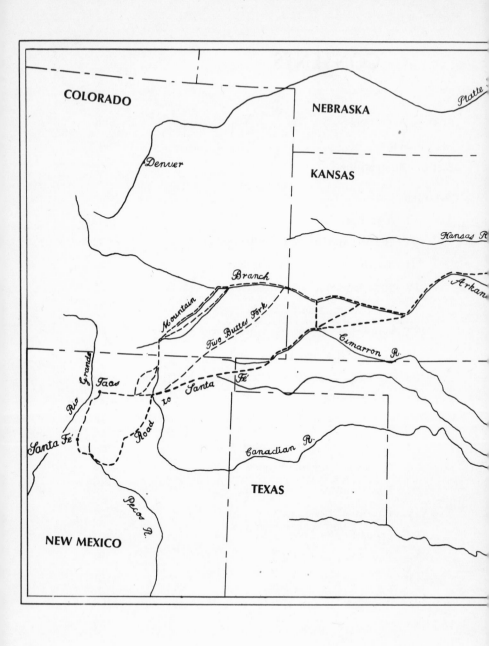

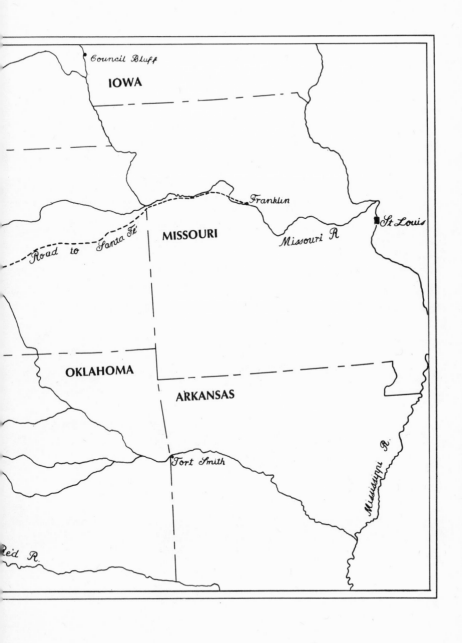

ACKNOWLEDGMENTS

THE BIBLIOGRAPHY is but a small measure of my indebtedness to others. To the several score, unnamed, in Missouri, Kansas, Oklahoma and New Mexico who courteously heard my request for information and promptly supplied it, I owe much. Without their patience I would know much less about the trace of the Road. The maps which show it were compiled from aerial photographs (frequently those of the Soil Conservation Service local offices), from land surveys and from U.S. Geological Survey Maps. My originals can be found in the National Archives.

I owe thanks to the American Museum of Natural History for permission to use much of an article concerning camels which appeared in *Natural History*.

On early surveys of land to townships, ranges and sections one may sometimes encounter the notation "Road to Santa Fe" on a curving line. The title of this book is an adaptation of that notation first used by Kate L. Gregg in a publication of the journal and diary of George C. Sibley.

To Christine Ward Schmitt whose skill in typing is exceeded only by her graciousness, I am grateful.

Most of all I am indebted to Helen Stocking for patient and painstaking work which did much to improve what was written. The faults remaining are mine.

Hobart E. Stocking

LIST OF MAPS

Map No.		Page
1	Missouri	8
2	Missouri	18
3	Missouri-Kansas	28
4	Kansas	42
5	Kansas	80
6	Kansas	84
7	Kansas	96
8	Kansas	106
9	Kansas	118
10	Kansas	127
11	Kansas	140
12	Kansas	152
13	Kansas	159
14	Colorado, Kansas, Oklahoma	170
15	Colorado, Oklahoma	178
16	New Mexico, Texas, Oklahoma	192
17	New Mexico	202
18	New Mexico	211
19	Colorado, Kansas	236
20	Colorado	244
21	Colorado	248
22	Colorado	264
23	Colorado, New Mexico	273
24	New Mexico	277
25	New Mexico	284
26	New Mexico	304
27	New Mexico	314

LIST OF ILLUSTRATIONS

Barbed-Wire Fence across Ruts of Road to Santa Fe   *title page*

	page
Ox Shoe	2
Township, Range and Numbered Sections	5
Marble Arch Gravestone of M.M. Marmeduke	14
Cannon at Fort Osage	20
Ox Cart Wheel	27
Conestoga Wagon Wheel	32
Tar Bucket	35
Conestoga Wagon	36
Ox Yoke	38
Meteor Shower	41
Oregon Sign	58
West Port Inn	60
Hi Jolly Monument, Quartz, Ariz.	70
Stage Station, One Hundred and Ten Mile Creek	76
Last Chance Store, Council Grove, Kansas	89
Mule Shoes	93
Bois de Vache	99
Diagram of Perennial and Permanent Streams	116
"Roglin '63" Inscription Carved on Pawnee Rock	124
A Cache	143
Yucca Blossoms	149
Picket Pin	164

Devil's Claw Seed Pod 166
Prickly Pear Cactus 167
Longhorn Steer Head 175
"D Willock 1849" Inscription at Cold Spring 184
"Norman Hamilton" Inscription at Cold Spring 185
Catkins of Cottonwood 187
Round Mound, New Mexico 195
Rabbit Ears Peak, New Mexico 196
New Mexican Ox Cart 197
Buffalo Skull 199
Henry Lorenzen Tombstone 213
Plan of Bent's Fort 233
Folsom Arrow Point 241
Arkansas River from Bent's New Fort 251
Los Ratones 269
Cholla Cactus 271
Cholla Wood 272
Charles Bent's Trunk 279
Inscriptions at El Morro
    Don Juan de Onate 280
    Ramon Garcia Jurado 281 top
    Simpson and Kern 281 bottom
Wagon Mound 286
Early Mexican Mining Lamp 298
Fort Union Ruins 302
Hand-Wrought Nails, Ft. Union 311
Bernal Hill, New Mexico 316
Church at San Miguel del Vado, New Mexico 319
Church at Anton Chico, New Mexico 322
Church at Pecos Village 334
Glorieta Mesa, New Mexico 338
Governor's Palace, Santa Fe, New Mexico 344
Casa Analco, Santa Fe, New Mexico 348
Metate and Mano 350
Barbed-Wire Fence across Ruts of Road to Santa Fe 352

CHAPTER I

The East End

ACROSS WESTERN MISSOURI, southwest across Kansas, the Oklahoma Panhandle and eastern New Mexico, is a line engraved in sod. Near its eastern end, runoff of a century of rainfall has erased the engraving save for short segments widely spaced. On arid plains of Kansas, Oklahoma and New Mexico the engraving—a line ten or so feet wide—is a shallow trough slightly greener than adjacent land. The dim thread is lost on floodplains of creeks and rivers but from any gentle divide on wide plains one may see it trending down and up again toward the next division of waters. In central Kansas the faint trace sometimes divides to two and these, in eastern New Mexico, separate to four. Here and there branches from it lead to springs and waterholes and beyond them rejoin. The engraving, less distinct each year, begins at Franklin in Missouri. Incised by toil beset with trouble the shallow trough, an antiphonary of history, is the mark of tens of thousands of rolling wheels. It is the Road to Santa Fe.

There is no other quite like it on North America. In the short span of half a century it was the path of hundreds of thousands of hooves, cloven and uncleft: the motive power of

1

commerce. It was the line of march of an army of aggression. And it was the route clearly marked for the uncounted who sought new life, new fate, new fortune somewhere in the western reaches of a new nation.

In an era of superhighways, few travel the Road to Santa Fe. Even so, their number is surprising: twenty to twenty-five each year. Whatever kindles their interest must be as diverse as the ways they learn of the Santa Fe Trail. My interest began in the Carnegie Library in Pittsburgh when I came on U. S. Geological Survey Bulletin 613: *The Santa Fe Route.* Between pages dealing with strata and structure along the railroad were small maps showing by dashed line, and in quite a general way, the Santa Fe Trail when rails and Trail were adjacent. I had forgotten having heard of the Trail and that moment recalled the first mention of it. In a small Texas town, Mr. Collinson's house was on the hill at the far end of the street on which I lived. He had been a buffalo hunter and I once heard him say he had freighted hides over the Trail.

Mr. Collinson's house was usual for the time and place, in a yard which was not. The latter was two or three acres of a region wherein trees are not volunteers and there was a thick grove of them just south and east of his house. They were planted, he said, to shut off view of the small college

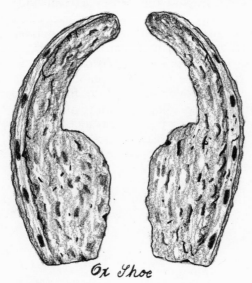

Ox Shoe

my father helped establish. The arboreal aspect of the yard was of some interest but what were more important were Mr. Collinson's peacocks in it. They were many and they were beautiful. Moreover, they had the darnedest screech anywhere out of doors. What use a one-time hide-hunter might have for peafowl I do not know, but it is certain he had them for I have checked recollection with others who knew him better. I have since learned from *Life in the Saddle*,[1] a posthumous collection of his writings, a great deal more which would have fascinated a man of my age (seven years) when I knew Mr. Collinson.

In Pittsburgh, I thought to plot on a modern map the old Road from Franklin, Missouri, to Santa Fe merely for the interest in learning how the geography of it conformed with the geology it traversed some 875 miles but I learned there were no topographic maps of most of the region through which it ran. When later we lived a few months in Socorro, New Mexico, and I searched the library for technical information, I came on a thin volume: *Down the Santa Fe Trail and into Mexico: the Diary of Susan Shelby Magoffin.*[2]

It was fascinating. Susan, a recent bride (in 1846) was then eighteen years old and the Trail, six years older, a well-beaten road. Susan accompanied her husband to Santa Fe and beyond to Chihuahua and she had written simply and with unconscious charm what she saw and did. Still, there were no suitable maps on which the road she followed might be plotted. About three years ago I came on a Yale University paperback of Susan's diary and re-read it with greater interest. By then this country had been photographed from the air and the Army Map Service had compiled from photographs a very accurate topographic map of the United States on the scale of 1:250,000, about four miles to the inch.

From journals of travelers on the Road I knew a good many of the landmarks. Invariably they wrote of river crossings for, on a road maintained only by those who used it, the earliest had cut trenches in steep banks for pack animals. Those later had beveled larger cuts for heavy wagons and they did so after nearly every spring and summer flood. But a river crossing was only an intersection of an indefinite southwest course which I did not know with a river on a map. And springs: in the southwest where rivers were few, generally small and frequently dry, springs were quite literally a matter of life or death to commerce powered by men, mules and oxen. Those who used the trickles of water which now issue from muddy banks, described them in words one might apply to Paradise. But on a scale of 1:250,000, springs are less than a pinpoint, hence rarely are shown.

By rare good luck, I found on a soil-map compiled from aerial photographs of Cimarron County, Oklahoma, a considerable segment of the Santa Fe Trail: a dashed line trending southwest and bearing that name. When wagons followed it, the line was the Road to Santa Fe. Only in later years, and most frequently since it was abandoned, has it become the Sante Fe Trail. Either end of the line on the soil map was a convenient point of departure for a journey over the Road. Fortunately for cartographic travel, much of the United States is laid out in sections, each a square mile. These in larger squares, six sections to the side, comprise a Township, numbered north or south from a base-line. The surveys which marked the land into numbered sections began about 1830 in Missouri and around 1858 in New Mexico. As then survey parties reached work by days on what roads there were, they commonly located by the mapping they completed, the roads they found. Many did; unfortunately, some did not.

From the National Archives in Washington one may secure for a price, well beyond the cost of production I came to think, a photostat of the original township survey of almost any part of the United States. Purchase of "landplats," townships, is an expensive hobby akin to lottery. One may begin by purchase of the township (thirty-six sections) which includes the end of the segment on the soil map, and the one adjacent and on them read, sometimes in Spencerian script, "Road to Santa Fe." With that plotted in fine dots on the photo-topographic map, one has an inch or so of the Road. Some ten feet of Road lie between Franklin, Missouri and Santa Fe if the scale is 1:250,000 and there is a strong temptation to deal in futures: draw lines between four or five points on the map known to be on the Road and buy,

R 16 W   R 15 W

6	5	4	3	2	1	6	5	4	3	2	1	
7	8	9	10	11	12	7	8	9	10		12	
18	17	16	15	14	13	18	17	16		14	13	T 26 S
19	20	21	22	23	24	19	20		22	23	24	
30	29	28	27	26	25	30		28	27	26	25	
31	32	33	34	35	36	31	32	33	34	35	36	
6	5	4	3	2	1		5	4	3	2	1	
7	8	9	10	11		7	8	9	10	11	12	
18	17	16		14	13	18	17	16	15	14	13	T 27 S
19		21	22	23	24	19	20	21	22	23	24	
30	29	28	27	26	25	30	29	28	27	26	25	
	32	33	34	35	36	31	32	33	34	35	36	

Santa Fe to Road (road label along the dotted line)

by the dozen, landplats which lie athwart the lines. It is the road to bankruptcy. Of the first dozen, perhaps three will bear "Road to Santa Fe." The remainder, by fault of guess or default of surveyor, will bear nothing save a neat grid of lines bounding numbered sections.

In time, I had on paper and between regrettable gaps, quite a bit of the Road from Franklin, through Independence and Kansas City, Missouri, southwest across Kansas and the Panhandle of Oklahoma, and beyond Las Vegas in New Mexico. Map in hand (18 sheets, each one-and-a-half by two-and-half feet) I began the trip to Santa Fe. I did not start at Franklin, Missouri, as had William Becknell (one among the first few, and in 1821), nor in Independence as had so many of his successors. Rather, I began at Jefferson City, quite a distance east of the Road to Santa Fe. There, in

State Archives, I picked up a few miles of the "Osage Trace" which early traders had followed from Franklin to Fort Osage on the westernmost frontier.

From Jefferson City to Columbia is but few miles and there, in a darkened room at the Missouri Historical Society, I read with fascination microfilm of the *Missouri Intelligencer and Boon's Lick Advertiser*, including the April 23, 1823 issue with Becknell's "Journal of Two Trips from Boon's Lick to Santa Fe, New Mexico." Published at Franklin, south and east of Boon's Lick,* the *Intelligencer* informed a town of about 1,000 of the Missouri Question, laws of Missouri, General Lafayette's visit to Lexington, Kentucky, and other incidents beyond the floodplain of the Missouri River. Banks were a consuming interest for although no one in Franklin owned one and only rarely used their services, they had on occasion a hard-won bank note. Banks then flourished as filling stations now, and folded in equal numbers. In a bank failure, a hard-come bank note might easy-go. When a bank in Carolina cashiered by Owen Moore ceased operation, comment on its failure, in the *Intelligencer*, ended with: "Owen Moore has gone away, Owing more than he can pay." The newspaper also spoke of the 1819 appearance of the Sea Serpent off Cobhasset Rocks. In the following year it was again seen off Nahant ". . . by a number of reliable gentlemen." It was last reported in 1823, forty-five miles northeast of Cape Ann where ". . . description (not given) agrees with that of earlier reports."

I found Old Franklin marked by a granite stone a hundred yards beyond the north abutment of the bridge across the Missouri at Boonville (Map 1). Two miles north is a larger stone on Santa Fe Avenue, the main street of New Franklin. From it one may read of Becknell's 1821 venture which was the first successful attempt to trade with Santa Fe, although there had been no New Franklin then.[3] Others out of Missouri and Illinois had tested New Mexican markets before. Their experiences had been unprofitable and disconcert-

---

* The Boons were Daniel M. and Nathan, sons of Daniel senior. The Lick was a seepage of salt water in soil, licked by whatever animal fortunate to find it.

ing. Lewis and Clark were scarcely beyond the horizon in the newly purchased Louisiana when William Morrison, a Kaskaskia, Illinois merchant had equipped Jean Baptiste Le Lande, Laurent Durocher and Jeanot Metoyer with trade-goods, and dispatched them to Santa Fe. It was a calculated risk proven an error. Le Lande and his companions boated up the broad Missouri to the Platte, and for a distance up that shallow stream. From it, they went south with Pawnees to Santa Fe. They were detained and there Le Lande, at least, prospered.[4]

Spaniards in Mexico, habituated by a century or two of practice of the direct technique of sending the missionary *with* the flag, understood less direct methods and knew the flag followed the trader. Neither was welcome in Santa Fe. However completely Spaniards on the Rio Grande might ignore the High Plains as an area of trade, they heard the slightest whisper from its eastern margin. What they heard, they heeded. When their Consul in St. Louis informed Santa Fe of an impending American expedition to the headwaters of the Arkansas, led by Zebulon Pike, action was prompt. Action in New Mexico collected 100 wagons, 500 militia, their lances, bows and arrows, and 2,000 carefully selected horses and sent them eastward with a purpose. Don Facundo Melgares and his men were to intercept all Americans on Spanish-claimed land, to explore the northeast frontier and to impress whatever Comanches, Pawnees, Kaws and Osages they might encounter. They did so.[4, 5]

Somewhere on the vast sea of grass, probably in the Texas Panhandle they gave a splendid performance. Three officers mounted on black horses led in maneuver 500 men mounted on white horses for the entertainment of 1,500 Comanche warriors, very probably each a better horseman than any who maneuvered for them. With that staging of a colorful extravagance well done, the army turned northward. Somewhere in Kansas, perhaps in Nebraska, they gave Pawnee chiefs medals and mules and very likely entertainment as well. When no invader from Missouri came to light, the performers went off-stage and back to Santa Fe.

Pike and supporting cast came onto the Plains later in the season.[6] By late November, 1805, they were in sight of the

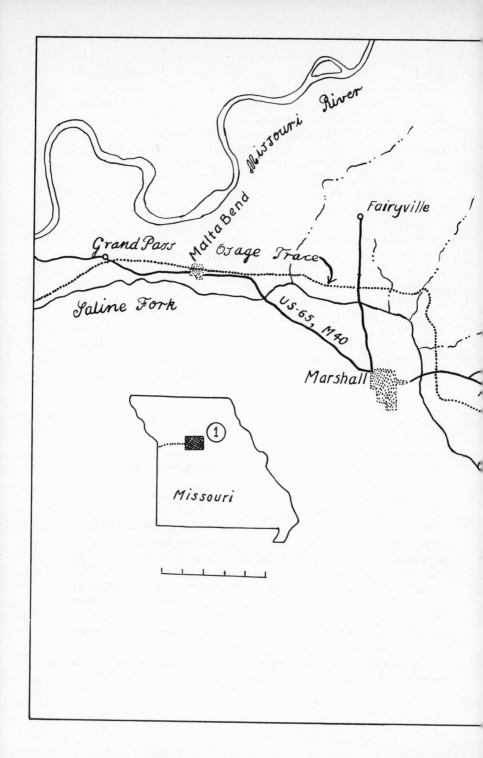

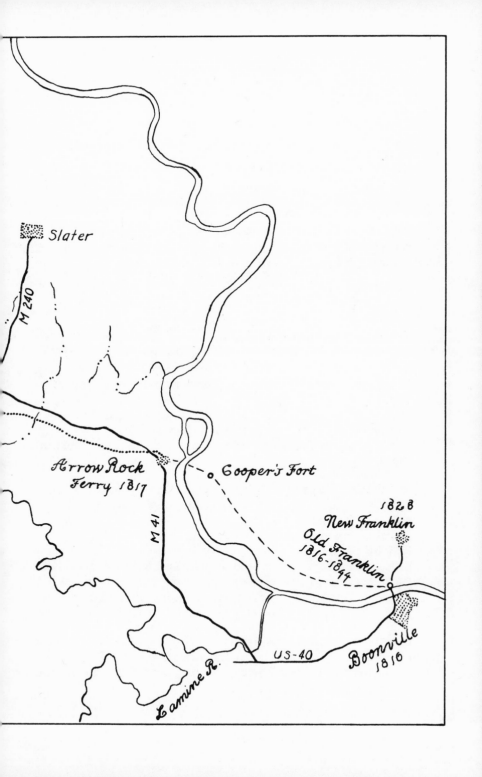

peak which became Pike's in name. Although it was not the month for travel in snowy mountains, the party saw a good bit of rugged territory before they turned southward onto Spanish land. On Rio Conejos, a tributary of the Rio Grande where Pike had constructed a stockade, they were found by Spanish troops who took them in hand, and to Sante Fe. There Pike talked with LeLande. In time, and with escort, Pike reached Natcetoches, Louisiana, and eventually New Orleans.

It seems improbable that Spanish hospitality left with Pike the impression his reluctant hosts least desired to make on one they regarded as an invader: that others from his country would be tolerated. But Pike's report of opportunity in the west (he wrote of imported cloth selling at $20 a yard) prompted others in that direction. As they lacked Pike's official cloak, they found hospitality chilling. Messrs. McLanahan, Patterson and Smith, with other traders out of St. Genevieve, Missouri, arrived in Santa Fe in 1810 to spend two years in jail. Alfred Allen, James Baird, Peter Baum, Samuel Chambers, Thomas Cook, Carlos Miers, William Mines, Michael McDonahough, Robert McKnight and Benjamin Shrive arrived in Santa Fe in 1812 with trade goods, and were immediately escorted to Chihuahua and nine tedious years behind bars.[7] As it has done with others in other times and places, revolution set them free. Mexican independence in 1821 released also the interest of eastern merchants in trade with Santa Fe.

William Becknell and his companions (four ?, history here is vague) were headed southwestward before the *Intelligencer* spoke of independence of Mexico from Spain, but it was a time of slow communication and slower reporting of it. With pack animals loaded with merchandise, the Becknell group went northwest through Missouri River bottom land for a day and ferried the river at Arrow Rock on September 1, 1821.[8] Perhaps a week later, traveling the Osage Trace, they reached Fort Osage, the westernmost post on the frontier.[9] There were several groups headed for Santa Fe that season and Becknell was the first to reach it. He was not the first to return but as he kept a diary of sorts, later published in the *Intelligencer*, it has been for a long time the source of information of an early mercantile journey westward and a source of credit to Becknell for scoring a "first." [10]

Pages of the *Missouri Intelligencer and Boon's Lick Advertiser* carried much of interest and from it I learned that Franklin, the town, was laid out in 1816, three years before the newspaper. By time the first issue was in type there were 120 buildings (two of brick, several frame and the remainder of logs) housing nearly a thousand residents (200 slaves), thirteen shops, four taverns, two smitheys, an equal number of billiard halls and sawmills, a post office and a court house costing $300. Among the shops was a saddlery to which Christopher Carson was apprenticed and from which he ran away to a career as trapper, trader, hunter and scout for the Army and, eventually, a General of it.

The first steamboat, the *Independence* (Captain Nelson) arrived from St. Louis in seven sailing days, just in time to be reported in the *Intelligencer* along with "Carlyle, who kept a book shop in Fleet Street, London, was sent to Newgate for selling Paine's 'Age of Reason' but afterward was bailed."

That year there were two practicing physicians (two more in 1820) and Dr. Lowery was librarian of the "Library Company." The death of Daniel Boone "at Charette Village in his ninetieth year" was reported in 1820. Six years later the newspaper carried an account of the very high water in the Missouri which began the doom of the town. Although Franklin escaped the flood, the great volume of it so altered the regimen of meanders in the river that in 1829 a new site two miles north and above the floodplain was selected. As buildings there were completed, New Franklin became the business center. By then the *Intelligencer* was three years in Fayette but it continued to report news from Franklin, Old and New, and from far afield. An 1831 dispatch spoke of the marriage of William Bean to Miss Sarah Greenfield, in Carolina, and:

> "If fate to their wishes yield
>   And fate to true love leans;
> Time may bestow on this Greenfield
>   A lovely crop of beans."

In 1831, 1833 and 1835 there was frequent mention of Asiatic cholera. It was everywhere: New York, Philadelphia, Washington, New Orleans. In Cincinnati 351 died in spite of a "cholera belt," a flannel cincture which, as nothing else did in the slightest, seemed to help some. Lawrenceburg, Kentucky, with a population of 250 before visitation, had 161 after. The *Intelligencer* in 1833 (it had moved to Columbus, Missouri, by then) carried a letter dated in New Franklin, speaking of cholera there (no deaths yet) and the severity of it among the few remaining in Old Franklin: four deaths in the Lee family, a Mr. Keil, and others unnamed. Old Franklin endured yet a few years after New Franklin saw adventurers leave for Santa Fe. Eventually a meander of the Missouri River claimed the ground, perhaps in the record floodwaters of 1844, and by some hydraulic vagary, restored it in a later decade.

Cholera which scourged the United States, came out of India (it is still endemic there) in 1831 to Europe and simultaneously to North America. Thereafter, until the last neap-tide in 1893, about every ten years it flowed and ebbed from seaboard to frontier in epidemic amplitude, each wave spreading death and terror. With an incubation stage of but few hours, at most a very few days, a strong and healthy man would suddenly be deprived of control of his bowels, and in an hour or so twist in violent muscular cramps between moments of uncontrolled vomiting. Within a day he would have lost eight to ten quarts of fluid in a fantastic dehydration which shrank the body to an incredible degree, but allowed it to live yet a brief interval uncontrolled by a clear mind. The rare survivor of the first onslaught was given a few hours of hope as blood pressure returned near to normal, body temperature rose from an incredible 75° F., and stools were less frequent. It was then that the poisons of uremia stifled the spark of life. All this was the havoc of a brief and terrible twenty-four hours. *Vibrio cholerae* is certainly the most potent dehydrator suffered by man.

The Osage Trace, a segment of the Road Becknell followed from Franklin to Fort Osage, went northwest along Missouri bottoms to Cooper's Fort (Map 1) on the northeast bank, opposite the few log cabins in the settlement of Arrow Rock. The Fort was a community barricade behind which settlers retreated in time of Indian troubles. They had them occasionally, and as Cooper's Fort was there before 1812, when war with the British began, they had more of them.

Scalping was an old custom initiated by the British and their friends and practiced on the French and their allies. It was a custom enthusiastically adopted by all Indians who survived the initial demonstration. When the British in Canada encouraged their Indians to hunt scalps along the Missouri River, Governor Howard of Missouri encouraged Colonel Cooper and settlers about his fort to move eastward. Cooper's reply was a succinct declaration of independence and courage: "We have maid our Hoams here & all we hav is here & it wud ruen us to leave now. . . . So we can defend this settlement . . . a fiew barls of Powder and 2 Hundred Lead is all we ask."[11]

Time and the River have extinguished Cooper's Fort and there is no ferry across the Missouri to Arrow Rock now. The latter is an 1815 settlement on an outcrop of carboniferous limestone containing many one- and two-inch nodules of chert. This substance was a chemical precipitate of silicon dioxide in small and sporadic quantities in an ancient sea, along with vast quantities of calcareous mud long consolidated to the enclosing limestone. Chert has a composition similar to glass. With much the same brittle hardness, it was suitable for flaking of arrowheads. The latter, in skilled hands otherwise unoccupied, was a task of fifteen to twenty minutes. Arrow Rock was a riverside spot much favored by Indians who wished to replenish their quivers and it appears on the earliest maps of the Missouri River in its original French: Pierre à Fleche.

To reach Arrow Rock from the site of Cooper's Fort, one need retrace the road to Franklin, cross the River at Boonville and follow Highway 41 northwest. This I did and found Arrow Rock, as are so many very old settlements bypassed by commerce, an exile of the past in the present. Those who live in the few houses about the block of mellow red brick buildings, mostly vacant, have done well with their heritage.

For the tourist there is a neat Tavern old enough (1837) to have seen a little of commerce of the prairie and it must have sheltered a few adventurers in the Santa Fe trade even when Independence, a hundred miles westward, was the main outfitting point. One is unlikely to find in any town larger or smaller than Arrow Rock, gutters so gleaming white. They are close-set slabs of pure white limestone, the careful and enduring masonry of artisan-slaves.

Informed by a filling station attendant of an old cemetery a couple of miles south, I found the wooded acre surrounded

by a low wall of limestone surmounted by an iron fence. On a morning bright with sunshine, above grass heavy with dew, doves mourned from massive cedars planted by hands long under the sod. More cheerfully, a mockingbird sang from an oak just outside the enclosure. Within was a small, deeply weathered marble arch and from the south wing of it one may read with difficulty: "M.M. Marmeduke, born August — 1779, died March 26, 1854, age 72 years, — days." To read the inscription was a delayed encounter with an old acquaintance, for his journal of a trip from Franklin to Santa Fe appeared in the *Intelligencer*.[10] From it I learned of some landmarks on the Road and something of the difficulties of travel between them.

The Osage Trace from Arrow Rock to Fort Osage is a road difficult to follow. Erosion has erased all marks of it from the land. No segment of it can be identified for certain on aerial photographs, where one can frequently see the Road to Santa Fe in central Kansas and westward. Becknell's Journal in the *Intelligencer* allows a few hints of location of the Trace and Sibley's journal of the survey of the Road to Santa Fe (in 1825) provides a few more. Major S. H. Long passed this way in 1819, and his account locates one point definitely. In a camp on the Osage Trace he wrote of the "Grand Pass": a strip of prairie between the Saline River and a tributary to it.[12] Grand Pass is yet there: a few houses on a trace made obvious by asphalt.

Early township surveys are more helpful in accurate location of the Road to Santa Fe, and one who has found a needle in a haystack can understand the pleasure of locating in Missouri State Archives segments of the Osage Trace and plotting them on a modern map. One may note from maps on these pages that the Osage Trace links no settlements between Grand Pass and Fort Osage. Later there must have been a branch from Lexington, laid out in 1821, connecting with the Trace for quite early in trade with Santa Fe, Lexington was a landing for goods shipped upstream by keelboats to waiting wagons. It is now a town with stronger southern than western ties. In front of the courthouse is a sign which calls attention to a Civil War cannon ball embedded in the wood near the top of a column supporting the portico. At the northeast corner of Main and Tenth Streets is the site, but only that, of the office of Russell, Majors and Waddell, for a short time operators of the Overland Stage Line from Fort Smith, Arkansas, southwest across Texas to El Paso and beyond to San Diego, California, and of the short-lived Pony Express from St. Joseph, Missouri, west across mountains to San Francisco. More tangible and a block west on the north side of Main Street is the building which housed the savings bank of John, James and Robert Aull, financiers of and participants in the Santa Fe trade. James Aull operated a store in Chihuahua, Mexico, wherein he was killed by an unsatisfied customer, in those days not always right.

East of Lexington, the Trace crosses creeks once named Petit and Gros Terrebeau (Little and Big Goodearth) (Map 2). In time they metamorphosed to Tabeau and, finally, Tabo. A few miles west, the Trace intersects two others, first named Petit Cheval aux Heber and Gros Cheval aux Heber. In a manner unknown, the names underwent translation to German which, in time, anglicized to Little and Big Snibar. "Cheval" once was idiomatic French for blunder, error, and one might surmise that Heber made two: one small and a second of the same sort, therefore big. Names on the land are as ephemeral as intermittent travelers across it. Of the scores of topographic features on the Road to Santa Fe, prominent landmarks for those who measured by them the long miles remaining to their destination, very few have their original names. It is just as well that ghosts do not trouble old haunts as they would be odd strangers in strange places, unfamliar in name or aspect.

It is doubtful that ghosts, which in the jet-age travel by UFO, would recognize modern Fort Osage, eighteen miles west of Heber's Big Cheval. It was a point of vantage high on a bluff above the Missouri noted by Lewis and Clark as they went northwest. It became the site of a considerable barrack, stockade and factory built under Clark's supervision after his return. For a time, Fort Osage was the westernmost civilization and a rendezvous for wagons headed for Santa Fe.

In the bargain obtained from Napoleon, a Louisiana

stretching from the Mississippi westward to merge in vague overlap with Spanish and British claims, there were uncounted nomads. Washington authorities sought to tie them to outposts by trade with Factories which made no goods and very little profit. They were loci of barter where an Indian might fairly exchange a beaver skin or buffalo robe for thinner calico. Fort Osage was a military outpost with a subsidiary Factory, the latter in charge of George C. Sibley. As primitive Americans had no standard by which to judge manufactured goods save their appeal by color or, sometimes, by use, a fur trader could offer a few cents in beads for several dollars in beaver. The margin of profit was always very large and frequently preposterous. Although economics or commercial accident might sever the financial arm of a fur trader, it was an accident regarded as a hazard of the game. But let the Government shave a millimicron from his profit or, at a Factory, offer a fair trade to an Indian, then the trader bled aortal blood straight from the heart, and very loudly. Senator Benton, in opposition to Government trade with Indians through Factories, spoke for John Astor, the Chouteaus, Manuel Lisa and others like them, but as no one spoke for Osages, Kaws or Kiowas, Benton easily made his point. Factories were abandoned in 1822 and so were Indians.

By then Sibley was a trader on his own account and in 1825, one of the three Commissioners of a survey of the Road to Santa Fe. It was at Fort Osage that Engineer Brown, under Sibley's direction, began the record of compass directions and chained distances that counted each foot to Taos in New Mexico: ostensible preparation of a map for those interested in the trade but unfamiliar with the road to it. Subsequent circumstances suggest it was covert preparation for invasion of New Mexico.

With establishment of Fort Leavenworth (1827) by a General of the same name, Fort Osage was abandoned to settlers in the vicinity.[13, 14] Logs from it went into construction of their cabins. In recent years it has been restored by Native Sons of Kansas City, acting for the Johnson County Court. From a small notice on the wall of the reconstructed Factory, I learned that restoration had depended on information supplied by Kate L. Gregg, and Miss Gregg's photo-

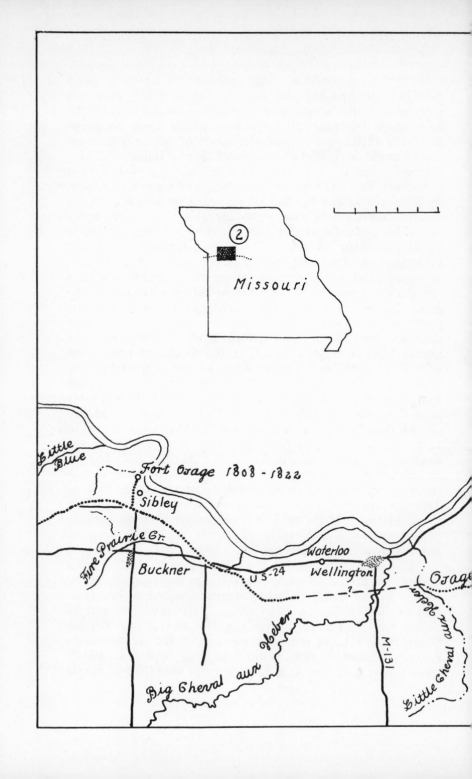

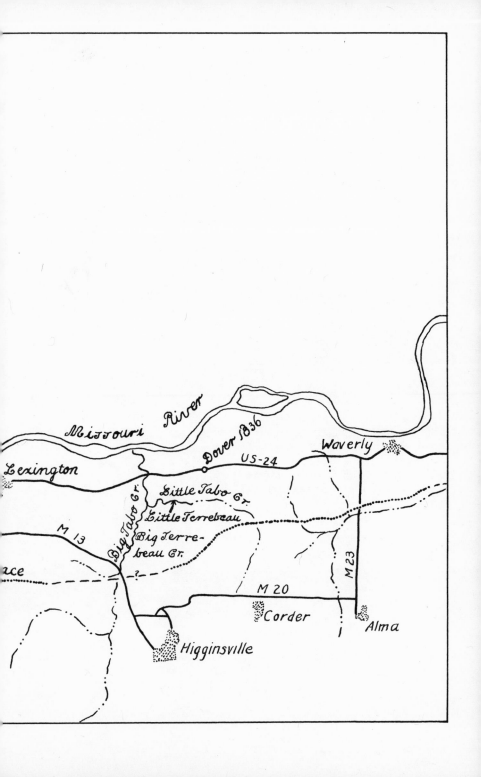

graph was adjacent. By then I had read a good many thousand pages, perhaps only one, probably less, about the Road: War Department Reports, House and Senate Documents, Historical Society publications, dry as dust, commonly turgid, shedding barely enough light to call attention to the surrounding gloom. There was always one exception: anything by Kate L. Gregg. Miss Gregg, until recent years, was Professor of English at Lindenwood College of St. Charles, Missouri, and custodian of Sibley documents there. It was with Sibley land that the College began. Miss Gregg taught

Fort Osage

English and wrote history with scholarly authority, with aptitude and charm. Occasionally she wrote of the Road but I came to read everything beneath her name, certain it would sparkle. The clipping on the wall of the Factory at Fort Osage was from the program of dedication of the restored Fort and it paid warm and deserved tribute to Miss Gregg. It was a pang to learn from an appended line that she had died at Chehalis, Washington, the following year: age 71 Yrs, 3 Ms and 22 Ds, as read so many stones over those of whom she has written. The photograph, taken at the time of the dedication, was an informal one at an angle which caught wrinkles of humor about bright eyes above a broad smile. Miss Gregg was a very pretty lady, and if she be judged by some of the lines she has written, she was one with a small corner of the heart always less than twenty-one. Among Commager, Schlesinger and Gregg, the latter is by far my favorite historian.

South a mile from Miss Gregg's monument, at the margin of the village of Sibley, is a cemetery. Hopeful there might be in it a name familiar to the Road, I read all the stones. Just outside the southeast corner of the enclosure, quite by accident I came on a few yards of the Road to Santa Fe where it mounted from the floodplain of the Missouri onto higher ground. Squarely in the middle of the Road that ran seven hundred miles westward into history, a Hereford bull and three cows were licking salt.

CHAPTER II

Before and After Fort Osage

To THE CASUAL READER of southwestern history, to one entertained by the everyday, commonplace circumstances different from now, to one who has passing interest in the trials and errors which in time evolved trade between the Missouri and Santa Fe, the indifference of Spaniards in New Mexico to commerce across the prairies appears a national deficiency. The confiscation of trade-goods and imprisonment of owners of it seem the despicable defect of arrogance, the Spaniards inferior because of it. Both impressions are purest chauvinism.

As Russia is now, for decades before and after the turn of the Nineteenth Century, Spain, Britain and France were what they were in both the Old World and the New, by ruthless gain at cost to each other and by ruthless domination of what they grasped, determined to hold. They knew, in fact had practiced, every maneuver obvious and subtle that might augment power and enlarge territory. They recognized instantly the overt innocent action of others as the covert intrigue of which they were masters. The recently United

States they saw as a tumor, a malignancy certain to grow at the expense of their prestige, their power and their territory. They would have been blind, deaf and indifferent had they not recognized the new nation as a competitor. They were what they were by aid of stereoscopic vision, microsonic hearing and an avarice for power which allowed no sleep.

In the new nation, scarcely a generation in being, there were monarchists uncrowned and expansionists unsatiated, even with the newly and legitimately purchased Louisiana. Alexander Hamilton, still a shining symbol, was among the former and Aaron Burr, now a tarnished character, among the latter. Hamilton, with every persuasion within his means, sought to insure for the Presidency a lifetime tenure, with absolute veto over legislative processes, with power of appointment that would make of state governors vassals from lifetime to lifetime. Burr, with matching fervor and less acclaim, sought an empire of his own in the surplus of Spanish territory or, if they were willing, in any of the states along the Mississippi. As their paths were not parallel, they were certain to intersect for they were of the same time, plane and category: domination of lesser minds by greater. As there was but one public and two appelants, personal animosity was as inevitable as political rivalry. There is no victory, save that of Pyrrhus over the Romans, quite the equal of that of Burr over Hamilton. The bullet fired at Hamilton by Burr took the mortal life of the one and the political life of the other.

James Wilkinson, commanding General of the Army, was the appointed Governor of Louisiana in 1805, at headquarters in St. Louis.[5] With the apparatus of his office he enhanced personal gain as he engaged in the fur trade; speculation in real estate added to his wealth. In what time there was to spare, Wilkinson composed and dispatched to the Secretary of War a plan for invasion of New Mexico. He knew Aaron Burr and it is a reasonable surmise that Wilkinson, then a traitor in the employ of Spain, or perhaps a double agent for as General of the Army and Governor of Louisiana he was responsible to Washington, was privy to Burr's ambition. If he shared it, he was one of a high-risk, short-lived elite group:

the triple agents of intrigue. It is certain he provided Burr with letters of introduction to acquaintances in New Orleans, presumed equally venal and provided Burr with river-transport that enabled him to deliver them.

When Lieutenant Zebulon Montgomery Pike left to explore the headwaters of the Arkansas, he did not travel the newly purchased land in the same capacity as Lewis and Clark: official representatives dispatched by the President. Rather, Pike went west at Wilkinson's command. To the Lieutenant, the General gave orders that kept him from Spanish lands. On an indefinite frontier, these were assumed by the United States to lie south of the Arkansas River; by the Spaniards they were assumed as far north of that water as they could establish a claim. No fool, Carlos Dehault Delassus, Spanish representative in St. Louis, advised the Governor of New Mexico of the explorer's destination: headwaters of the Arkansas. Pike, as clearly his letters and journals reveal, quite as clearly understood he was to scout Spanish land. His travel and his trespass was the covert beginning of the Road to Santa Fe, and one is led to conclude by events of the following two decades that it was to be a road for invasion.

With written orders to avoid Mexican territory, Lieutenant Pike built within it a stockade, a fort, on the Rio Conejos, a tributary of the Rio Grande and not the Arkansas.[6] With the stockade completed and with Dr. Robinson* as bishop-piece, Pike then placed himself in checkmate. It was so stupid a move as perhaps to obviate suspicion or so clever as to defer retaliation. From the stockade, Dr. Robinson went to Santa Fe to collect for William Morrison, a trader of Kaskaskia, Illinois, the debt owed him for merchandise by Jean Baptiste LeLande. Robinson, as he spoke with LeLande, collected no debt but as he located for Spanish authorities the stockade on Rio Conejos, he made Pike's venture a success: a trip to Santa Fe as a captive with the immunity of an official military representative.

---

* John Hamilton Robinson was a "civilian volunteer" whose status on the expedition remains unexplained by any of the documents related to it.

It appears that Pike's record of exploration was confiscated by Spanish authorities. In Santa Fe these somehow were regained (Pike does not explain how) and the sheets rolled for insertion into the barrels of muskets among his men. Perhaps this is so. Record of his exploration now extant are in notebooks.

In time and in that virtue which always ornaments whatever success (a peak he barely saw bears his name and the stockade built for intrigue has been rebuilt as a monument of it), the Lieutentant delivered to his General in St. Louis the information Wilkinson needed.

Pike was too late. Wilkinson "by his duplicity had ruined his associates, had failed in his attempt to blackmail those who formerly bribed him, and now found himself fighting to keep the office he had disgraced." [5]

When Becknell and his companions began their journey for trade with Sante Fe, they must have had in hand a copy of Pike's published journal or at least a copy of his map. It was low-grade cartography but in the absence of better it was necessarily adequate. It suggested by general delineation of topography that the better route through unknown country between Fort Osage and New Mexico was up the Arkansas River. Near where the stream emerged from mountains, the map depicted a tributary, "2nd fork," entering the Arkansas from the southwest. On a day unrecorded in 1821, the party left Fort Osage, headed southwest.[16] On September 24, a Monday, they camped on the Arkansas River. Between floods it was a shallow stream; without difficulty next day they crossed into Mexican territory through water scarcely more than a foot deep and three hundred yards wide. Becknell recorded they soon passed through a ten-acre prairie-dog town and later killed a rabbit as "large as the common fox," their first jack-rabbit. High hills entirely of sand were unusual in their ken and it was noted these they found after four days upriver travel. If they made a reasonable fifteen miles a day and encountered sandhills after four such days, as the hills are yet there one may calculate they must have struck the Arkansas a few miles below Wichita in Kansas. With Pike's map it was fair navigation; if they traveled by instinct and hearsay, it was very good indeed.

However the course was charted, the journalist of it was more mercantile, even more poetic than geographic-minded. Becknell's journal covers some 875 miles between Franklin, Missouri, and Santa Fe, New Mexico, and twenty-six days travel in a minimum of detail. On "October 21: arrived at a fork in the River. Took left one." There are a myriad small drainages entering the Arkansas from the south (Becknell's left) and without foreknowledge of when and where to choose one, perhaps Pike's map, the party would easily have been lost. Even so, the choice was not a good one. "Cliffs became immensely high and rugged." They had left the Arkansas and must have been ascending the Purgatoire River in Colorado. The road for men and horses was to become a great deal worse before they found yet a better. "October 28th: Ascended cliffs after two days removing rocks. One horse fell and was killed." [10]

Once the party was out of the canyon of the Purgatoire, there were the Raton Mountains to cross by Raton Pass or some other unnamed. South from the mountains, perhaps somewhere on the Mora plains of central east New Mexico, the adventurers met Mexicans and with their aid reached Santa Fe. It was a brisk and profitable market with its independence from Spain newly won.

Becknell's journey was a difficult beginning to a circumstance with a remarkable end. His return was doubtless advised by Mexicans, probably *Ciboleros* (buffalo hunters) who knew the plains, for his route eastward was a great deal smoother, easier, and suitable for wagons. It was on or very near what was to become the Road to Santa Fe. It carried thousands of merchants to southwest markets and it directed the march of a portion of the Army in 1846, to the acquisition of acres nearly the equal of those already claimed by an aggressive United States.

As traffic across the prairies increased each year Fort Osage, point of departure of Becknell and associates, quickly became the point of rendezvous for wagons heading southwest. Before many had left that outpost, wheels of their predecessors had cut in the fertile earth clear tracks easily followed. Moreover, landing points on the Missouri shore for merchandise destined for Santa Fe moved with the years up-

stream. From Fort Osage upstream half an ox-wagon day, seven miles, was Owens' landing, later Blue Mills Landing.[15] Southeast from it three miles, wagons crossed the Little Blue (Map 3). A small creek, it offered adequate water in a well-watered land and little difficulty to loaded wagons, partly because men and teams were fresh. Most miles lay ahead. The Aull brothers of Lexington built Blue Mill on the east bank near the crossing some fifteen years after the first wagon crossed the Little Blue en route to Santa Fe. Each year it was a landmark for fewer caravans as each year, more left from Independence, Missouri. But it offered flour to many Oregon-bound pioneers that failed to bring an adequate supply from points east.

Three miles west of Little Blue, and the later Mill, a wagon road from the Missouri River joined the Road. On the river shore Samuel C. Owens had whatever structure necessary for a freight landing. The Aull brothers formed a partnership with Owens soon after the mill began grinding and Owens' Landing was renamed Blue Mill. One may reach

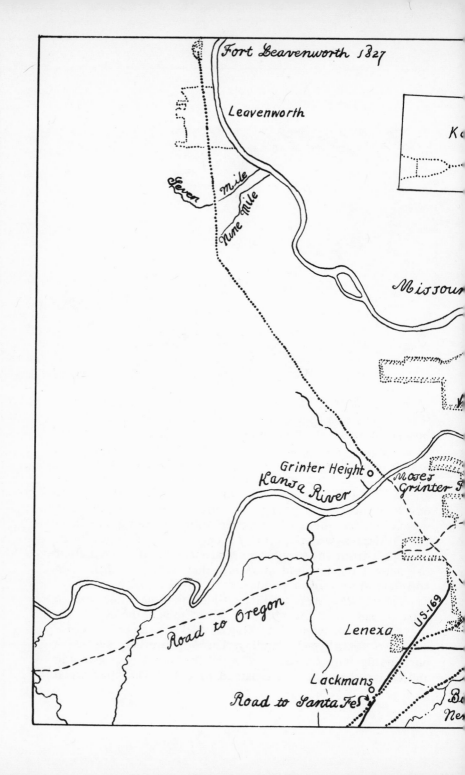

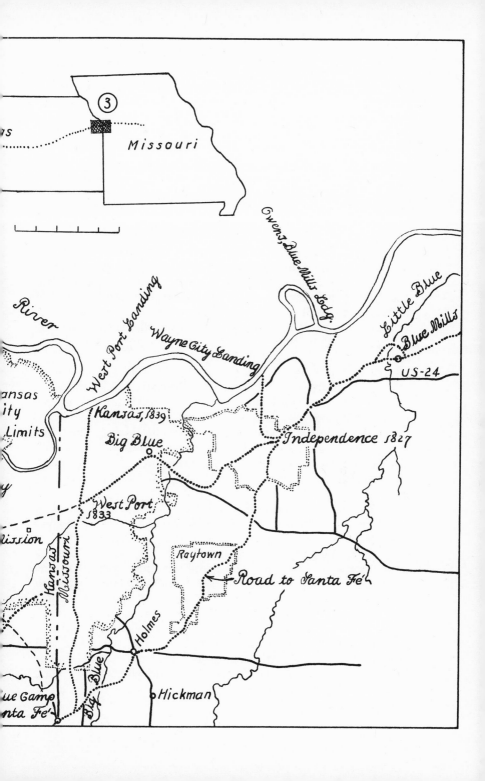

the spot now by a steep road down limestone bluffs to the floodplain, a narrow strip of terrain crowded between river and cliff. It is wide enough to hold a huge cement plant which neither Owens nor the Aulls dreamed of. Cement, the raw stuff of concrete, is a finely ground mixture of limestone which supplies calcium, of shale to provide aluminum, and the proper amount of sandstone to supply silicon. The mixture is heated to fusion and the melt, coarse "clinker" from the furnace, is ground to dust and sacked as cement of commerce. In the furnace all water is driven off, and the calcium aluminum silicates developed in the heat and finely ground, readily take up water. In doing so, they form new compounds which, when the absorption is complete (the interval in which cement "sets"), is concrete. Certainly Owens and the Aulls could have put the product to use, but the mill is a development of a later day. Below the strip of floodplain holding the cement plant are rails which carry away the finished product. Blue Mill Landing is as busy now as ever it was before or during Owens' time.[16]

River landings in time of the Road could not have been elaborate affairs, else the expense of construction would not have allowed so many of them. Four miles upstream was another: Wayne City Landing. Who Wayne might have been, other than the optimistic founder of a city, is forgotten. But his landing, and that of Owens as well, linked the cabins which later were to become Independence, Missouri, with the eastern seaboard as now do the rails which pass that spot also.

The road up the steep bluff at Wayne City Landing must have been a very difficult connection between the river and the cabins of Independence, and it is fortunate that it was short. Wagons on it were smaller than those carrying goods across the plains. Merchandise came upriver to the landings for several years by keelboat, and later by small steamer in the months between March and November when the Missouri was free of ice. For the time and place, keelboats were economical transporters of freight but on the Missouri, half a voyage was always toil and the other half frequently trouble with snags and shifting channel.[17] The boats were sixty to seventy feet long and eight to ten wide at deck-level. They had a rudder and mast but as a river transport they rarely had room in which to tack, hence could use the wind, when it blew, only if it came from a few points off the stern. There were usually four pairs of oarlocks and en route upstream these were frequently in use. En route downstream steerageway was necessary in order to avoid snags and shallower water. Without aid of wind, against the current, keelboats were frequently poled or towed with ropes by men ashore. When brush was thick along the bank, the crew simply pulled from limb to limb. By whatever progress, fifteen miles by keelboat was a day well done. By whatever means, river transport was an advantage over equally slow, or slower, wagons as the latter were quite often in difficulty at river crossings. In the hours and days of high water, they were helpless at any stream.

The 1821 adventurers in the Santa Fe trade used pack animals for transport. The following year Becknell returned with merchandise to Santa Fe and according to the February 23, 1823 *Missouri Intelligencer*, part of it was carried in one wagon costing $150 in Missouri and sold for $700 in Santa Fe. In the settlements along the Rio Grande, merchandise was exchanged for Mexican coin (legal tender in Missouri) or for bullion. If these were lacking, goods were bartered for beaver skins where they could be found or for mules, jacks and jennies. By 1834, merchandise was traded for wool and blankets of it. The Missouri mule has Mexican antecedents. Because a hybrid is commonly of fibre tougher than either of its parents it was not long before mules replaced horses at wagons which had quickly supplanted pack animals.

Throughout the United States, wagons were the main transport of commerce. Railroads were few and the first constructed in 1828. As population multiplied, wagons which supplied it increased and turnpikes lengthened to accommodate both. Then, as now, a turnpike was a toll road with a fee for use of each ten or fifteen miles of it. At each such interval the collector of revenue for maintenance of the road barred the path of an approaching wagon with a pike. When toll was paid the pike was turned to open the road.

In those days, Harrisburg in Pennsylvania was a freight point for wagons rolling down from hills about. In the settlements around, artisans made wagons by hand to fit requirements of freighters to Harrisburg and beyond. Teamsters were as interested in profits as were their employers. To the freight they guided they added rough cigars, rolled from leaves of Maryland and Virginia tobacco for sale at any inn or ferry they passed. As many wagons from which cigars were sold were made in the Conestoga Valley, the tobacco shared the name of the wagons, in time shortened for the cigars from Conestogas to "stogies." [18]

Earliest wagons rolling the long miles from the Missouri River to New Mexico were those available on the frontier. In but few years they were Conestogas made in Pennsylvania, shipped down the Ohio and the Mississippi and up the Missouri to Franklin. Later, freight went further upriver to Lexington, to Owens Landing, then Wayne City and event-

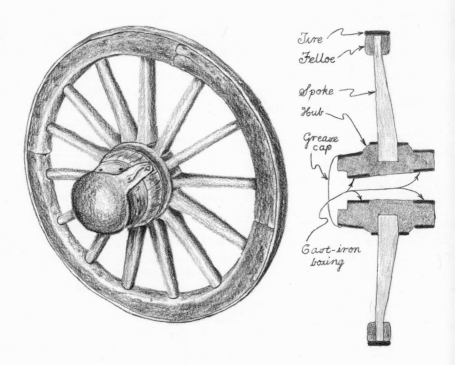

Tire
Felloe
Spoke
Hub
Grease cap
Cast-iron boxing

ually, where the Missouri River turns north, to West Port Landing, the westernmost and the progenitor of Kansas, later a City.

The Conestoga was fashioned by skilled hands for a specific purpose: efficient transport of heavy loads on any road. As they did not always travel a smooth turnpike, their wheels were large: fifty-four to seventy inches in diameter. With large wheels they rolled over and not just against an obstacle. The high center about which they re- volved held the load above high centers on a rutted road. Conestoga wheels were "dished": each slightly convex toward its opposite, and it was a clever utilization of physics. Spokes were slightly inclined inward from rim to hub and as "they were as large as a medium-sized bedpost" set deep in sockets in felloes and hub, they had the strength to sustain a heavy load. The sideward lurch of a loaded wagon on a rutted road was an enormous strain on the down-slope wheels. The stress that moved the spokes from their slight inward inclination to the hub, outward toward the vertical, simultaneously thrust them more firmly into their sockets. As under compression solids have their greatest strength, then at the moment of greatest stress the spokes were in positon to sustain it. They did not pop out as so many match-sticks, as certainly they would have had their position of rest been in the vertical and a sideward lurch of bed and load moved them outward from it.[18]

Narrow wheels under a heavy load cut deeply into the road and require a greater pull to surpass the restraining friction. Moreover, on a turnpike, narrow wheels were charged a higher fee as they demanded a greater toll of the teams. Conestoga wagons rolled on iron rims three to four inches wide, forged to exact circumference. Reheated evenly throughout, they were quickly driven onto a rim of oak felloes and as quickly quenched to confine, by contraction consequent on cooling, the felloes, the spokes and the hub in a quite literal grip of iron. The average Conestoga rear wheel weighed three hundred pounds.

Joining opposite wheels were massive axletrees of oak, each supporting a bolster: a stout timber joined at the lowest point of its lower convex surface by an iron pin to the axeltree. On the flat upper surface of the bolster rested the wagon bed. The lower surface of the bolster, curving upward from the point of contact with the axletree, allowed a single wheel to roll over an obstacle, allowed a few inches of lift of that end of the axle, without lifting wagon-bed and box. Forward from the running-gear (wheels, axles, bolsters and hounds) extended a thirteen foot tongue, once rigid but eventually made to rotate about a stout iron bolt which allowed it to rest on the ground when not suspended by harness or yoke.

The wagon-bed, floor of the wagon-box, was about three feet wide and eleven to twelve feet long in a gentle curve upward toward the ends. On it rested the wagon-box, the ends flared out fore and aft so that as their lower margins were the length of the wagon-bed apart, their upper edges were six or so feet more. Sides were vertical or near to it, their bottom and top edges matching the curve of the bed upward toward the ends. Sides and ends were of planks reinforced outside by a grid of hardwood and they enclosed a box three feet wide, eleven or twelve long at the bottom, eighteen feet long at the top, five feet deep and higher at the ends than at the middle. Securing the sideboards across their tops were as many chains as might be required to prevent their spread from the sideward thrust of a full load.

Historians who have never on-loaded a flat wagon-bed at the forward end and after a drive of five miles over rough road, off-loaded the shifted cargo at the rear, write of the curved bed as a touch of artistry. Those who have, regard the curved bed of the Conestoga as a means of centering the cargo and hampering its shift.

Over the box arched the bows, eight to sixteen of them, and over all spread an "Osnaburg": a heavy weave of hemp and flax fastened well down on the sideboards. Two such sheets with a layer of blankets between were a proof against falling weather of almost any duration. Ready to roll, the Conestoga did so at a cost of about $225 and a weight of around 4,000 pounds. It rolled the 775 miles from Independence to Santa Fe under 5,000 pounds of merchandise. They were colorful vehicles, at least as they began to roll: white top, blue box and red running gear, and the earliest

Tar bucket

without brakes to hamper movement. Secured to the box at the midline on both sides were chains for locking the rear wheels. To lubricate them was pine-tar and tallow in a bucket suspended at the rear of the bed.

Among teamsters on eastern turnpikes were men of pride. They maintained wagons in good repair and whatever they drove with jerk-line and jockey-stick, they made better teams of them. "Leaders" were the forward team. "The leader" was the left (nigh or near) horse. Extending back from the bit-rings of the leader were two straps to join over his shoulders, the left rein an inch shorter than the right. From the junction a single strap, the jerk-line, passed through rings on hame and hip of the nigh swing (left horse of the middle, swing team) to the hands of the teamster mounted on the near wheeler. The span hitched direct to the wagon were wheelers; swing and leaders pulled by a chain secured to tongue and wagon.

A firm, steady pull on the jerk-line with simultaneous shout of Haw!, related pull on bit to command and the leader turned left, ultimately on command alone. Fastened loosely but securely to the leader's collar was a slender hickory stick with its opposite end snapped to the left bit-ring of the off-leader. Whatever the near leader did, the off-leader was led to do by pull or push of the jockey-stick.

A series of sharp jerks on the line pulled the bit of the leader both right and left. But pressure of the shorter rein on the left side of its neck, simultaneous with the shout of Gee!, taught the leader to Gee-right. Whoa-stop came easily as all learned while resting. Whatever the leader did his team-mate was bound to follow and as the leaders, so did the swings and wheelers.

A skilled teamster let his teams boast for him. In a field open for maneuver, lying flat on his back and to one side of the wagon, the driver started his teams by voice. And by voice he carried them through a circle, straightened the axis of teams, tongue and wagon and moved that axis, flanked by thudding hooves and massive wheels rolling under 9,000 pounds, straight down the axis of his prone body. It was impressive drama, as it need be with never an amateur in the cast.[18]

Conestogas dominated the Road southwest for three decades but it does not seem likely that caravans bound for New Mexico included many so accomplished. Skill on

that Road was less a necessity than endurance: 1,500 miles of it in the round trip between Independence and Santa Fe and 1,300 more to Chihuahua and back if they went so far. Horses had some, mules more but it was plodding oxen that came to pull three of four wagons to the Rio Grande. In 1828, Major Alphonso Wetmore, an Army paymaster (an appointive office in his day) went over the Road to Santa Fe and south to Chihuahua. In a province which had ample of both, Wetmore was impressed with the superiority of ox-power over mule teams. He recorded his observations in a letter to the editor of the *Intelligencer* which kept Franklin informed of happenings beyond the valley of the Missouri. Wetmore's words became news the next year, just as the freighting season opened. That year six yokes of oxen pulled two military baggage wagons of an escort of the caravan by Major Riley and troops out of Fort Leavenworth. There were some who thought oxen slower than mules and horses, and perhaps they were in the first week of travel. Wear on wagons was less than on livestock and among them, least on oxen. The latter with less effort in later days easily kept abreast of failing mules and horses and could have out-distanced them. Oxen on the Road to Santa Fe came to outnumber mules three to one and by then there were ten mules to one horse.

The bullwhacker who supplanted the muleskinner walked at dust-level alongside the nigh wheeler all the 1,500 miles to Santa Fe and back, all the 2,800 miles to Chihuahua and back to Missouri if he went so far, and about half did. Clad in flannel shirt, tattered and stiff with grease and pine-tar before the trip was done, tucked into buckskin breeches or store-jeans ending at rough shoes, sometimes moccasins, he was variously described as a rough character, a bully, a ruffian and, by one among them, a hard working man of determination, loyalty and recklessness.[19] In different men he doubtless was all of these. When a newspaper of the day spoke of "adventurers in the Santa Fe trade" it might be referring to merchants from as far distant as New England. When a Missouri paper observed that the teamster's "most intolerable nuisance was their speech" it was speaking of homefolk.[20] Without New England frugality, the teamster out of Missouri spoke well and loudly the language of his trade. It was mostly profanity, according to the few ladies who knew him on the road.[2, 21] Some bullwhackers were reputed to strip the bark from an oak at less than twenty words and among witnesses to such feat, two turned gray and one bald before the week was out.

Their vocabulary included Gee!, Haw!, and Whoa!, and without jerk-line or jockey-stick, they did not spare the rod as they taught their lead, swing and wheel-yokes those words. But teamsters were not truly acorn-fed and bark-clothed; they merely behaved as if they were. They were a poor-risk group with a high-survival rate.

The bullwhacker's lead yoke were fast-stepping steers when he could secure such; wheelers were the sturdiest his employer could provide. The swings (usually two yokes, sometimes more) might be untrained, but only at the outset of the season. The rod he did not spare was the bullwhip. Of weight around five pounds, it had a short stock of ash in a sheath of oiled supple rawhide extending in plaits to around ten feet in length, ending in a buckskin cracker. It was no mean weapon and with it a drover could, but rarely did, flay an ox. Four yokes of oxen started the heavy wagon on signal from the cracker, menacing and sharp as rifle-fire over their heads. With such a whip, a bullwhacker walking alongside the near wheeler, could lift a fly from the ear-tip of the off-ox of the lead yoke, and never disturb a hair.

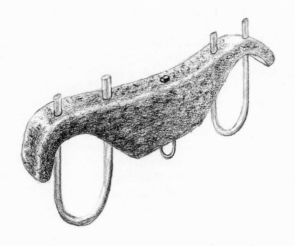

CHAPTER III

To the Rendezvous and Beyond

ONE MAY FOLLOW southward across the night the curving handle of the Big Dipper and on that line find Arcturus, the star which presides over the migration of birds and the growth of grass. It was the arrival of Spring on the plains that governed commerce across them. April and May were the months for caravans leaving Missouri and in the first years, pack-horses the means. Grass is food and food is fuel. Without it there was no motive power in horses nor in the mules and oxen which soon replaced them. Rolling a heavy wagon, made heavier with merchandise, 875 miles from Franklin in Missouri to New Mexico was not light work. A depressing refrain in every account of freighting was the common notation, "livestock are failing." Generally they made it, sometimes in fair condition, more frequently in poor, and sometimes in shocking state.[22] Those which did not were left to shift for themselves on the prairie, an easy kill for wolves or, if they recovered and remained near the Road, they were sometimes picked up and put to work by a passing wagon train.

In the last years of traffic, when most cargo was government freight, contractors, if not more humane were careful of their contracts and by necessity of their livestock. In those days there were more oxen to the wagon and less work for each. As an added touch, teams were matched: four to ten yokes, all black, pulling one wagon; an equal number, all white, drawing another. The lead, swing and wheel yokes of a third might all be red. In the herd of loose stock following, were their duplicates as spares.

The first traders went west in small parties but as Indians were always a problem never solved, they later collected at a rendezvous and traveled in groups as large as might be mustered by public invitation. It was probably indirect invitation to join in the trade that was most heartwarming. One such appeared in the *Missouri Intelligencer* for November 10, 1832: "Captain Bent and company have just returned from Santa Fe with $10,000 in coin, $25,770 in silver bullion, $1,847 in gold bullion, 3,182 pounds of beaver furs, 355 buffalo robes, about 1,300 mules, 17 jackasses and 15 jennies. Total value is about $190,000." Another appeared in the St. Louis *Argus*, July, 1838: "There arrived here yesterday a wagon from Chihuahua, via Santa Fe, with $50,000 in bullion and $30,000 in specie. This and the company arriving in May, together brought about $200,000."

Despite the profits of commerce, there was an uneasiness about the land, residue of an omen from Heaven. On the night of November 12, 1833, to the astonishment of every inhabitant awake on the continent, stars descended in torrents as sleet in a storm.[23] From out of frigid interstellar space they hissed down in alarming velocity in sizes from mere pinpoints to that as large as the apparent mass of the moon. From rooftop to incalculable height, in streaks as bright as lightning, the filaments vanished in balls of fire. Exploding with the menace of a pistol-shot, they left ephemeral clouds of phosphorescent vapor, vivid and angry reminder that all was *not* well either in Heaven or on earth.

There was no oracle nearer than Delphi and no need of one anywhere. Each interpreted what he feared in accord with conscience. In Missouri the heavens warned against repetition of recent whipping of Mormons for their peculiar beliefs. In Santa Fe, the government was threatened for its denial of privilege to the Church. Denison Olmsted, astronomer at Yale College, rejected the probability of thunderbolts thrown by Jove or the possibility of sparks from Vulcan's forge. He was so naive as to think the display a shower of meteors and others were so crass as to recall a similar phenomenon in the night of November 12, 1799, when the earth passed through the Leonid cluster of meteors.

With little heed of omens, merchants sold and traders bought goods for sale in the southwest. Fort Osage was an early rendezvous for wagons; later Independence, then Blue Spring and later yet, West Port four miles inland from a landing on the River and now about the center of Kansas City. When the vicinity of West Port had been thoroughly cropped of grass and some plowed under, Big Blue Camp (now the small settlement of New Santa Fe on the Missouri-Kansas line) was a point of encounter for individual traders joining a caravan (Map 4). Later yet, Lone Elm four miles

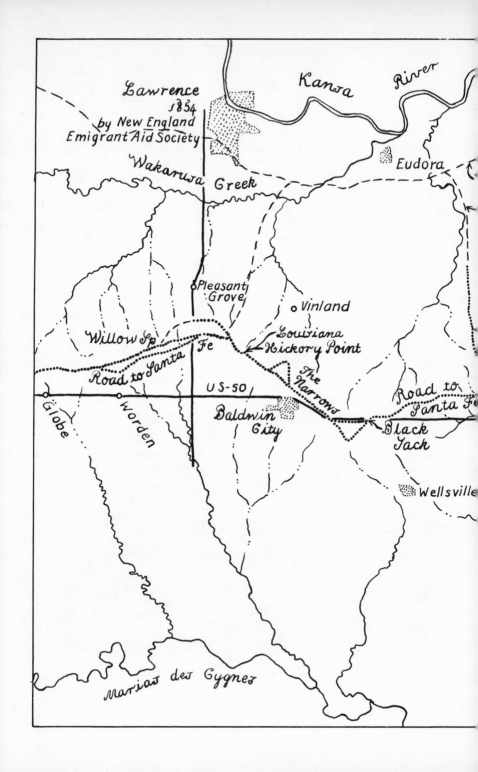

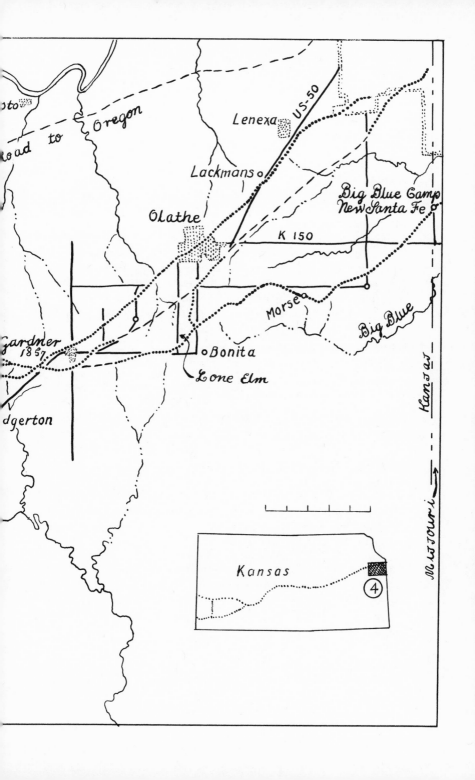

Road to Oregon

Lenexa US-50

Lackmans

Olathe

Big Blue Camp
New Santa Fe

K 150

Gardner
1857

Morse

Bonita

Lone Elm

Big Blue

dgerton

Kansas

Kansas

Missouri

④

west of the present Gardner, Kansas, was a rendezvous. An 1848 diarist noted ". . . this lone tree stands on the bank of a small stream with no other tree or shrub in sight. All branches have been cut from it by traders and emigrants for fuel." [24] By 1853 only a stump remained of Lone Elm and there is no one left to explain why the locality was variously mentioned as "Round Prairie," "Round Grove" and "Caravan Grove" since there was no other timber in sight.

Eventually, Council Grove in Kansas, one hundred and fifty miles and fifteen ox-cart days west of Independence (for years the main point of supply) came to be the rendezvous. There the "Ne Ozho" flowed ample clear water over a gravel bed; hills about were carpeted with grass three and four feet high and on the floodplain was a magnificent stand of oak, hickory and ash and softer woods that never failed to impress the transient. Their high arched foliage was the entrance to a school of experience reaching six hundred miles westward. It had a sound, solid curriculum, slow instruction and tuition was sometimes very high.

At Council Grove teams were unyoked or unharnessed to graze for hours or days as early wagons waited for those later. Teamsters generally cut a log or two of hickory or oak, suspending these beneath wagons for the time when strains and stresses on the road ahead demanded replacements of axletrees, hounds, tongues or yokes. Westward from the Neosho River, hardwoods thinned out and soft cottonwoods, massive in girth, were few in number. Even fragile willows were so sparse as to make firewood a problem. A fortunate teamster might carry a log of hickory from Council Grove to Chihuahua and back to Missouri.

The *Missouri Intelligencer and Boon's Lick Advertiser* of June 15, 1824 reported wagons recently departed from Franklin and downriver settlements encamped on Missionary Ridge ten miles southwest of Forth Osage and the men in meeting to elect a Captain, First and Second Lieutenants. A committee was appointed to draw up a set of rules for government of the party. It was organization to facilitate group travel and protection of it, and the meeting set a precedent for caravans in decades to come.

A captain of a caravan had not much authority (in exasperation more than one threatened to resign) but he had responsibility. The captain set the order of march and the scheme of rotation in it. Daily he went in advance with a work party to select the next river crossing and to direct its improvement with spade and mattock, and with axe if it was necessary to "bridge" boggy margin and soft bottom with brush.[22] Where that was unavailable further west, a thick mat of grass was laid on the crossing with a layer or two of sod on it. The whole was capable of sustaining the crossing of three score wagons, all heavy. The captain divided the men into watches for wagons and herders of livestock, day and night. In addition to animals drawing wagons, there was an equal or greater number of replacements loosely herded behind the caravan during the day. On the return, the herd was enlarged by the jacks, jennies and mules accepted in barter.

Wagons generally reached the rendezvous safely as Indians between the Missouri and Council Grove were Osages. The Osages, as did the Plains Indians whose specialty was other people's horses, took what they could from passing wagons: gifts of coffee, flour, bread or bacon by day and sometimes livestock as booty at night. Unlike Plains tribes, Osages were wards of the government, living in their own relatively peaceful way on annuities. From them, through their agent, a trader might recoup losses if they were properly witnessed, confirmed and a list presented, but only after patience was exhausted. A common item in the *Intelligencer* was a list of Indian damages claimed and allowed. They ranged from a few dollars claimed and fewer allowed to several thousand of both.[10]

To Council Grove, wagons traveled singly or in small groups. Beyond they traveled as a unit, generally in a single column, to Cottonwood Creek in the vicinity of Durham, Kansas. West of that crossing they traveled in two parallel columns to about Walnut Creek draining into the Arkansas River at its Great North Bend. Thereafter, they traveled in four, rolling parallel.

It was the captain, presumably on advice of his lieu-

tenants (more frequently a category than an office as sometimes it included most within earshot, but so many voices
added little to the specific gravity of the discussion) who
selected the night camp, always for grass, wood and water.
It was he who signaled the approaching wagons to corral.
During the day, on sight or sound of Indians no signal was
necessary. At the moment of alarm the two outside columns
swung outward at increased pace (it was now that the buckskin cracker of the bullwhip raised a thin red mist of blood
and hair) and converged to a point as the two inside columns
slowed and spread to complete a rough diamond of defense,
open at the front and rear points to receive loose stock as
herders pushed them within the barrier of wagons, left front
wheel of each interlocking with the right rear of the preceding, and teams within the enclosure. The openings at front
and rear were closed with chains.

What the earliest pack animals and wagons carried to
Santa Fe is not known. Obviously, it was whatever was
available in a frontier settlement such as Franklin. Within a
year there was a steady stream of merchandise from the
East to Franklin and other river ports as the frontier moved
upriver. It came at a cost of $8 to $12 a hundred pounds
(10% to 25% of cost of goods); freight to Santa Fe was $8
to $10 a hundred pounds. Of "light goods" an 1845 assort-
ment included: prints, fancy white, pink and mourning;
sheeting, brown and bleached; muslins, striped and checked;
drillings, blue and white; cloth, scarlet and zebra; alpaca,
blue, black and green; flannel, red and white; cambric, striped
and plain; linen, French and Irish; edgings, white and fancy;
bandanas, silk, cotton and black; German shawls; cotton hose;
hickory shirts; blue denims; black silk ties; suspenders, fine
ivory combs, beads, necklaces, gold rings, hairpins, fancy and
gilt; buttons, pearl for shirts, gilded for coat and vest. And of
heavier hardware: needles, scissors, razors, strops, coffee
mills, sad-irons, and shaving soap; shovels, saw files, pocket
knives, log chains, axes, padlocks, percussion caps and
candlewicks.[25]

On the Road the bullwhacker was up before the sun.
His stock had been on the move earlier, having been brought
by night-herders from the bedground to the corralled wagons.

If it was Indian country, and beyond Cottonwood Creek it was safer to think it so, livestock spent the night within the corral. At the captain's shout, "C a t c h UP! C a t c h UP!" the bullwhacker shouldered a yoke and went in search of the leader. Once found, he transferred the heavy hickory to its shoulder. Fastened by habit and dangling yoke to the ground, the animal waited until joined to its mate. Whatever choice of lead, swing and wheel yokes the driver had made on a first morning a couple weeks ago was his to the last day, or could be exchanged only with spare stock, as generally it was every few days of travel. Alternates were about equal in number but second in choice.

There was competition to be the first to shout: "All SET!" and yet more not to be the last. When all were set, they heard the captain's voice: "S t r e t c h OUT! S t r e t c h OUT!" Commonly, the last words were lost as in a volley of musketry, when buckskin cracker impelled oxen to lean against their yokes. The wagons rolled into columns, commonly four west of Walnut Creek. Some miles and breakfast lay ahead.

Around ten in the morning the captain, having selected the spot, signaled the oncoming wagons to corral. Livestock, generally in harness and yoke, were put to graze under day-herders who had pushed the loose stock along in the rear of the columns. Outside the circle of wagons and at intervals about it, the eight or ten members of the separate messes converged, some having rustled water, others wood or buffalo chips ("It burns like Irish peat," wrote one.)[26] as cook of the morning rattled pots and pans. He rattled very few: a Dutch oven in which bread was baked for the meal or the day, and if he did not use the top of the oven for frying bacon, he rattled a skillet. Always there was a coffee pot. Each driver provided his own tin plate, ample cup and utility knife. The average monthly salary of bullwhackers and muleskinners was $25 "and found." For him and his boss (the wagonmaster in charge of several wagons belonging to a single adventurer, trader), their employer "found" flour for bread, salt pork or bacon, coffee, brown sugar or "long sweetnin" (West Indian or New Orleans molasses) and, besides salt, very little else. In Missouri and eastern Kansas, for himself the bullwhacker sometimes found a deer in the river bottom; in more open country an elk along a divide (they were common in Kansas then) or an antelope on the margin of high-grass country, but he did not eat well until short-grass country, beginning about the Little Arkansas River. There were a conservatively estimated sixty million buffalo spread from the Gulf to Saskatchewan and always an astounding tens or hundreds of thousands right on the Road.[27] With rifles provided by wagon proprietors, teamsters took their toll and lived high on the hump of tenderloin.

From the east margin of buffalo country and into New Mexico a number of wagons in every caravan traveled in a cloud of flies hovering about the thin sheets of buffalo meat hung from the sides to dry in prairie sun and wind. Even though the teamster ate a larva once in a while, it did him no harm. The blowflies that laid eggs on the drying meat had relatives in the high grass of eastern Kansas and western Missouri: always a dread and in some seasons a menace. They were "prairie flies," the common horse fly, several times larger than their cousins. While they were not true proboscidians, horse flies had a proboscis sharp as a needle and nearly as long. Settling, ten or a hundred, on a plodding ox or mule team, they frequently jumped the animals ten feet into a dead run that overturned wagons and tore up furniture.[28] In a particularly bad fly season, when there was no breeze to blow them away, caravans traveled through tall grass country only at night. Mosquitoes were hungry everywhere from Missouri to New Mexico. The female of the species is a great deal more deadly than the male for without a gut-full of fresh blood they could lay no eggs. That catalyzer they took from whatever mammal was handy: herbivores if they were convenient and carnivores, including humans, if they were not. Without unguents and insecticides to discourage them, mosquitoes were as much a part of the Road as the scenery, and equally impressive in wet years. In such seasons they rose above the level of mere Arthropoda to become a sharp reminder that some day insects must rule the world. Susan Magoffin, a bride at eighteen, en route with her husband to Santa Fe in 1846, wrote of mosquitoes at a camp on the Little Arkansas crossing (about fifteen miles southwest of present McPherson, Kansas). The clouds of them were a torment to livestock which, unharnessed, fled. Susan, with feet tucked under her dress and a shawl tightly about her head, recorded: "There were millions of mosquitoes and their noise knocking against the carriage reminded me of a hard rain." [2]

From ten in the morning until about two in the afternoon, livestock grazed and rested. A caravan wholly mule-powered would have had a shorter rest but cattle are ruminants. Herbage they crop goes to the rumen and when it is filled the ox lies down, contemplates the landscape, regurgitates a cud (a wad of grass) and chews it. Thoroughly ground and mixed with saliva, it is returned to the rumen and another takes its place. Beyond the first stomach in ruminants is another receptacle for masticated cuds and the abode of bacteria which make, or assist in making, vitamin B_{12}. Without it even an 1830 ox was in a bad way. Mules and horses make their own, without aid of bacteria.

By two in the afternoon the columns were moving again, and if the sod was dry they made another six or seven miles on a cool spring day or under a hot June sun. While water was an absolute necessity for livestock, falling water taxed some, quite literally, to death. On open rolling prairie, a day of soft benediction of rain on dry land bogged wagons everywhere. Four yokes of oxen could handle nine thousand pounds on massive wheels but on soaked prairie fourteen, even twenty-four, could not budge a mired wagon. Generally they could move out when the cargo was off-loaded, as always it was. Bullwhackers and muleskinners were indeed hard working men. They did not travel to work; they worked to travel.

The night camp, hopefully on good grass, good water and wood, twelve or fifteen miles beyond that of the night before, was usually made before sundown and always before the next meal. For creaking wheels there was pine-tar and tallow to be applied every four or five days. There was such a thing as a wagon jack for the grease job, but usually it was a hickory pole that provided leverage of a high order even to 9,000 pounds of wagon and load. If repairs were necessary they were done with tools carried for the purpose. Wagons constructed in Pennsylvania and even those later put together in Missouri (Independence by 1846 had seven wheelrights and nine blacksmiths) were in equilibrium with a humid-temperature climate. They left it for an arid one, drier each mile west. Spokes loosened in hub and turned in felloes; wheel rims shrank from iron tires. After dark, the camp rang with hammers, more of them and louder beyond the Arkansas than east of it. Stop-gap remedies achieved permanent status. Wedges cut from steel barrel hoops and driven between iron tire and wood rim were a sovereign remedy and where it failed, recourse was had to "buffalo-tug": rawhide fresh or soaked and wrapped as tightly as possible about a loose joint. It shrank as it dried but it was at best a temporary measure. It could be renewed from time to time, for however many the miles there was always green rawhide on the hoof.

James Webb, an adventurer in the Santa Fe trade in the middle 1840's, wrote of a wagon of his returned to Missouri after a trip of 8,000 miles past Chihuahua deep into Durango and beyond, on wheels of diameter three inches less than the original.[25] The spokes forced through hub and felloes were reduced by chisel as they protruded. The whole wagon: box, bed and running gear, was held together by *varas* of rawhide and barrel-hoop wedges. That it was coherent for so great a distance even with that aid, speaks highly of the hands that made it for it bore a heavy load for most of the distance.

In the night camp, what muleskinners, bullwhackers, captains and lieutenants had for supper was not much a variant of breakfast, but hunger is a potent sauce. Exceptionally there might be something out the ordinary. All were adept at spotting bee trees in timber as far west as it went, as bee hunting was a profitable occupation for many frontiersmen between seed time and harvest. In settlements such as Franklin it was not a casual one as it occupied men, teams and wagons in journeys of several days. After reviewing the time expended and those who spent it Nathaniel Patten, editor of the *Missouri Intelligencer*, tartly advised his readers to pay less attention to wild honey and more to their cultivated crops. There were wild grapes, currants, onions and greens for those lucky to find them. Along the Arkansas there were acres of plum thickets on the sand-hills. Plum Buttes, three conspicuous hills of sand ten miles west of Cow Creek in Kansas, were landmarks on the Road until the wind which put them there long before the first wagon passed, took them away a decade after the last. At whatever stream crossing, for a transient who had the time and took the trouble, there were fish to be caught. Except for buffalo meat on the plains, all these variants from a salt pork diet were ephemeral and, after a few years of caravans, depleted. One writer, having crossed in brief succession Running Turkey Creek, Turkey Creek and Dry Turkey Creek, all just southeast of present McPherson, Kansas, protested the names as there was not a feather to be found. In a pinch, and these were of a frequency to toughen drivers and drovers, there was always tougher beef or mule meat, or sometimes wild horse when buffalo were elsewhere and goats (antelope) were elusive.

Predecessors of caravans, the "Mountain Men": trappers and drifters across the frontier, sometimes developed odd appetites. With an abundance of buffalo, fish or venison on hand, they might trade for a horse to savor that meat. And, given a choice between venison and dog, sometimes chose the latter as the meat course.[30]

Major Wetmore, an 1828 diarist on the Road, recorded a delay by high water in the Neosho River at Council Grove and the savor of "alderman's (turtle) soup." [28] There were no teetotalers west of Council Grove if they could help it and one who could, spoke of the pleasure of mint-julip at Diamond Spring in central Kansas, the mint having been planted by someone before 1844.[25] It is a spot visited now by few and by none in Conestoga wagons but the mint is there yet. So, too, are the springs, four of them flowing clear and cold beneath fern and oak. On a hot August day, one can easily understand George Sibley's pleasure when first he saw them in 1825 and named them "Diamond of the Plain" in a journal of the survey of the Road, after Diamond of the Desert, an oasis in Arabia.[31, 32]

As common as major and minor pleasures were major

and minor hazards on the prairies. Rain on the plains was a welcome armistice with a scorching summer sun and a cursed war with mud. It bogged wagons as it replenished ephemeral lakes and overflowed rivers. River crossings were difficulties separating easy miles and it was a rule of the Road to cross rivers as they were encountered, even when crossing meant a late camp. If not crossed then and there, rain in the night might make them impassable for days. Stream banks were frequently steep as spring and fall rains renewed those beveled the previous freighting season. If rear wheels were not locked by chains, then twenty to forty men on tail ropes eased wagons down the slope, at least partway for momentum and the strength of doubled and tripled teams was necessary to mount the opposite bank. On occasion there was a broken hound, yoke, tongue or axle to be mended on the far side of a difficult crossing.

In sunshine, life was easier for men and teams even within clouds of dust and flies. Behind the columns, loose stock raised more dust. Ahead there were occasional rifle and pistol shots as extra hands, never many, either on foot or mounted, killed a rattlesnake, more numerous then than now. As one might surmise, the rear of the train, the least desirable post, was usually unguarded save by herdsmen and teamsters who had a position to maintain and a responsibility in it. Front and rear, all saw and wondered at the liquefactions of a mirage which sometimes gave to the landscape the reality a shroud imparts to a ghost. Mirages were unexplained miasmas rising from the soil and as sometimes they were as disturbing as the sight of real frogs in an imaginary pond, they halted more than one caravan. Trees or scattered buffalo in the distance appeared as horsemen, suspected always as Indians. And horsemen appeared as giants of substance, but of form unrecognizable. The unfamiliar, the unidentifiable, was always a potential danger. Having been warned of Indian raiders led by a warrior on a white horse, one caravan halted to examine by spyglass a man approaching on a white horse, accompanied by another on foot. It proved to be only fifty yards distant, a raven on a white buffalo skull with another alongside, neither recognizable until they flew above the level of the heated distorting air.[25]

For a decade after 1822, wagons left Missouri only in the spring and, somewhat slower than a flying carpet, reached Santa Fe fifty to seventy unaccelerated days later. If goods were not sold immediately to local merchants, there was delay in return. Perhaps half of the time, markets could be found only *Rio Abajo*, downriver (the Rio Grande), or perhaps yet further south in Chihuahua, sometimes in Durango or even Sinaloa on the Pacific coast. Delay in search of markets meant a return in winter or the following spring. In the 1840's, energetic freighters might leave Missouri, find good luck and quick sale in Santa Fe, and return eastward to make a second trip in September or October. It was autumn and fall which were hard on men and a great deal more difficult on mules. Although faster than oxen, they were not so durable and neither ox nor mule moved fast without food. Fall grass was high and filling but from it most nourishment had quite literally evaporated. A wagon loaded with freight, well guarded by armed men, had little room for grain for mules. Pawnees, Comanches, Kiowas and Apaches, while not generally willing winter travelers, did move on occasion. What wagons they could not plunder, the well-guarded, they sometimes hampered and quite as frequently, a careless trader left difficulties for those who followed. Fall and winter grass, brown, crisp and dry, ignited readily and in a fanning wind, flames leaped high and far enough to span creeks. At night a prairie fire was a sight to see. In rolling country the arcs of fire waxed and waned beneath a glowing red sky, visible for scores of miles. On flat land slender crimson fingers groped skyward and retracted to a low wall of flame: an impressive and dangerous barrier. In day, huge clouds of grey smoke rolled high along a front miles in length, the number increasing every hour. The caravan that crossed fifty miles of black ground breathed a choking atmosphere for three or four days; worse yet: livestock did so with full lungs and empty stomach. James Beckwourth, "an old campaigner returned with the mail from Fort Leavenworth" after a December trip across the plains, reported to the Santa Fe *Republican* of February 12, 1848, that there was "little snow on the prairie and grass was burned from Pawnee Fork to Council Grove," a distance of 150 miles.

Descendants of those who set fire to the prairies are now the mainstay of forest fire-fighting in the Northwest. Indian reservations hold a mobile labor force instantly available by air transport to sporadic forest blazes beyond a size manageable by local fire-fighters.

Wherever a train camped for the night, about the corral of wagons was another of scattered campfires and about each of these, groups of teamsters and an occasional tourist. The latter were welcomed by most caravans provided the tourists brought their own rifles, stood turns at watch and helped when they could. As fires burned lower, tales were taller. When in reasonable time they reached unreasonable height, teamsters rolled into blankets beneath a buffalo robe, wool-side inside and inside outside and, with a yoke for a pillow, slept. Somewhere about, the the night watch passed the tedious hours, perhaps drowsy until an ox snorted in real or fancied alarm. Thereafter, every object took on its typical night-time distortion.

If the camp was on short grass, the night guards generally had no difficulty remaining awake for likely there would be buffalo about. The millions on the plains were attended by hundreds of thousands of wolves, themselves followed by coyotes. Night was their time to howl in units, in tens, by hundreds in chorus. Occasionally a guard leaned an ear to a distant rumble. Commonly it was a summer storm. By thunder or stinging hail, picketed horses or ruminating oxen often were stampeded. Wild stock, like those domesticated, sometimes panicked in hailstorms or when lightning cracked near. A night stampede of buffalo was a wonder to hear, although not a welcome one. George Brewerton who, in 1848, rode the Spanish Trail from Los Angeles to Santa Fe, and beyond joined a caravan for Missouri, wrote of hearing in a camp on the Cimarron in southwest Kansas the thunder of a distant storm out of which later came the rumble of hooves to pass within fifteen yards of the corral of wagons.[33] It was Brewerton's recollection that for nearly an hour a solid mass of buffalo, darker than the starlit night, thundered past the camp. The imminent threat, the impending disaster, is larger by night than by day.

If "nearly an hour" is forty-five minutes; if a "solid mass of buffalo" is a stream twenty animals wide, and if each might run for forty-five minutes at ten miles an hour, each animal measuring ten feet from panting nostrils to flying tail, Brewerton heard about 80,000 animals on 320,000 hooves. Quite probably he did. Others by light of day passed through masses of grazing buffalo and from promontories overlooking measurable miles, calculated by density-distribution, herds much greater in numbers. One who estimated he saw more than ten times as many had his guess checked by others who estimated yet more. Second only to Indians, stampeding buffalo were hazards to livestock of a caravan. Many lost part and some lost all their animals to them.

CHAPTER IV

Independence and Westward

THE ROAD TO SANTA FE was born a pair of wheel tracks leading west from the end of the Osage Trace at Fort Osage. By the early 1830's the Trace had become the "Missionary Road" when Friends, Methodists and Baptist missions were established five or six miles west of West Port, now about the center of Kansas City. No one seems to know, and not many care, who built the first cabin near a spring between the crossing of the Little Blue (Blue Mills) and West Port, a locality which became Independence.[29] By 1827 Samuel Weston had a blacksmith shop at the corner of what were to be Liberty and Kansas Streets. It must have been of sturdy construction, as in it Conestoga wagons were repaired for nearly two decades and the building served other purposes for at least a century.[34] Someone with more thought for the present and the future than of the past, razed it. Few such shops and few towns projected their influence so far and none for so long into the the west as did Independence. From the time of Weston's smithy until about 1850, Independence was *the* start of the Road to Santa Fe.

By 1844, West Port was a bustling town and Kansas, at West Port Landing, was soon to be. In but few years, Independence came to be less, West Port more and Kansas a City.[35, 36] But by 1827, Independence was the county seat of Jackson County with a courthouse and a square about it. There, trade with Indians came to exceed trade in furs and, in turn, was surpassed by trade with Santa Fe. By time the Army went west in 1846, Independence housed seven hundred readers of the *Western Expositor* who supported four churches, two taverns (reverse of the ratio now), Washington Hotel, Independence House, nine blacksmiths, seven wheelrights, one tinsmith, a gunsmith and four saddleries.

April and May were the months for departure of wagon trains. They came to be the months of arrival in Independence of Oregon-bound wagons from points eastward. What had been a season for good business became a better one for supply houses. At the beginning of the gold rush in 1849, twenty thousand passed through Independence bound for the promised land. Some unfortunates stopped permanently there for that year Asiatic cholera struck savagely at frontier settlements. As then medical science leaned heavily on calomel and castor oil, recovery depended a great deal on constitution.

As far as ten miles west from Independence, there were scattered houses and "plantations" by 1825. James Jennings, John Campbell, Robert Johnson, J. C. McCoy and others owned land in that direction. Because there were others about, McCoy added a general store to his. Jennings subdivided his quarter-section and from it sold town lots. For no reason of record, the neighborhood of some fifty people was called West Port. By 1837, John Sutter, a Swiss, came to be one among them. Another, Pierre Roy, cut a road through timber to the Missouri shore near the mouth of the Kansas River. Francis Chouteau, a fur trader, had long had a warehouse there, a replacement of an earlier one a few miles downstream washed away in the flood of 1826, the high water that doomed Franklin. Soon there were other warehouses at West Port Landing, storage for upriver freight and furs from the far west: beaver, buffalo, otter, fox, wolf and weasel. The landing came to be "Kansas on the River" and by 1850 the east end of the Road. By then around Independence, what had been pasture so necessary for livestock of caravans was partly farm land, mostly fenced.

While West Port was a very small settlement casting a shadow on Kansas, Washington Irving had begun there *A Tour of the Prairies* and Francis Parkman ended at West Port *The Oregon Trail*.[10] A Bostonian with little interest in the marvels of California, Parkman turned south from the Oregon Trail somewhere near Fort Laramie in Wyoming, to strike the Arkansas River, turned east down it to visit Bent's Fort and went on downstream to intersect the Road at the Upper Crossing of the Arkansas. Once on that broad track, he followed it to the east end and in due time left West Port for Boston.

It was some years before Kansas-on-the-River pretended to be a City. In 1849 it had four brickyards, ten stores, three taverns, a livery stable and a population around seven hundred. Next year, and again in the following, cholera struck. In 1851, less than 300 lived there. But slowly houses spread from Kansas-on-the-River to include Big Blue Spring, a spot on the road connecting Independence and West Port, and later West Port itself. Before then John Sutter, who had lost money speculating in West Port real estate, was building a mill on the American River in California. John Walker, who had worked with George Sibley in the survey of the Road, had a hand in the construction of it. There was a *Santa Fe Republican* by then and an August, 1848 issue reported the return from California of Mr. B. Chouteau and quoted: "A man found two pieces of virgin gold near San Francisco, worth $3000." More accurately, less gold had been found in the tail-race of Sutter's mill, washed in with gravel by water which powered the machinery. Sutter collected very little California gold, unfortunately, but a few who in the years following made of the Oregon Trail a well-beaten road, collected fortunes.

The modern traveler on the Road to Santa Fe, accustomed to ox-cart pace, will find Kansas City and Independence maelstroms of traffic. So they seemed to me as I tied sections of it into knots, searching for landmarks older than the Truman Library. At Independence, down by the waterworks, I found "Emigrant Spring" (a sign reads: Water Unsafe!). The spot must have seen a great many more wagons headed for Santa Fe than for Oregon, but as is commonly the case, the last to come is the longest served. In Kansas City I located West Port Inn. Its owner had been a versatile man: a Shawnee Chief, a West Port merchant and a Captain in the Seminole War. His Inn, versatile too, is now "Bill's Bar," serving Coor's, Hamm's and Budweiser beer. As I recrossed the street from photographing it, I was astonished to see completely filling a large second-story window, an heroic-size figure in Confederate uniform.

Long before there was either a West Port or a Kansas, or even an Independence, wagons left Emigrant Spring on a

West Port Inn

southwest course to strike the Big Blue about twelve miles south of what was to be West Port Landing. Major Wetmore wrote of the Big Blue in 1828: "We spaded banks and crossed by easing wagons down the slope with twenty men on a tail rope. Saw two bee-hunters . . . (and) one prairie fly this morning." [28]

Beyond the City, in the suburbs just east of Redbridge Shopping Center, I located what must have been (I hoped) the exact crossing of the Big Blue. Never the current its name suggests (it is barely larger than the Little Blue), now it is a willow-studded flow three feet wide and as many inches deep over limestone gravel between newly-eroded mud banks. All around ground was wet with recent rains. Missouri mud has some of the strength of Missouri mules and the slipperiness of politicians. Even so, I would never have found the Road without its aid. Walking a gentle slope a hundred yards from the Big Blue, I improved matters greatly by falling flat on my face in the mud. Recovering to knees, I scraped the muck from shirt, chin and cheek. There, straight ahead ran the Road: a gentle notch in the near ridge-crest and visible beneath trees only from knee-height. Climbing a fence about well-mown acres of some estate, I walked the ground: a shallow wheel-cut trough twelve or fifteen inches deep and one wagon wide. Long abandoned (the last wagon for Santa Fe passed here a hundred years ago), elms a foot in diameter rise within it, shading ground once as slippery for oxen as now it is for man.

Many wagons from Independence passing here, having crossed their last stream for the day, went a few miles beyond and camped on grass adequate for livestock. The general vicinity came to be known as "Big Blue Camp" and many who used it knew it to be on the line between Missouri and the Territory of Kansas. James W. Magoffin, U. S. Consul at Saltillo in 1825, and whose bride Susan wrote so well of what she saw on the Trail, had some sort of bachelor quarters there. As frequently there came to be on ground frequented by many wagons at the same time, a settlement grew there: New Santa Fe. It is not a great deal larger now than when wagons and later stages passed this way. In 1850, Waldo, Hall and Company began, on contract, a mail and stage line from Independence to Santa Fe, and New Santa Fe was the first stop. Fare from end to end of the line was $150 during winter months and $125 during the summer season, with a baggage allowance of forty pounds. W.W.H. Davis, newly appointed Attorney General for New Mexico Territory, rode the stage west in 1853, and one who reads his account is convinced that passengers, as well as stage company, earned every cent of the fare.[26] Davis' departure from Independence was delayed a day by a telegram from one Captain Reynolds, U.S.A., en route from St. Louis:

> "Fink's stages are so rickety,
>   His horses so slow,
> His drivers such drunken sots,
>   They scarcely can make them go.
>
> Then, hold your horses, Billy,
>   Just hold them for a day;
> I've crossed the River Jordan
>   And am bound for Santa Fe."

Rhyme was more valued than reason in Reynold's day, even when it bore a higher toll. Fink was operator of the Stage from St. Louis to Independence; Billy McCoy was manager of the Independence-Santa Fe Line and the River Jordan was a small tributary to the Missouri below Jefferson City.

Davis rode in one of three light wagons drawn by four mules. Another was pulled by six as it bore a heavier load of baggage, corn and oats for livestock and food of a sort for passengers. In addition to drivers, there were two "outriders" (men on horseback) to whip up the teams.[37] The group numbered twelve, seven of which were passengers. New Santa Fe was a night stop and the stage company had an agent there, Mr. White, but not much else for convenience of passengers. Without supper, Captain Reynolds slept in a bed; Padre Donato, an Italian priest and Carlos, a lay brother, slept on the floor and the remainder in the wagons. One would hope that baggage allowance of forty pounds did not include bed-roll, for it was a cold November. Stages started early and stopped late. Next morning they drove fifteen miles to Lone Elm and breakfast. Stump of the landmark provided fuel for warmth and for cooking such food as they found among the stage company supplies in the baggage wagon.

West of New Santa Fe some fifteen miles, I toured gravel and dirt roads, hunted section corners, searching for Lone Elm, without success. I had the section number on a file card along with the notation: "Pritchard, May 3, 1849 . . . this lone tree stands on the bank of a small sream with no other tree or shrub in sight. All branches have been cut from it by traders and emigrants for fuel. At this place we found 40 or 50 emigrant wagons."[24] It was unreasonable to expect the trunk lasted much longer, but hope dies hard. I had not known then that Davis, more than a hundred years ago, cooked breakfast with part of the stump. He thought the felling of Lone Elm the work of vandals. For thirty years Lone Elm had been a landmark on the Road, the only timber for miles around casting a shadow. Even after the Elm was gone, the spot was a common camp. One who stopped there four years after Davis, recalled dust six inches deep at Lone Elm in that year of drouth, the soil pulverized by thousands of wheels and twice as many hooves.

It was raining and five P.M. when I passed through Gardner, Kansas, but as there was a light shining from a window beneath the sign, "Public Library," I stopped to question the librarian. She was busy closing shop but she courteously phoned two friends who might, she thought, know something about Lone Elm. Unfortunately, they were not at home.

Quite early on the Road I learned: *Never* question the idle man. From him or her you are certain to get an endless flow of history all the way back to Him who made the first earth here, none of it related to the starting question. If you wish information, select the busiest person in sight, state precisely the question and you are certain to receive an equally precise answer: no more, no less, than you asked. Your informant will not be interested in your name and he will regard explanation of your need for information as unwarranted imposition on his time. Bless the Busy Man! She was a librarian in Gardner, he was a postmaster in Burlingame, a cowboy on Kansas plains, a highway laborer in Oklahoma, an engineer in Las Vegas.

About a mile and a half west of Gardner, long before there was a town, there was a branch in the Road. It was marked around 1844 with a crude sign by someone who had thought for those who followed. It read simply "Oregon," as it pointed to the right fork.[38] The few earliest emigrants followed the Road to Santa Fe and some route west from there. In 1839, Thomas J. Farnham and a party of fifteen left Independence for Oregon and three years later Marcus Whitman led a larger group of hopefuls from West Port, northwest across the prairies and South Pass in the Wind River Mountains.[39] In later years, as discovery of gold in California increased numbers, Oregon wagon trains were guided by Moutain Men, trappers, who knew well the roads across the plains to the Continental Divide. Some unknown among those emigrants placed the sign. After 1847, most such trains left civilization from points higher up the Missouri than Independence or West Port, of which St. Joseph, Missouri was one.

Beyond Gardner eight or ten miles in the rain, I found "Black Jack," a small grove of scrub oak. Wood, water and grass were the trio which determined morning and night stops for caravans. Black Jack in tall-grass country had all three and for many camping there, legions of horse-flies as well. The spot was marked not only by flies but twice by history: first of the Road and then by dissension leading to Civil War. Lawrence, Kansas, about fifteen miles north of Black Jack, was unofficial "free-soil" headquarters.[40] The newspaper there, outspoken in those sentiments, was destroyed in May, 1856 by pro-slavery raiders. In retaliation, John Brown collected a group and killed five, presumably holding those sentiments, in a small settlement on Pottawatomie Creek. Five lives for a machine was an even exchange in an odd time. Reaction was prompt as Henry Pate led a mob in an attack on Palmyra, just beyond the north margin of present Baldwin. Early of a June morning, Brown and his men found the Pate group camped at Black Jack. It was an indecisive encounter with several wounded on both sides, but it fueled the zeal of John Brown who aspired to a higher level of conflict. That, and immortality, he attained in the futile raid on the Arsenal at Harper's Ferry, Maryland, in 1859. Black Jack, an inconspicuous spot and minor incident, contributed to Brown's career. John Brown yet moulders in grave and song while the Road and Black Jack have been abandoned, forgotten for a century.

CHAPTER V

Windwagons and Camels

BEYOND THE OUTPOSTS of civilization, the Road to Santa Fe was rarely rutted for, with prairie unlimited on which to roll, wheels swung to one side or another of the marks of a bogged wagon. Across a wet swale of prairie there might be a hundred or more deep ruts, avoided by later wagons until time and hooves leveled them. Thirty years after the first wagons on the Road, one who saw it recorded: "For about four rods (64 feet), not a spear of grass grows on the Road. There are but few and occasional ruts and the ground is tramped . . . hard by the feet of cattle. We could count in the Road in sight perhaps thirty wagons, including six or eight Pikes Peak emigrants on their return. . . ." [41]

In the last years of the Road it was yet a wider swath and in the unused widths, sunflowers quickly took root in the pulverulent sod. When then spring came to the prairie the Road was a winding thread of gold in a waving sea of green. By then wagons were a great deal longer, lengthened by a "tail," a smaller wagon with a lesser load behind the first, the two pulled by ten to fifteen yokes of matched oxen, generally hauling military freight.

65

When the Road had been beaten to a broad track, it sometimes saw innovations in place of Conestogas. Two of these were "windwagons." [42] Charles Post, one of a multitude headed for Pikes Peak and a fortune in gold, on Friday the 13th of May, 1859, four or five miles northeast of Olathe, Kansas (a two-year-old settlement by then), came on an anomaly on four wheels beneath a large sail. So long as the "windwagon" was not sheltered by a hill, Kansas winds, insistently pressing on man, beast or machine, pushed it across prairies wet or dry. Below the wind, a deep valley was always a shoal certain to founder the prairie schooner. [43] Post was not witness to the last voyage of Mr. Thomas' windwagon out of West Port.

After some five or six years of experimentation and expenditure of $800, Thomas had devised a prairie schooner, powered by Kansas winds which then, as now, were considerable. Hopefully she was launched on an April Monday: a body like a sloop with bow and stern cut off, of width about nine feet and length unrecorded. Wheels, four of them, were about six and a half feet in diameter with hubs hollow as a barrel and about the size of a small one. Presumably there was a tiller aft and a mast forward for the contraption carried sails estimated twenty-five feet high. Appearing as "an overgrown omnibus," there were seats for twenty-four. Designed with a gross tonnage of one and a half, arrival of the vessel at the port of Council Grove "forty-eight hours running time out of West Port" was reported in the *Kansas Press* of July 23, 1860. The *Press* that day also reported transit for the period April 24 to June 25 of 1,400 wagons bearing 3,562 tons of freight and 11,705 oxen, 3,868 mules, 372 horses and 65 carriages bound for Santa Fe.

Mr. Thomas' windwagon was designed to tack a hundred miles of prairie in a day and to complete a trip to Denver and back in twelve. Her failure, if she met that fate, could not have been for lack of wind in Kansas.

As Mr. Thomas was testing, Samuel Peppard of Oskaloosa, Kansas, set sail with a crew of three in another, a "compact" among windwagons. [44] Weighing only 150 pounds, it was "a cross between a spring-wagon and a sail-boat" with a body three feet wide, eight long and six inches deep resting on light axles and four wooden wheels. Above it rose a mast bearing a sail nine by eleven feet, presumably square-rigged. With less weight beneath a hundred square feet of canvas, Peppard's windwagon outperformed the fleet. Whatever unrecorded difficulties she met in storm and calm, she stoutly weathered them all save the last. A "dust-devil," a whirlwind, demolished and foundered the craft on an unmarked shoal about a hundred miles east of Denver. It was a worthy try and had it been an age of plastics, prairie commerce might have been revolutionized. It was nearly so by camels.

Three years later, the June 29th issue of the *Kansas Press* reported for the week the passage of 162 wagons with 512 tons of merchandise; 850 men, 1,150 oxen, 185 mules, 80 horses and 5 carriages. The following week the *Press* spoke of Kiowas camped at Cow Creek, in Kansas ". . . becoming more insolent. They take from wagons whatever they wish."

The fratricidal fury of a Civil War tormented the nation and the *Press* made August note of it: "The train from Kansas City of July 31st is reported attacked by bushwhackers" and: "The three camels captured by General Curtis in Arkansas and up to now in Des Moines, Iowa, were recently sold in St. Louis for $545." At the other end of the line, a year later, the Santa Fe *Republican* noted: "The dromedary owned by Mr. William Kroenig of Barclay's Fort, passed through with the train of Mr. C. G. Parker, en route to Chihuahua."

Beyond these reports lay an experiment on eighty-nine camels. It had begun in 1836 when Major G. C. Crossman called attention of the War Department to the possibilities of camels as pack animals in the arid western wilderness.[45] When Jefferson Davis became Secretary of War, steps were taken to try them. In 1855, Major H. C. Wayne and Lieutenant D. D. Porter were dispatched to the Mediterranean on the *USS Supply* to learn as much as they could of the use of camels and their care. In the following year the *Supply* returned with the first of two loads landed at the Powder Horn, three miles south of Indianola, first capital of Texas: one *boghdee* (hybrid offspring of a male Bactrian and an Arabian female), nine Bactrians and twenty-two Arabians.

The confinement of a sailing voyage is a hardship on animals and particularly difficult for those so top-heavy as camels. When seas roughened the captain of *Supply* had the animals brought to their knees; when rolling increased, he rigged a harness to hold the kneeling animals upright. The *boghdee*, a gigantic brute, was a special problem because of its height, but a hole was cut in the deck above to accommodate its hump.

Among the Bactrians and Arabians aboard the *Supply* were four *pehlevans*, trained wrestling camels. On their native heath, camels defend their harems from interlopers by throwing a foreleg across the neck of an intruder and bearing it to the ground. A buck camel thus vanquished sought companionship elsewhere or else the rivalry was carried to a bloodier finish. This natural wrestling tendency was cultivated in the Levant where camel-wrestling was as common as cockfights in Louisiana. By time a calf born on the high seas (christened "Uncle Sam") was a month old, the Arab tenders had coached the youngster into a first-class wrestler. With sea legs at birth, it was eager to wrestle any other animal similarly equipped. The calf had the run of the ship and as it stalked unsuspecting seamen occupied with their tasks, the infant *pehlevan* invariably won in a matter of seconds the first fall of innumerable wrestling matches. By order of the captain of *Supply*, the champion was securely tied.

Seventy-four camels, costing $100 to $400 each (oxen then sold in Kansas City at $50 to $75 a yoke and mules about $10 more for a team) were landed at Indianola. With fifteen Arab tenders they were given a permanent home at Camp Verde, about fifty miles west of San Antonio. As they had neither horns nor hooves, camels were not regarded with favor in a country over-run with both. But traders were impressed when they saw a camel lift 1200 pounds—a load that would have flattened a mule—and leisurely plod away with it.

In September, 1857, a brigade of camels, mules and a few wagons, in charge of Lieutenant Beale, went west from Camp Verde. At the outset, the camels lagged behind but very soon they were accustomed to the work and thereafter their placid efficiency was taken for granted. At El Paso, the group struck the road so familiar to traders, south from Santa Fe to Chihuahua. Northward on it they reached Albuquerque and there turned west with the aim of laying out a road from point to point with water, grass and wood, feasible for emigrants bound for California over the Road to Santa Fe. Each camel packed 600 pounds of food for men and mules. In the desert the Levantines were expected to rustle their own, and did.

In the malevolently arid terrain of Arizona, the guides lost their way and under a broiling sun the circumstance was quickly acute. Camels laid aside their burden of food and placidly packed water from the last waterhole, a journey beyond the strength of their long-eared associates. On another occasion, a water shortage sent searchers from camp in all directions. Lieutenant Beale returned alone and long after dark. Pausing on a rise overlooking the sleeping camp, he was affronted by the lack of vigilance. This was Indian country and careless regard for his orders was certain to be lethal. He taught them a lesson: drew his pistol and fired a shot as he loosed a war-whoop. Before his mouth was closed a volley of shots whipped about his ears. His horse wheeled in fright and raced through the night in uncontrolled panic. Miles from camp the animal stumbled and Beale spent the night recovering from the jolt.

Through 4,000 miles from Texas, past what now are New Mexico and Arizona, across the Mojave desert to Fort Tejon (near Bakersfield), California, and back to Texas, the camels performed with imperturable efficiency. Beale's report to the War Department reckoned the value of one camel in the southwest the equal of four mules. In 1862, the California-Nevada Camel Company imported fifteen Bactrians from Mongolia and employed them in transport of salt, the evaporite of an ephemeral lake in the desert, to a silver reduction mill at Washoe, Nevada. Government and private experience with camels was an unqualified success but the Civil War put an end to the federal experiment. Only one camel remained indefinitely in Government service: his mounted skeleton stands in the National Museum. Several were sold, one to Mr. Kroenig of Barclay's Fort (now Watrous, New Mexico) and some escaped to happy freedom in the arid southwest. In the 1890's the U.S.-Mexican Boundary Commission reported several along the line of survey. But with the hand and gun of every man against them, the camels did not survive. The last wild camels, two, were reported by the Rhyolite, Nevada, *Journal* in 1907, as visions of an itinerant prospector in the desert.

Of those associated with the camels, probably none achieved such favor as Hadji Ali. Beginning on the shore of the Mediterranean under Wayne and Porter, he remained in faithful service until 1870. Mustered out, he became a prospector and for years a colorful character in the southwest. It is certain he left enduring friendships for alongside a stretch of bleak gravel road near Quartz, Arizona, is a monument, a pyramid of cobbles held in cement, topped by the silhouette of a camel and bearing on one side a bronze tablet with tribute to Hadji Ali who lived history as he tended camels. Doubtless he remained a Levantine at heart, but not in name. Hadji Ali appears briefly and favorably in the memoirs of several pioneers, and always as "Hi Jolly."

The last camp of Hi Jolly
born in Syria about 1822, Died Dec 16, 1902.
Came to this country Feb 10 1856. Camel driver,
Packer, Scout; over 30 years of faithful aid to
the U.S. Government. Quartz, Arizona

CHAPTER VI

From the Narrows Southwest to Council Grove

BETWEEN BLACK JACK and Baldwin City begin the Narrows (Map 4). It is a divide, in places barely a Conestoga wagon wide, between waters draining north to Wakarusa Creek and those discharging southeast to Marias des Cygnes.[22] It was the route of wagons from low onto higher ground, up an outcrop of Carboniferous clay. The stratum, scarcely a hundred feet thick, dips so gently westward that the Narrows carved from it span nearly six miles of Road. Even when the surface was dry, clay on the Narrows was deceptively soft beneath. Wheels cut the thin crust and sank to the hub in mud. From time to time after every soaking rain on the Narrows, teams were doubled, in places tripled and all hands leaned hard against the wheels to plow the deeper mud. There is scattered timber about the Narrows now, as there must have been when wagons had troubles there. Some who found a dry road wrote of finding bee-trees on the divide.

Where the Narrows widen to higher and drier ground there is a spring. Although many camped there, it got little mention in accounts of the Road, presumably because any spring in eastern Kansas was not far from the next. Farther into the arid west where water was sparse and more welcome, sometimes in spite of a strong taste of calcium sulfate and epsom salts, springs rose in status from unnoted landmarks to goals of desperately thirsty men. Hickory Spring, near the higher, west end of the Narrows, had another kind of fame. At various times and places there have been gold rushes, silver stampedes and oil booms. In early Kansas there was the real estate equivalent: townsite promotion. In files of the State Land Office are plats of some two thousand townsites now extinct. The locality of Hickory Spring, Hickory Grove or Hickory Point, as it was at various times called, is one.[40] "Louisiana" was the name chosen for the budding frontier community destined never to blossom. The small settlement became less rather than more, and finally nothing. Even so, it remains unique among defunct townsites. Before Hickory Spring pretended to be Louisiana, it was the site of the "Wakarusa War." The conflict began in 1855, with the murder of Charles Dow and ended a few weeks later with the killing of Thomas Barber, a neutral unfortunately convenient to the wrath of avengers. Thereafter, free-soil and pro-slavery blood flowed easier and more frequently.

None of this early turmoil between opposite sociological views affected caravans pausing momentarily at Hickory Spring, en route west and hopeful of avoiding greater danger at the hands of Indians or headed eastward certain they had. In later years when dissention divided the States to North and South as definitely as Jupiter fissioned Biela's comet, freighters to Santa Fe felt the weight of war as bushwackers fell upon bullwhackers. By then there was a *Kansas Press* in Council Grove to inform that on August 17, 1863: "The train from Kansas City of July 31st is reported to have been attacked by bushwackers."

I passed Willow Spring with regret as it could be reached only by roads deep in mud. It was "good water" according to several who "cooked with willow twigs." [46] It was at Willow Spring that a part of the Army of the West, out of Fort Leavenworth, came onto the Road in their march to invasion of New Mexico. They, too, thought well of spring water there. To all travelers on pavement who get their water, iced, in a glass across a cool counter, the constant reference to water in accounts of the Road—water poor, bad, good, sweet, bitter, sparse or abundant, is tiresome repetition of trivia. On the Road, water was life.

Between Globe and Overbrook in Kansas is a hill (Map 5). It is a modest elevation, only moderately conspicuous in a subdued terrain. But it was one of the very few spots of the 1825 Survey of the Road by Brown and Sibley that I could tie to the ground with certainty. Brown's "way-bill" map, compiled from compass directions and chained distances, here notes "hill" alongside the map-symbol for one.[32] The line of survey ran straight over the rounded crest but the Road bent gently around the south flank of it, somewhere between the high radio-relay tower at the top of the slope and Highway 56 at the base. Be advised that when you phone east or west your voice is relayed from a tower very near the most famous of the slower means of communication. But I could not find it. Soil run-off has filled the ruts and although I traversed the plowed field from tower to highway several times, I found no mark. The two young men who operated the station knew of the Road elsewhere but they had never seen trace of it on this hill. It was pleasing to stand on the crest and know that right here nearly a century and a half ago, men ran a line westward into history and it was disappointing to look down the gentle slope and only know that between here and yonder, less than a quarter-mile, the path of thousands who followed is concealed by silt and clay a century accumulating. With back to radio tower, plowed fields scattered about, Herefords grazing the grass between, with traffic on asphalt winding among scattered farm houses, even with eyes closed it took imagination to make Francis Parkman a part of this scene. But certainly once he was.

Rock Creek on the Road, just east of Overbrook, offered no difficulties for trains save in time of high water. On other days it even offered minor conveniences. Here, in 1828, Major Wetmore, who wrote with more zest than most of the few who wrote of the Road at all, dined on wild strawberries and fish from the creek.[28]

Because the Civil War looms larger than lesser events of the same time and because many events leading to War happened near the eastern end of the Road, one tends to relate that part to moments younger than the remainder. Buckets of blood were shed all over Kansas by encounter between those who owned slaves and those who would set them free. The first settler at Rock Creek Crossing was a Mr. Baker, in 1852. Nine years later he and his brother-in-law, George Segur, were killed by the Anderson gang.[40] This latter was one among many which in the shadow of war took wholeheartedly to brigandage for personal profit. By then the Road was in its forties; it saw most of its traffic before their time. Rails lay west of the east end of the Road less than a decade after.

Stopping in Overbrook beyond Rock Creek to mail a letter, I inquired of the postmaster did he know of relics of the Road in the vicinity. He gave me the name of an oldtimer who might. From Mr. Gerwin I learned that near the crossing of One Hundred and Ten Mile Creek, buildings of the Harris stage station of later years of the Road still stand. By Brown on that first survey it had been named "Oak Creek" but two years later as Sibley marked shortcuts on the original survey by mounds of sod, it was calculated that by Road, Oak Creek was one hundred and ten miles from Fort Osage; hence the second, more enduring name.

I followed Gerwin's directions and a rarely traveled farm road. When it softened I walked, for Kansas mud that bogged ox-powered wagons is even more receptive to horse-powered automobiles. The stage station is a small, brown sandstone, two-room house with an abnormally steep shed-roof, and a considerably larger two-story stone stable. Both are crumbling a little now but they rise anomalously, untenanted and untended, above rows of corn and rank johnson-grass. Stage stations such as that at One Hundred and Ten Mile Creek are relatively new to the Road. Waldo, Hall & Company, the first mail contractor, had but two: New Santa Fe and Council Grove. By 1861, increased traffic and a new contractor accounted for stage stations every fifteen or twenty miles between Independence and Santa Fe.[47] I think it was Barnum, Vail and Vickery who had the contract then. Every fourth stop was a "home" station and a driver rode from one home station to the next. Between, at "swing" stations, tired teams were exchanged for fresh. By that time some of the vehicles were "Concords" made in New Hampshire, seating either six, nine or twelve passengers and cost $775 to $1050.[48] Their average speed was four miles an hour but as their hours were long, they made fifty to seventy miles a day and the distance from Independence to Santa Fe in eighteen. Sometimes, probably frequently, they

Stage Station

had in the wild west an escort of ten to fifteen soldiers. If they were not horsemen at the start of the day, they were not in the saddle at the end. And if their mounts traveled so far on consecutive days, it was because they were sons of Pegasus. Fifty miles is not too much for a horse with steel ligaments but seventy on consecutive days is more than muscle can do. If they rode mules it is certain their animals got all the nine pounds of grain allowed by Army regulations, and more (twelve) if they were horses.

One Hundred and Ten Mile Creek

The Concord coaches were brightly painted efficient transports for their time, of design pleasing to the eye. But few of their lines were drawn for comfort of passengers, other than those which shut out part of cold winter winds and shut in all the summer heat. Drivers and outriders were armed to "fire 136 shots without reloading," as one hopes they had few occasions to do, from a Colt's revolving rifle, Colt's revolving long pistol and Colt's revolving short pistol. For emergencies they used bowie knives.

At One Hundred and Ten Mile Creek, beyond the station a hundred yards or so, I found the Road, now a thicket of small trees in a deep trench eroded by drainage into the Road as it came down the slope, traversed the narrow flood-plain and intersected a meander of the creek (Map 5). In reading journals of the Road, one unconsciously comes to share the regard of writers for difficulties encountered. Here, as at all crossings I saw, there was nothing spectacular. It did not even appear difficult to a man afoot with no intention of crossing. But accounts of wagons at this and other streams speak of the considerable labor in beveling banks re-formed by high waters, of felling trees and cutting brush to "bridge" the worst portions, of doubled and tripled yokes (sixteen to twenty-four oxen) goaded to do what they could do only under the bullwhip. The miles to Santa Fe were easy distances between formidable barriers.

One Hundred and Ten Mile Creek meanders about a small floodplain thickset with oak, elm and lesser growth, pressed closely now by plowed fields. It is a pretty segment of landscape. Susan Magoffin was pleased with everything about it when she saw the crossing in a more primitive state: "Oh! This life of mine I wouldn't exchange for a good deal. . . . It is the life of a wandering princess, mine!" [2] It was a life more difficult in later miles for Susan, her husband and nearly five hundred other drovers who were the ruck of the Army en route to invasion of New Mexico. The Army, its freighters and Susan went past Santa Fe and deep into Chihuahua, and the Army to the Halls of Montezuma. Susan spent worried weeks in El Paso del Norte at the home of her husband's Mexican friends, their political affiliations being despoiled by an army but their hospitality remaining unbroken.

Beyond One Hundred and Ten Mile Creek about seven miles, the Road passed what was to be Burlingame. It began in 1857, as so many others, at a river crossed by the Road: a cluster of log cabins roofed with walnut "shakes" and floored with walnut "puncheons," boards split from logs.[49] The stream, anomalously, was first "Bridge Creek," so named by Brown. But the Road, forty-five years older than the town, had no bridge there until twenty-five years after the first wagons when John Switzler, a citizen of Saline County, Missouri, built one for tolls in 1847. The water beneath his bridge became Switzler Creek, as still it is. In that time, and for those who had it to spare, the creek provided bass, perch and catfish.[50] Through a narrow pass beneath the railroad, pavement enters the settlement which began as "Council City" and changed its name to honor Anson Burlingame, a strong free-soiler. The boast of the town: "Where rails and Trail meet" is apt, as certainly they did somewhere close by, but not in the life of either. There were no wagons on the Road bound for Santa Fe when rails crossed it here. At the height of the Pikes Peak (Denver) gold rush in 1859, the Road carried through Burlingame from twenty-five to an unusual five hundred wagons in a single day. As then wheels rolled slower such a traffic was perhaps a congestion not met on the pavement through it now. Before rails reached Burlingame it was near a stop on another railroad on which trains traveled only at night: the underground carrying illegal passengers, slaves en route north to freedom. In Harveyville, seven miles off the Road and northwest of Burlingame, Henry Harvey's loft was a station on the underground and Enoch Pratt's, in Wabaunsee, the next.[51]

West of Burlingame the Road crosses Dragoon and then Soldier Creek. The former was named by Lieutenant Fields who brought a company of Dragoons out the Road in 1852. Dragoons are mounted infantry, as they need be if they were to cope with mounted Indians. To the layman, a soldier on horseback is cavalry but as a Dragoon carried no sabre, in the table of military organization he was an infantryman on a horse. Dragoons were distinguished by other indices apparent even to the uninitiated. By custom, less mutable than law, they cultivated as bushy a mustache as nature allowed

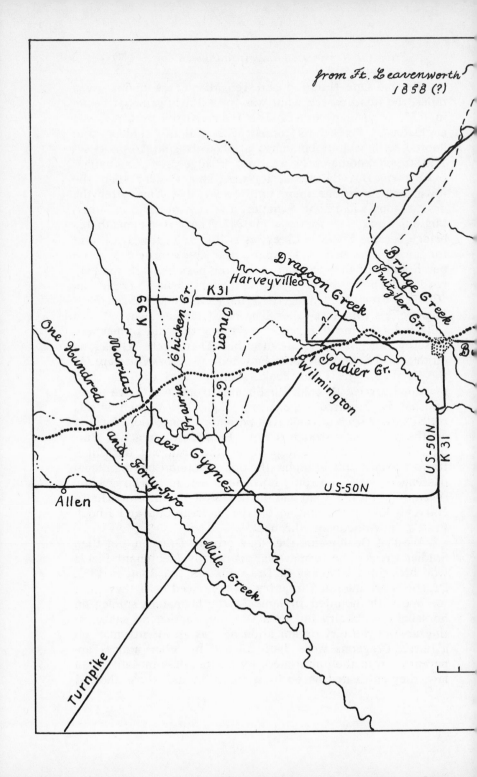

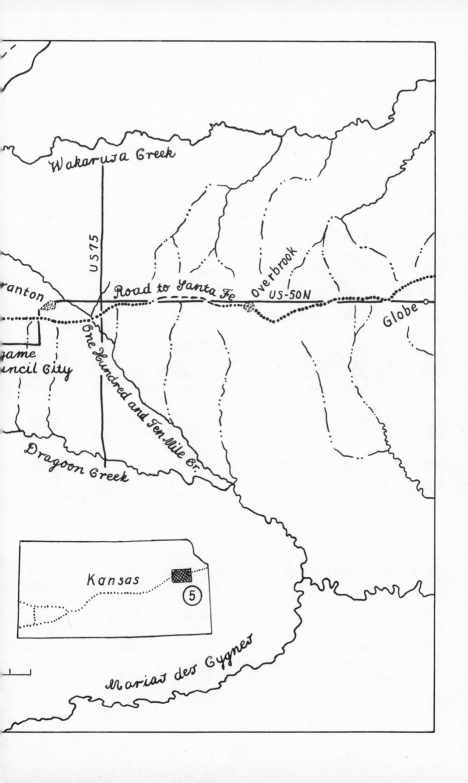

them, grew hair as long as comfort permitted and, until some General concluded they were unmilitary, Dragoons wore ear-rings.

Soldier Creek had no name among traders. In May 1851, an army group left Fort Leavenworth and camped here to fight a bout with cholera. To it they lost thirty-eight men. The stream was named for the detachment. Beyond it, somewhere near modern Wilmington in Kansas, a road from the north joined the Santa Fe Trail. After 1846, Army men in numbers and military freight in considerable tonnage passed to and fro. Most came out of Fort Leavenworth or was headed in that direction. Always they sought a shorter route. There was first a trail and then a road southwest from the Fort to cross the Kansas River at Pappan's Ferry, now the site of Topeka, Kansas, and on to the vicinity of Wilmington. One would guess that the route had some use before that by the military as the ferry at the Kansas River was there by 1842. It came to be a point on the Oregon Trail. During the Civil War the road from Fort Leavenworth to join the Trail near Wilmington was much used by military and commercial wagons headed for Santa Fe as they detoured around Confederate raiders out of Missouri.

Onion, Prairie Chicken, Marias des Cygnes, One Hundred and Forty Two Mile (from Fort Osage), Bluff and Rock Creeks were names on the land and crossings of creeks before wagon trains reached Council Grove (Map 6). For a time longer than at any other point, traders met in council at the Grove to elect a Captain, his lieutenants and sometimes to make formal record of rules which organized their traverse of the miles ahead. By 1846, it was the westernmost point from which a man might return alone and safely to Missouri.[46] It was not always that. This was the country of Kaws and Osages, relatively peaceful after treaty with George Sibley and the other two Commissioners of a survey of the Road. But before the treaty and for a time after, they were whimsical to the extreme of taking all livestock in sight and quirting owners who objected if they were few in number or poorly armed. Westward, caravans might encounter Pawnees from the Platte, scourge of the Plains and enemies of all, or Comanches from the south.

Contrary to folklore, the tall timber at the rendezvous of traders on the Neosho River is not known ever to have been the site of conferences among Indians.[31] They were a people of primitive resources and for countless generations trained to survival by an unyielding environment. Indians were a great deal more apt in action than they were with words. The stately oaks, tall elms and tough hickories shading the Neosho River spoke for themselves to every transient and they spoke eloquently. Rarely, if ever, did they speak for moderation, as they appealed to the sense that perceives beauty. In their cool shade Sibley camped in 1825: ". . . as we propose to meet the Osage chiefs in Council here to negotiate a treaty . . . I suggested naming the place 'Council Grove' . . . & Capt. Cooper (was) directed to Select a Suitable tree & record this name in Strong and durable characters—which was done. . . ."[9] They proved to be the casual words of a man with a sense of responsibility and the wit to discharge it.

Senator Benton of Missouri had urged the three Commissioners, of which Sibley, for himself at least, was an unexpected one, to keep in mind that the survey they were to make was not of a road between States but a survey of a highway between Nations. Now nearly a century and a half later it seems odd that words of a political opportunist were, by random chance, to fall on ears of a person of Sibley's character. His associates, as their advisor, did not have it. Where surveyor Brown calculated the Hundredth Meridian intersected the Arkansas River, the former extending southward and the River westward to mark the boundary between Mexico and the United States, Sibley's associates would have impatiently given up the survey as they waited for permission from Mexico. Bored with the wait, they did in fact, and having had little to do with work to that point they had less thereafter and returned to the comforts of civilization in Missouri. It was Sibley's drive which made his objections to termination of the survey a part of the official minutes of a formal meeting of the three Commissioners on the barren margin of the Arkansas and its unseen intersection with the Hundredth Meridian, and it was Sibley with a smaller group of teamsters, hunters, chainmen and engineer Brown who

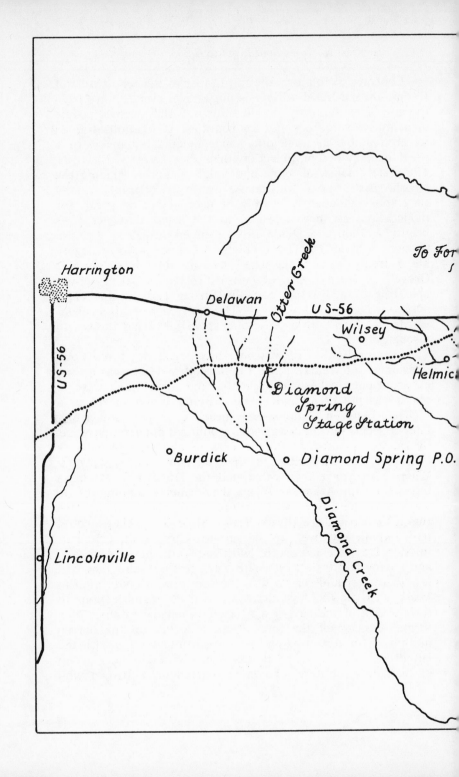

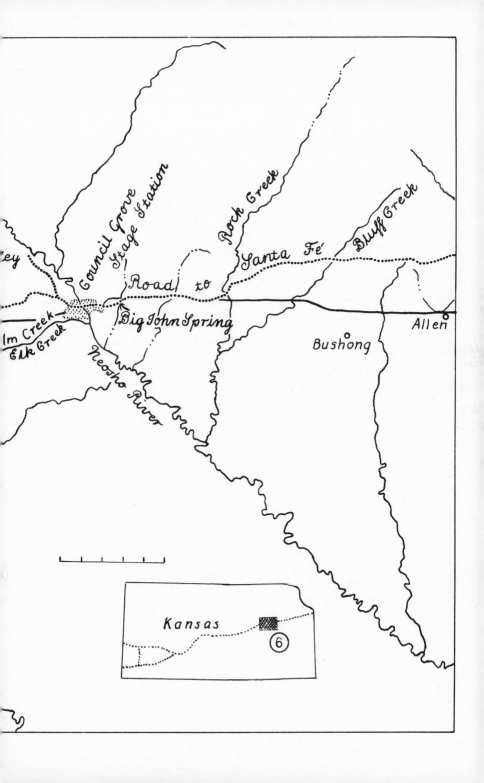

without permission (later given) carried the survey across Mexican Territory and the Sangre de Cristo Mountains to San Fernando de Taos, sixty-five miles north of Santa Fe. The former was a frequent terminus for pack-trains out of Missouri before many wheels marked the Road.

Sibley, once the Factor at Fort Osage (point of beginning of the survey), when Factories were closed to trade with Indians had purchased the residue of trade-goods there. He had mortgaged what property he owned and as he was without other resource, there was difficulty in "overtaking the interest and catching up with the capital." [9] While Sibley was in the West, engaged in the survey, the reputation he left in Missouri was maligned by vituperation written in venom and printed in the *Missouri Intelligencer.*

By time the survey began at Fort Osage in 1825, there had been four years of wagons over the Road: perhaps a hundred or so wagons altogether. They were loaded and they were heavy. They did not skim the prairie; they cut into the sod. Even if the second did not follow exactly the tracks made by the first, it is quite probable that in the second year of wagon traffic, most vehicles followed tracks left by the first few. One need not be a pedologist to know that in a semiarid and arid climate, as that of the southwest, the marks of a heavily loaded wagon on soil a thousand years in the making, do not vanish in a single season. Nor are the eyes of Deerslayer needed to follow them. Moreover, a frontiersman with merchandise for Santa Fe had every reason to follow the tracks of the wagon that reached that market, unless he knew of a better route, as it seems probable few did. By time the survey began in 1825, there *was* a Road to Santa Fe traceable by all but the most casual eyes, and Sibley in his journal of the survey mentions more than one encounter with it.

In Congress, Senator Benton spoke in flamboyance adequate to conceal a purpose and he urged constituents, who could read the road on the prairies, to lobby for passage of a bill for the survey. With no serious difficulty the bill was approved. Sibley's journal of the survey was recorded in the years 1825-1827 (the survey was complete in 1825 but Sibley later spent time and appropriated money in marking short-cuts on it) and Brown's map was complete in 1825. Despite Benton's hullabaloo and fanfare in Congress, the journal was not published until 1955 (edited by Kate L. Gregg) and Brown's map is still in its original manuscript form, unpublished.

Most who write of the Road to Santa Fe speak of the delay as typical Governmental bungling and intimate the data of the journal, landmarks and distances between them, was kept from those who needed it most: the traders. If this be so, there is the anomaly that *Gazeteer of Missouri* written and published by Alphonso Wetmore in 1837 included two names given by Sibley.[52] In particular, Sibley named Diamond of the Plains (i.e. Diamond Springs) after an oasis in Arabia. That the same name, at least one so esoteric, might have been conceived by different men does not seem likely. And also, Josiah Gregg in *Commerce of the Prairie* (1844) speaks of Big John Spring, Council Grove and Diamond Spring, landmarks named specifically by Sibley.

It is a reasonable conjecture that survey of the Road in 1825 served the probable purpose of its sponsors: a map for invasion of New Mexico. If this be so, there was no reason for its publication and every reason for its secretion in Senate files forever. That such invasion was in the minds of many, in the writings of a cautious secretive few, is apparent from the time of Pike's expedition. Invasion of Mexico (in 1846) must have been nurtured in many Washington minds, Senator Benton's among them, as early as 1825; and before him in General Wilkinson's in 1805—as certainly his letters prove.[53]

Beneath an oak in Council Grove the Commissioners, Sibley, Mather and Reeves, bargained with Osages "Great and Little" for right-of-way to Santa Fe and for unhindered passage on it, presumably for so long as the grass shall grow. To the Head Chief they gave $300 in trade goods and an order for $500 more on Augustus Chouteau, then a trader in their village. Congress had appropriated $20,000 for treaties. As the Commissioners spent little here and later an equal amount, they remained within the budget.

Between caravans for many years no sound disturbed

the Grove save the murmur of spring and fall breezes through tall and stately foliage. In winter there was absolute silence beneath a blanket of snow. When contractors began hauling freight for the Army there was the clangor of hammer on anvil in a Government smithy and, soon after, the bustle of a trading post set in the Grove by Boon and Hamilton. Susan Magoffin and her husband saw Council Grove in a quieter time, passed the oaks and camped a short distance beyond. Susan climbed a gentle promontory and ". . . to the west as far as the eye can reach there is nothing but a waving sea of green . . . I thought I had never seen a more imposing sight."[2] It grew a great deal thicker and much higher than now when cattle crop grass near to its roots. Davis saw grass here three and four feet high.[26] Waldo, Hall & Company, mail contractors, had a hay-cutting crew at Council Grove, a repair shop and an agent, Mr. Withington, who provided beds and breakfast for Davis and others. They had, of course, other breakfasts, but no dinners and only sometimes suppers on the Road and this was their last bed east of Santa Fe. Withington began immediately repairs to the stage and shoeing of mules which drew it. He told Davis that the day before he had given food to a stranger, one of a party whose last meal had been several days before, their strength enduring to a point several miles west of Council Grove. They had sent the strongest member for food, else they would have frozen in the low November temperatures.

About as quickly as the stranger received succor at Council Grove the modern traveler receives information. There is "Council Oak" beneath which, according to a sign by Daughters of the American Revolution, Sibley and associates dealt with Osages. It is now a sheltered stump some four feet in diameter, as recently time laid it low. Convenient and well marked on the north side of Main Street, the stump stands less than 1,100 feet east of the Neosho River. According to Brown's measurement made at the time, the oak marked by Captain Cooper and beneath which Sibley, Reeves and Mather held council with Osages was 1,650 feet east from the river.[32] Time, and the Daughters of Revolutionists have changed the distance. Nearby is a sign pointing to "Postoffice Oak" crowding the front steps of a residence on

Main Street. It informs that east and westbound traders left letters in some crevice (not there now) beneath the tree confident they would be delivered by others bound for Santa Fe or Independence. Certainly it would have been much a convenience if only traders had known of the depository and if vagrant Osages had not.

On Main Street a few feet west of the small bridge over the Neosho is Hay's Restaurant, once Hay's Tavern of the middle years of the Road and at the corner of Main and Chautauqua Streets, Last Chance Store ten years younger than the Tavern. First a post office with quarters more

Last Chance Store, Council Grove

spacious than the crevice at Post Office Oak, it later housed a general store. The name "Last Chance" was more of an advertising slogan than a guarantee, as by then there were a few others farther west. Davis mentioned the half-dozen log cabins about the crossing of the Neosho in 1853, and a missionary at work among the Kaws and Osages of the vicinity. Not long after his time an imposing stone mission was built at Council Grove by Methodists [54] and now it is a neat museum (as is Last Chance Store, but closed) housing relics of the day. In it I heard a tourist introduce herself to the curator as "third cousin to Vice President Curtis," and recalled he was some-part Kaw. It was about the only distinction he brought to that office and greater than any he achieved in it.

Having searched east of Council Grove for "Big John Spring" without success, I checked at a photographic shop to make certain I gave the correct exposure to film I so frequently used, and inquired of the courteous proprietor the whereabouts of the spring. In 1825, Big John Walker of Sibley's party had found it and on Sibley's order had carved on an oak overhanging the water, that name.

"Before my time," replied the photographer. "Never heard of it. Maybe you're looking for Fremont Spring. As a boy I used to trap muskrats there. See so-and-so at the Chamber of Commerce next to Hay's Restaurant. He knows all those things."

I found Big John Spring hidden in dense brush and trees. From a segment of twelve-inch pipe set vertical in the ground comes a thin flow of clear, cool water, quickly lost in reeds and weeds thick along Big John Creek. The water flows, I think, from above a bed of limestone but so thick is the growth about that it is impossible to tell for certain. In 1843, Captain Cooke returning eastward from escort of a caravan to the Arkansas River (limit of U.S. territory), where he had disarmed and sent home a marauding band of Texans, had stopped at the spring on a hot July day, parched from weeks on the dry prairies.[55] In parting, all took a long drink of that cool water. Richardson, a private in the army three years later, caught "black trout and catfish"[56] as did Marcellus

Ball Edwards of a later detachment. He found Big John Spring cold and clear beneath a huge oak carved in dates, some as old as 1819; known, then to others before Big John Walker.[50]

Fremont whose name Big John's Spring now bears, proved himself an avid seeker of publicity in an ill-conceived winter expedition to the Rocky Mountains. He proved himself a fool by his evaluation of advice from those hired for their familiarity with geography he did not know. When Fremont reaped what he had sown, and the harvest included bodies frozen by bitter frost during his folly, he proved himself a monster of indifference and cowardice as he laid blame on those whose advice he had ignored. Fremont was a General by marriage to the daughter of Senator Benton of Missouri.

As Big John Walker had none of these characteristics and held no rank, time and publicity have given his spring to another and the oak beside it to some unknown.

Council Grove is a point on pavement of a character not stressed by the Chamber of Commerce: here the West begins. I saw here the first ten-gallon Stetsons, the first boots and over a cup of breakfast coffee strong enough to etch zinc, listened to ranchers discuss prices offered for beef in Kansas City, once the beginning of the Road and now the end of another for fat Herefords on the prairie.

CHAPTER VII

Beyond the Neosho and the Turkey Creeks

BEYOND COUNCIL GROVE, searching for Diamond Springs was a hopeless quest. A mile off in count of crossroads on section lines, I took the wrong one, plowed out muddy ruts and shaved down high centers. There was no spring, not even a creek where I sought both. I knew the Road to Santa Fe; had, in fact, a map of it. But there was no landmark by which I could be certain of my position on Road or map. Named in full "Diamond of the Plain" by Sibley after Diamond of the Desert, an oasis in Arabia, the Springs might have been that far away from where I searched. En route back to the highway, I waved down a pick-up truck and inquired: "I'm looking for Diamond Spring. Can you direct me?"

"You want the post office or the water?"

"The water."

"Just follow me. I live there."

"Can I make it? This car is low-slung and. . . ."

"Sure," he called, as he drove off. "I'll lead you."

Very likely the only high points Detroit knows are those of production and sales. There are others less comforting in Kansas and I was certain I would leave my transportation on one of them. Diamond Spring ranch house is a short distance up-slope from Diamond Springs: four points of water closely spaced, one enclosed in a small concrete box from which, years ago, a hydraulic ram pushed water up to the house. (It was an innovation regretted by Miss Gregg who confined her indignation to a footnote.)[32]

Bob Waner, Kansas cowman, courteously showed me the springs and later pointed to an oak, once the shade of the blacksmith shop of the stage station built after Davis passed here. In a drawl pleasant to hear, he allowed it must be so because "Jim is always finding mule-shoes there, them little Mexican mules. And I found an old sledge there last week."

"You wouldn't part with one of the mule shoes, would you?"

"I might, if I can find one up at the barn."

Later we rummaged through assorted junk, always a filling in every such ranch shed, and in another without success. By then we had a following: nine cats, four dogs, and later Jim who located half-a-dozen small mule shoes once thin from wear and now thick with a crust of rust, hanging on the frame of a gasoline storage tank.

According to my information there was nearby a considerable stone foundation of the stage corral and I asked if I might see it.

"No," Waner replied.

By then he had given me quite a bit of time and a mule-shoe, and I was not offended that he could not spare more. I was about to ask would he point the locality and let me search, when he continued.

"Nope. They're under four feet of dirt. No one here knew what they were and when ground was leveled for that barn yonder, the dirt was shoved onto those old rocks."

As I thanked him for his courtesy, and the muleshoe, I asked Waner if he had many visitors searching for the springs and the Trail.

"Well, about twenty or twenty-five each year. In 1960, when there was some sort of anniversary, we had near forty. And a couple years ago there was an old man, around ninety I guess, in an ox-wagon. He said he had been over the Road when he was a boy and just thought he'd like to see it now he was a man."

The visitor would have been one of the many after Colonel P. G. Lowe who had camped at Diamond Springs with a small group of cavalry en route to Fort Leavenworth in the fall of 1852.[19] Lowe had written of the crisp weather and the high wind (it still blows) they had endured all day. He had seen, morning and afternoon, five or six Indians riding a mile or so from the Road on one side or another.

Lowe and his men camped east of the Springs and were finishing supper when a ring of fire rose about them. Flames leaped high from tall grass and higher yet in the strong wind. In frantic minutes they set back-fires controlled with beating blankets. Within few moments they were safe and badly burned near the center of widening acres of black ashes. Antelope-fat was their only unguent and hands coated thickly found some comfort in the cool water of Diamond Springs.

Davis the following year staged nine miles before breakfast to find Diamond Springs safe and very wet in a cold November rain.

Lost Spring post office is on the highway and Lost Spring is only two miles northeast (Map 7). About fourteen miles by Road and several more by mud and pavement from Diamond Springs, there was a stage station here also. Maintained by George Smith, the stage-house was a three-room structure of siding roofed with sod. At least one old-timer recalled details of interest to few. "It had four outside doors and five windows each with twelve lights and rooms were papered with newspaper. A short distance southwest was a stockade, a hollow square of posts about eight feet high, with loopholes. There were nine graves a little way west of the station, said to be of cowboys frozen in a blizzard and five more to the northeast, said to be of bullwhackers." [57]

Lost Spring now discharges to Lyon Creek and around the spring cottonwoods grow. Long ago it was Lost Creek "with not a tree or shrub in sight." One who saw it then wrote that the spring "rises suddenly out of the ground and after rushing over the sand a few yards, as suddenly sinks and is seen no more."[56] Lost Spring still flows clear, with less drama and no great rush. It is certain that with grass more sparse than when wagons passed this way, run-off from rainfall is greater from the whole region. With less water sinking into the ground, the watertable is certain to be lower, hence there is less volume to rush from Lost Spring.

In the last year of heavy traffic over the Road, Jack Costello, a New Mexican cowboy headed for the bright lights of Kansas City, stopped at Lost Spring stage station in 1866.[44]

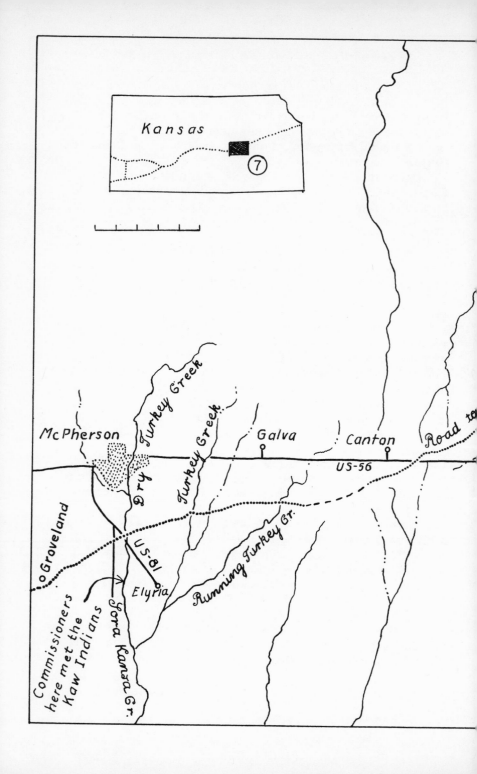

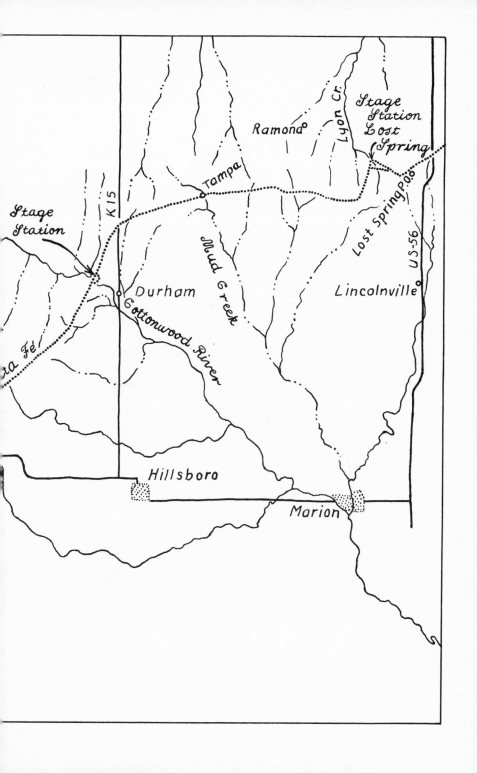

It may have been a dry year for Costello drank whiskey. He awakened next morning with a heavy head and a heavier pocketbook. He learned to his surprise that he had won Lost Spring ranch in a poker game the night before. It is not of record that Costello ever saw Kansas City but it seems reasonable that he had cows which did.

One of the smaller streams in central Kansas is the Cottonwood River flowing southeast to join the Neosho. One of the smaller towns in Kansas is Durham and through it the Cottonwood flows. A mile upstream from Durham the Cottonwood River winds through an S-curve and there the Road to Santa Fe branched, each crossing a bend of the S to join immediately beyond the stream. Although the Cottonwood is small, the narrow channel with steep banks was adequate discouragement for a tired ox or mule so that if a barrier of wagons were thrown across the neck of the bend, a caravan might have the convenience of a natural corral. Quite a few did.

It was at the Cottonwood that wagon trains bound west generally set the first night watch. The stream was appropriately named as here westbound wagons saw their first *canadensis populus sargentii*, the Plains cottonwood. From here to New Mexico only these and occasional willows grew. Firewood became a problem for a few days. In the time of covered wagons, buffalo no longer ranged so far east as Cottonwood River, hence there was no *bois de vache*, the mainstay of cooks of caravans. When the military went to New Mexico, it included quite a few from homes on the settled side of the frontier. To them, food cooked with buffalo dung was repugnant. Until a day or two of hunger dissolved prejudices they marched without food. A couple hundred miles farther west, as food supplies dwindled and soldiers marched twenty or so miles each day on half-, then quarter-rations, food cooked by any fuel or cooked not at all, was more than welcomed.

The quiet of green fields and small trees along the Cottonwood tell nothing of difficulties sometimes met by traders camping at the crossing. To a summer transient, the locality is ordinary. Even for the winter traveler, so long as

Bois de vache

the car heater functions and the radio is on, it is difficult to comprehend that Kansas blizzards were lethal to livestock and men who drove them. In 1841, Don Manuel Alvarez with a few wagons and men camped on Cottonwood River in a winter storm. In but few hours, two men and all the mules were frozen. The remainder survived only because they kept constantly moving. As now the Cottonwood is a thicket of small trees, the circumstance seems improbable with so much firewood about. Surveyor Brown noted on most creeks in this vicinity "no timber" and for Cottonwood River noted "Cottonwood Grove," probably small. Streams with few trees would likely have been stripped of firewood by a few years of travelers on the Road. Since those days, there has been a considerable change in the ecology of the land and streams then barren of timber are now shaded by dense growths of a variety of trees.

Ten years after Alvarez, Colonel Sumner and his group met another blizzard at the Cottonwood.[7] One man and nearly three hundred mules were lost to the storm. Winter winds are still cold in Kansas but now few livestock and fewer men meet them by necessity. When they do, at least the livestock are fortified by a diet with calories adequate to withstand low temperature and high wind, the colder the faster it blows.

Beyond the small wooden bridge by which the country road crosses Cottonwood River, I found a young farmer mowing weeds along the highway. He courteously shut off the tractor to hear my inquiry: "Are there ruts of the Trail nearby?"

With him I walked up a slope and as we came onto a stretch of short grass he remarked that it was virgin sod. A few more steps and he stopped to say: "You're in the middle of the ruts now."

They were so gentle a mark of a time so old that I had not recognized them. We stood in a long curving trough a few inches deep, ten feet, perhaps twelve wide quite as well-grassed as the adjacent soil, indeed a little more so as the farmer pointed out. Although virgin sod all about bore buffalo grass, it was perhaps an inch higher within the trough than without, watered by runoff from soil adjacent. It was always reassuring to find the marks, proof that wagons *had* passed this way, crossed these rivers, camped at those springs. Without such evidence, the tourist on the Road comes to feel he is following a phantom. As far west as Council Grove and perhaps this far beyond, wagons commonly traveled in one dusty column. When rains softened the sod, the column swung aside to cut new tracks parallel to the old. Somewhere between here and Council Grove, the one column sometimes divided to two. Somewhere along the Arkansas River, generally near Pawnee Fork but sometimes before if it was a hazardous Indian summer, the two columns divided to four.[22] Far west in New Mexico I frequently came onto four endless troughs, two rather close together and, fifty yards distant, a second pair. From around Cottonwood River where the first night guard was posted, to El Vado de las Piedras on the Canadian River, the cloud of dust hanging over caravans was a penumbra of caution. Around here and westward to the Arkansas was the margin of Kaw country. Over it Kiowas, Comanches and even Pawnees might sweep. If their road was to war, and generally it was, and if on it they met a caravan, they saw the columns swing apart and converge to a point as the rear wagons remained nearer together, the maneuver completing a rough diamond for defense.

By the casual tourist, ruts are a great deal easier to find in the unplowed west. Where rains are adequate to support crops, the plow is a very effective eraser. Decades ago but years after the abandonment of the Road, the ruts were a great deal easier to see anywhere in Kansas, not so much because of their depth but because of sunflowers. They were the first claimants of the pulverized soil and had not yet given way to a much slower but more enduring competitor, the buffalo grass. For several years after the last wagons, the Road where sunflowers grew was a ribbon of gold through an immense expanse of green, winding down a gentle slope and up across a distant crest.

In and southeast of McPherson, Kansas, are the Turkey Creeks: Running Turkey, Turkey and Dry Turkey Creek. There were thousands of those fowl along creeks crossed by the Road. Settling on the prairies to feed, huge flocks were in numbers so great as to be mistaken at a distance for buffalo. The latter were the universal standard for comparison of all animals in numbers too great for counting.

Westernmost of the three is Dry Turkey Creek, crossed by the Road two miles south of McPherson (Map 7). About an equal distance farther downstream, Sibley and the other Commissioners camped on a Tuesday in the middle of August, 1825, to await the arrival of the Kaws.[32] Old Bill Williams had been sent a few days before with invitation for them to meet in council on Sora Kansa Creek, later Dry Turkey. Kaw, Konza, Kansa and Kansas were alliterations indiscriminately applied to the tribe which roamed country through which the surveyed Road must pass. Their permission and tolerance was required for unhindered traffic on it. Sibley that day recorded: "The morning fair & pleasant . . . the treaty was read . . . after which we delivered them good to the value of Three Hundred Dollars, St. Louis Cost, and gave them an Order on Curtis & Healey, Traders . . . for such as they may want, to the value of Five Hundred Dollars at fair cash prices."

It was a bargain in a way but it weighed little as an obligation on the Kaws. From time to time when the notion struck, they plundered a caravan of livestock. Plundering was a part of their heritage, a way of life, a means to virtue in this world and the next. Moreover, by then, livestock were a part of their economy. A strong, energetic and in-conspicuous brave could start with nothing save daring and with luck become conspicuously wealthy in horses as he made others poorer. In older times before Indians had horses and lived a sedentary life amid small fields of corn and squash, about the only thing a brave might covet from an-other tribe was a slave or a wife. Raiding for squaws was risky business as later raiding for horses came to be. With squaws the point of diminishing returns was quickly reached but with horses never. On ample prairie grass they main-tained themselves and served as currency in purchase of wives, should more be needed, or for slaves. Generally, slaves were captured squaws or the young of either sex and on occasion they were by captors exchanged for horses. When frontier settlements moved west to the domain of prairie Indians, whites came to be slaves of Indians as well as other captured enemies.

As a general rule, with marauding savages it was women and children last. Which is to say: when they could, they killed men and made captives of women and children. On occasion they killed all, but again only some. Always attack-ing Indians were fast operators, knowing well that surprise and speed were their sharpest tactics as they enlisted their greatest ally: panic among victims. Who, then, might be killed and who spared, depended on instant evaluation of confusion. Mary Jane Luston must have owed her life to just such hasty decision.

On the Llano Estacado, near the headwaters of the Colorado River in Texas, on the outer edge of settlements in June 1867, lived a Mr. Babb, his wife, three small children and a summer visitor: Mary Jane Luston, young, and a widow since the preceding year. That month, Babb drove eastward a small herd of cattle to markets several days distant.[58]

On the fatal day of his absence, the two older children were playing in front of the cabin and one called to their mother that men were coming. On looking out the door, Mrs. Babb was terrified to see mounted Comanches racing toward the cabin and already very close. She screamed to the children to come. Perhaps it was the very terror in her voice that held, rather than prompted them. The instant of delay was that much too long and left no time in which to bar the door. In that second, Mary Jane leaped for the ladder to the loft. As one savage seized the children, another raced after Mrs. Babb. Strong hands grasped her hair, jerked back her head and slashed her throat.

The sight was something more than could be witnessed in silence. Mary Jane, who saw it all from the loft, screamed. They dragged her down, put her and the children on horses and rode northward. It was all a matter of fleeting and bloody moments and these preliminary to hard days. As fast as the horses could stand the pace, Indians and prisoners rode for several days and nights making frequent but short stops to rest and graze the horses and for quick food and short sleeps for their riders. In hurried days of travel mostly unremembered by Mrs. Luston, the party crossed the Brazos, the Red, the Wichita and Canadian Rivers. Always, Mary Jane judged the horses. With care she noted those of greatest speed and endurance, how they were guarded, when they were not and how they were picketed during night stops. Late of a dark night after a day of hard riding she crept from the two children in sleep of exhaustion, caught and mounted the best horse. Without saddle and with picket rope for a bridle she rode off at a walk. Once out of hearing of the camp, she urged the mount to a gallop. By Polaris she went north and in the day following, by the sun maintained that direction. She could only guess that the nearest settlement lay northward. For a full thirty-six hours she made the most of the endurance of her horse. When it was completely exhausted, so was she. With picket-rope about her waist, Mary Luston slept.

She awakened as the focus of a circle of Kiowas, Little

Wolf's band. They took her to camp, gave her food and opportunity to rest. They did not offer release but in the days following, treatment by Kiowas was better than that of Comanches. She noted the departure northward of a small band of Indians and their return six days later with ears of green corn. On one futile attempt at escape at night, she caught a horse but as by then she had aroused camp dogs which barked in alarm, she crept back to the lodge, fortunately unnoticed.

Another attempt was successful and Mary Jane rode very fast in the direction from whence the corn came. Accounts do not make clear how long and how far Mrs. Luston rode, but one can guess it was northeast and on leaving the Kiowas, that it was on the order of five days. Coming to a large river in flood, with difficulty she forced the jaded horse across what she later learned was the Arkansas. At no great distance beyond, it was with astonishment and infinite relief that Mrs. Luston came onto a broad well-beaten road. It was the Road to Sante Fe some fifteen miles west of Dry Turkey Creek. East a short distance on it she met a wagon train headed west in charge of an employee of the Bents. As she told her story, they gave her food and while it seems unlikely, the account states she continued alone, unescorted to a settlement on Dry Turkey Creek. At Fort Zarah, on Walnut Creek, about three days and forty-five miles west of the encounter, the teamster spoke with the Indian Agent, even then in council with Little Wolf of the Kiowas who had just told him what he knew of Mary Luston's ride. A messenger was dispatched to escort Mrs. Luston to Council Grove. The two children were ransomed at some later date and returned to their father.

CHAPTER VIII

Between
the Little Arkansas
and the North Bend

HALFWAY BETWEEN McPHERSON and Lyons, Kansas, was the crossing of the Little Arkansas River, and in later years a stage station (Map 8). One who crossed the Little Arkansas a century ago saw it ". . . a ribbon of stately trees winding to the main river through a broad flat valley of green, dotted with fat black buffalo and groups of antelope." [59] In an earlier time it was a point important to all caravans as it was near the margin of buffalo country. By then weeks beyond the frontier, westbound wagons with yet a supply of bacon or salt pork welcomed a change in diet and those without regarded buffalo tenderloin better than tough beef. Certainly it was easier to secure than wild elk, wary deer or timid antelope. There were millions of buffalo on the plains and always an astonishing fraction of that total right on the road. Gibson (one of the Army of the West) found the country between the Little Arkansas and Arkansas Rivers like a slaughter pen: carcasses of buffalo in every stage of decay, skulls, ribs, femurs and fibulas scattered all about. [46]

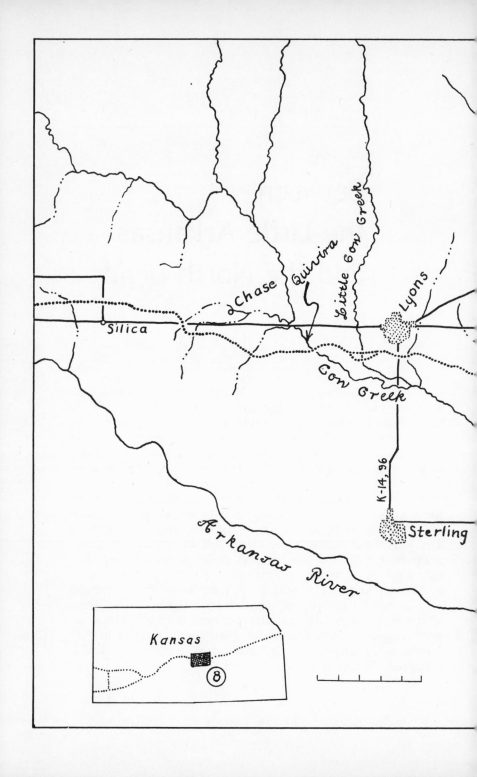

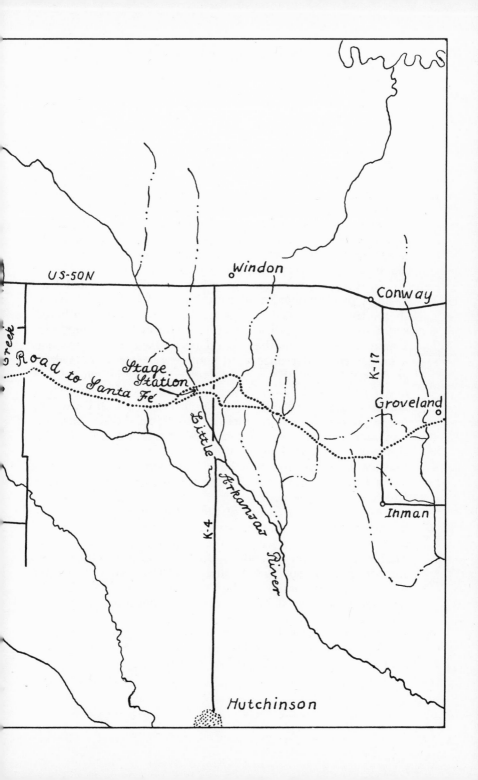

The Little Arkansas is now a crowded line of small trees trending across field and prairie. I found a stone marker for the Trail on the county road that bridges the river but in the thicket of the river itself I found only vertical mudbanks, a pumping oil well, a small boy and two dogs. From the wooden bridge across the Little Arkansas the boy showed me two carp, each a foot long, he had herded into a shallow pool and blocked by stones at either end, and he urged I come to his house to see a piece of iron found on the Road. It was obviously old, thick with rust and curved as one end of a crow-bar. He spoke of "lots of old iron" in a pile in a nearby field and we went to see, together with his sister, about six to his seven years.

Gravely we inspected the pile of bent pipe, rusted bed-springs, truck fenders and frames, bottles and fragments of them. The boy tugged at a stirrup attached to a weathered saddle-tree and together we pulled it free. He thought, and I agreed, that his mother would be pleased to have so fine a saddle. His sister uncovered another real treasure: a deep green bottle once the container of prunes, and two others larger but less in color. With saddle, bottles of several sizes and a fragment of old iron, we walked back toward the house. As his sister bore a lesser burden on shorter legs, she now and then skipped to come even or gain a lead. As she skipped, she chanted softly. When at last I caught the words I would have given, would have had to have given, a good many years to join in: "I like coffee, I like tea; I like Kenneth and Kenneth likes me."

As we turned a corner of the barn and came in sight of his mother in conversation with a middle-aged couple along-side a car in the driveway, the boy insisted he carry the saddle. If we were an odd sight, none of the adults gave sign of thinking so. To my question: "Can you tell me the location of the crossing of the Trail on the Little Arkansas?" the man replied as if he answered that question every day: "No, but my wife can."

She could and did. She was the only unbusy person I met who overflowed with lore of the Road: "My grandfather said . . .; my grandfather-in-law told me. . . ."

I followed the couple down the road a quarter mile, where she pointed to the line of dense-set trees along the Little Arkansas. "That's the actual crossing. You'll find a white granite marker, a stone put there several years ago by the Old Settlers Association. And in the creek bed just beyond are limestone slabs which floored the crossing."

With her husband's aid, I lined her up so that through her head and a fence post just beyond, an imaginary line led to the one tree she intended among a host in the dense line of them.

"As for the stone corral here when the stage came this way, my grandfather-in-law said that if you were on horseback, you could just barely look over the wall. He ran a herd of about 400 cattle around here a long time ago and to keep them from rustlers, he penned them each night in the corral, so you can guess how big it was. Grass then, he told me, was as high, was as high as. . . ." Here she looked at her husband who offered no help.

"As high as a horse's belly?" I supplied.

"As high as a horse's belly everywhere and shoulder-high on the bottoms. Years ago, a long time ago, someone tore down the corral and sold the stones to house-builders in Sterling. You can see houses in Sterling now made of stones from right over yonder in the north end of that maize."

In dense small trees I found the stone marking the crossing of the Little Arkansas and a few paces beyond, dark in dense brush, the channel cut some twelve feet deep in mud banks holding a minor trickle of water between small pools. So thick are the brush and small trees that the Little Arkansas winds through twilight even on a cloudless day. A startled heron sailed from a log and around a bend in the dark tunnel; a turtle glided from the mud, deeper into a pool. There was no footing, but with aid of branches and roots, I slid down into the channel, a morass of mud. About two feet above water level, I found projecting edges of limestone slabs and on the river bed a heap more of them stained by discharge from oil-water-gas separators, for this is oil country now. Selecting a small one, I toted it back to the car. I have it yet, a nondescript chunk of calcium carbonate of no earthly use and certainly nothing I could take with me. Now and then it rattles in the trunk of the car. Common sense and my wife insist that it be removed but I listen to neither. Mementos so hard come by, without close care are certain to be lost. It is true I have no pressing need for it, but somewhere, somewhen, somehow I may. It is the only trophy I have of the Road, save the muleshoe which I frequently place on the coffee table and which reappears as frequently on a bookshelf in the bedroom.

With the aid of good luck and a good map (so I had come to think) I found the crossing of Jarvis Creek. Nearby is a pump-jack which moves up and down ceaselessly as it lifts sucker-rods and, by them, oil from a shallow well. Jarvis, it is said, and I believe the lore, is a corruption of Chavez. The latter is a common name in New Mexico.

Quite early in the commerce of the prairies, there were Mexican wagon proprietors out of Santa Fe, El Paso del Norte and Chihuahua. The *Missouri Intelligencer* of June 9, 1826, remarked: "Six or seven new, well-built wagons owned by Mr. Escudero, a Native of New Mexico, left here loaded with goods. This marks a new era in the trade as he is likely to be followed by his countrymen." It did and he was. They came in such numbers that about half the trade was handled by Escudero's countrymen.

Don Antonio Chavez was one among many who came east. He started with two wagons and five employees but as a storm sweeping across the prairies killed some of his livestock, he abandoned one wagon on the plains. Chavez intended to purchase others in Independence or West Port and merchandise with which to fill them. What Chavez brought in rawhide bags ($10,000 to $20,000 in coin, bullion and furs), depends on which historian one reads but there is agreement as to what happened to him.[36, 40, 60] He was robbed and murdered.

It was a time shortly before Texas annexed the Union, when roving bands on the frontier from the vicinity of Austin had provided themselves, at no great difficulty, with papers signed and sealed by Sam Houston or his Secretary for War. These made privateers of them, so they believed. As a man believes, he commonly acts. Even in those days there was a tendency to confuse the endless swells of the prairie for those of the seas. From such imagery came the impulse to put poetic analogy to practical use by raids on prairie schooners in trade between Missouri and Mexico.

Having somehow made their way to West Port, Missouri, perhaps guided by a geiger counter instinct for the dollar but as likely in quest of riff-raff to join in a raid on the Mexican frontier, a band of Texans learned in Young's tavern of the impending arrival of Don Antonio Chavez with several thousand dollars for purchase of merchandise. Spreading casual word they were leaving to raid the Mexican frontier (a legitimate pastime in Texas), they left West Port and several days later encountered Chavez on the Road, perhaps somewhere in the vicinity of the creek bearing his name. The Texans took their prisoners some distance from the Road, robbed Chavez and shared the booty among themselves. Disagreement among the brigands split the group; some left for Texas and some remained. The group holding Chavez prisoner drew lots and, for reasons known only to those whose blood runs cold, as in reptiles, shot him. Jarvis Creek, once Chavez's, is scarcely a hand-span wide.

Westward traffic on the Road crossed in succession Little Cow and Cow Creeks, just beyond modern Lyons. They flow through country drier than the eastern part of the state and Cow Creek ran but little water between banks perhaps twenty feet high. But they were firm, easily beveled, hence offered little difficulty to loaded wagons. About a mile upstream from the crossing was a spot visited by Europeans nearly four hundred years before there was a Road and some seventy years even before there was a Santa Fe. In 1541, Francisco Vasquez de Coronado ventured across the mountains flanking the Rio Grande, onto the endless Prairies.[3] With him Friar Juan de Padilla recorded on June 29, their arrival at the southern bend of a river which natives called Nepestle, named by Coronado the River of St. Peter and St. Paul, now prosaically the Arkansas. A week later, beyond its great North Bend, on a small tributary, now Cow Creek, they found a considerable settlement: Quivera (Map 8). It was a cluster of grass and reed huts, the home of Wichita Indians amid small fields of corn, beans and melons. Indians settled there partly because in numbers there is strength and partly because then prairie tribes were agriculturalists in villages more or less permanent near small fields of grain and vegetables in soil they found to be fertile. It was not the land of milk and honey, nor of gold and silver Spaniards hoped for. Padilla thought it a fertile field and returned the next year. His good works were short-lasting for some dissident heathen or apostate took his life soon after.

Between the time of Coronado and that of traders, Indians became nomads on horses. Quivera and similar settlements were abandoned for tipis, the roving life and a diet higher in protein. By secret treaty, France relinquished to Spain all of Louisiana west of the Mississippi in 1762 and for the next forty years there was one less among the many hazards to commerce between the Mississippi and Santa Fe. Difficulties remaining were adequate to discourage all save the completely brave or the completely ignorant. By then plains tribes from the Missouri to the presidios of New Spain were centaurians. Even in the judgment of Iberian experts, "as horsemen they have no equal."

Among keys to conquest, horses were a large one. To a man on horseback the world has an aspect different to one afoot. It is his to ride through and if he is motivated by avarice, it is his to ride over and to ride down. Even his language evolved connotative words to fit the unique perspective. In Spanish he was a *caballero* and in French a *chevalier*. By the time Pizarro had collected a "room-full of gold" and the life of Atahualpa whose ransom it was, a continent had been subjugated. By the time Cortez had taken a Mayan mistress from one captain, used her and given her to another, those who made her civilization were slaves.

Horses, and the mobility they gave to men in armour, made these dark deeds possible. Spaniards raised them by tens, then by hundreds and eventually by thousands at Gu-yamo in Cuba, Tlaltizapan in Guatemala and at Oaxaca in Mexico.[61, 62] When Spaniards came north from destruction of Cuzco in Peru and Tenochtitlan in Mexico, they came on horseback to conquer a harsher land. From Spanish in-vaders, Apaches and Comanches collected strays and strag-glers and became themselves *caballeros* and horsemen with-out equals.

With one hand heavy on the Rio Grande, the other on the Missouri, Spanish governors sought to pass from one to the other merchandise surplus in each. To do so they needed a road and from their hope came the scant record of one of the few journeys from west to east across the plains. To mark a road, they employed a Frenchman itinerant in Santa Fe.[63] On May 21, 1792, from that village Pierre Vial, accompanied by Josef Villanueva and Vincente Espinosa, rode seven leagues to Pecos. Three men comprise a short party for so long a venture but Vial was armed with specific instructions comforting in their assurance. Blandly the of-ficial paper stated he was to overcome all obstacles to the advantage of the Province of New Mexico. To smooth the road to St. Louis, as yet unknown, it stated he would, of course, meet only Comanches friendly to New Spain. This must have seemed reasonable at the time because a few years earlier, Spaniards under one Don Carlos had defeated Comanches in the vicinty of Don Carlos Creek and later fought with them a drawn battle somewhere near Round Mound (both points on the later Road to Santa Fe) which resulted in agreement to be friends.[26] Vial was instructed to keep a diary in detail so that others might follow his path. It was a fine bureaucratic beginning.

As a diarist, Vial was parsimonious and most days got no more than a line: "Marched easterly over plains; many creeks. Made ten leagues." Striking the Rio Colorado (Cana-dian River), Vial and his companions followed it for eleven days when illness delayed them for eleven more. Greater hazards lay ahead and illness barely won mention. Vial, Villanueva and Espinosa rode north from the Canadian somewhere beyond the center of the Texas Panhandle. Crossing two streams (North Fork of the Canadian and the Cimarron) and now traveling in Kansas, they met the Arkansas River and rested horses for a day.

In another day of travel down the Arkansas they came on buffalo killed by Indians, judging from signs about and, reassured no doubt by the confident note of official instructions, Vial followed the trace to find them camped on the opposite side of the river. Firing a gun for attention, he got it: mounted Indians swarmed across. The first shook his hand warmly, the next few took the horses and others, drawing knives, hospitably cut off the clothes of their guests. Immediately some drew bows as others shouted: "Kill them with hatchets!"

Among Indians excited with a zest for killing, one shouted above the melee: "Let them live!" Suiting action to words, he hoisted Vial up behind him just as a late-comer to the excitement hurled a spear. Vial's savior grappled with his tribesman, leaving the prisoner mounted alone. Yet another shouted: "Don't kill! I know him!" and spoke to Vial in good French learned, he later said, in the settlement at Saint Luis.

As the two savages grappled, one for life and the other for death of the prisoners, a brother of one of the wrestlers mounted quickly behind Vial and, faster yet, rode with him across the river to camp.

"Eat fast, friend! It is our custom that after eating our food no visitor is killed!" Vial, Espinosa and Villanueva ate for their lives. The latter could not have had much appetite for across his abdomen was a wound which would have been fatal had the knife not first cut the arm of an Indian who sought to save him.

For two weeks the travelers remained naked in the village; then, without clothes, went north with their hosts to a village on the Kansas River named later for the tribe. About mid-September came a French trader who supplied them with what clothes they needed to be dressed among savages and better yet, with tobacco, rifle, powder and balls. A few days later with three French traders, they went down the Kansas to the Missouri and on to "San Luis de Ylinnes,"

Saint Louis of Illinois, a settlement of about 2,250 freemen and 200 slaves. There on October 6, one hundred thirty-nine days and a thousand miles after they were begun, Vial gave to the Governor his instructions and his diary.[63] The venture was half failure, half success. All the king's horses were lost; three of the king's men were safe.

The Cow Creeks in Kansas marked the beginning of short-grass country, herbage favored by buffalo. It was grass only a couple or three inches high, very short indeed in comparison with that two and three feet high in tall-grass country eastward. Teamsters accustomed to high grass were skeptical that nourishment adequate for livestock could be had in the shorter, sparser blades. Although in time convinced, they never found it so convenient. Short grass required that livestock graze a longer time over a wider range. Since Cow Creek was truly Indian country, the longer and wider oxen cropped, the greater the hazard and probability of loss to raiders.

Twelve miles west of Cow Creek and the site of Quivera rose Plum Buttes.[64] There were three and in mid-summer the thickets which grew on and about them provided plums for many transients, including coyotes and wolves. They were not buttes in a topographic sense; rather they were unusually high sand dunes standing perhaps a hundred feet above the prairie. Long, long ago, winds sweeping eastward across the great North Bend of the Arkansas had mobilized the rock debris, moved it from the floodplain and heaped it in dunes out on the prairie. And long ago, their slow migration had been temporarily halted by brush and grass on them, springing up after some mild wet winter and damp spring. They were there when the first wagon passed but soon after the last, by some whim of weather, wind erosion began their reduction. By the time rails lay across the prairie, what had been three prominent hills of sand along the Road had become three minor depressions near the rails.

Soon after leaving Plum Buttes, wagon trains were in sight of the Arkansas River, their goal for weeks and their guide for more. The Arkansas is a line of water two-thirds as long as the Missouri. Heading near Leadville in Colorado, it crosses South Park and slices through the Front Range by a gorge made Royal for tourists. Free of mountains near Cañon City, the river carries a load of rock waste from eroding mountains out onto the high plains. With velocity less on a lower gradient, deposition of the sand makes the plains yet higher. Beyond Pueblo, the Arkansas has a wide gentle valley and in Kansas it is yet wider. Entering that state on a southeast course, it turns northeast for about fifty miles, then by a great bend, resumes the southeast direction. The Road struck the Arkansas at its great North Bend, near where Ellenwood now stands. For some reason unknown, "Camp Osage" was the general locality of the first stop on the river which wagons were to follow for the next week or two.

Early description of the Arkansas, "clear, about two hundred yards wide on a sandy bed and not more than four feet deep anywhere," does not fit closely its appearance now. At Ellenwood town dump I found it clear, about ten feet wide and half as many inches deep (Map 9). A lower water-table and much irrigation higher up have depressed its status at Ellenwood and garbage of the town has not raised it.

Traversing arid country, its course a guide for wagons, the Arkansas has many intermittent and few perennial tribu-taries for some two hundred miles in western Kansas and eastern Colorado. This is commonly so with streams which

rise in mountains and flow through dry country. Rivers flow constantly only where their channel has incised the land to a depth adequate to intersect the watertable, and the Arkansas is one of very few of that region of a size adequate to do so. In arid land the watertable is always low, and the infrequent rainfall filtering slowly down from the surface is insufficient to raise the watertable to shallow depth. As then few streams cut it, subsurface water moves slowly from pore to pore in rock untapped by any save the deeper stream channels.

Tributaries, either intermittent or perennial, were for wagons along the Arkansas a nuisance. The river itself provided a superabundance of water save in the driest of years and tributaries to it, wet or dry, were interruptions, major or minor, on the Road. This was not so when the Army came to build forts for protection of its traffic, for commerce and later for immigrants. To a fort water is as essential as a wall: indeed, is a fifth one without which the fort is always vulnerable. It was not feasible to place a fort on the plain of a river so frequent in flood as the Arkansas. There it would be vulnerable to a hazard less common but greater than Indians. A favored location was on high ground amid unlimited grass and with water adequate within the walls. Next best was water within an arm's reach of the fort. Along the Arkansas this could be only on some flowing tributary of it.

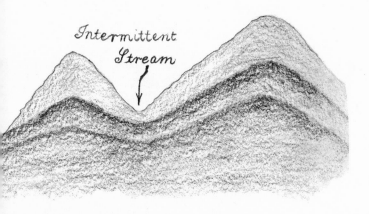

Intermittent Stream

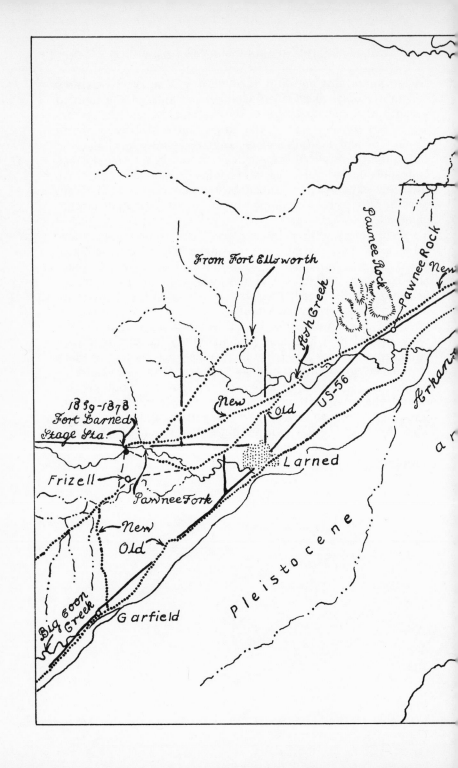

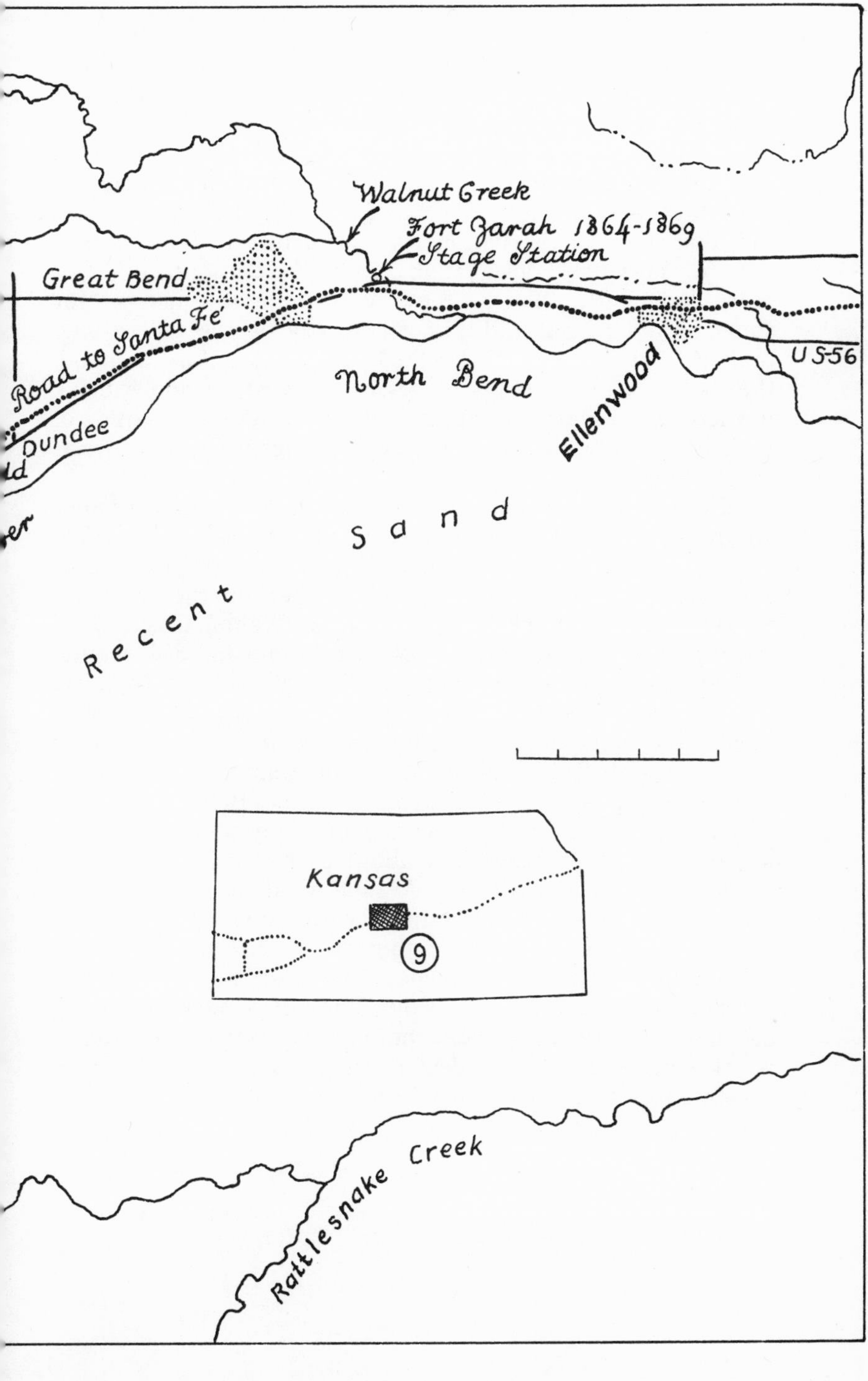

Walnut Creek
Fort Zarah 1864-1869
Stage Station
Great Bend
Road to Santa Fé
North Bend
Dundee
Ellenwood
US 56
Recent   Sand

Kansas
⑨

Rattlesnake Creek

Walnut Creek was such a branch of the Arkansas at its great North Bend. On it, perhaps two miles above its junction with the Arkansas, the Army in 1864 built Fort Zarah.[13, 14] The numerous scattered points of minor military concentration through the west were not imposing structures. From the moment of construction they were intended to be temporary. Variously designated "Camp," "Cantonment" but more frequently "Fort," they were generally named for someone among the military, frequently by the officer who built it, and for himself. Formed of material close at hand, they were of sod in many places in the west; of adobe brick if there were Mexicans about who knew the technique; of timber if there was any but this was rare in the southwest; or of stone.

Fort Zarah was one of the several built that summer and Major General Curtis named it for his son, Zarah, killed in the battle of Baxter Spring, Missouri, the preceding season. General Dodge built another farther up the Arkansas and named it for himself. Fort Zarah on Walnut Creek, from its beginning was temporary and at its end in 1869, melted into the landscape. A marker on the north side of Highway US 50-N has in recent years resurrected the site, an historical invocation of the shroud but not the ghost.

To wagon trains for most of the years, Walnut Creek was an index to travel deeper into danger. Before the Road was abandoned, there had been a good many treaties blanketing the land with peace and about as many of these were abrogated along Constitution Avenue as along the Arkansas. Without treaties and sometimes with guns, wagon trains protected themselves as best they could. It was somewhere around Walnut Creek or Pawnee Fork that the two columns of wagons divided to four. Four lines of vehicles traveling parallel was the convenient number for maneuver into a rough square late on a quiet afternoon or a rough diamond for defense at any moment of the day.

CHAPTER IX

The Arkansas

ALONG THE ARKANSAS BEYOND Walnut Creek and the great North Bend, there was a diversity of dangers to satisfy the adventurous. The shock of surgery generally was not among them. When, by chance, it was, adventure commonly ended. Christopher Carson, an eighteen-year-old fugitive apprentice from a West Port saddlery* is reputed to have been a member of a successful surgical team with serious work in hand somewhere between Walnut Creek and

---

* *Missouri Intelligencer*, October 1826: "Notice—To Whom it may concern: that Christopher Carson, a boy about sixteen years, small of his age, but thick set, light hair, ran away from the subscriber, living in Franklin, Howard Co., Mo., to whom he had been bound to learn the saddler's trade, on or about the first day of September last. He is supposed to have made his way to the upper part of the State. All persons are notified not to harbour, support or assist said boy under penalty of law. One cent reward will be given to any person who will bring back said boy.

David Workman

Franklin, Oct. 6, 1826"

Pawnee Rock. Andrew Broadus, the patient, had been a hunter with Sibley the year before (date of the operation is variously assigned to 1826 and 1827) and was now an employee of Charles Bent, along with Carson, Stephen Turley and others. As the Bent train went into camp one evening not far east of the Arkansas, perhaps in the vicinity of Little Cow Creek, Broadus hastily drew his rifle, muzzle first, from a wagon, intending to shoot a prairie wolf. Snagged on a piece of baggage, the gun discharged, the ball lodging in his right arm. What treatment Broadus got, certainly primitive, was inadequate and within a few days the arm was swollen and odorous with gangrene.[32, 65, 66]

A reader of western history can never know what is fact and what is folklore, or when either becomes legend. It is said by a great many, only one of whom was there, that Carson, with aid of others, honed a butcher-knife to razor sharpness, filed the coarse teeth of a saw finer and sharper and anesthetized Broadus with whiskey. The ex-apprentice in saddlery, certainly as skilled in cutting and sewing of skins as any of the group, sliced Broadus' arm to the bone and with the saw, cut it through. If truly he did then someone else must have applied the hot wagon-bolt in cauterization of the stump and yet another applied a coating of warmed resin and tar, the common lubricant of squeaking wheels. They must have worked fast, for if they had the wit to know why they need do as they did and ingenuity to devise a means, experience as hunters must have taught them a mode, for spurting arteries and shock of surgery wait for no man. Andrew Broadus survived many years but not so many as the Carson legend.

Southwest from Great Bend, Highway 50-N, the Road and rails travel a distance in close company and in some places the Road is beneath pavement and rails (Map 9). Along here the northwest skyline, margin of the valley of the river, is higher than is common in plains country and the height is the Dakota sandstone: the forerunner, the beach deposit of a Cretaceous sea advancing onto the continent. At a time when a great revolution had folded some fifty thousand feet of sediments into what became the Appalachian Mountains on the east margin of North America, the interior of the continent, once a sea-floor, had been gently raised without folding to the status of dry land. In a later geologic era, the Mesozoic, while the east remained high and dry, the western and mid-portions of the continent were depressed for an epoch of Cretaceous time to be the floor of a colossal arm of the sea, receptacle of sands from the continent.

Invasion of a continent by the sea signaled a prodigious development among dinosaurs to a size heretofore unequaled by any organism, aerial, marine or terrestrial. Ponderously they stalked a domain in domination unquestioned, save by their own kind. When great carnivores among them of which *Tyrannosaurus* was an incredible one, sought prey among herbivores nearly as large, lesser reptiles fled the thunder of giants. What brought an end to reverberations of such and the extinction of dinosaurs is yet a moot question.

The Dakota formation had its beginning with the invasion of the continent by the Cretaceous sea. Its end is yet to be but its career includes induration, cementation to stone, its uplift and exposure to erosion by the Arkansas River which cut in it a valley and left a prominence which is now Pawnee Rock, highest on the Road east of New Mexico (Map 9).

At Pawnee Rock, the Dakota is a deep red-brown soft sandstone, a landmark to all men, red or white, passing this way. On its surface, stained dark by iron oxide, the rust of steel and stone, the earliest Spaniards carved inscriptions found later by the French. So, too, did travelers on the Road. As a register of transients, Pawnee Rock came to hold thousands of names, a few among them distinguished as those of authors of narratives of travel on the Road to Santa Fe. As they tarried behind departing wagons and while her husband and servant stood watch on the warm morning of July 4, 1846, Susan Magoffin left her name among the myriad there.[2] So did several hundred Kilroys of the Army of the West. It was at Pawnee Rock overlooking miles of the plains that some among them had their first sight of the tens of thousands of buffalo and a consciousness of the uncountable, unnumbered millions of them. They were then, and frequently there, a dark brown mobile crust on an ocean of green, and some who saw it from Pawnee Rock estimated it a crust of a million separate pieces. It was a thin one, reaching a thousand miles south and twice as far north. Before many generations, the brown spots which made it were to be red and, for a few years before they returned to the dust from whence they came, bleached white. In but few years more, Pawnee Rock itself was to be a monument to the rails which antiquated the Road and to a competitor of them, the pavement. Much of the Rock was indiscriminately quarried, Spanish inscriptions and all, for railroad ballast, and those who travel the pavement have followed the impulse of those on the Road. On weathered sandstone now there is no place for another name and rare indeed is one which antedates the pavement. I found just one, "Roglin 63," remaining to be obliterated.

For two hundred years, Pawnee Rock served as a sign-post far out on the prairies and for a century as register of Road and pavement. It once served as a cemetery. Richardson, an Army private en route west a few days after Susan, climbed the rock and saw buffalo everywhere, merging in the distance to a dark blanket from horizon to horizon. He saw also the grave of Nemiah Carson of Glasgow, Missouri, dead and buried there three days before. Just south of Pawnee Rock, on Ash Creek, was another marked by a fragment of Dakota sandstone carved "R. T. Ross," and around it the same horde of Buffalo.[56]

Half a wagon-day beyond Ash Creek, the Road crossed Pawnee Fork, the second of the flowing tributaries of the Arkansas, at a point very near the southeast corner of Larned, Kansas (Map 9). In later and wetter years, there was a branch of the Road near what now is Dundee. The west branch was the "Dry Route" which crossed Pawnee Fork higher up where Fort Larned was to be. The Dry Route was in use before 1843, and it was indeed very dry. A part of its course southwest of Pawnee Fork was in sight of the Arkansas River but in the fifty miles across the South Bend of the River it passed no flowing water and only in wet seasons did it pass water stagnant and odorous in buffalo wallows (Map 10). It was feasible only in wet years and in dry seasons only for men in haste or with little care for their livestock. There was enough of both to cut ruts still visible on the parched sod. Davis, by stage, traversed some thirty miles of the fifty of the Dry Route on some path unknown but which crossed Coon Creek, a dry arroyo which lies nears the Arkansas and by its tributaries drains the region of the Dry Route. Davis' stage had crossed Pawnee Fork by moonlight after Mr. Booth, wagonmaster, made reconnaissance of it because with banks high and steep it was an "excellent ambuscade" for Indians.[26] Somewhere next day they crossed Coon Creek and Davis had reason to recall it. The mules ran away, full speed down the steep bank. The wagon bed was thrown from the running gear, landing ten feet away. Davis was thrown on his head, stunned, and Reynolds was bloody from a deep cut over an eye. The mules raced over the prairie with a light load made lighter as linch-pins fell from hubs, setting wheels free and dropping the axle to skim the sod. The outriders caught the runaways and after a delay of only an hour, had the pieces together again and were under way. With kegs still holding water from Pawnee Fork, by time of the evening camp there was plenty for men but the mules were so dry they could not or would not eat. Later, in such darkness that Davis and Reynolds took turns walking ahead to scout a suitable path, the mules were driven yet farther, this time for their own good to water in the river.

Lieutenant Royall, an earlier traveler on the Road, also had occasion to remember Coon Creek.[67] With new recruits out of Fort Leavenworth destined for Chihauhua, he left the Fort as escort for Major Bryans, Army paymaster, as far as Fort Mann. At Leavenworth, the detachment had been equipped with breech-loading carbines newly arrived from Germany. They were an innovation in armament as they could be loaded to fire five shots a minute. In the hands of backwoods boys they were fearful weapons, throwing a one-ounce ball each twelve seconds, dangerous to soft flesh although perhaps not lethal, at four hundred yards. Although the black powder of their cartridge made an impressive noise and much smoke, it failed to drive the ball through as much as two dried buffalo skins at a short distance or even one at a greater.

En route on the Road, the mounted troops found the crossing of Pawnee Fork so steep that wagons were let down by ropes, and Pawnee Rock so crowded with names that they had difficulty in finding places for their own. Lieutenant Royall followed the old Road on the northwest bank of the Arkansas and crossed Coon Creek at its mouth. Upriver they camped on the slope of the ridge separating the Arkansas from drainage to Coon Creek, somewhere near modern Kinsley, Kansas. That day, Tandy Giddings, an old plainsman and their guide, urged Royall to double the guards for he was certain Indians were about. When questioned, he pointed to the absence of buffalo in a season and region where usually there were thousands.

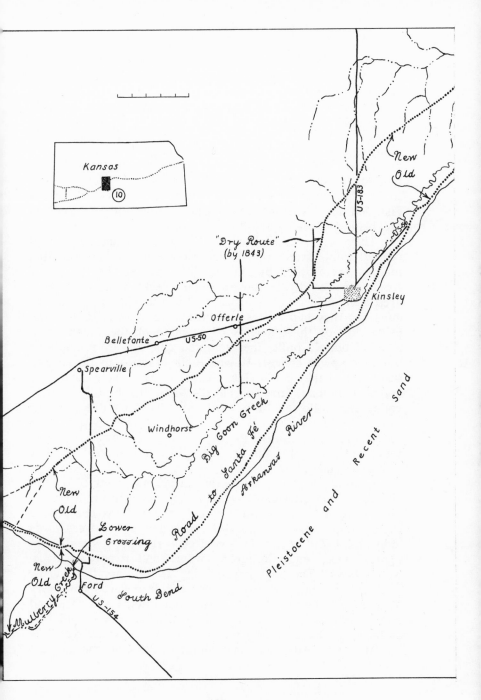

Before dawn next morning, men were sent with horses to a nearby depression where grass was thick. As they returned to camp, they heard wolves howling on the opposite side of the river, answered by others downstream and from the divide between Coon Creek and the River. Giddings spoke sharply: "Look out, boys! I've heard them wolves many a time. Them's Indians!" But no one believed.

Even as Giddings gave warning, some of the boys sighted buffalo, several hundred, galloping toward camp. They rushed for their guns, intent on fresh tenderloin for breakfast. Giddings' warning was sharper: "Hold on thar! Indians are behind those buffalo!"

They were, and clearly seen as the stampeded herd veered aside from the tents. Moreover they were, that moment, reinforced by Indians from across the River and from over the divide toward Coon Creek: some eight hundred Comanches and Apaches on the warpath. They had no guns but they had lances and bows and arrows. Behind the protection of thick shields of rawhide of the tough neck-skin on buffalo bulls, they tempted rifle fire by precipitous but incomplete charge. It was their practice to do so and then, fast as they could ride, charge to lance their opponents before they had time to reload. When the first ineffective volley was followed by a more effective second at shorter range, Indians retreated. As it had never been within their experience and confident the rapid fire could not be repeated, they charged again. On the field they left several as they retreated once more.

A mile or so distant the attackers assembled and "howled for a quarter of an hour." Perhaps the howls were directions and orders, for suddenly the Indians charged: a racing solid front of warriors, perhaps a hundred yards long and eight or ten horses deep. "It was a standing-up fight between eight hundred savages and twenty-six backwoods boys." The boys began firing at four hundred yards; fired still at three, at two, at one hundred yards with very little effect. The lead balls striking the shields was "a sound like striking a board fence. It looked as if they would ride us down as the front line was held in place by the rear."

At fifty yards, someone shouted: "Shoot the horses!

Shoot the horses!" The effect was instantaneous and astonishing: horses and riders fell in heaps. Those who could, turned and fled. By the time the attackers had crossed the River into the sandhills, Royall had made some order out of the confusion. At his command: "Mount and pursue!" the troops galloped across the river and ascended a sandhill to see Indians half-way up the next. With Royall leading, the backwoods boys charged down and up the slope. When they were half-way up, Indians poured over the crest. The soldiers retreated with savages close behind. Smith Carter dropped his carbine, dismounted hastily to recover and as he remounted, his horse threw him. That moment a racing Indian leaned forward to lance him, but Carter exactly at the right moment dropped flat to the ground. Dave Rupe paused to fire an old Missouri deer rifle and the gun snapped as an Indian charged with upraised lance. Instead of a government issue "US" belt, Rupe wore a hunter's belt with a large iron buckle. The lance, tipped with a segment of officer's sabre, struck the buckle, wedging between frame and tongue. Instantly grasping the lance with one hand, pistol in the other, Rupe shot his assailant.

Retreating to the crest of a sand hill, the boys used their carbines with murderous effect as they dodged arrows. One of these, fired at a high angle, arched up and down to pierce the thigh of a soldier, pinning him firmly to the saddle until the shaft could be cut off. Just as the Indians turned and raced away, a last volley killed a splendid grey horse. Scrambling to his feet, the rider turned to retrieve the saddle, only to be killed by a last long shot. On the instant an Indian boy, some thirteen or fourteen years old, turned from the retreating group and with the speed of light raced back. As he reached the body, he plowed to a stop. Hitting the ground running, the boy fastened a lariat about the corpse, leaped to mount and dragged it from the field. Not a shot was fired as the backwoods boys watched the plains boy in admiration.

As some dressed the wounds of five injured soldiers, others counted seventy-three dead Indians in the sandhills and about the camp.[67]

The Arkansas around the junction with Coon Creek was always dangerous water. Colonel Easton camped on it in 1847 and sent a wood-gathering detail across early in a morning.[25] From out of the high grass on the floodplain Indians rose from ambush to kill eight and wound four. A relief party drove off the attackers and found seven of the eight bodies. Next day another party searched for the missing body but unsuccessfully. Colonel Easton was unwilling to leave without another search by a larger group. They found the soldier badly wounded, yet alive and completely scalped. He recovered to live through several years of dangers on the frontier.

Coon Creek country had long been within reach of war parties of several tribes before the Army had difficulties there. Pawnees from the region of the Platte River frequently passed there en route to raids in Mexico. About where the backwoods boys fought Comanches and Apaches, twenty years before them James Collins, James Fielding, Solomon Houck, Edwin Ryland, Elisha Stanley, Thomas Talbot and William Wolfkill, returning from a year in Santa Fe where they had exchanged merchandise for coin and about a hundred horses, mules and asses, camped on an October night. Pawnees crept near the sleeping group and with a sudden whooping rush, stampeded all but three hobbled animals. Scouting next day, the traders found sixty-six animals abandoned in the rush. Back in Missouri, they petitioned Congress for reimbursement of losses as it had happened on U.S. land.

North from Coon Creek, the Army built Fort Larned in 1859 on Pawnee Fork.[68] It began as "Camp on Pawnee Fork" and became "Camp Alert." Next year an adobe structure was begun three miles upstream on the Fork and this was named for Paymaster Benjamin Larned. The adobe buildings were soon replaced by stone quarried from an outcrop of Dakota on Lookout Mountain, now Jenkins Hill. Five years after its beginning, Ketchan saw Fort Larned and was impelled to remark that "dissipation, licentiousness and venereal disease prevail in and around the fort to an astonishing degree." [64] Abandoned by troops in 1882, the seven or eight stone buildings yet stand and one may see them partly equipped as in their earlier days. For years part of a ranch, the stone barracks, saddlery, smithy and officers' quarters enclose a parade ground perhaps three blocks long by half as wide. Within a building on the north side, a visitor may descend a few steps, walk crouched a few yards of tunnel and emerge at the margin of a meander of Pawnee Fork which supplied the Fort. In the August I saw it, there was a pool adequate to meet the needs of many although the river was not flowing. From old accounts, one would guess Pawnee Fork the largest among those discharging to the Arkansas. One traveler judged it as large as the Neosho which is but a small stream now. Another recorded a width of twenty yards and a depth of one to three feet at the crossing. A stream so small might be counted peaceful, save in days of flood. Part of the dangers it carried must have been washed from land about; although commonly dry and always arid, it nurtured many.

Indians on horseback were marvels of skill. On horseback and bent on plunder, they were marvels of efficiency. With it they reduced professional generals to fumbling sergeants and alert lieutenants to rear-rank privates. General Custer at the battle of Little Big Horn was a glittering example of the former in a later day. Lieutenant Love on the Arkansas, near the mouth of Coon Creek, was an outnumbered example of the latter.

In June, 1847 Love commanded a detachment of cavalry out of Fort Leavenworth, escort for some $350,000 to meet the expense of the Army in New Mexico.[19] At the crossing of Pawnee Fork, some miles above its junction with the Arkansas, Love and his men came on two wagon trains encamped, one bound for Santa Fe, the other for the States. The day before, Indians had attacked the returning caravan and within sight of it had killed most, if not all, the oxen. As the marauders were known to be still in the vicinity, Love took both trains with him, presumably until encounter with another eastbound on the Road would provide the strength of union.

The slow march of a day brought the group to the

Arkansas. There Love disposed the wagons in corrals within a short quarter-mile of the River, his men midway between and less than two hundred yards from either. A corral of heavy wagons is a fortification of greater military weight than mere pounds. With his men encamped between, their horses on short pickets and immediately at hand, the Lieutenant had that mobile unit so vital in defense against mounted Indians.

That night, oxen ruminated placidly and safely within the enclosure. Next morning, just as oxen were turned out of one corral to graze north of the wagons and as livestock were about to be released from the second, Indians swooped. Scattering as sort of a lethal chaff, with whoops and waving blankets, they stampeded the livestock and with arrows wounded three herdsmen. On the instant, cavalry were in the saddle seconds after, rather than minutes before the fact. In those seconds, from out of nowhere across the river, fifty Indians charged the camp. Instantly Lieutenant Love split his decision and his men: twenty-five guarded the camp as the remainder raced with Sergeant Bishop to recover the vanishing livestock. Words for the action are a euphemism for high velocity bedlam. As Bishop and mounted men descended on the galloping oxen and their tormentors, three hundred savages came over the rise on the northwest side of the river and another two hundred from the south bank. As much a part of their speeding mounts as were their manes and tails, whooping Indians raced as demoniacal whippets among frightened rabbits. With blankets as terrifying as now commonly they are comforting, they stampeded horses of the cavalry. With the speed of lightning and the skill of malevolent sorcerers, whooping savages transferred blankets from hand to mouth and flashed arrows from bows to soft flesh.

In minutes countable on three hands, five soldiers were dead and five more wounded. In fewer intervals of chaos and confusion, savages and oxen were across the River beyond sight among sandhills. Lieutenant Love and his men had received their first seasoning lesson in high velocity maneuvers.

To General Jones in the safety of Fort Leavenworth, a rueful Lieutenant reported that his detachment was encamped with both wagon trains and would remain so until reinforcements arrived. He estimated that time elapsed between the first warwhoop and last sight of Indians was no more than half an hour.[25]

Beyond Kinsley in Kansas the older line of the Road is difficult to follow in its course along the Arkansas as the highway swings away from the river. An interested traveler may intersect the Road by pavement reaching the small town of Ford at the South Bend (Map 10). The settlement is well named because Mulberry Creek, which enters from the south side, was the site of a ford of the Arkansas, the "Lower Crossing." The earliest wagons used it until a better was found upstream. Anyone willing to walk half a mile along fences can readily find the junction of the thin, slightly cloudy flow from Mulberry Creek with the clear and not much larger of the Arkansas. It was, in a very large space, a very small spot at which wagons were pointed from distant Missouri. The combined streams are scarcely ten feet wide now, but cooling to hot feet in August. The two waters differ slightly in color and after they join in a flow a few inches deep they remain distinct in the few tens of yards they can be seen downstream before willows close densely about them. Somewhere nearby, wagons crossed here between 1822 and about 1825 until an easier crossing was found upstream, but on occasion the Lower Crossing was used in the 1850's. Somewhere about, many wagons must have camped before they continued up the Mulberry. The creek does not now flow from any great distance upstream but there must have been flowing water for a greater part of the valley when wagons came this way. From a head somewhere near the modern village of Ensign, the Mulberry flows parallel to the Arkansas for about twenty miles, then turns northeast for ten more to join the river (Maps 10 & 11). Following the Mulberry upstream, wagons must have had in most years at least a trickle of water;

thereafter they depended on pools and beyond them found occasional water by digging in the creek bed. Having followed the Mulberry for about thirty miles, on leaving it the Road was a great deal drier. West lay nearly thirty miles of the "Waterscrape," the Cimarron Desert, very dry now and incomparably drier for mules and oxen pulling heavy wagons. Taking heed of reports of mule and man-killing terrain, most caravans went some forty miles past the mouth of Mulberry Creek to the Middle Crossing, beyond the present towns of Cimarron and Charleston on the Arkansas.

Before many wheels marked the Road, traders with merchandise on packhorses sometimes left the Arkansas and the Lower Crossing at Mulberry Creek. An 1822 company of thirty-one out of West Port, captained by Joel Walker and Benjamin Cooper, struck the Arkansas and bad luck at the North Bend.[32, 69] Osages stampeded their grazing guarded horses. More determined than discouraged, but considerable of both, four of the party returned to the frontier for replacements and in twenty-two days were back at the North Bend. By experience both wary and cautious now, the company traveled upriver to the South Bend and the mouth of Mulberry Creek. It must have been an unusually dry year and no flowing water in the creek, for in recounting their trials, Joel Walker remembered that "From this point we traveled west a day and a half without water."[69]

An account of the physiology of thirst is parched reading; the experience of it a torment. A mere day and a half without water is adequate to induce a mania for liquid, any kind so long as it is wet, and the psychology of thirst produces in some an inertia that becomes resignation to dry death. Joel Walker and seventeen of the thirty-one went in search of water; those resigned remained. Fortunately they found a small stagnant pool and Walker sent five men back to camp while he remained to guard the odorous fluid, strong with buffalo urine, from other thirsty animals. When his companions did not return in reasonable time, Walker killed a stray buffalo, from it removed the skin of a hindquarter, filled it with putrid water stained with blood and went in search of them. By 10 P.M. he, too, was done in;

on the prairie he slept. Next morning, somewhat refreshed and no longer thirsty he resumed search for the camp. Encountering two strays of his company, he left a small group on the plain not far from the Arkansas with its ample water and he returned to the main camp with seven others. No doubt he was welcomed. As the thirsty men recouped strength, Walker saw in the distance a large party on horseback. With a companion and precaution against surprise, the two went out to meet the strangers, certain they were Indians. To Joel Walker's unlimited astonishment, the leader of the group was a brother, Captain Joe Walker, whom he had not seen for more than a year. Joe Walker had been trapping in western mountains and sometime in that interval had cached merchandise on the Arkansas, returned for the goods and was then en route to Santa Fe. It was a happy reunion on the wide prairie and a reassuring one, for Captain Joe Walker's company had an Indian guide, one Francisco Sargo, who knew the country well and assured them there would be no more difficulty for lack of water. The group now numbered fifty-five and together they drove 200 mules and horses. As on the desert there is safety in number provided there is water adequate for all, the joined parties traveled westward, Francisco Sargo well in advance to scout the best route.

Having again exhausted what water they carried, the parched men followed Sargo, generally a minute speck in the distance. That night, still without water, they saw the guide, scarcely visible even in the clear air, as a small speck atop a distant mesa. By nine o'clock they had found neither water nor guide and they were again within the grip of dehydration and near-panic.

Early in the cool dawn they went west without water, in what soon became a hot and parching June day. Desperately they turned northeast, aiming for the Arkansas. Sometime around mid-afternoon, the men encountered a buffalo, shot it and thirstily drank its blood. It was not enough for all and it marked the spot where twenty-five remained, resigned and exhausted. About an hour before sundown the remainder waded into the Arkansas and quenched their thirst. Immediately Joel Walker filled eight or ten canteens and began the return. When in the dark he could not find his weaker companions, Walker hobbled his mule and slept fitfully. Next morning, he was awakened by shots and from a promontory looked down on his company welcoming another who, by good luck, had located the exhausted adventurers lying about the dead and dry buffalo. From among them, one was missing.

With adequate water they went in search. By good luck they saw in the distance their companion, Will Huddard and a buffalo he had killed for its blood. On closer approach, they heard him croak: "Water?" They filled him, or thought they had but Huddard, perhaps semidelirous, crawled back into the animal to lap more blood. Next day the recollected group returned to the Arkansas where they gave Huddard a much-needed bath and access to water adequate even for his monumental thirst. Wiser, weaker and still dry men, they continued up the Arkansas to Chouteau Island at the Upper Crossing, and south from it they reached Lower Cimarron Spring without difficulty. Meeting no other hazards they arrived safely at Santa Fe. "We had two bales of domestic which we sold for $45 a bale. We could have sold calicos and cottons for any price. . . . A little looking glass worth ten cents was easily sold for a dollar."

From Fort Larned southward across the Dry Route or on the older Road at the margin of the Arkansas, is empty country even now.[70] It was a great deal more so when wagons raised dust within it. Captain Phillip St. George Cooke had been warned that some part of it might prove dangerously crowded. Cooke and his troops were the guard of a wagon train as the season before had been fruitful of Indian depredations and traders expected another vintage year. Captain Cooke and the caravan had followed the Dry Route to strike the Arkansas perhaps three miles upsteam from the mouth of Mulberry Creek.[55] Earlier in the trip, the party had encountered Ceran St. Vrain, partner of the Bents in Bent's Fort on the upper Arkansas, who had warned of a group of armed Texans raiding commerce on the Road. Coming from the Dry Route, Cooke saw Colonel Sniveley's group of Texans camped on the south side of the River, perhaps on Mexican land.

From Red River (between Texas and Oklahoma) north to the Arkansas, the Hundredth Meridian was the boundary between Mexico and the United States (Map 11). Westward the boundary was the Arkansas River. The Meridian intersects the River at the site of Dodge City. On a modern map, Snively and his marauders would be about ten miles east of the meridianal boundary and that many miles within U. S. Territory. Lacking a chronometer and a technician experienced in making observations for longitude, ten miles would have been a reasonable error in location of the critical meridian. Cooke had neither chronometer nor technician. He had only a suspicion and, as an officer and gentleman by act of Congress, strong prejudice for a "store-keeper's clerk" he had "known in Nacogodoches in 1832" who called himself a Colonel, as Snively did.

Cooke collected his officers and asked their opinion: should he disarm the Texans, probably on U.S. territory, even if it meant a fight? The majority of No's carried less weight than the Captain's decision and Cooke sent an officer to fetch Snively from across the River. When Snively came, the Captain examined the Colonel's commission. By it, Texas authorities empowered Snively to organize a company, equip it at his own expense and with it raid New Mexico commerce. The commission read clearly that a proper accounting of booty would be made by an appointed representative of Texas and that the State would share in the loot. Cooke thought it a preposterous paper, unbecoming of any nation and he later spoke of the Texans as no better than pirates. The Captain ordered the Colonel to disarm his men.

Before he left to do so, Snively informed Cooke he had 107 men, and ten days earlier had attacked a hundred Mexicans, the advance guard of General Armijo's army (in camp at Lower Cimarron Spring on the Cimarron River, a point sixty miles southwest and a distance somewhat greater than generally separated the main body from an advance guard), en route to the Middle Crossing to take over escort of the caravan. Snively reported he had killed eighteen and wounded about as many before he had defeated and disarmed the remainder. Magnanimous in victory, Snively had set the Mexicans free, returning to them twenty muskets so that they would not be without arms on their return to Santa Fe. The battle, hard-won by brave men, had taken place on Mexican land for Snively stated the encounter had been on the Road fifteen miles southwest of the Middle Crossing. It was as true as anything he said but as all other details proved false, it does not seem likely that Snively inserted in the web of fiction a word of fact.

Some of the Texans turned homeward with the few rifles allowed them by Cooke for defense against Indians. Others remained in camp for Cooke's return, to accompany him back to the Missouri frontier.

Upriver at the Middle Crossing, the soldiers and traders went into camp. That day or the next, the merchants and their teamsters (130 armed men) began the work of crossing twenty-four American and thirty-two Mexican wagons. It could not have been an easy job as it required ten hours. Remaining in camp, Cooke sent out a hunting party which returned with a Mexican who had escaped the Snively attack, along with a companion who had just died. The Mexican reported his group had numbered fifty, of which four were armed with muskets, the remainder with bows, arrows and lances. These were common armament of Santa Fe militia. Another hunting party encountered a second survivor who stated the group attacked by Snively had numbered forty-eight, four carrying muskets.[55]

CHAPTER X

La Jornada

THE DRY ROUTE FROM FORT LARNED met the older Wet Route along the Arkansas, at a point west of the South Bend and east of the Hundredth Meridian (at Dodge City), near where was to be Fort Dodge, forty years younger than the Road. Because in that region all trains on the Dry Route were in need of water, there must have been hundreds if not thousands of tracks on grass where wagons went direct to the nearest point on the River. Fort Dodge began in 1864, near the junction of the Wet and Dry Routes, as a few huts of posts set close and upright in the ground and roofed with sod.[13, 41] Next year there were two adobe buildings, later veneered with stone and these still stand. I found Fort Dodge a cluster of a few stone and many frame houses amid flower-beds fronting on Sherman, Custer and MacArthur Streets and Patton Drive. On almost every porch sat an old soldier and sometimes his wife. As the only traffic at a late afternoon hour, I waited long as a very old soldier tapped his way blindly across Dewey Street.

The tourist on Highway US-154 crosses the Hundredth

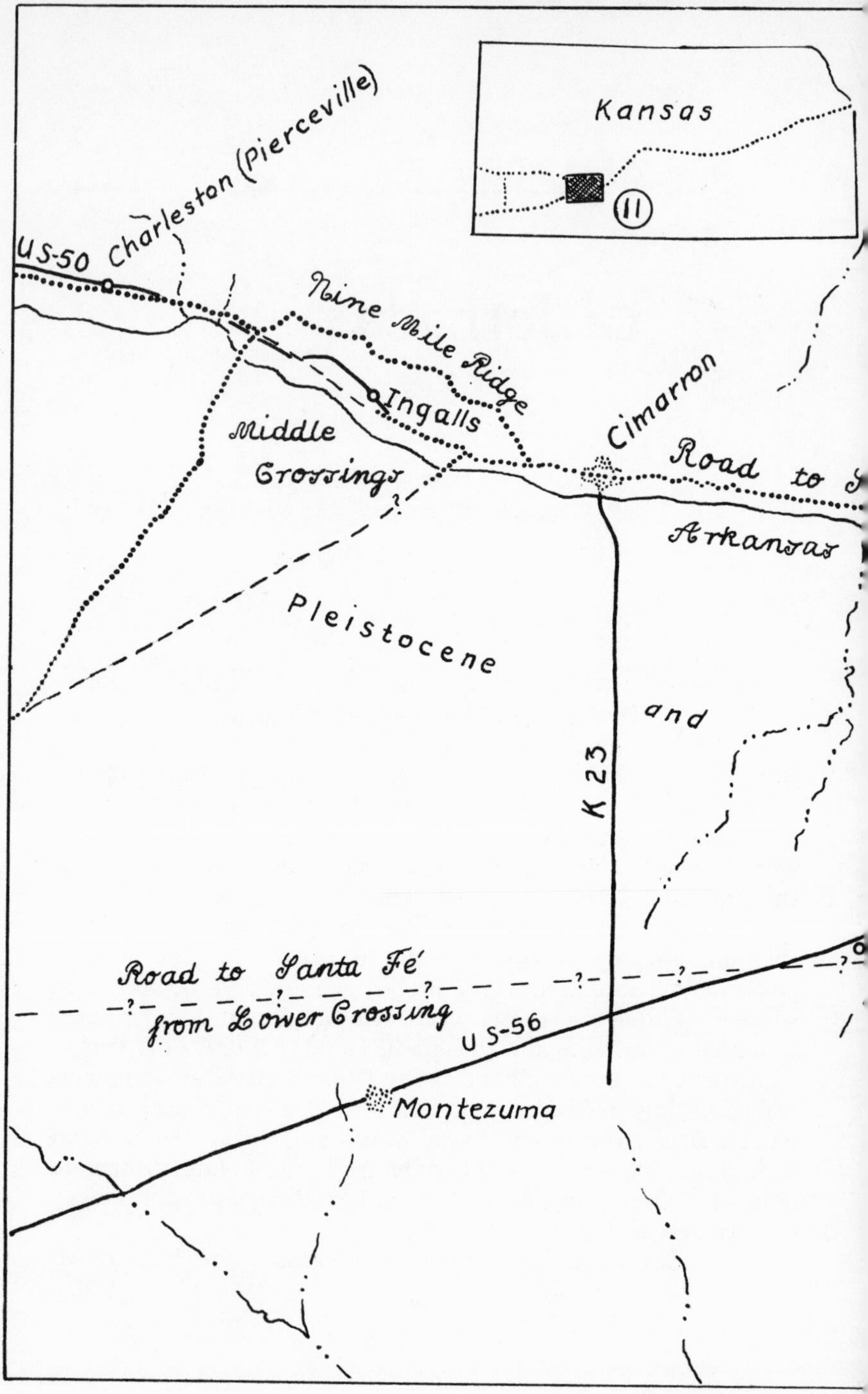
Kansas
11
US-50
Charleston (Pierceville)
Nine Mile Ridge
Ingalls
Middle
Crossings
Cimarron
Road to
Arkansas
Pleistocene
and
K 23
Road to Santa Fé
from Lower Crossing
US-56
Montezuma

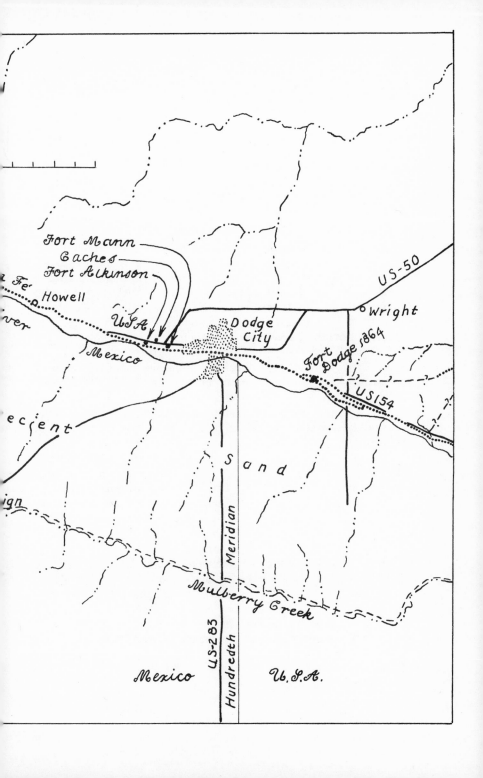

Meridian at the east margin of Dodge City (Map 11). Its intersection with the Arkansas was once a corner common to Mexico and the United States. An indefinite mile west of town is the site of Fort Mann. For the military it was a way-station in 1847 with a wheelwright, blacksmith shop and minor storage facilities. In the two months of its occupation (May and June) three of the guard were scalped. George Brewerton, an Army regular who did not lose his, spoke lightly of the men stationed there.[33] He passed the Fort en route from Los Angeles to the east and recalled Fort Mann as a "little government post garrisoned by a handful of volunteers who drank whiskey, ate Uncle Sam's bacon and hardtack, drew their pay regularly and otherwise wore out their lives in the service of the country." Brewerton had traveled as far as Santa Fe with Christopher Carson who carried dispatches from General Sherman, Military Governor of California, announcing an important discovery of gold at Sutter's Fort on the American River.

About a mile west and four years after Fort Mann was abandoned, Colonel E. V. Sumner supervised construction of Camp Mackay, later Fort Sumner and finally Fort Atkinson. Colonel Lowe of the Quartermaster Department saw it in 1851 and thought it a comfortable sod building.[19] Others who knew the establishment spoke familiarly of it as Fort Sod and Fort Sodom. If Fort Sod resembled Fort Larned in reputation it was, aptly, Fort Sodom. Major Fitzpatrick, Indian Agent, had assembled there a considerable group of Apaches, Kiowas and Comanches for a "Big Talk." Lowe estimated them at 30,000 but a careful census would not have found so many in all three tribes combined. That year or the next, Washington and the tribes agreed upon a treaty. For $18,000 in red calico, red beads, red blankets, copper kettles ($1.00 a pound), knives and hatchets but *no* guns, Apaches, Kiowas and Comanches would leave inviolate everything on the Road. Doubtless the Indians, as did Washington, took all the agreement seriously, save the promise of peace. Treaties between Washington and its western wards were quite surely worth the paper they were written on, for paper in that quantity has value.

Davis, passing by stage in November the following year, saw Fort Atkinson abandoned and falling to ruins. Next year it was reoccupied by the time Lieutenant Beckwith, engaged in one of several surveys for a transcontinental railroad, marked a reconnaissance line up the Arkansas past the Fort.[70] He counted there 280 lodges of Comanches, their horses and mules spread for miles around. As a successful brave might have fifty to a hundred and a prominent sub-chief or chief 500 to 1,000 horses, the landscape must have been crowded. From Major Chilton at the Fort, Beckwith secured wood for cooking bacon and coffee, because with so many campfires on a treeless land, there was neither drift-wood on the river nor buffalo chips on the prairie.

The sites of Forts Mann and Atkinson just west of Dodge City are about a mile apart. Somewhere between them was an older mark on the Road: the Caches. In the quarter-century before there were forts or their ruins in the southwest, the Caches were seen and remembered by many.[2, 32, 38, 40] A cache is a hide, a concealment, for something of value. Constructed by a plainsman it was a task done with care, else another plainsman, red or white, would find and loot the cache.

Site for a cache was a spot conspicuous for nothing but one which could be found a year or two later. A circle of sod a couple of feet in diameter was carefully cut and removed intact. In the soil beneath, a shaft was dug about two feet deep and below that the excavation was enlarged to hold what was to be hidden. Overall shape was that of a bottle: narrow neck and wider body. All soil removed was carefully collected on a blanket and dumped into the nearest running water or, if none were convenient, it was carried a distance and widely scattered. There was a layering of sticks across the top of the hidden goods to support the soil and rock returned as filling of the neck. When this was packed and the plug of sod returned, if there was any sign of disturbance of the ground, a fire might be built there or livestock driven across it or picketed to graze on the site. If well done, and it was useless to complete any other, the cache was undistinguished from any spot around.

Very early in the trade, James Baird, who had gone to New Mexico in 1812 and to a Chihuahua prison for nine years, returned as a member of a trading party in the fall of 1822.[5] An early winter storm halted them on the Arkansas River near the sites of the future Forts Mann and Atkinson. Winter did not relinquish its bitter cold grip, merely added snow to their difficulties and in no great time their starving animals froze. When weather permitted, they cached their merchandise, went west for pack animals and returned for the goods. The hole left by the cache was a conspicuous scar on the slope near and north of the Road (Map 11). Few who had not seen it could pass by it, although they knew it to be only an empty caving hole and why it had been dug. By the time the first wheels rolled past, the Caches were a curiosity which remained a legend long after the last.

Near Ingalls, Kansas, upriver eighteen miles from the Caches was the Middle Crossing: two points, perhaps three, at which the Arkansas was forded by a great many wagons in all the years of the Road (Map 11). There were other crossings nearly as important and as long used, and there was not much difference among them. More important was the route beyond. The River had been for many miles a certain guide and an equally certain water supply. South from the Arkansas was a strip of very dry country, very sandy soil at best and sand hills elsewhere. The slope up from the River was gentle but slow for loaded wagons and exhausting for livestock. It was a very bad beginning for any day and as there was no water anywhere along the Road across the desert, the end was always worse. Distance to water from the Arkansas depended on which crossing one might choose. And, sometimes, so too did life.

Before Sibley, Brown and the survey of 1825, there had been four years of light traffic on the Road.[32] With the survey party were two employees who had been to Santa Fe one or more times. Just what crossing they had made of the Arkansas and the Cimarron Desert beyond is not known; perhaps it was at Mulberry Creek or near the Caches, or even both at different times. What they told Sibley of their experience in the Cimarron Desert is certain to have had bearing on his choice of a point at which to leave the river for the very dry land. A second factor influencing Sibley's choice must have been what information he could wring from Pike's map and Dr. Robinson's recollections. Robinson, a civilian volunteer on Zebulon Pike's expedition, had worked at Fort Osage with Sibley, after returning from the west. With the best information available, Sibley chose to extend the survey some seventy miles beyond the Caches, even then a landmark, to another: Chouteau Island in the Arkansas.[32, 40, 64] On an azimuth due south from that point they left the river and passed the sands with no trouble. It must have been a wet year, for Sibley's journal speaks of ponds and Brown's map shows them. Few transients of the Cimarron Desert had so little trouble; more than a few found it very difficult and none found it easy. South of the Arkansas is still unwatered land, still a menace to anyone afoot, on wooden wheels, or horseback.

When the survey was done and parts revised, Sibley was of the opinion that the vicinity of the Caches was probably the most advantageous point of departure from the Arkansas. Neither his journal nor Brown's map was published during the life of the Road. Even so, it seems likely that much useful information was available to those who needed it, if for no other reason than Sibley was an associate among them. In any case, it did not much matter for Indian troubles quickly forced individual wagons into caravans and in any such collection someone always knew the Road to Santa Fe.

A mile west of Cimarron, a town on pavement and river, the Dakota sandstone pushes close to the Arkansas and nine miles west, swings back from it. This is the locality of the Middle Crossings: one just before the steep slope comes close to the river and another after the Road has climbed the high ground (Nine Mile Ridge), crossed it back a ways from the Arkansas, and descended again to the stream. The first, east, Middle Crossing is between modern Cimarron and Ingalls. The second, west, is between Ingalls and Charleston (Map 11). Of the Middle Crossings, the most or last used was the western, because it is the only one which can be followed with certainty on aerial photographs.

Across the plains, the Arkansas River has flowed uninterrupted millennia on a course slightly south of east. In great bends alternately northeast and southeast, it winds across Kansas. Always the stream has carried from the Rockies vast quantities of sand from wasting mountains and, in time of high water, spread the debris over the floodplain. In another epoch, the course of the River lay transverse to winds of a climate different from now.

Somewhere in the north of this continent, eventually the home of man, somewhere east of Hudson Bay, a little snow falling in a shaded spot during a remote winter endured the following summer. On it fell flakes of the next season and although much of both melted in summer warmth, still there was a surplus, a foundation on which subsequent snows accumulated. The Pleistocene, the Age of Ice, had begun.

In uncounted millennia and by tedious increment, the thickness of the accumulation reached near ten thousand feet. Long before that magnitude was attained, all but the thin upper layer was compressed to ice. Frigid in temperatures uncommon even in arctic climates, compressed by unmeasured weight, the lower levels of ice were stressed to mobility. In every direction from the area of greatest accumulation, it flowed in ponderous movement. From somewhere in Labrador, on a slope of ice some ten thousand feet above the sea, ice flowed down ice. It flowed outward in all directions, up and over whatever hillocks were in its path.

Much water had been evaporated from the sea and, by meteorological whim, precipitated as snow to remain as ice on the continent. The inevitable consequence was lowering of sealevel by micron, by millimeter and in a hundred thousand years or so, by more than two hundred meters. It was a circumstance so infiinitely slow as to be unnoted by primitive man, or any other organism such as he, motivated only by hunger and urge for survival.

All over the world continents grew larger as seas grew less. In Bering Strait which, then as now, separated easternmost Asia from westernmost America, what had been a shallow habitat of fish, became the dry path for Asian man. Without motive other than hunger, man drifted westward to inhabit a continent unmarked by feet such as his in all the three billion years in which that continent had grown to its now ice-laden magnitude. His Eurasian contemporaries, generation by generation, retreated southward before ice gliding infinitely slowly out of Scandinavia. Long after ice melted from Eurasia and America, descendants of both were to meet on North America some twenty or thirty thousand years later and again, after much less time, on the moon.

On North America, with man now its witness, the mobile frigid desert, a ponderous sheet of ice, reached far southward into the heart of the continent. When eventually the blunted prong lay on what was much later a city in Missouri, it met there an immutable warmth of climate. Along the line, in the zone of that encounter, ice flowed south at exactly the rate it melted. Meltwater cut from rock, hard and soft, the valley in which the Kansas River now flows eastward to join the Missouri at Kansas City.

The longer any process continues, the more likely it is to be interrupted. At long as motion continues, for every swing of a pendulum there is another opposite in direction. Where once ice advanced into a warm climate faster than it melted, where once it flowed at a rate equal to melting, it now came to melt more rapidly than it flowed. Steadily, sometimes intermittently, the continental glacier diminished in rate of movement and thickness as its southern margin retreated by melting. During one pause in retreat, its edge lay where the Missouri and Ohio Rivers now flow. There and then, meltwaters in volumes unmeasured but certainly immense, carved valleys in which those rivers now wend. It was their combined waters which made the Mississippi then, as they contribute much to it now.

As everything must eventually, the ice disappeared, waning as slowly as it had waxed, some ten to thirty thousand years before now. But when the massive thickness of ice bore heavily on the interior of the continent, southwestern climate was a great deal more humid than now. Streams draining from western mountains, of which the Arkansas was one, were frequent in flood. Winds common in gale strength bore southward in high velocity from off the sheet of ice. Lifting sand dried on the floodplain of the Arkansas, polar winds constructed a huge ridge south of the River and parallel to its course. A hundred miles long, nearly two hundred feet above the river and twelve to twenty-five miles wide, the ridge in the Pleistocene was a region of dunes creeping as waves in largo. The height is there yet, arrested long ago by a thin veneer of buffalo grass, sagebrush, scattered yucca and infrequent cactus. In covered wagon days, it was the Cimarron Desert, the "Waterscrape," *La Jornada*, and it is no more temperate now.[10, 25, 71] In the average year it was an expanse of fifty parched miles from Middle Crossing to the next water, found with very good luck by digging in the dry bed of Sand Creek and without it, ten drier miles to Lower Cimarron Spring. A good many mules and some oxen did not make it.

Crossing the Arkansas at whatever point began with reconnaissance of its shifting sandy bed. A line of stakes was set to mark the best route and with doubled and tripled yokes, wagons followed it. Once moving in water they did not stop, else wheels sank deeply and irretrievably in the sandy bed. Eight hours to cross fifty wagons, fifteen or sixteen to cross a hundred is an average of fifteen minutes for one wagon. Fifteen minutes to cross a wagon does not seem much. Nor was it when measured in time and distance. Measured by effort it was a great deal more and when all were across, livestock were rested. While they grazed under guard, water-kegs were filled, pork-barrels cleansed of salt and filled with water. No man was willingly without it in the Cimarron Desert, although mules and oxen without choice always were, and sometimes to the extreme of fatal thirst. As teams grazed, watered and rested unaware of the long thirst ahead, cooks prepared food for the next two days. There were few buffalo chips and much less wood in *La Jornada.*

After a day of rest and generally around four in the afternoon, passage of the Waterscrape began, and with difficulty. The first ten miles or so was on Recent sand: soft, loose and hard pulling as the track wound between hummocks. The slope to the top of the aeolian ridge and firmer Pleistocene sand was gentle but on a soft road, miles were always long for heavy wagons and livestock worn from many of them west of Independence. The few who spoke of the terrain be-

Yucca blossoms

yond the ridge crest described it as flat with scattered shrubs. Yet one who described it so, mentioned that a French doctor lending support from downslope side to a tilting Dearborn carriage, was beneath it when finally it upset.[22] Flat, then, must have been a relative term as it is to one who crosses the desert now and conveniently on asphalt.

The Cimarron Desert, to traders the Waterscrape and, if they were Mexican, *La Jornada,* was a region of sparse grass, common mirages, rare wood and no water, save in the very wet years. *La Jornada* is idiomatic Spanish for "The Journey" hopefully completed in a single day. The route from the Middle Crossing, near the town of Cimarron, was shorter in miles to Santa Fe and longer in miles of desert than any other except the Lower at Mulberry Creek. Although in rare wet seasons it offered no difficulty because in wind-carved depressions there were ephemeral ponds, in any season it was an enormous draft on the strength of livestock. One wonders that men willingly drove them to it in dry years. A great many chose the shorter Upper Crossing.

Just east of the Middle Crossing in the small town of Cimarron, I stopped at the courthouse on a tree-lined street to search records for segments of Road to fill gaps on the map. I intended to visit the office of the Soil Conservation Service and there examine aerial photographs of Gray County, confident they would show the Road where I had not found it in other sources. It was near the noon hour but the County Clerk courteously laid out the bound volumes of earliest land surveys, data to be found in every courthouse and duplicates of the originals in Washington, made long before there were Counties in the West. As I thumbed the pages, she called a lawyer up the street who, she explained, had written a history of the region which might be helpful. As he was willing, she generously offered to duplicate the sheets of manuscript in the few minutes remaining before noon. I left off search among musty folios, hastened up the street, grabbed the manuscript and scarcely thanking the lawyer, promised to return it by 12:15. As the obliging lady unstapled the pages I glanced at the first, the second, and hastily all fifteen. I knew them by heart. Certainly it would have been more tactful had I simply accepted her offer but so keen was the disappointment that I explained the pages were excerpts from Gregg's *Commerce of the Prairie.* She courteously offered to return the manuscript as I collected gear and left the office closing for the day. Five miles east, regretting my lack of tact, I remembered my promise to the lawyer. Fortunately he was waiting; moreover, he was courtesy itself and confident the manuscript would be returned. He explained the pages bore no original composition, were merely part of the data collected in support of a petition for a marker on the Trail here. Twenty miles west I remembered I had had no lunch and had forgotten about the aerial photographs. Seven hours later I was to learn that I had left my baggage in a motel in Cimarron. Such great days are hard won but fortunately short lasting.

Garden City, just beyond Cimarron, flourishes with water from the Arkansas (Map 12). This is dry country and it is drier westward. Caravans left Council Grove and flowing waters nourished by frequent rains. Coming this way it got drier and drier and finally never did rain. An early issue of the *Missouri Intelligencer* quoted Captain Cooper recently returned from New Mexico to report "No rain in Santa Fe for three years and no complaint about it." [10] At the east end of the Road, Spring comes to the trees; at the west end it comes to the people.

There is scarcely a mile of Road between Missouri and New Mexico that has not witnessed some bizarre fragment of southwestern history. The incidents were normal to the time, and by time so far separated from the present as to belong to another world. It is a world now peopled by good white and bad red men. Good and evil have random distribution, which means more good than evil in some and more vice than virtue in others, with or without color.

For much of its course along the Arkansas, the Road traverses huge swells on a vast sea of grass, undulations differing as ocean waves: unequal in amplitude and wavelength but identical in form. Such is the land between Charleston and Garden City and somewhere in that section, I think, was an incident in the career of David Meriwether

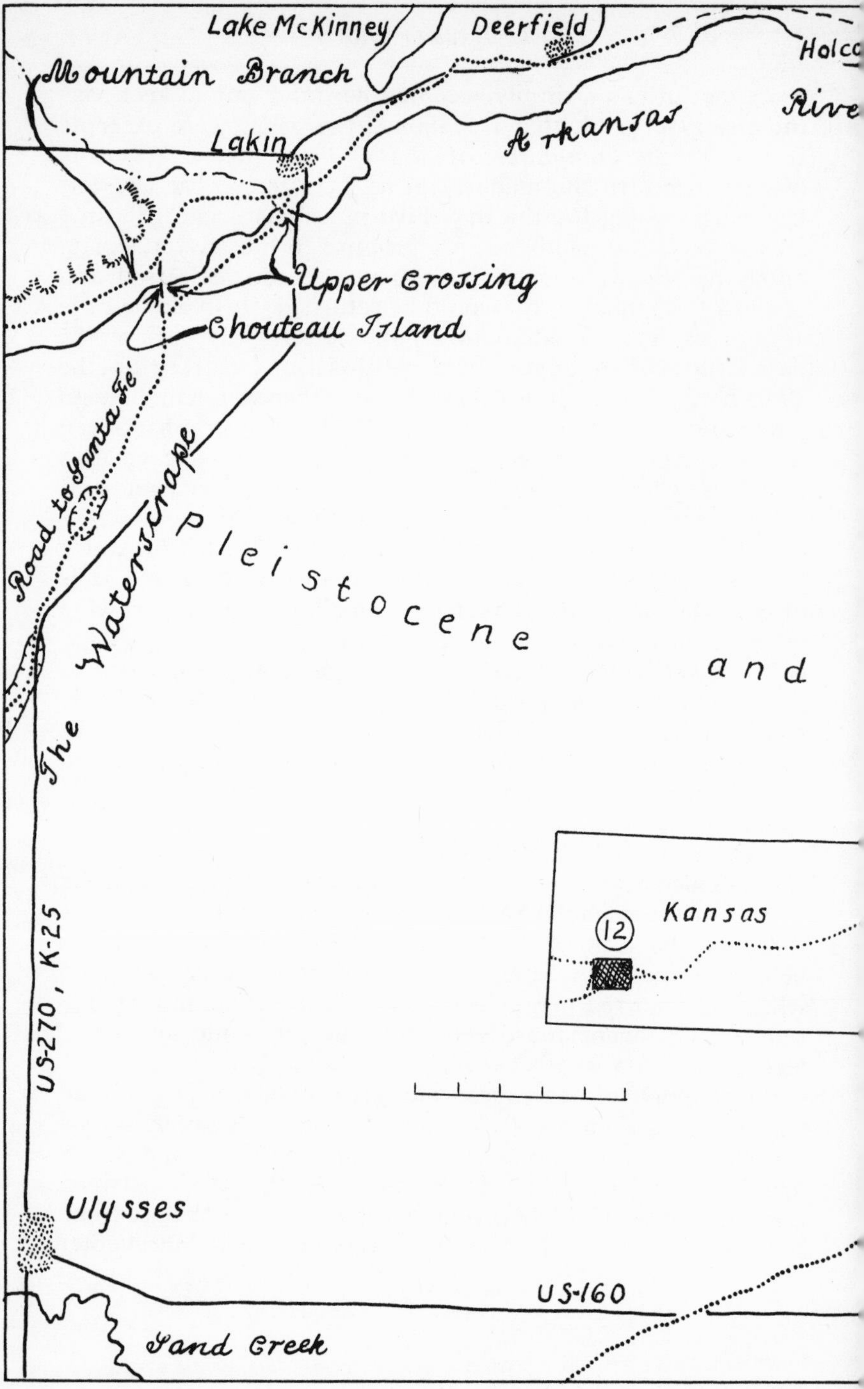

Lake McKinney   Deerfield

Mountain Branch   Holco

Arkansas   River

Lakin

Upper Crossing

Chouteau Island

Road to Santa Fé

The Waterscrape

P l e i s t o c e n e   a n d

Kansas

⑫

US-270, K-25

US-160

Ulysses

Sand Creek

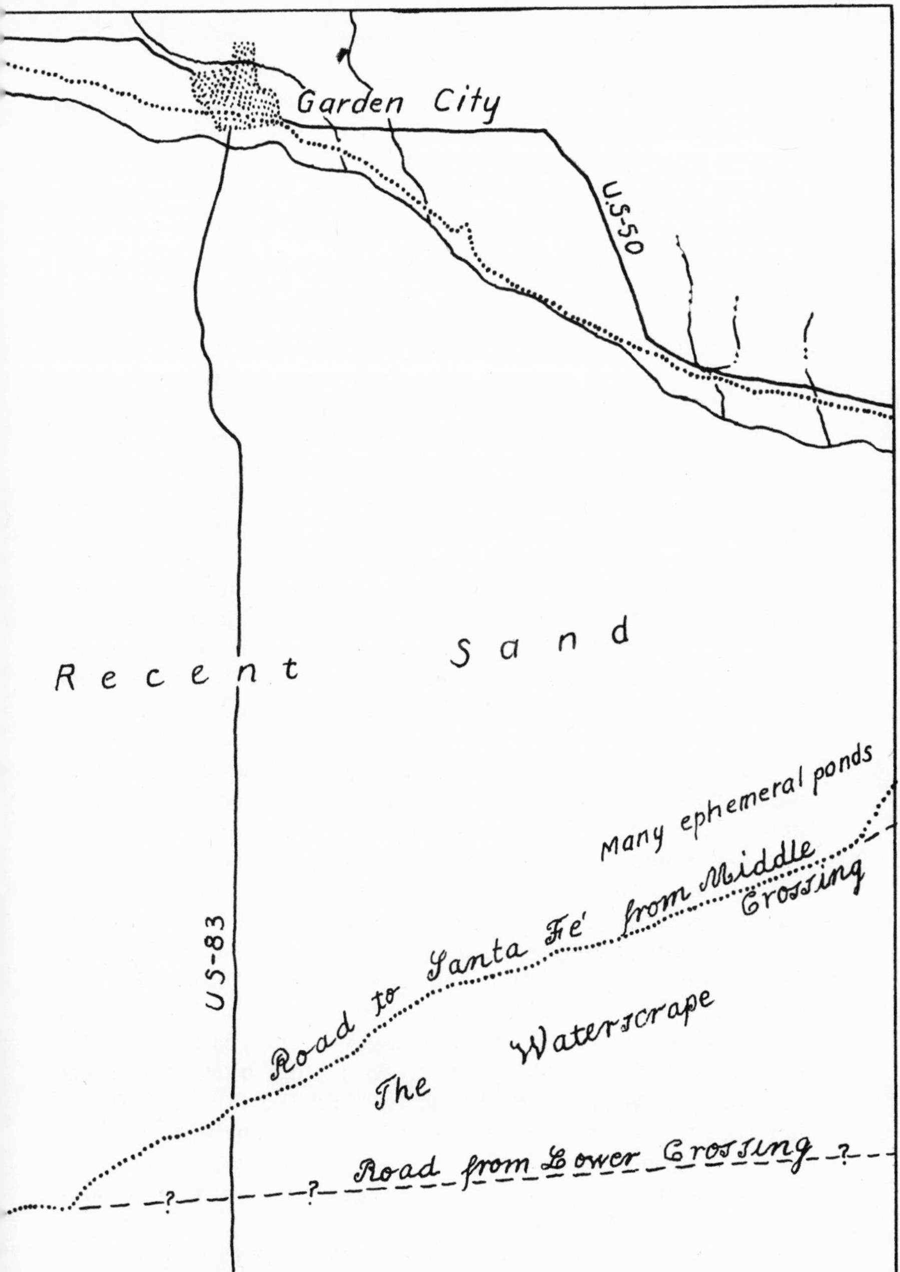

Garden City

US-50

Recent   Sand

US-83

Many ephemeral ponds

Road to Santa Fé from Middle Crossing

The   Waterscrape

—?— — —?— Road from Lower Crossing —?— —

o Santa Fé

en route to New Mexico.[72] Riding a short distance in advance
of wagons and escorting troops, Meriwether topped a rise.
On the slope below he saw Indians whooping like madmen
about a wagon train. General Garland and the troops scattered them. The train was that of Mr. Cooper of West Port,
and cause of the whooping was two Mexican girls, ages about
ten and thirteen.

The children had been captured in Chihuahua by Comanches a year or so before and traded to Kiowas. The day
before Meriwether saw them, they had been sent along with
Kiowas their own age to herd horses. Toward evening, not
long before time to drive the horses nearer the Kiowa
camp, the girls had seen Cooper's train pass. They decided
then and there to escape to it. As later the herd and herders
moved toward camp, the children rode covertly down some
arroyo onto the Trail and to the corraled wagons. Next
morning, Kiowas appeared with demands: first for their
captives and then for search of the wagons. Cooper refused
both. At Meriwether's sighting, the braves were whooping up
enthusiasm for attack. The children accompanied Meriwether
to Santa Fe from whence they were returned to Mexico.
From the Governor there came a warm note of thanks.

Yet more bizarre and tragic is Meriwether's account of
another captive: Adeline Wilson. Born a Howard in Missouri
and an emigré to Texas with her father, where she married,
she had come to Meriwether's attention through the inter-
vention of Lieutenant Adams and his wife. En route down
the Rio Grande to duty at some post on it, they had met in
a Pueblo village a ragged, haggard girl, newly escaped from
Comanches. Mrs. Adams had given her a dress and the
Lieutenant had urged the Pueblos to inform the Governor at
Santa Fe. A messenger was sent to escort the girl to Santa Fe.

Adeline Wilson told her harrowing story bit by bit as she
remained in Meriwether's care. He paid the Pueblos $50 for
her return and spent another $250 for her rehabilitation and
support. Reimbursement of it was cooly refused in Washington, promptly paid by Governor Pease of Texas, and later
allowed in the Capitol.

A bride of five months, Mrs. Wilson, her husband, his

father and two small brothers began, with others, the long trek to California in the spring of 1852. Ascending Phantom Hill (in Jones County, Texas), a piece of harness broke and the Wilsons dropped out of line to mend it. It was recourse never risked by experienced traders on the Road. There, when one wagon stopped, all halted.

At a time when few wagons passed, Indians always knew of transients through their country. Even now, or at least but few years before asphalt threaded the modern reservation of the Navajos in Arizona, no stranger on the dirt roads could stop his car in the unlimited, and to city eyes, uninhabited space without the spot being later examined by the sharp-eyed owners of it.

Comanches fell on the Wilsons, alone on Phantom Hill, killing the husband, his father, and making captives of his wife and two small brothers. There followed a long summer, a very difficult fall and a winter of torment during which Mrs. Wilson collected wood, made fires, cooked for her captors and otherwise served as they demanded. Comanches were nomads, roaming trails of eastern New Mexico and adjacent Texas. It was the practice of this band when they moved, as frequently they did, to order Mrs. Wilson to rise in the night, build fires and begin the roast of the morning meal and then, on foot, pack a load on the trail in the direction pointed for her. When, perhaps in mid-morning, she was overtaken, from some mounted brave she received a few lashes about the shoulders, presumably for being so slow on bare feet under a heavy load.

Gathering wood about an evening camp of her captors, on a spring she had no idea where, to roast an antelope newly killed, Adeline Wilson came on a stump, a large hollow cottonwood some ten or twelve feet tall. As she pulled from it bark for fuel, she thought it a more comfortable shelter than she had seen in recent months; reasonably dry, at any rate. Having roasted the animal, Mrs. Wilson was commanded to pack meat and, as soon as the moon rose, start on the trail. She did.

To modern tourists western miles are very short and it might seem to a hurried traveler on asphalted trails that only a mental defective, given such opportunity as frequently Mrs. Wilson was, would long endure the casual cruelties of slavery. Comanches were born and raised children of the plains. As very sharp-eyed juvenile delinquents on them, they learned to read blades of grass as the FBI reads a suspected document. From a confusion of moccasin prints on bruised grass, those of sharper eyes among Comanches could not say with certainty that Chief Flowing Robe and his band had passed but with confidence they could read the number and the tribe that made them, and when. And they could read that the travelers had passed in haste or in leisure.

All this Adeline Wilson knew from painful instruction. When a mile or two from the sleeping camp, lighted by the rising moon, she came on the graveled bed of an arroyo, she walked with bare feet and with care on the gravel, disturbed no ground when she left it and circled back to the camp. Tossing the bundle of meat into the opening well above her head, she scrambled up to follow it into the hollow tree trunk. It was in sight of the camp and some hours later, through a knothole, she saw the sleepers awaken, break fast and depart. Yet more hours later she saw three Comanches return and search the vicinity. She must have breathed very softly, or not at all, as they moved near the stump but they did not find her. All day and all night she remained concealed, hoping some friend might pass but as she had none nearer than Texas, none did.

The spring, wherever it might have been, was as all waterholes in dry country: a point on a trail passed by Indians in their aimless and sometimes purposeful wandering. Having no place to go, Mrs. Wilson stayed and so long as to lose track of time. As she had when in need of water, when food was exhausted she left the stump at night, searched for and found an occasional terrapin, the shell of which she crushed with a rock and ate raw. A few frogs captured in the dark at the pool about the spring were likewise raw and relished. All this was something less than a minimum diet of calories and vitamins and eventually Mrs. Wilson had not the strength to climb from the stump. Sleep must have then occupied most of the day as well as the night, for it is the only defense, a conservation of energy, of a starving body.

Three or four days without water or food, Adeline Wilson awakened to see through the knothole five Indians recognized by their dress as Pueblos. She shouted, but so weakly her voice was not heard. As she watched, she prayed and as she prayed an Indian collecting firewood came near. With mouth to the knothole Adeline shouted again but he fled. Prayer then, was her only sustenance. Meanwhile, the five Pueblos, now armed, surrounded the stump and one peered within. With lariat they hoisted the girl from her prison, took her to camp, gave her soup and a blanket on which to sleep. In a few hours she was awakened and fed more.

Her rescuers were indeed Pueblos from the Rio Grande, en route to trade with Comanches. They assured her that should she accompany them, Comanches would reclaim their slave. It was agreed that in a few days Adeline Wilson would return to the stump with enough food to carry her through until they returned. Mrs. Wilson resumed life in the hollow, clambering out each night for water. As best she could recall, she remained two more weeks in the stump apprehensive always, sometimes terrified as wolves howled in exasperation about the tree and the meat within.

Wild things have much patience and Adeline Wilson, one of them, had enough. The Pueblos returned and on a bareback mule she rode with them to their village on the Rio Grande some four or five days distant. If her accounting is correct, and several days would be an excusable error after such an experience, the spring and the stump, if it still stands, are somewhere in the longitude of Tucumcari, but this is only a vague guess.

It was through the Pueblo settlement that Lieutenant Adams and his wife chanced to pass and not long after they had, Mrs. Wilson was in Santa Fe. Lodged there with a minister at Meriwether's expense, she spent some months recuperating. When Meriwether's accounting was refused in Washington and promptly paid by Governor Pease of Texas, the latter requested aid and offered guarantee of expense in recovery of the two small boys. Eventually they were ransomed and returned. The fibres that made of Meriwether a competent Governor on a rough frontier were sometimes bent by bureaucratic accounting but they did not break. He marshaled precedent, persuasion and pressure. When eventually reimbursement came from Washington, Governor Pease's check was returned.[72]

For most of its course in western Kansas, the Arkansas River is now much too small either to build or maintain an island on its bed. When caravans followed it, the water was a great deal wider and deeper and islands, small to large, were common. But even then, as with islands in all rivers, they were temporary. They were thought by some to be especially fertile because they supported thick tangles of willows and sometimes huge cottonwoods. Trees do not attain girth so large in a single season; some islands in the Arkansas must have spanned several generations. Even so, they were temporary and Chouteau's Island which served him well, is no longer there (Maps 12, 13).

Returning in 1816 from a winter of trapping in the Rocky Mountains, Auguste Chouteau and men in his employ were attacked in a camp on the Arkansas about four miles west of modern Lakin, Kansas. With one killed and another wounded in the first moment of surprise, the party retreated to an island in the River and behind makeshift barricades, successfully discouraged the Pawnees.[73]

Chouteau Island was near a slight southward bend in the River and it was the point chosen by Sibley on "Tuesday, 27 Sept 1825: The morning fair & cool & windy. At 35 M past 8 we resumed our journey. And as now we take our departure from the Arkansas & must find our way thro the Sand Hills, of which such fearful stories have been told . . . I shall . . . take notes for a correct chart of our course." [32]

Theirs was an easy transit of the Cimarron Desert to water at Lower Cimarron Spring (Map 12 & 13). Others before and after found the same route savagely unfriendly. Traders out of Missouri were inured to hardship and most took to yet another naturally. It is well they did, for south of

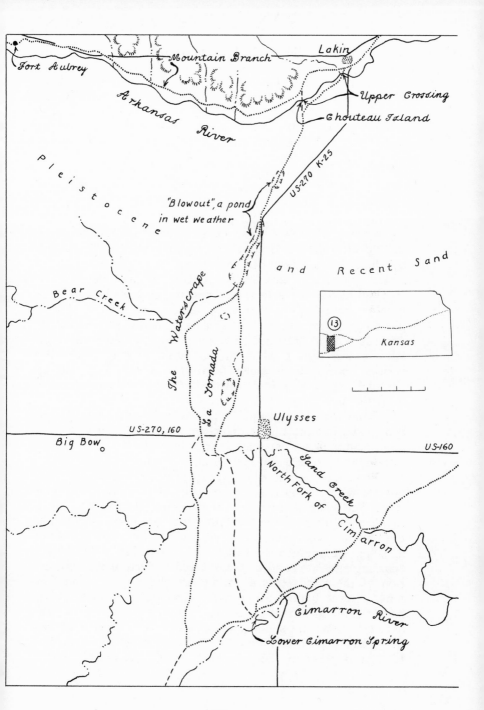

Fort Aubrey

Mountain Branch

Lakin

Arkansas River

Upper Crossing

Chouteau Island

P l e i s t o c e n e

US-270 K-25

"Blowout", a pond in wet weather

a n d   R e c e n t   S a n d

Bear Creek

13

Kansas

The Waterscrape

La Jornada

Ulysses

US-270, 160

Big Bow

US-160

Sand Creek

North Fork of Cimarron

Cimarron River

Lower Cimarron Spring

159

the Arkansas the odds were against them. They met most difficulties in stride and across the Cimarron Desert it was the unexpected with which they strode. The year before Sibley, M. M. Marmaduke crossed the *Jornada* and recorded in his diary: "I never in my life experienced a time when such general alarm and consternation pervaded every person on account of the want of water." [71]

At the Upper Crossing, of which Chouteau Island was the landmark, the same preparation for the desert was necessary: a day of rest, filling of water kegs and cooking food for the next two days. Traverse of *La Jornada* usually began in late afternoon and continued until midnight. Sometimes by then the slightest dew dampened the sparse grass and given opportunity and moist herbage even a very thirsty ox would graze for a time and rest as long as allowed. After two or three hours they were under way again. By mid-morning, Lower Cimarron Spring was in sight and the *Jornada* behind. East-bound wagons with lighter loads might leave Lower Spring when the sun was three or four palm-widths above the western horizon and traveling through the night in one uninterrupted plod, reach Upper Crossing with the sun.

From Chouteau Island in the Arkansas to Lower Cimarron Spring on the Cimarron River is now almost exactly in gasoline-minutes what once it was in ox-cart hours: twenty-five. Near to where the highway leaves the south margin of the Pleistocene sand ridge, it drops slightly into a "blowout," a wind-carved depression scooped from sand by polar gales. The scale of my map did not allow it to show by contours so slight a depression but even so, one may recognize the blowout from words written nearly a century and a half ago. ". . . we pursued the valley South 10 west 3 miles further (passing another Pond of Water) and arrived at the termination of the Sand Hills & found ourselves upon a most extensive level Plain." Sibley was unaware that meteorology had intervened to make their passage of the *Jornada* an easy one. Dry now, the shallow elongated bowl of the pond has the bleak aspect common to all lands parched to aridity. It is a depression fed by water from the rarely flowing drainage of Bear Creek entering from the west. Only after infrequent rain of such volume as to soak the dessicated sands is it possible for runoff to coalesce in flow in the arroyo discharging to the depression.

From the blowout, the highway runs south a few miles through Ulysses, Kansas (Map 13). Just beyond, it crosses North Fork of the Cimarron, the "Sand Creek" of caravans which sometimes found in it small stagnant pools. Those which did not, dug in the dry creek-bed hopeful of encountering water within three or five feet. Eight miles south of Sand Creek, Highway US-270 bends from south to southeast to cross Cimarron River at right angles and beyond it, turns southwest for a mile or two. Near the top of the slope toward the river, the pavement resumes its south course. At this last bend is a sign, courtesy of the Kansas Historical Society. It informs that at no great distance west (it is about two miles) and within sight, is Lower Cimarron Spring. West beyond the sign is a wide gentle valley of short grass all parched brown the August I saw it, and about its floor meandering in wide sweeps, a thin green line of small cottonwoods marks the Cimarron River, dry now as it was when most caravans reached it. Jedediah Smith saw this, very near his last sight of things terrestrial.

With a name so common, Smith was an uncommon man. He was as experienced a frontiersman as one might be who twice had crossed the mountains to the Pacific before he was thirty. He had traversed California from south to north, sold beaver to the British on the Columbia River and spoken from the Bible to the Flatheads.[7] Smith was a church communicant who practiced what he preached and those who knew him were in agreement that very few miles west of the Mississippi bore men of his stature. He had been a partner in a small fur company and proceeds from the sale of it had been invested in merchandise for Santa Fe.[74]

Jedediah Smith and some eighty others had left Middle Crossing and the Arkansas to encounter bad luck in the *Jornada:* no water and a Road so dim they lost it. They were practical men and did not dilute common sense with quadratics. Perhaps even for that reason, their encounter with the *Jornada* was the hopeless opposition of the transitory to the timeless. As men of the frontier they knew the dispiriting effect of hunger; they were to experience reduction to algal status by thirst. Without water, hopelessly lost, for three days they wandered in the desert, perhaps some oxen dead and all men nearly so. Searching on horseback in advance of the caravan, Smith followed a buffalo trail to the Cimarron. As commonly the river is dry some miles below Lower Cimarron Spring, it seems likely that somewhere within eye-compass here he found water. From a long drink of it, doubtless thankful beyond words, Jedediah Smith rose: one among the best friends the Indian ever had. On the instant he was lanced or shot. With yet all instincts for survival in command, he remained erect, tugged pistol from holster, killed two Comanches. Generous, even compassionate to their kind, he died with their blood on his hands.

CHAPTER XI

Springs Along the Cimarron

SOUTH FROM THE Historical Society sign, on the outskirts of Hugoton, Kansas is another, speaking of a museum. With directions from three small boys I found it: a low broad building in the picture window of which a small card listed visiting hours: nine to five. My watch read 5:10 but I tried the door and found inside an attractive matron drawing numbers for a small boy. I remarked that it was late and she responded that she was about to lock the door. Intending to return in the morning, I inquired did the museum contain a relic of the Trail.

"Why, yes, we have a picket-pin, found north of Rolla, Kansas."

I looked at one for the first time: about eighteen inches long, of iron about the diameter of a little finger, bent into a loop at one end. The remainder was exactly like a giant corkscrew. Twisted into the ground, it must been an effective hold for any animal tethered to the loop. I had read of horses of cavalry picketed along the Road, terrified by the lash of hailstones in summer thunderstorms throwing

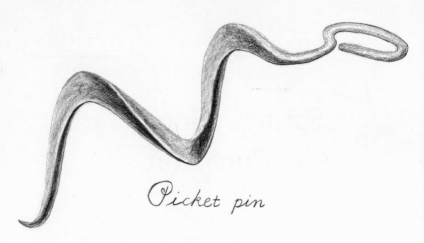

Picket pin

their weight against the picket-rope. If the rope held, the ground gave and picket pins at high velocity sometimes killed and more frequently wounded animals not yet free.

"Are you interested in the Trail?" inquired the curator.

I said I was. It was as if I had opened a valve on a high-pressure line for Mrs. Pfaff is Executive Secretary of the Santa Fe Trail Association, an organization of towns along Highway 56.

"You'll be interested in this; this too, and this," she said as from a nearby rack she plucked pamphlets setting forth the virtues of towns along the highway. I learned something of the Chamber of Commerce aspects of the Road and something of the hopes of the Secretary.

"We need an angel," she mused, and set a high feather-count. "Someone to donate $10,000, or even $5,000, for the preservation of landmarks. Of course the ruts are being washed away more every year and we could do nothing about that. But there was a stageline along the Trail with stations every few miles. They shouldn't be expendable but they are fewer every year."

It was an hour after closing time for the museum and at a motel that I learned my baggage was yet at Cimarron in another. By then having searched for the Road in all directions for quite a few miles, a round trip of 166 more for a clean shirt seemed little enough. On pavement far removed from expressways I drove alone in a stationary car as hypnosis of bright lights pushed back the night and allowed asphalt to flow beneath. To interrupt the monotony of the passing road I once stopped and walked a quarter mile in darkness through the sage. Underfoot the sand gave to the night the heat of the day. The multiplicity of empty miles all around constituted a solitude and within it, it was easy to believe that civilization is the manifestation of the powers of men rather than those of Heaven.

Next morning, by aid of roads from gas well to gas well, producing from an enormous subterranean reservoir for consumption as far away as Chicago, I found Lower Cimarron Spring. It was ground walked for a few and dangerous moments by Jedediah Smith, whose assailants had showed his arms and other loot, perhaps his scalp, to Mexican traders more wary or less vulnerable. It was only by hearsay that his companions learned of Smith's death.

The Spring had been renamed "Wagonbed" long after the Road lay unused, for the finding there of a wagonbed serving as a trough for seepage. There is neither bed nor seepage now and the Cimarron River a few feet distant is likewise dry. Thin cottonwoods closely spaced, overhang the yellow ribbon of dry sand fifteen or twenty feet wide. Now and then a gentle sough of air among the leaves left a corresponding flicker of bright points on the sand. These and the muffled roar of absolute silence all around are the plasma of Jedediah Smith's monument.

Dry, too, is the landscape and in dry months, ruts of the Road are no greener than elsewhere. It took quite a bit of searching to decide where they ran. The Spring was the junction of the route southwest from Middle Crossing and due south from the Upper Crossing of the Arkansas. Both were used throughout the life of the Road and the Upper Crossing much more than most writers credit it. It may have been that exclusive use for a time of the Middle Crossing allowed Upper Crossing to be forgotten. Quite some years after Sibley, Francis X. Aubrey, a flamboyant spirit

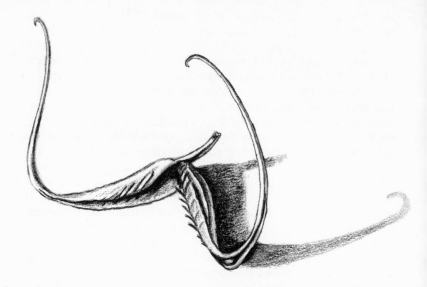

among phlegmatic traders, scouted a "cutoff" used by many, which could not have been much different from the route surveyed by Brown. When David Meriwether returned to New Mexico Territory in 1853, officers at Fort Atkinson recommended the Upper Crossing as better than the Middle, for its shorter distance between waters.[72] Meriwether followed their advice, directions and the route traversed by Sibley and Brown with no more difficulty than had they. He and others made much use of the Upper Crossing and proof lies in the marks they left so deeply cut that they remain yet to be seen.

Francis X. Aubrey who rediscovered the route from Upper Crossing to Lower Cimarron Spring, or one not far from the original, was an energetic trader given to innovation. When no one ventured to freight merchandise to Santa Fe in mid-winter, Aubrey did so and with success in spite of blizzards. Once, in kinder weather, finding prices in Santa Fe pleasingly high, he persuaded several returning caravans to take along a mount for his use.[25, 36] By the time Aubrey had sold his goods, he had several mules and horses out on the plains with different wagon trains. With others Aubrey began the return east and when he outdistanced companions, he rode alone on relays of mounts from the several trains. Aubrey reached Independence, Missouri, in five days and twenty-two hours, having walked, it is said, thirty of the 776 miles when one mount gave out.[75] An average of five and a half miles an hour for nearly six days does not appear high velocity in the jet-age, even when one knows it was more than ten times ox-cart pace. But so fast a journey across the prairie was truly a feat at considerable cost to flesh and blood of several mules, horses and Aubrey. Presumably it was returned in dollars and cents, with profit, as Aubrey made a second trip that summer of high prices in Santa Fe.

After the *Jornada*, the Waterscrape, Lower Cimarron Spring was a real oasis in a real Cimarron Desert, not of heaped sand and barren rock, but of sparse grass, yucca, prickly-pear cactus and sagebrush on a parched land. As the only water for miles around and the best for more, it was a striking spot of green with cat-tail rushes growing thickly

Prickly Pear

about the spring. Many of the Army spoke glowingly of the sweet water and several spoke of the curious "gravel rock" which separated the plains from the gentle slope to the Cimarron River. Clear white and colored pebbles set free by weathering of the conglomerate, carpeted the ground. The rock is a coarse phase of the Dakota sandstone, first met at Pawnee Rock and it was the decomposed soft outcrop into which the Caches were dug. It is marginal to the small valley of the Cimarron for miles and the Dakota sandstone, the beach deposit of a Cretaceous sea advancing onto the continent, came to be the acquifer, the reservoir, of water at Middle and Upper Cimarron Springs and at Cold and Cedar Springs as well. Wagons had last use of it at El Vado de las Piedras, where it floored the crossing of Rio Colorado, now the Canadian.

To pass Lower Cimarron Spring, Cimarron River flows out of the southwest (Map 13). Nearby, the Road follows the same course "in the bottoms and on the hills." It is a region of poor soil supporting sparse grass and sagebrush, the "artemesia of bitter taste and terebinthine flavor." [38] And it was along here that observant freighters saw their first horned frogs and other reptiles of dry country. Rattlenakes were still with them and in exceptional years so was a plague of buffalo gnats and millions of grasshoppers. No one thought highly of water in the Cimarron. There was very little of it standing in rare stagnant pools. Most frequently it was found by digging in the sand for several feet. What slowly seeped into the excavation was disagreeable in taste, strong with calcium sulfate and epsom salts. Both are common precipitates from intermittent streams in dry country. When travelers on the Cimarron did not taste the dissolved compounds, they saw them as a "white crust," an efflorescence of tiny fragile white crystals here and there on the moist river bed. Both salts have a cathartic effect. It was not serious for men but it was an added handicap for working animals. In a dry atmosphere, hard work made them thirsty. What they drank when they could along the Cimarron made them weak by diarrhea and dehydration and, therefore, thirstier yet. Cimarron water killed more slowly than prussic acid but in large doses on hard work it was lethal. Should ever a philanthropist set on the Cimarron a monument to the animals which made possible commerce of the prairies, the ox and mule of it need be standing with head low, feet wide apart, very lean, with gaunted ribs and protruding pelvic bones as becomes those which, without water, traversed a desert to work along water sparse and cathartic.

About eight miles north of Elkhart, Kansas, pavement crosses a bridge and the Cimarron River where the sandy bed, dry the August I saw it, supports a considerable growth of feathery tamarisks (Map 14). It is a shrub two to fifteen feet high, adjusted to a soil so salty that few other plants compete with it and adapted to a climate so aridly hospitable as to support little else. Sometimes called "salt cedar" because of the appressed leaves, they only remotely resemble members of that family to which they do not belong. Leaves of tamarisks, comprising a feathery sort of foliage, are so reduced as to offer a minimum of transpiration surface and very little of the water taken in by their roots is lost through their leaves to dry air. With a slender stem, too thin to be called a trunk, tamarisks growing on a sandy bed bend before high water and unless a persistent current scours out their roots, are as viable after a flood as before. In another and distant arid land, it was manna which sustained the Children of Israel in the Wilderness and it was the manna of tamarisks. From desert air and parsimonious soil, the shrubs extract sustenance and with the aid of chlorophyl and complex chemistry put carbon, hydrogen and oxygen together to make mannitol, a sugar. The manna of tamarisks is an exudation from a puncture, by an insect, in a slender twig. In the cool of a morning it is a solid which becomes a viscous liquid on a warm afternoon. No caravan ever collected manna along the Cimarron nor did any ever see a tamarisk there. The shrubs are immigrants from Asia and from the first forgotten transplant, winds and waters have spread tamarisk seeds so far and wide that now they are a common growth on sands of streams all over the southwest.

North of Elkhart and the abutment of the bridge over

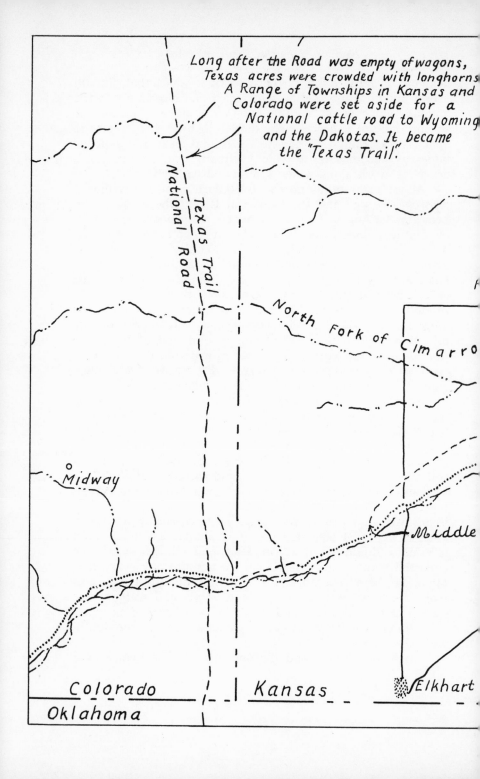

Long after the Road was empty of wagons,
Texas acres were crowded with longhorns.
A Range of Townships in Kansas and
Colorado were set aside for a
National cattle road to Wyoming
and the Dakotas. It became
the "Texas Trail".

Texas Trail
National Road

North Fork of Cimarro

Midway

Middle

Colorado | Kansas | Elkhart

Oklahoma

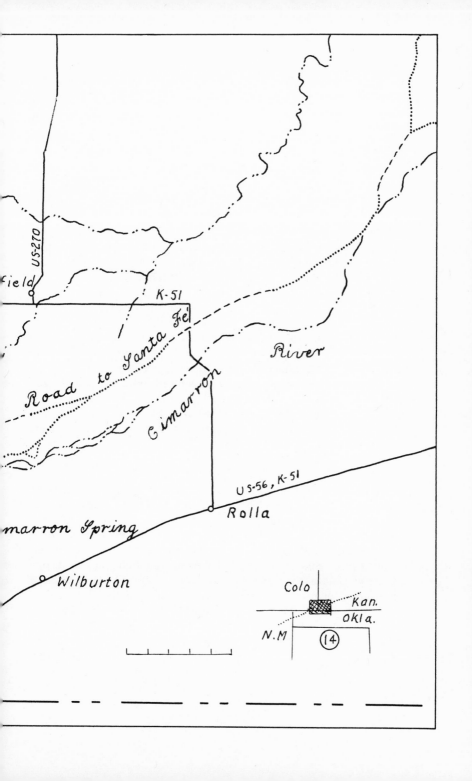

the Cimarron the Highway crosses the Road. This is still the region of the Hugoton gas field, largest on the globe. Across the area, ruts of the Road lie fallow but there are many field roads within a few feet of it along here. They are more frequently used by pick-up trucks of well-gaugers than ever was the Road by wagons. A hundred yards or so from the bridge, one may turn west from pavement onto a gas field road and about two miles from the highway cross a strip of sand between tamarisks thick on the river to the south and a narrow cat-tail slough extending north a few hundred yards. At the end, near the head of the very slight open valley, is a small clear pool, dense set with rushes. The pool is Middle Cimarron Spring (Map 14). Northward from it, the slope rises to an outcrop of the Dakota which here holds up the plains. A hundred yards or so west of the spring, a prong of the Dakota reaches close to the river, becoming steeper the nearer it approaches the sandy bed. Within a few tens of feet from the Cimarron rises a promontory which pinches the Road between steep cliff and stream to a single pair of ruts on rough stone. The soft rock bears quite a few names but I found none older than the pavement which brought the engravers this way. Back at the spring, it is the Dakota formation from which seeps the water: clear, fresh and sweet. Overflow from it supports a contrast of green rushes to the parched yellow sand of the river.

In another dry August, that one of 1848, Phillip Ferguson, a private in the Army, found at the foot of the bluff a grave about which wolves had been scratching and nearby a board on which had been noted that John Goose of the Missouri Batallion had died August 2 (1846 ?) from infection of a tarantula-bite nine days before. The boy was from Philadelphia and had been buried two years to the day when Ferguson passed here and Ferguson reached the spot one hundred nineteen years ago.[76] As several hours yet remained of that afternoon, his detachment had gone a few miles farther up the Cimarron to camp before dark. At that unknown spot another soldier, one Russel, while picketing his horse, failed to see in the twilight a rattlesnake which promptly bit him. Russel got immediate rough and effective treatment. A Mexican guide had him down a pint of whiskey and then, tying a cord about the bitten finger, cut it to the bone so that free-flowing blood might remove the poison. Other men with a thirst beyond that remaining from the Cimarron Desert complained they, too, had been bitten. But the Mexican argued that correct treatment required the cut be made first and only then whiskey administered. Having made one error in haste, he was not willing to make others at leisure.

Cimarron country held surprises for many transients of it. They were not invariably fatal; some were not even painful and James Webb wrote wryly of one of his own in that country. Loss of livestock on the Road was a moderately common and always a serious circumstance. Near-loss was yet more common and sometimes only a moderate inconvenience but few who experienced it could speak of the circumstance with even a trace of humor. Webb wrote of a November in 1844 when his returning caravan camped seven miles northeast of Middle Cimarron Spring (in the southwest corner of Kansas) where there was no water save by digging in the dry bed of the river. Awakened around midnight by stampede of his mules, Webb jumped from bed in shirt, vest, trousers and moccasins and without calling anyone, took after them.[25] As it was from there some three hundred miles to Council Grove and two hundred back to Santa Fe, it was not the moment for discussion of ways and means. In the darkness behind he heard another man who had been equally prompt and negligent in collecting clothes adequate for the very cold night. Together they followed mule tracks to the Road and down it, hearing in the distance the bell on the lead mare. They were much afraid Indians had stampeded the animals, yet were determined to recover the mules if possible. When sound of the bell faded, the two would run a distance, then kneel and search for tracks in the snow. Three or four miles down the Road the marks disappeared. On backtracking, they heard the bell-mare off to the side and judged from the tempo of sound that the animals were feeding. Cautiously Webb and his companion approached and when they were reasonably certain no Indians were about, made the whistling sound to which the animals were accustomed. With no difficulty each caught a mount and herded the remainder toward camp. Within a mile or so they met two Mexicans of their party following the trail (presumably the night guard; Webb does not say). They generously parted with their blankets but none of the four was dressed for a winter night. Back in camp, Webb learned that others had awakened but none joined in pursuit as one remarked, in effect: "leave it to Webb," and rolled over and went back to sleep.

When one has read of Indian depredations which befell other caravans of those years, Webb's pursuit was folly and the concern of his companions fantastic indifference. As danger was always with them, presumably they thought of less common things, or perhaps months of unrealized fear had given them unfounded optimism.

For a few miles above Middle Spring, the sandy bed of the Cimarron is a braided pattern of short, shallow intersecting channels (Map 14). It is the pattern characteristic of overloaded streams. Some fifteen miles west the Cimarron comes from land held higher by lava flows. These outpourings were the easternmost signs of the great contortions which folded the Rocky Mountains. Out of fissures deep enough to tap reservoirs of magma, flowed molten rock to congeal as lava on the surface. In that region the Cimarron has a less permeable bed on a much steeper gradient, hence greater velocity which enables it to transport a larger volume of sand from eroding rock. Once out of the higher land and on lesser slope, velocity of the river is less, hence the bed on which it flows is built higher by deposits in the channel. When a shallow channel is partly filled so that it can no longer contain that volume of water, the excess overflows to make a new thread of current an inch or two deep and a few wider. The result is a braided pattern. The sandy bed of a braided stream makes a poor road for "travel in the bottoms" and wagons avoided it when they could. When the stage arrived at Middle Spring, it had left the river about fifteen miles downstream, returning to it for water at Middle Spring.

Six miles west of Middle Cimarron Spring the River and the Road which follows it, cross the line between Kansas

and Colorado (Map 14). It was, of course, a point unknown to caravans. Once out of Missouri they traveled in Kansas Territory to the Arkansas, and beyond it on Mexican land. A mile or two into Colorado the Road is crossed by another, a great deal younger.

After the Road lay empty of wagons, Texas acres were crowded with longhorns. Stockmen there had a great many more cows and steers than dollars and cents. The state became yet more crowded when the Llano Estacado, the western portion of it, was cut into ten-section pea-patches by fences enclosing land bought rather than claimed by use. By then the larger outfits, fat with British capital, found the range crowded. North from the Texas Panhandle eight hundred to a thousand miles was unfenced, unmeasured land, inviting by its emptiness. Because of climate, northern ranges were a happier land for cattle. Texas ranches supported a great deal of livestock and every head, including ranchers', supported a host of ticks. No tick could survive a northern winter and longhorns transplanted there, and free of ticks, became fat on rich grass.

The larger cattle companies rounded up crowded stock and ticks, cut them into herds of two or three thousand and burned on each uncooperative steer a simple road brand.[77] When the dust settled, the cattle were turned north toward higher grass and wider spaces in Wyoming, Montana and the Dakotas. A long herd moved under the eyes of two cow-punchers on the drag (the rear), two on the swing, two on the flank and two on the point. Ahead, the foreman scouted the route and off to one side was the cook on a wagon loaded with suggins (bedrolls), Arbuckle coffee and a few sacks of flour. Somewhere around was the remuda and the horse wrangler. Together they made the trip, with a few stampedes, in about two months and in all the weeks on the trail they never tasted their own beef, probably would have choked if they did. They trailed through long miles of grass supporting the scattered stock of other ranchers. A few of these, either as volunteers or recruits, joined the line of march. Strays, all cattlemen agreed, had the better flavor.

Because in the years the number of trail herds and strays increased, all of them cropping grass claimed in oc-cupancy by others, a Range of Townships, a strip six miles wide on either side of the Kansas-Colorado line and its north-ward extension, was set aside for a "National Road." As scarcely anyone but Texans used it, and none more aggres-sively, it became the Texas Trail. The Trail crossed the Road and the Cimarron near the common south corner of Kansas and Colorado and northward it crossed the Mountain Branch of the Road and the Arkansas River at the modern settle-ment of Coolidge, Kansas. There, across the line in Colorado, was "Trail City" which supplied hard liquor and harder re-laxation for thirsty cowhands. Trail City is now uninhabited, a point found only on old maps and the Trail an untraveled line missing from all but the most detailed.

In the southeast corner of Colorado the Cimarron River curves to cross into the Panhandle of Oklahoma (Map 15). As it bends southwest to do so, its course is athwart the prevailing winds and the south margin is a line of shifting sand dunes. The Road follows the north margin of the Cimarron and just within Oklahoma it crosses and leaves the Cimarron River at Willow Bar. The island was but one of many willow-studded strips of sand in the river, undistinguished from any save as a crossing, a point of departure and an occasional raid. A caravan in mid-channel was half-prepared for danger and Comanches knew it. So, too, did traders. It was only when the one did not take precautions that the other took livestock and sometimes a scalp or two.

Summer caravans, save in time of storm or exceedingly dry season, rolled with comparative ease. Fall and winter trains rolled with the unexpected. The caravan of Albert Speyer, outbound late in the fall of 1844, camped just south of Willow Bar in the teeth of a growing blizzard.[25] The mules, gaunt on hard work and dry fall grass, clustered as closely as the hundred or so bodies would allow. Starving animals freeze quickly and as one by one they dropped, those yet on four feet gnawed the ears of the dead and dying. In time the heaps of bodies became heaps of bones. The transition was the accomplishment of a season as winter wolves, coyotes and foxes were ravenous. In the summer following, a whimsical teamster-artist arranged the hundred or so bleached skulls in a neat row above another of tibias. Artistry became a pastime if not a compulsion for every caravan camped there. Circles succeeded rows and squares replaced circles. Until the vicissitudes of time dispersed bones and artists, it was Op-art at its best. With material native to the heath, integrity of the canvas remained inviolate, as even now it does.

There was yet more difficulty waiting that year for Speyer. Having secured a second set of teams from New Mexico and finding no market in Santa Fe, he went south toward Chihauhua. Near Fray Cristobal, Navajos ran off 150 of Speyer's stock. It could not have been a profitable trip by the time he bought a third set.[25]

When the Army passed Willow Bar two years after Speyer's unfortunate loss there, in a time long before the less organized examples of the Chimpanzee School of art, the arrangement of skulls and bones caught the eyes of

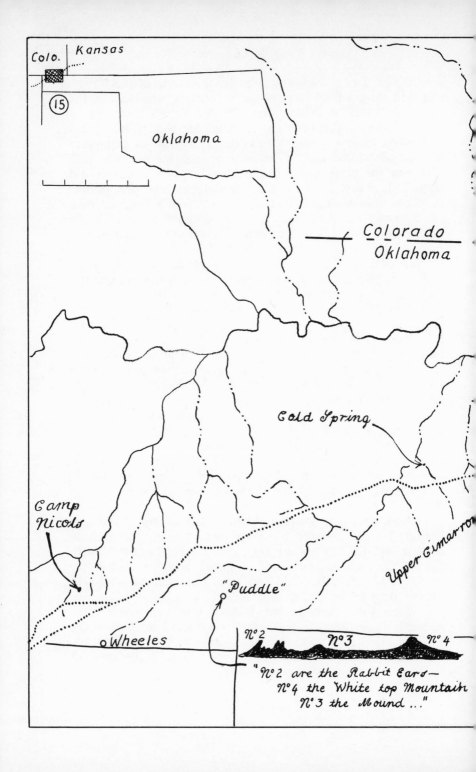

Colo. Kansas

Colo.

⑮

Oklahoma

Colorado
Oklahoma

Cold Spring

Camp
Nicols

Upper Cimarron

"Puddle"

Wheeles

Nº 2   Nº 3   Nº 4

"Nº 2 are the Rabbit Ears —
Nº 4 the White top Mountain
Nº 3 the Mound ..."

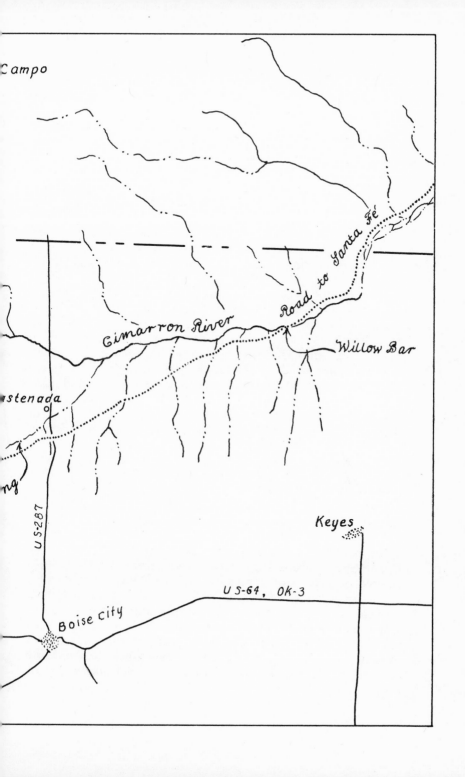

several soldiers who kept diaries. The Mormon Batallion, en route to California via Santa Fe, found a human skull among those of the mules, identified by their surgeon as belonging to an Indian.[78] One of his patients wrote of the Doctor in words so vivid that a reader might surmise he would have been pleased had the skull been that of the physician. Dr. Sanderson counted fit every private able to stagger to medical examination and for any complaint less than a severed leg administered large doses of calomel. As the men had marched weary miles on a starvation diet, haggard much of the time by thirst, many were unfit and some died from combined exhaustion and disease. If Sanderson was a capable doctor, he was unheralded among his patients.

That same year Speyer was again on the Road, headed southwest with a very fast mule train and but a few days ahead of the first military detachment en route in 1846. In Missouri there was rumor the Army was about to march and Speyer was in haste to reach New Mexican markets. All other wagons had been halted by the military and ordered to follow rather than lead. Escaping their guard and once on the Road, Speyer pushed his mules to the limit, making twenty and sometimes thirty miles a day to stay ahead of Captain Moore sent after him. James Webb, who met Speyer on the Road beyond pursuit, states Speyer told him of the state of war between the United States and Mexico, and that two of his wagons carried arms purchased by Armijo, Governor of New Mexico.[25]

North of Boise City, Oklahoma, Highway 287 crosses the Road and two miles west of the intersection, wagons came to Upper Cimarron Spring (Map 15). It was a waterpoint not on the river as are Lower and Middle Springs. Upper Spring seeps from the Dakota formation rising in a jumble of dark brown rocks at the head of a small valley about six miles from Cimarron River. Along the small flow of clear water are a few stout cottonwoods in the shade of which loaf stolid Herefords doing their hardest work: chewing cuds. With careers carefully planned for leisure and obesity, they do much better on buffalo grass than did any of their predecessors on the Road. It is not likely any of the trees about Upper Spring shaded wagons as they are probably younger than the Road and caravans did not generally camp on any spring. Grass there was quickly overgrazed. Moreover, while springs were a blessing in a dry land they were likewise a curse. As the only water for empty distances around, they were a frequent camp for Indians as they might have been for wagons, but their vicinity was the radius of greatest danger.

Twenty-five men of a five-wagon train bound east in October 1828, found Upper Cimarron Spring very dangerous indeed. It was their bad luck to arrive late in the day, simultaneously with a hundred or so Comanches. Hospitably the Indians invited traders to camp with them. As the merchants had about 150 mules, sundry equipment in the wagons and twenty-five scalps, all a temptation, they thought themselves too few to accept a spider-to-fly invitation. As they pushed on, Captain John Means, with Bryant and Ellison, guarded the rear of the small train. It was a brave purpose that deserved a better end. Captain Means was shot out of the saddle and scalped as he hit the ground. Bryant and Ellison raced to safety of the group and together they stood off attackers.[7, 10, 79] Moving when they could between assaults, the traders made a few more miles by nightfall, one among them seriously wounded. In the darkest hour of hopelessness, perhaps near Willow Bar, they abandoned wagons and mules. Taking only some 10,000 Mexican silver dollars and what little else they conveniently could, the Missourians rode slowly and quietly out of hearing of the Comanches. That perilous night, all the next day and into the next night they rode as fast as exhausted animals could go. At the Upper Crossing of the Arkansas they cached most of the silver and pushed on at a slower desperate pace. By the time the fugitives traveled the 200 miles to Walnut Creek, men and stock were completely done-in. Confidence is an attribute of a full stomach and despair the adjunct of hunger and exhaustion. In desperation, the five best fit men and mules were sent ahead and on their arrival in Independence a rescue party was quickly organized. On the Road they found the exhausted men scattered in small groups as widely separated as their strength allowed and all near to starvation. The silver, hidden somewhere near Chouteau Island, was recovered the following season when Major Bennett Riley and troops out of Fort Leavenworth escorted a train to the limits of U.S. territory.

Cold Spring, next to the last on the Road flowing from the Dakota aquifer, lies at the foot of a small bluff of sandstone in the Oklahoma Panhandle (Map 15). Wislizenus, a German physician and naturalist who traveled with Speyer just ahead of the Army, thought it "best water since the Arkansas River. Beyond Cold Spring the scenery is beautiful where mountains and prairie meet." [38]

Cold Spring is the unique part of the Road I saw in wintertime. From Stillwater in north central Oklahoma, westward to Guymon in the Panhandle (once "no-man's land") is a long 234 miles of dull road when driven alone on a late February afternoon, even by way of a settlement named Slapout. By arrival in Guymon it was very cloudy, very dark and the wind gusty. There was no snow on the prairie and the pavement was likewise clear but in the barrow pits were piles of snow three to six feet high, now being reduced by gusts of the gale as if they were confetti. It seemed the better to stop in Guymon but as a quick glance at the roadmap showed only thirty miles to Boise City, I drove on in wind of whatever velocity that makes driving a heavy car difficult on an open road. Soon it began to snow very thickly in horizontal streaks. A second, more careful, look at the map now read thirty miles to a vacant highway intersection and thirty-five beyond to Boise City. By then the choice ahead and behind was only the difference of about ten miles and I chose the former.

As yet the ground was bare but in the air was as much snow as ever I had seen and all of it horizontal. For long minutes the flakes made a very small world of thick opaque white, with one dense wall of lateral streaks which concealed everything save the front fenders. In such minutes, three miles an hour was dangerous speed. Occasionally the world expanded a bit, allowing sight of the road shoulder and a speed of fifteen miles an hour in gusts that rocked the car.

I understood better the difficulties of those who traveled the Road in winter and one reason so few did. It was not even a good night for car trouble and there would have been trouble of a lethal sort for men and oxen.

As the cold white world contracted to barely a fender-length, I slowed to a crawl to let the opaque white streaks unravel. As five billion streaks whipped by, followed by ten billion more, the car coasted to a stop, half on, half off the asphalt. Cheerily the red lights spoke of no oil pressure, no generator, no car. Completely, irrevocably dead, there was no life in the cylinders. As the snow moved in high velocity horizontal streaks, the car rocked gently. An oddly gentle hiss made the whole circumstance unreal, but not the sort of fantasy I would have chosen.

As the frigid white striated world shrank to less than a car length, the clearest and only impression was a recollection from a childhood in the southern Texas Panhandle wherein one might each winter hear of one or two men, sometimes six or seven, freezing hard as stone in a blizzard on the plains to the north. The pavement I could not see was on those plains and I had them all to myself. There had not been a glimpse of a car since Guymon. I later learned the highway had been closed to traffic. On it there was but one car other than my own. That statistic was pleasant not to know as I sat bundled in everything that would wrap around, including a chilling oppressive claustrophobia.

The minutes passed, each in its own leisurely way. When thirty-four of them had and much in contrast to the streaks of horizontal white outside, so dense as to leave no space for time, there was a glow of light behind. So thick was the snow, all in the air, there was scarcely time to open the door and step into the bitter searing frigid blast before the car went past. The driver stopped, backed up and pushed my car off the road. He said he would be glad to give me a lift to town and congratulated me on having one.

It was scarcely three miles before we ran out of the small tight world of white into the dark night of transparent high-velocity air that leaned heavily against the car, and only five or so miles more to a motel in Boise City.

Next day with a new coil ("Without one you've got a

pile of old cold iron.") and by courtesy of Mr. Gorman on whose ranch in the Oklahoma Panhandle both rise, I visited Cold Spring and the sandstone bluff alongside.

Of all the registers on the Road the sandstone at Cold Spring was nearest to what I hoped to see. Some years before Mr. Gorman bought the ranch, a part of the bluff had been quarried for a spring-house. Even so, it was worth the trouble of searching out the remote spot just to read: "D Willock 1848" lightly cut in Roman letters by a surprisingly skilled hand. From Pentagon Archives, and for a fee, I learned that David Willock had been a Captain (an elective office in his time) of the Special Batallion, Missouri Volunteers. It was a part of Doniphan's Brigade, a fragment of the Army of the West and the only one to reach New Mexico by the Road as it was marked by commerce. The remainder, followed by some 1,600 wagons belonging to freighters, had gone past the Upper Crossing, and up the Arkansas to Bent's Fort. From it they turned southwest to follow the Timpas of "bitter water" to its head, crossed the divide to El Rio de las Animas Perdidas en Purgatorio (shortened by their guides to "Picator"),[80] which they followed to Raton Pass. Through that rough gap in mountains they made a road rather than followed one.

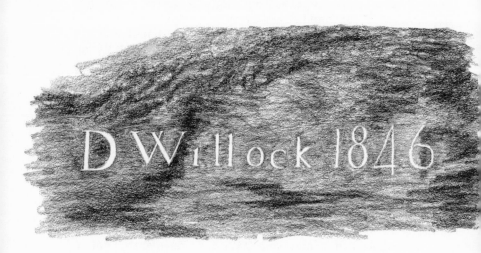

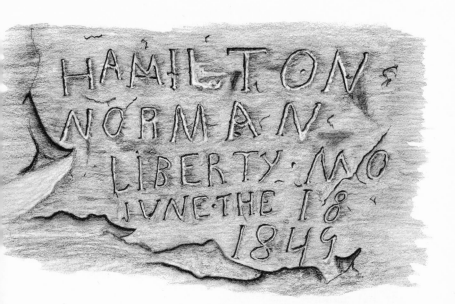

There were other names than Willock's at Cold Spring and all less skillfully, more deeply incised. "Hamilton Norman Liberty Mo June the 18 1849" is one and "C B Haynes Mar 16 75" is another. The latter date is some years after the last wagon is known to have left Kansas City. In 1865, the railroad was west of that settlement and its west end was the east terminus of the Road. But Cold Spring was a stop on another trail, one of Mr. Collinson's day.

The National Road, the Texas Trail, was a vague network of hoofprints in the Texas Panhandle converging on the common corner of Colorado and Kansas on the north line of the Oklahoma Panhandle. To reach the National Road, trail herds crossed "No Man's Land," now the Oklahoma Panhandle. It was land beyond the authority of sheriffs and jurisdiction of courts, claimed by many with gun in hand, and owned by none. In it ranged fugitives from all. When by chance or intent they gathered in a group, they levied on passing herds bound for northern grass a tax of five cents a head. Although $150 does not now seem much tribute for passage of 3,000 head of cattle, nor was it then, it was more than drovers were willing to pay to no good cause, and they were frequently taxed by more than one group of outlaws. The average herd of 3,000 was accompanied by eleven men: two on the drag, two at the swing, two on the flank, two at the point, the foreman, the cook and Little Joe the Wrangler. They generally outnumbered any random collection of outlaws that might seek tribute. But a trail herd is uncommonly vulnerable to two determined bandits and it is at the mercy of just one. It is no trick to race at night into a bedded herd and with whoops and waving slicker, stampede 3,000 steers in all directions. If, by chance and outlandish luck, they were all collected next day, it was even less a feat to scatter them a second time. By the third night it could be done with a whisper. It was less wearing on livestock and men, and even cheaper to pay the tax. It was nearly as simple to avoid it altogether by driving west in the Texas Panhandle, beyond the hangout of most outlaws, then north to the National Road. Cold Spring was a stop on that detour.[77]

Along Cold Spring Creek, a rivulet from the spring, are scattered cottonwoods and willows. Both trees were a part of Indian economy. Bark of willows was an ingredient of plains Indian tobacco. When winter snows were deep and all grass concealed, the bark of cottonwood twigs was all the forage Indian horses had. Both cottonwoods and willows are wet-ground trees and grow rapidly in about the only environment they can endure. As cousins in the same family, both have inconspicuous flowers, "catkins." On both they appear early in the spring before leaves are out, and early in the summer from small green pods on the cottonwood, spread cotton and seeds. The latter are tiny specks surrounded by radiating fiibres like, but lighter than, thistledown. So buoyant are the seeds, so much more fluff than body, they travel endlessly on the lightest of breezes. On airless days, the ground around a seeding tree is thinly white with cotton and a myriad of hopes.

Around Cold Spring I knew I was running out of time for travel on the Road, which is to say: money. Even with it I could afford only to glance off the country to the west. At a bank in Boise City, Oklahoma, I asked if they would cash a check if I paid for the telephone call necessary to confirm my account.

"*He* might. He's president," responded the cashier, pointing to a middle-aged gentlemen at a desk behind a railing. For him I wrote and spoke my name in full and that of an acquaintance in my bank and heard him mispronounce both to the cashier in a distant Texas town. As he laid out the cash, the president inquired with friendly interest what I might be doing in Boise City. I hesitated, and yet longer as I reached for the money and tucked it into my billfold, thinking that once with it beneath my hip, he might think me as crazy as he wished.

"Oh, I didn't intend to be inquisitive. I. . . ."

"I'm following the Santa Fe Trail," I interrupted, and knew my concern was wasted as he hauled out a map.

"You must see Middle Spring and Willow Bar, although the Bar might be difficult to reach by car now. And Inscription Rock (he meant the bluff at Cold Spring) is loaded with names carved. . . ."

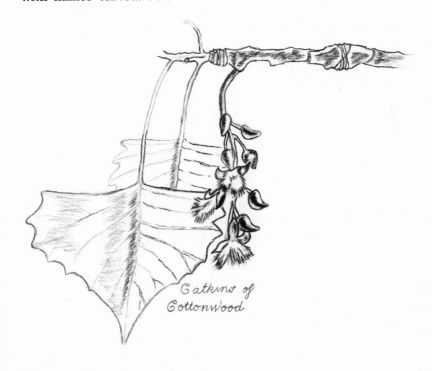

Catkins of Cottonwood

It was an hour before we had shared mutual interests and it was yet another before I stopped a passing truck not far from Keyes, Oklahoma, to inquire about Camp Nicols.

"Don't believe they've used it for some time but the old stones of the rock walls are northwest of that windmill."

On the northern horizon were three tiny pegs a resident might recognize for what they were.

"Which one?"

"The west one. Head off northwest from it about two mile. Wind around the rocks out there near the breaks of the Cimarron and if you don't rip a crankcase you got a fifty-fifty chance of finding the old camp."

With what I hoped was the right fifty in pocket, I turned off on a ranch road that led past the west mill and just beyond it opened a wire gap, a gate of sorts designed by Samson for use by Hercules. Heading northwest beyond the gate it was a considerable pleasure to come onto the Road: two faintly greener stripes twelve or so feet wide trending down a long slope and, yet parallel, up and over a distant crest a mile or so away. About the proper distance from the windmill I came onto a peninsula of land between two rocky drains northward toward the Cimarron. Having in mind a clear recollection of a map of Camp Nicols, a fort of sorts, Colonel Christopher Carson commanding, I knew exactly where it should be in relation to the drains.[82] It was not. As I searched on foot in bright sun nearing the western horizon and a mile from the car I was surprised when a sharp, sudden very cold rain and hail pelted down. To the west the sun was clear; off to the southeast towered an immense thunderhead, the very top edge of which had spread overhead. As I drove back toward the windmill across the short grass, glaucous in the low sun and crossed the Road, it was pleasant to follow by eye the long stripes aimed east, squarely at the center of the arc of a rainbow.

It was another day when I found Camp Nicols on another peninsula of grassland between rocky arroyos holding trickles of water (Map 15). The westernmost held Cedar Spring, water for the Camp and campers on the Road. On the tableland between the small creeks is a quadrangular line of jumbled flagstones, fragments of the ubiquitous Dakota. They mark the crumbled walls about an area adequate to hold a considerable number of the three hundred cavalry commanded by Carson. Dividing the nearly square area in half is a wide pavement of sandstone slabs which must have been the picket line, the feeding ground. Regularly disposed about the low linear mound of stones were small heaps of others, once ordered in floors and low walls to which tents provided roofs. It was easy to locate ruins of that one which had housed Lieutenant Russell and his bride. Marian Russell, in another age, wrote of the history she had lived in words so exact, so simple and so clear as to leave the reader nostalgic for a time he never knew. It required no magic to find where Private Barda's grave must have been and where Carson's tent stood but the haystack marked: "Warning! Government Property," when the Camp was abandoned in the fall of 1865, is gone.

During the first two decades of the Road, traders mostly looked after themselves and between scrapes with Indians, complained to Senator Benton of Missouri for protection by the Army. After 1846, there were Generals of it in New Mexico. They, and the Government to which they complained, took care of military freight on the Road and, incidentally, of merchants. During the Civil War there were, of course, all varieties of raiders out of the Confederate States near the east end of the Road. Inevitably, unrest spread to the Plains, raising disputes with Indians from quartan to quotidian incidence. Christopher Carson, who began as a runaway apprentice from a Franklin, Missouri, saddlery and rose to General, built Camp Nicols in the spring of 1865. From Fort Union in New Mexico, cavalry escorted wagon trains through Comanche land and camped at Nicols. From there, contingents under Carson led them northeast to Fort Dodge. Returning with wagons collected on the Arkansas, his troops passed them to others waiting at Camp Nicols for return west to Fort Union and beyond to Santa Fe.

CHAPTER XII

To a Crossing
on Stones

TO THE MODERN TRAVELER through the dusk, from Camp Nicols in the Oklahoma Panhandle toward Clayton, New Mexico, is a traverse of dark green velvet. Valleys are deep folds in that cloth, in twilight each much like the last and little different from the next, save one. The small arroyo at the bottom bore a sign: "McNees Crossing" and the drain is the North Canadian River (Map 16). It was "Louse Creek" to Sibley and Brown in 1825, and three years later it became "M'Nees". It is only occasionally a flow of water from its head westward near Sierra Grande where, without geographic embarrassment it simply changes its name to Corrumpa Creek. Just west of the Oklahoma-New Mexico line, very near to Mexhoma in the former state, M'Nees Creek has a valley of depth out of proportion to the small flow. In twilight, one may know this is high land, for in the clear air stars are close. With land high, gradients are steep and on steep gradients little water does much work in eroding a valley.

Somewhere a few miles upstream from the highway

crossing of M'Nees Creek, the Road divides into several branches to cross the same drain. The *Missouri Intelligencer* for September 12, 1828, carried the note: "About seventy or eighty recently returned from Santa Fe with a handsome profit. Captain Daniel Monro was killed by Pawnee Indians and also the son of Samuel M'Nees of Franklin." [10, 22]

The brevity was characteristic of the *Intelligencer* and of a time before eye-witness accounts amounted to much. Major Wetmore's diary for the same year makes note that on July 16th: ". . . reached upper Semiron spring at the base of a rocky hill, on the summit of which is a cross standing over the bones of two white men . . . slain while asleep . . . by Indians." Josiah Gregg in *Commerce of the Prairies*, tells what little else is known of the circumstance.

Monro and M'Nees were riding in advance of a returning caravan and on reaching the crossing of what was to become M'Nees Creek, dismounted and lay on the bank, awaiting the arrival of the wagons. Perhaps it was a warm afternoon; perhaps they were tired men. With nothing of urgent hold on their minds, they fell asleep. Creeping up on the men, Indians gently lifted their rifles and even as wagons came down the opposite slope, shot the sleepers with their own guns. M'Nees was dead on arrival of his companions; Monro was desperately wounded. No caravan was equipped to offer more than the roughest first aid and sincerest good wishes. On that, Monro survived the rough thirty miles of road to Upper Cimarron Spring. By then, from loss of blood, shock or infection, perhaps all three, he died.

Just at the moment of burial at Upper Spring, six Indians approached. It was an advance no savage who had recently killed a member of the group would have dared. There was a moment of heated argument among the pall-bearers but the words were made superfluous by rifle fire from the lesser of wit. Five Indians lay dead and the chain of misunderstandings between Red and White was lengthened by another bloody link.

M'Nees Creek is a few miles beyond the area where "mountains and prairie meet" and from any ridge crest, muleskinners and bullwhackers had clear sight of outliers

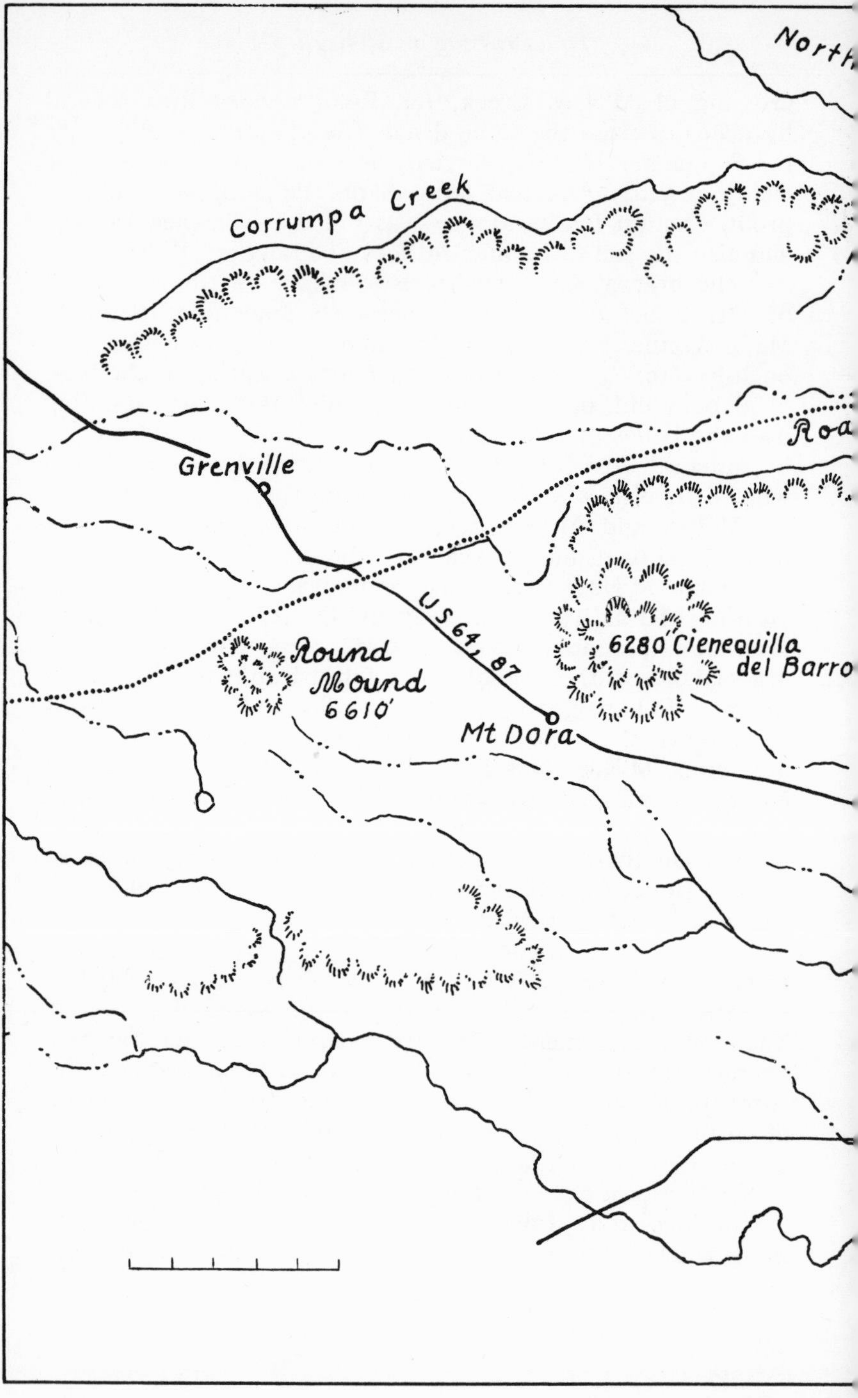
North
Corrumpa Creek
Roa
Grenville
US 64, 87
Round Mound 6610'
6280' Cienequilla del Barro
Mt Dora

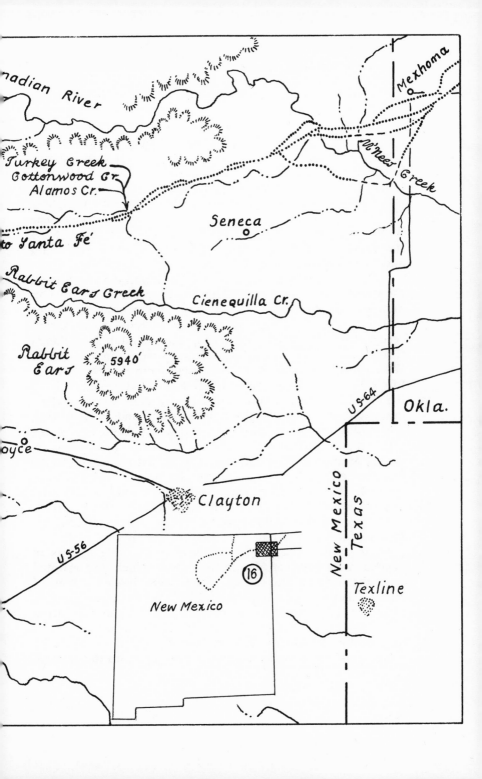

of the Rocky Mountains and, far beyond, the faint blue of
the backbone of the continent. Sibley kept both an official
journal and a personal diary which differ but little and
both contain a definitive profile of the landmarks on the
horizon, seen from a point about midway between Cold
Spring and Louse (M'Nees) Creek (Map 15). It was a sketch
intended to guide those who followed.[32] "Tuesday 11th October (1825) . . . the direct course from Upper Sem-
erone Spring to this puddle is S° 62 W—16 miles—straight—
(We) steered first S° 75 W 1¼ M to top of the Ridge. The
Rabbit Ears bear S° 56 W—N° 2 are the Rabbit Ears; N° 4
the White Top Mountain— N° 3 the Mound . . . not very plain
and to which we now steer. . . ."

The two knobs of Rabbit Ears Mountain, if viewed from
the correct angle and with imagination resemble, at least in
number, the ears of a rabbit. The first prominent height
(5,940 feet) encountered by westbound wagons, it was always
recognized. "N° 4 the White topped mountain" is Sierra
Grande sixty miles in the west from Sibley's point of view.
With a height of 8,720 feet, it is always capped with snow before other peaks gain theirs or after they have lost it. "N° 3
the Mound" is Round Mound of later travelers who had their
first sight of it forty-eight miles distant and in line with
Cienequilla del Barro Mountain (Once Mt. Dora and sometimes Mt. Clayton) only forty miles away (Map 16). As
Round Mound is 6,610 feet and in line with Cienequilla del
Barro of only 6,280 feet, caravans did not at first sight dis-
tinguish the two. When they did, the Mound higher and
nearer the Road got more attention and a few climbed it.

The contortions that bent great masses of strata into
Rocky Mountains broke the crust of contiguous plains by
great fractures. The deeper of these intersecting masses of
magma, were the loci of volcanoes from which lava erupted
onto the surface and about which were heaped cones of
cinders. Time and erosion have destroyed the cones, leaving
huge roughly cylindrical pipes, once the fluid in the throat
of volcanoes, long congealed to the knobs of Rabbit Ears,
Cienequilla del Barro, Round Mound, Sierra Grande and
scores of others. From around here and for miles to the west,

the Road traverses stretches of lava from ancient volcanoes, the congealed throats of which now rise without cones. South of the Road a few miles, the Don Carlos Hills are mesas capped with basalt lava and west beyond the Canadian River are scores more.

The Road, as wheels marked it from Lower Cimarron Spring, past Rabbit Ears and Round Mound and on to Santa Fe, must have been a trail well known in reverse: Santa Fe to the Cimarron and perhaps to the Arkansas, by people along the Rio Grande before ever a merchant traveled it. Becknell followed it on return from Santa Fe in 1822, noting the way as feasible for wagons. He could not have known of that route from data collected en route westward by way of the Raton Mountains. Even as later traders used the path (the first few went south of Rabbit Ears) they met on it *Ciboleros* who must have been Becknell's source of information. [1, 22, 26, 28, 38]

There had been Pueblo Indian villages along the Rio Grande perhaps a millennium before Don Juan de Onate was

Round Mound

there in 1598.[83] Their need of protein was met with buffalo meat and long before the first wagons appeared out of the east, centuries of hunting had driven most buffalo in that direction and out of New Mexico. It was the custom on the Rio Grande for parties to head east each summer for buffalo country on a trail about where the Road to Santa Fe was to be. Wetmore in 1828, met such a group in the vicinity of Round Mound; Josiah Gregg had encountered another in 1833. Wislizenus, thirteen years after Gregg, had encountered a third in the Cimarron Desert east of Sand Creek and Davis in 1853 spoke of yet another. Old man Collinson, who lived on the hill with peacocks in his yard in a small Texas town, had known them in the Panhandle of Texas, years after rails west of Kansas City had replaced most of the Road. By then *Ciboleros* traveled east more miles to find meat.

Rabbit Ears

Those who wrote of *ciboleros*, Mexican buffalo hunters, gave much the same description. In a century they had changed but little in dress and equipment and not at all in technique and purpose. They were eighty to a hundred men wearing broadbrimmed, flat-topped hats in Gregg's time, leather trousers and jacket, probably buckskin. Each carried a quiver of arrows and a bow in a leather case on his shoulder. Their chief weapon on the hunt was a long lance carried in a case hanging from the saddle, point high overhead and with a tassel of bright color at the tip of the case. Their wagons were two-wheeled ox carts with solid wooden wheels screeching on wooden axles. The cart bed was of rough hewn planks rather than sawed and the enclosing sides were an arrangemnt of stakes set close in a frame. There was not a splinter of iron in the whole assemblage.

Collinson met them at Blanco Canyon near the middle of the Texas Panhandle in 1875. The group numbered about 200 men, women and children with fifty wagons and they had come the 900 miles from Chihuahua in some three months. Their wagons were drawn by two to six yokes of oxen and some by buffalo captured as calves and broken to harness to draw the dried flesh of their brothers. *Ciboleros* were skillful riders and their mounts were equally skilled surefooted horses trained to the chase. A fall in a stampeding herd meant death or, with rare good luck, serious injury beneath hooves of animals weighing up to 2,000 pounds.

Even in Collinson's day, *ciboleros* killed with lances pointed with the long blade of a steel bayonet. On sighting a herd, *ciboleros* rode as closely as possible at a slow pace.[1] Once the animals turned away, hunters closed in. The faster they ran, the closer packed was the herd and it was then *ciboleros* struck, chiefly at cows and young stock as they were the better meat. Racing alongside a fleeing cow, the hunter leaned to thrust hard and deep at a point behind the ribs or through them, reaching for the lungs. A skilled *cibolero*, and those who survived a hunting season always were, could stop ten to fifteen animals in a long run and by the time he returned to the first, it had bled lifeless from lacerated lungs. The lance, some six or eight feet long, had in the end a hole through which was threaded a strip of rawhide four or five feet in length. Should the lance be caught between the ribs, the rawhide was quickly "dallied," looped about the saddle-horn and, by slowing the horse, jerked free.

When a run was over, the few wounded animals were finished off with bow and arrow and cutting of the meat began. At this, too, *ciboleros* were artists. An entire hindquarter would be sliced into one continuous sheet of meat so thin it dried quickly in drier air. In the carts were stakes and hundreds of feet of rawhide rope. With stakes driven into the ground, with ropes tied from one to the next and the whole supporting the thin sheets, sometimes there were acres of meat drying on the plains. Without a fire, curing required several days or a week but the hunters had time to spare and there was other work to do. Buffalo tongues, a delicacy, needed attention as they were fire- or air-dried or, later, salted. All tallow need be rendered over slow fires of buffalo chips and when the meat was dry, it was tightly rolled, fitted into rawhide bags and over it the tallow poured. The packet was the *carne seco* sold by the *vara* along the Rio Grande and in Chihuahua long before traders were there and as frequently long after. The "big hunt" was over by 1879 or 1880 and *ciboleros* no longer visited the plains.

Collinson himself was no mean *cibolero* with a Sharps rifle. Each season, in pigs of twenty-five pounds, he bought five hundred pounds of lead, 100 sheets of patch-paper (for separating powder from lead in reloading cartridges), and up to five kegs, each twenty-five pounds, of black powder. One among several successful seasons was the spring of 1877: 6,000 buffalo tongues (dried or salted) at $1.00 a pound, 4,000 hides (around $4.00 each) and 45,000 pounds of dried meat.

A decade later, only few stragglers escaped slaughter and in 1885, Collinson killed the last wild buffalo he saw: south of Clayton, New Mexico, on Trampero Creek.[1] Collinson wrote of an estimated 20,000 participating in the "big hunt" in the middle and late 1870's and of an acquaintance who, in thirteen years of hunting, killed around 40,000 buffalo. When all was done, more than sixty millions were dead. It was an appalling slaughter, a gargantuan waste, and some who made it had second thoughts. I never heard Mr. Collinson voice regrets but there was an age-differential of some sixty years, a barrier to easy conversation. Much later he left the Texas Panhandle for El Paso and there, old and frail, recorded in his memoirs that it was hide-hunters who decimated the buffalo. By then the big kill was not a pleasant recollection, although he still thought the buffalo had to go.

Collinson's memoirs are likely one of very few written by specific request as a favor to another: the son of one among Collinson's contemporaries had taken up art as a career and wishing to become an illustrator, persuaded his father's friend in retirement in El Paso to record his recollections which the young artist illustrated.

As only in recent years have beef cattle on fewer acres come to equal the buffalo in number, there might be some who would argue the point of necessity if Mr. Collinson were still around to support the premise. He would not have readily conceded, for Collinson was British by birth and it was the tenacity of those people, of which he had ample share, that made him a successful hide-hunter, a comfortably fixed rancher on acres empty of buffalo and, with years which most sustain with torpid resignation, a vivid writer of times and places by then known to very few. His peacocks have gone the way of all fluff and feathers, but Trampero Creek I saw just last year.

Beyond Round Mound, thirty miles north of where Collinson saw his last wild buffalo, creeks were no more frequent than east of it but as many flowed on basalt, pools were common. Whetstone Creek was frequently wet, although grass around was not the best (Map 17). It had its name from some early transient who thought the sandstone outcropping there would be a profitable source of whetstones. Beyond is a small drain, the Don Carlos, a branch of Ute Creek. It was somewhere in that vicinity that Spaniards under one Don Carlos won a decisive battle from Comanches.[26] Two years later 250 of them were in pursuit of other Comanches who had raided Tome, now in Valencia County, New Mexico. Spaniards came upon the Indians in ceremonial dance about the scalps they had lifted. Following a battle lasting three hours and more or less silent save for whoops as arrows are quietly lethal and the Spaniards had few guns to speak of and Comanches had less, the Indians retreated with many dead and wounded. They regrouped and swooped down on the men from the Rio Grande, neatly cutting off their horses. The Spaniards, in their turn, retreated. Result of the two encounters was an agreement between the two peoples and the official reassurance given to Vial as he was about to leave Santa Fe in 1792, on a pathfinding journey across the plains to St. Louis.[63] The creek and an extensive outcrop of basalt holding up mesas five miles south of the Road both bear Don Carlos' name.

Westward from Don Carlos Creek is Point-of-Rock of elevation 7,060 feet, an ancient volcanic plug of syenite, a type of igneous rock named from its outcrop in another arid land, that about Syene, Egypt.[38] At its south point is a spring, well known to men on the Road. From the modern highway several miles south of it, Point-of-Rock appears the southernmost extension of high hills and low mountains rising from rough country reaching northwest to the Raton Mountains. Point-of-Rock and the spring were frequent stops on the Road. As it was then, so it is now: a landmark of tragedy.

Those interested in history of the Road eventually come to read "Calhoun's Correspondence," a compendium of official letters from James S. Calhoun, the first Indian Agent of New Mexico Territory, to the Bureau of Indian Affairs in Washington.[84] With ink now dry more than a hundred twenty years, the letters have lost little of their flavor. A reader

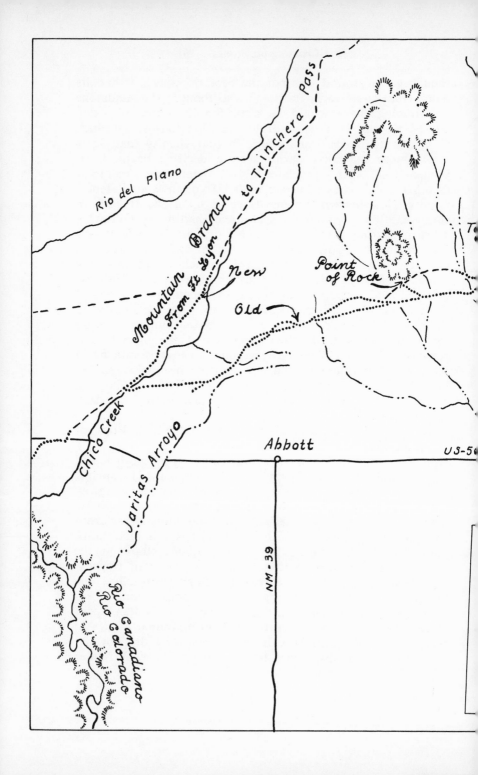

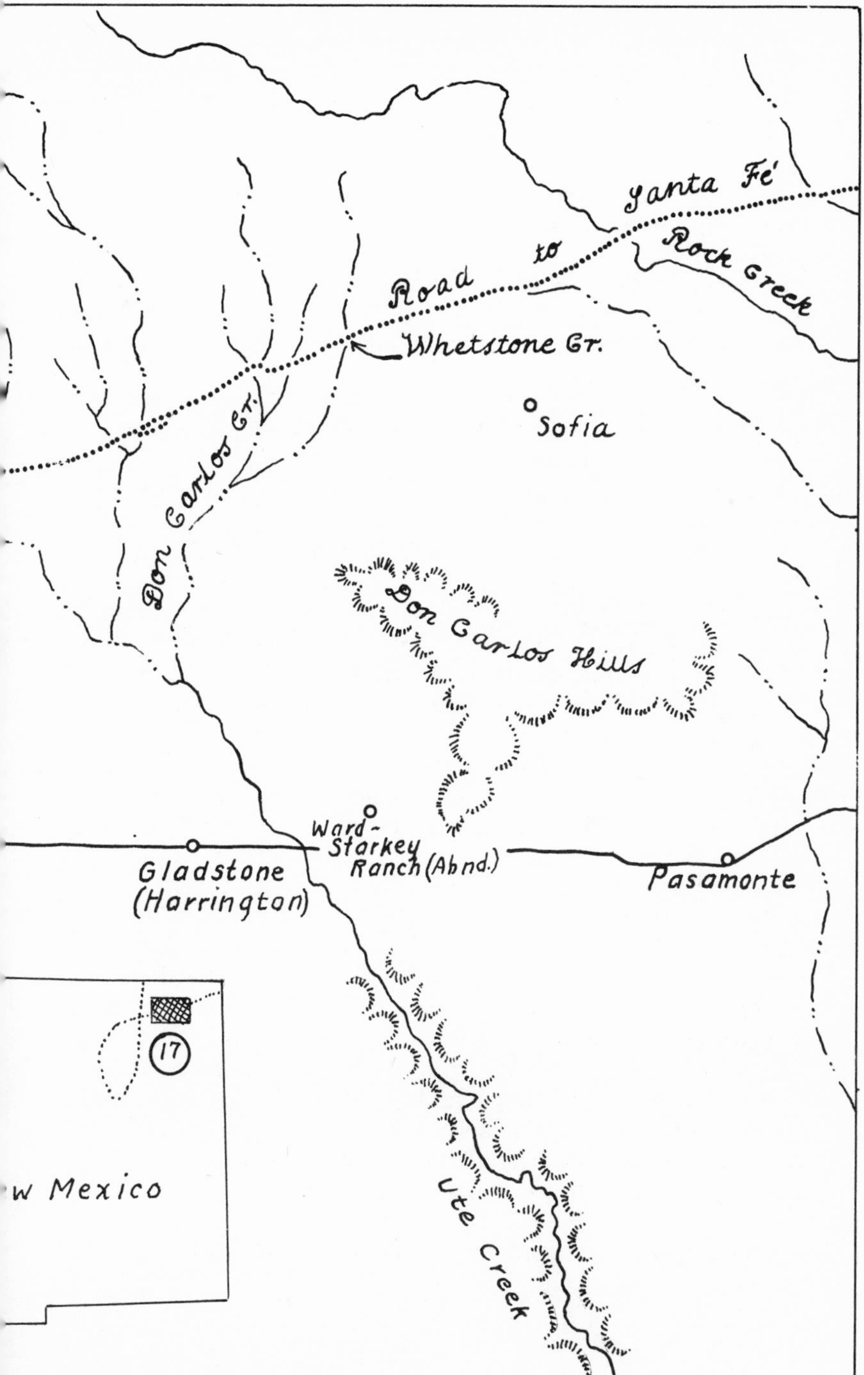

Road to Santa Fé

Rock Creek

Whetstone Cr.

Sofia

Don Carlos Cr.

Don Carlos Hills

Ward-
Starkey
Ranch (Abnd.)

Gladstone
(Harrington)

Pasamonte

(17)

New Mexico

Ute Creek

comes to believe that few men attempted so much and fewer yet did so well. Had Calhoun ever fully realized how difficult his job was, he would have given it up. His letters are always interesting, even when Calhoun writes of house-keeping chores of his position, and they are sometimes de-pressing. One learns from them that when an administrator comfortable in a Washington office truly sets his mind to the task of hewing to the letter of regulations, he is some-thing more than two thousand miles removed from reality and sometimes even farther from justice and mercy. Ac-counting is done in cold ink, and when done by rule it is icy. When sometimes in Santa Fe, logic, common sense or even justice petitioned for mercy, it was read in Washington through dark glasses by minds attuned to shorter wave-lengths.

Quite early in his tenure, Calhoun reported Indians living in the Territory were an estimated 12,000 Comanches, 7,000 Navajos, 1,500 Cheyennes, 1,600 Arapahoes and about as many Pueblos, the latter relatively peaceable in adobe houses along the Rio Grande. Of these, only the Navajos were thought to be increasing. Indians were not fertile folk. Some were altogether barren and many supported spiro-chetes of syphilis. Two offspring were the average and a number were stillborn. Perhaps because of sturdier genes and chromosomes, Navajos had more. At any rate, they now number around 110,000 on their reservation in Arizona. By Charles Bent, first Governor of New Mexico Territory, they were judged industrious, intelligent and warlike. With these attributes they were, even then, proprietors of considerable livestock: an estimated 300,000 sheep, 30,000 cattle, 10,000 horses and mules, and uncounted slaves. Most of the quad-rupeds were coups scored on villages along the Rio Grande. Many of the slaves were from the same source and others from Chihuahua, Durango and Sinaloa. Mexico was a com-mon hunting ground for several tribes. Navajos raided there and quickly retreated northward as did Apaches, Comanches and even Pawnees from distant prairies around the Platte River.

One need only read the "Correspondence" to know that

one man's hands, Calhoun's, were overflowing with problems impossible of solution, injustices impossible of redress, captivities impossible to end. Through the pages run dark threads of tragedy and none darker than the words which connect Mrs. White, her small daughter and colored servant to the present. The thread of words appears in the warp of Indian depredations in October 1849, and paraphrased, reads:

> Four or five days ago, Mr. Spencer, an American merchant on return from the United States, saw east of Point of Rocks the bodies of Mr. J. M. White and five or six others of a party returning from St. Louis. Next day Mr. Spencer met a group of Pueblo Indians who had recently seen in a camp of Apaches an American female and daughter, supposedly Mrs. White and child.

Mr. White was a Santa Fe trader returning west with the caravan of Francis X. Aubrey and at some point east of Whetstone Creek had concluded Indian dangers lay behind. In haste to reach Santa Fe, Mr. White, his wife, small daughter, Negro servant and three men, a carriage and a wagon or two, had left the protection of the caravan and forged ahead. Camped for the night about half-way between Whetstone Creek and Point-of-Rock, they were visited by Apaches whose tribal policy was malice toward all and charity toward none. The Indians demanded gifts, a common levy on the Road and generally met by offer of food, perhaps a drink of rum. Mr. White ordered them from camp. Later they returned and meeting the same refusal, opened fire, killing White, Lawbarger, an unidentified Mexican and an unknown American. Mrs. White and her daughter of about ten years were taken prisoner.

It was not the custom of raiding Indians to make captives of men. As warriors however unwilling, they must be defeated and if valiant, scalped. Children of either sex were amenable to slavery and women subject to rape, or death if they resisted.

A November letter from Calhoun adds very little, but all the information then available:

> Mr. Barclay passed Point of Rock soon after the murder and thought all the bodies among upset carriages and wagons were Mexican. His information from a party of Pueblo Indian buffalo hunters indicated that Mrs. White, daughter and colored servant are captives of Jicarilla Apaches.

One may know that Washington was stirred to the extent of a word or two, as a letter from there concludes with the statement: "This will be handed you by Mr. Isaac Dunn, brother of Mrs. White who goes to New Mexico to aid in the search."

Letters following are sundry accounts of Indian raids and one speaks of a twelve-year-old boy captured in Durango by Apaches or Comanches, whose freedom was bought in New Mexico for four knives, one plug of tobacco, six *fanegas* of corn, four blankets, and six yards of red cloth. There is an account of another captive, a girl about twenty-five, whose husband and daughter were killed at the time of her capture, bought by New Mexicans who gave her freedom for two striped blankets, ten yards of cotton drilling, ten yards of calico, ten yards of cotton sheeting, two handkerchiefs, four plugs of tobacco, one bag of corn and one knife. It was little enough for emancipation without proclamation. And then in March 1850, is the letter one hopes not to read:

> Mrs. White was killed in retreat of Apaches before the attack upon them by troops under Major Grier. The child is believed killed perhaps the day after.

From other sources, one may learn that soon after the murders east of Point-of-Rock, Major Grier collected troops and guides, one of which was Christopher Carson living then in Rayado, and followed the Apaches. Just how far, how long and to where is not certain, but for a considerable time and into the Texas Panhandle.

Captors and captives traveled in dry country, necessarily from running water to spring to *tinaja*. Departing any hasty camp, the Apaches scattered but as Carson was quite as familiar with the country as those born in it, no great time was lost in tracing misleading signs. Eventually Carson, scouting ahead, returned to inform Major Grier he had sighted the Apaches. Carson urged an instant charge. Grier hesitated, hoping to negotiate release of the captives. Carson, who not only knew Indians better but knew them very well indeed, must have argued hurriedly, certainly briefly, for in that instant there was report of a rifle and the whistling ball passed through the slack of Major Grier's coat. The charge was instantaneous and too late. Mrs. White was killed by her captors.

Hope which springs eternal, dies never. Among the "Correspondence" is a letter dated six months later, from Jasper H. Dunn of Abington, Virgina, in which he states that reports reaching him from Captain Aubrey of Santa Fe, inform that his niece is certain to be alive, and another in the next month from Calhoun speaking of the $1,500 appropriated by Congress for "redemption of the daughter of the late Mr. J. M. White now supposedly in captivity of Apaches." In March a year later, he advised Washington that inquiries among Utahs concerning Mrs. White's daughter and colored servant met no success.

One may read now from microfilm of a tattered copy of the *Santa Fe Weekly Gazette* for Saturday, November 27, 1852 and learn the last word. It is an account of a conference with Indians gathered at Abiquiu, where Chacon, Chief among Apaches, related that the massacre of the White party was a joint venture of Utahs and Apaches led by White Wolf. Angered by their expulsion from the camp, they killed Mr. White, the Negro servant and others. Mrs. White and the child were killed somewhere on Rio Colorado (the Canadian) as the fight with Grier's troops commenced.

Highway 56, west from Clayton, New Mexico, and south of Point-of-Rock, is a very long tangent with very few interruptions. The most populous is a combined store and home with a gasoline pump in front and a second house, abandoned: Gladstone, New Mexico, southwest of the Don Carlos Hills (Map 17). On the interminable pavement not many cars pass and those generally quickly. Separated by hours, now and then one may slow and turn from the highway and now one did, to stop beyond the pump. From it an apparently sane man got out, approached the two men passing the time of day and asked an insane question.

"Can you tell me where I might find the cemetery?"

There was a considerable interval but not a raised eyebrow before the younger replied: "Follow that dirt road a mile south, then turn left for half a mile. The graveyard will be on your right."

There was a longer silence as I surveyed the expanse, limited only by a far-distant mesa of basalt, wondering if curiosity would prompt a question. They merely surveyed the landscape also.

"Are those the Don Carlos Hills?"

"Yep."

"Where is Ute Creek?"

"Between here and the Hills."

I explained that a good many years ago I had spent a summer over yonder on a ranch owned by an uncle and that my grandmother was buried here. I mentioned the few names I could recall and the older of the two men remembered his father had once pointed to a crumbling corral as headquarters of the old Ward-Starkey ranch. The younger repeated his directions, simple to follow.

The Don Carlos Hills lay several miles and more years distant than I cared to count right then. Long before I had ever seen the basalt-capped mesas I had read with avid interest Ernest Thompson Seton's word-sketches of animals, accepted them as fiction and enjoyed them as an unfettered imagination allowed.[85] When Seton wrote of "Lobo, King of the Corrumpa" who repeatedly raided at night herds of O T O sheep, killing a dozen and slashing a score more, I took it to be fictional and royal prerogative. When King Lobo led his blind mate to the feasts I worried lest she be shot by a vengeful herder. When a cruel trapper by unfair means caught and killed the blind wolf, I was near to tears. When by foul use of the scent of her skin he caught and killed the King, I shed them.

And there was the story of the "Pacing Mustang" in words so vivid as to free any adolescent soul as certainly it did mine. On that wild stallion and free on Seton's words we ranged fanciful Don Carlos Hills. It was a torment when, by relays of lesser horses, cowboys literally ran the pacing stallion to death.

When I visited the ranch somewhere distant in the haze, owned by others now, my uncle had met me at the nearest point on the railroad in a Model T. With rear heavily loaded with supplies, we drove country completely different from what I knew. I knew prairie but none so unlimited as this; I had never seen a mountain or mesa. On the horizon was the thin blue of mountains and here the road led gently up to cross a gap between mesas capped by basalt, the first interruption in a smooth and fascinating hour. I examined them with interest, particularly the dense black layer; all rock I knew was yellow, red or white. A few turns of the track and we were past the crest and on the descending slope beyond. I turned to see more of the lava-topped hills and inquired of my uncle did the place have a name.

"Don Carlos Hills," he replied.

Startled, I searched his face, then quickly looked back at the Hills, embarrassed that somehow he knew of my fascination for the Pacing Mustang. For quite a few long and uneasy minutes I kept eyes on the receding Hills and only after the car came to a stop did I turn to face the road and ridicule. We had come onto a huge flock of sheep and now they crossed the tracks ahead. It was a welcome interruption and I watched with interest then, suddenly, with heart leaping free, free of everything: every sheep in the hundreds crossing from left to right was clearly and unmistakably marked: O T O.

There are moments out of a liftime of which one might speak, if only for their fullness. That one is unmatched by any other I know.

The ranch was a small outfit, purely a working concern and in truth they had no time for a visitor. My uncle dropped me off at one of the four small tar-paper houses, each on the

corner of a "claim," and drove off southwestward to an unknown Ute Creek Canyon where my aunt ran the camp while
his two daughters and a couple of cowhands took care of
livestock remaining after three disastrous winters and a
summer rich in loco-weed, poison to cattle.

With time adequate for the responsibilities, I became
Listener to Winds and Inspector of Sunsets, Don Carlos
Division as, with another aunt and my grandmother, I spent
a summer mostly alone but never lonely. I thought the return
of my uncle, aunt and two cousins a few days before my departure, an intrusion on a place I had come to regard my
own. But only for the first few minutes; for the few days
remaining I was dazzled. My cousins, whom I had not known,
were about the prettiest girls I had ever seen and the older,
just my age, was a beauty. It was a detached observation,
as her work allowed no time for itinerant relatives. On a
ranch perilously close to foreclosure, she was a very busy girl,
a ranch-hand in every sense of the word thirteen years, a
sharp mind and firm training would allow. She went about
work, anything that could be done on horseback, each day
twelve or fifteen hours of it. For her one morning my admiration was unbounded when the horse she mounted broke in
two. She stayed in the saddle, girl and horse achieving a
grace of motion that countered gravity, or at least put it to
work. When in later years I came to know her in Denver, I at
least old enough to be a grandfather, we spoke of the ranch.

"Yes, it was wonderful there. But, you know, all the years
at the Don Carlos I had a constant itch and the welts of hives.
I didn't know until long after we left the ranch that I was
allergic to horses."

Quite some miles west of Gladstone and a few east of
Springer, the highway bridges the Canadian River, barren
of brush, shrub or tree (Map 18). A short distance beyond
the west abutment I turned sharp left and south through a
cattle-guard. Immediately the tracks dipped steeply to ford
a small creek in a wide gentle valley at which watered three
mares and a yearling that behaved as if he had never seen

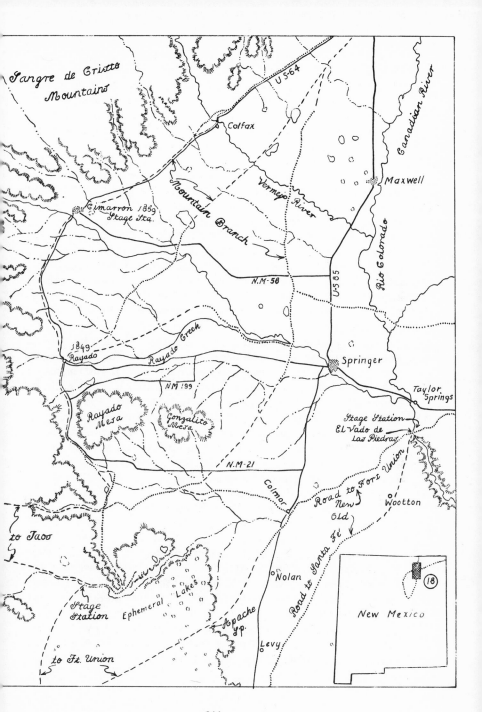

Sangre de Cristo Mountains

Colfax

US-64

Canadian River

Maxwell

Vermejo River

Cimarron 1859 Stage Sta.

Mountain Branch

N.M-58

US-85

Rio Colorado

Rayado Creek

1849 Rayado

Springer

NM !99

Taylor Springs

Rayado Mesa

Gonzalito Mesa

Stage Station El Vado de las Piedras

N.M-21

Colmar

Road to Fort Union

to Taos

New

Old

Wootton

Nolan

Road to Santa Fé

Stage Station   Ephemeral Lakes

Apache Sp.

New Mexico

18

to Ft. Union

Levy

an automobile before, although at any time he had only to lift his head from grazing and see all sorts pass on the highway. Following the rough road a couple of miles south, as I stopped to open a wire gate, I knew I must be somewhere near El Vado de las Piedras, the ford of stones.

East a mile was the margin of the valley: clay hills topped by thin limestone. Somewhere between the wire gate and the clay slopes ran the Canadian River. Off to the west smooth prairie slanted gently upward and on it half a mile distant was a small spot of white; I had the pleasant feeling which so comforts the student who, for once, has done his homework. I knew where El Vado de las Piedras was for I was certain that spot of white marked Henry Lorenzen's last stop. Cedar posts holding planks enclosed a white marble stone on which one may read: "In Memory of Henry Lorenzen, Native of Schleswig, Born September 30, 1837. Died March 13, 1879."

I never learned who Henry Lorenzen might be save a marker on an abandoned Road leading west out of Missouri. He may have been an employee of the old Taylor ranch, a crumbling adobe and nearby stone shed half a mile south, or at the Stage Station on the opposite side of the river. From a stone so terse in meagre virtues: born, died, one could not know but Henry must have been well thought of in these parts. It seems improbable that in 1879 a marble slab would have been available so far west of Missouri or hauled so far to mark a grave. I would guess the stone quite a bit younger but I never found anyone who knew.

Due east of the grave, the Road to Santa Fe crosses the Canadian River on El Vado de las Piedras, truly a ford of stone. Here the Dakota formation, overlain by younger clay, outcrops in the bed of the river, paving it with sandstone for several hundred yards. It was for heavy wagons the firmest crossing west of Franklin, Missouri. The Canadian is now a flow of sweet water eight or ten inches deep between shallow stone cisterns, and about as many feet wide. Bare of shrubs the sod slopes gently to the water-edge. Somewhere upstream, it must flow on red shale and sand for Marmaduke (beneath the marble arch at Arrow Rock, Missouri) wrote on July 17, 1824: "Crossed Red River . . . a very deep red color, resembling thin, weak blood." [71] To the Spanish of long ago it was El Rio Colorado and in name confused by their eastern contemporaries with another Rio Colorado, Red River, which flows between Texas and Oklahoma and once was a part of the boundary between New Spain and the United States. It is commonly a jolt to Texans living a distance from it when they learn, as they spit in Red River, that they spit in Oklahoma. By Supreme Court decision the south bank of that stream is the north margin of Texas. Commonly they spit a second time, as if in water not worth owning even by a dry state.

At the ford, the Canadian offered no difficulties to loaded wagons and for miles upstream it was no barrier to mounted men. Pawnees from the Platte commonly passed this way, en route to the annual raid into Mexico for horses, slaves and other such booty as good luck might allow. In the summer of 1820 Pawnees camped somewhere upstream not far from El Vado de las Piedras of later wagons. With them was a twenty-year-old Kentuckian soon to be prisoner in Santa Fe.

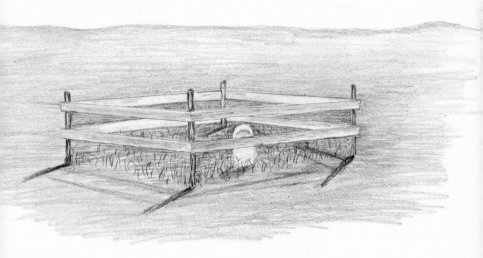

David Meriwether, employee of a St. Louis fur company, on their behalf was a licensed Indian Trader and sutler (civilian merchant) to a detachment of the Army at a small post on Council Bluff in Iowa.[72] There he came to know Pawnees as sometimes unruly customers and as captors of two Mexicans, father and son. The latter was a ten-year-old "bright sprightly little fellow" and the former "old and morose" as might be a man with the dismal future of a slave. The captives were allowed considerable freedom as it was thought they could not escape or could easily be captured if they did. But the old man managed the one and avoided the other. Some weeks later the boy in tears appealed to Meriwether as he had been told he was to be burned at the stake. Pawnees were addicted to esoteric spiritual diversions, including cannibalism of captives when the moon was right or perhaps when it was wrong, to set it right. The *Missouri Intelligencer* had carried an account of a feast of Pawness on the flesh of a squaw captured from another tribe. Meriwether, with two other traders at Council Bluff purchased the boy for about $150 in trade goods as Pawnees, like other people, were sometimes more susceptible to appeal of things material than spiritual.

Before the father of the boy had dropped from sight, he had shown Meriwether a hollowed stem of a feather, a quill, filled with gold dust recovered in New Mexico. Meriwether suggested to his employers that he visit the region to learn if there was more such loose dust. They agreed, and as it was soon convenient to do so, Meriwether with Albert, a Negro boy, joined a southbound party of Pawnees led by Big Elk, on their annual raid into Mexico. The summer prairies offer no difficulties to horsemen provided they do not meet a larger band of Comanches or Apaches. As Pawnees were enemies of many and friends of very few, there was always some danger in their presence.

Southward the group encountered the Arkansas River and followed it west, upstream, for a time. Crossing the shallow water they entered dry country, the "Waterscrape" of later wagons. Near the southwest edge of buffalo country, the group paused long enough to kill a few, smoke-dry the meat and conceal a part of it in a small cave which they blocked with large stones to discourage wolves from provisions stored for the return journey.

Eventually Big Elk and his men led their guests to the Canadian River, somewhere not far above the Ford, crossed easily to the west bank, and camped. Hunting for fresh meat not far upstream, Meriwether and Albert came on a sand bar bearing tracks of earlier visitors. To Meriwether they were new and a threat. To Big Elk they were old and no warning. As the Chief would not move camp, Meriwether and Albert recrossed to the east bank and made camp among sparse cedars in a small tributary cove a mile or so from the Pawnees.

Before daybreak next morning Meriwether heard shots and from a hilltop near could see the Pawnees were under attack. Very soon, and in haste, Big Elk and another arrived and later a third, badly wounded. The five remained concealed and Meriwether, at least, contemplative. By mid-morning he concluded it an opportune time to separate from the Pawnees. He knew that with them he would be counted an enemy by every Spaniard in New Mexico, as all had a warm, even heated, regard for Pawnees. With the excuse that he wished to learn who the attackers were, Meriwether and Albert left despite Big Elk's objections and with agreement that if he did not return by nightfall, the Pawnees would wait at the meat cache.

With a flag of truce, the left-over of a shirt torn to provide bandages for the wounded brave, Meriwether and Albert approached the battleground where a few Spaniards remained. They were immediately taken in hand, led four or five miles upriver where their captors set them afoot and relieved them of everything save the clothes they wore. En route soon to Santa Fe, the footsore Meriwether persuaded his captors to allow him to ride one of the extra mules. They camped that night at "Cicuique," the Pecos Village of later caravan years. Next day they followed the trail through Apache (Glorieta) Pass and on northwest to Santa Fe.

In the capital Meriwether was brought before Don Facundo Melgares, Governor, but as neither could speak the language of the other, the interview was not informative to either. Separated from Albert, Meriwether spent a few days in a room in the northwest corner of the Palace of the Governors, an adobe structure, where he was certain he would be eaten alive by bedbugs and fleas. Through intercession of a priest whose French Meriwether could speak, the prisoners were released on parole and the Padre provided food and lodging. In return, Meriwether worked in his garden. Governor Melgares recalled the invasion of Florida by General Jackson and he was not kindly disposed toward citizens of the invading country. The priest was a most persuasive man, for soon the prisoners were given freedom and each a gaunt mule for the journey eastward, in return for a promise never to return to New Mexico. As by then there were the uncertainties of cold weather, and snow, Meriwether argued with the Governor that it would be as merciful to shoot them then and there. A journey without arms across the prairies would be equally certain and a great deal more uncomfortable. Don Facundo was more amenable to reason than most Governors of New Mexico. Departure of the prisoners was delayed a few days while he recovered Meriwether's rifle, one pistol and provided Albert with a musket of sorts.

It seems improbable that Melgares bid his captives *buena suerte y adios,* but if he did by rare grace not usually the award of prisoners even from Spaniards who are born to courtesy, Governor Melgares spoke to the boy who, in but three decades, would return a man to the flea-and bug-crowded room and to the Palace itself in the very capacity Don Facundo occupied it. David Meriwether returned in 1853 to New Mexico Territory as Governor.[72]

Unaware of the future and that as Governor of it he would be burned in effigy, Meriwether, with Albert and under escort of two Mexicans, left New Mexico in humble circumstances and with criminal intent. He was determined to steal one of their mules as his own was much too gaunt for a journey across the plains. The freemen, and their escorts, passed Pecos Village and from it went northeast across a fold of the Sangre de Cristo Moutains. Somewhere on the trail which emerged in the vicinity of present Las Vegas, the

Mexicans lagging behind called to the prisoners ahead, waved *adios,* and turned back. Meriwether and Albert headed for the only landmark they knew: the Canadian River. Intersecting the stream and turning down it, they found Pawnee bones on the battleground. Now on a familiar trail, they followed landmarks without difficulty and somewhere between the Cimarron and the Arkansas Rivers, found the meat cache and the three Pawnees, the wounded one nearly recovered.

The group remained in camp a few days, and then traveling northeast forded the icy Arkansas. North of it, on a tributary of the Platte, weather became so severe and snow so deep that they made camp for the remainder of the winter, on water and near wood. With tomahawks they cut slender poles, set them in the ground with tops leaning against the overhang of a rock ledge. Killing the lean mules, their skins were stretched over the framework which, covered with snowfall, was insulated yet more by throwing spring water over it to freeze into a plains igloo of a sort. Within the shelter, a crevice in the rock wall served as a fireplace and carried smoke to the top of the cliff where they took turns at watch. Days passed slowly as weather encouraged no hunting, unnecessary so long as mule meat lasted. Meriwether made rude candles of mule tallow, moulded by hand about willow twigs. He found a cobble the size and general shape of a human head and, following a whim, stretched over it a scrap of green rawhide. When this was dry and removed, holes for eyes, nose and mouth were cut. Set with a candle behind it on a rock shelf in the dark rear of the shelter, the glowing mask made a startling conversation piece. It proved a very useful one.

Albert, on watch, announced what all feared and hoped to avoid: the approach of Indians, nine, who had spotted the campfire smoke, a necessity in the bitter weather. The ratio of nine visitors to five hosts argued for peace and no provocation. Quickly Albert and Meriwether concealed their arms, a temptation, behind a blanket curtain hanging from a rock ledge at the back of the shelter. With apprehension they waited. The strangers first wished food and when fed, wished to know what lay behind the blanket. The superior number of guests allowed no real choice; it merely encouraged the diplomacy survival required. Meriwether spoke in signs of strong medicine there and revealed nothing as he stepped behind the barrier and lighted a candle behind the mask. When the visitors persisted, and pressed aggressively their inquiry, Meriwether arranged three of them in front of the curtain and dramatically pulled it aside. In the dim light, the luminescent mask was a startling apparition, medicine too strong for the visitors. They scrambled out and left immediately.

They were scarcely out of sight before Meriwether, Albert, Big Elk and the two braves packed up: arms, blankets and meat. For a full twenty four hours they walked northwest, hoping for as many miles as possible between them and the strangers, should the latter have second thoughts. A few weeks later, in March 1821, the year of Mexican Independence and the opening of the Santa Fe trade by Becknell and nearly a year after his departure, Meriwether was back in Council Bluff. His later biography included a time at Fort Osage when it was reoccupied by troops to which he was sutler, his return to marriage, farming and politics in Kentucky, and in 1853 a return to New Mexico as Territorial Governor.

Among those least distinguished by historians for a journey, Santa Fe to St. Louis, across the plains and nearly half a century before commerce on them, are John R. Peyton, Charles Lucas and Annette Ximenez.* Theirs was a

* The lack of distinction is for good reason:

College of William and Mary   August 22, 1968
Office of the Registrar,
Williamsburg, Virginia 23185

The following is in reply to your recent request for information regarding John Rowzee Peyton. There seems to be no existing College records listing John Rowzee Peyton's name as an alumnus of the College of William and Mary. Unfortunately, our earliest matriculation book dates from 1827, which would be a goodly period after the time to which you make reference. We do not find his name, either, on any of the Faculty minutes or Bursar's book which go back further than flight to freedom, important only to participants hence a trivia among ventures in commerce and exploration.

According to his grandson who, in 1867, wrote *The Adventures of My Grandfather*, John Rowzee Peyton of Stony Hill, Virginia, was a 1772 graduate of William and Mary College and son of a planter. The twenty-three-year-old graduate sailed from Alexandria, Virginia, to see something of the western hemisphere before settling to confining responsibilities. Letters told of his travels: one from Jamaica where he engaged a servant, Charles Lucas, a half-breed Indian conversant with Spanish; another locates master and servant in Cartagena, Colombia (now Panama) in July, 1773 and in New Orleans two months later where they embarked on the British ship *Swan*, with Captain Jones, for St. Augustine, Florida.[86]

An ill wind dismantled the *Swan*. As it drifted on rough seas it was sighted and boarded by Spaniards. As was sometimes a custom in those days the Spanish captain claimed the *Swan* an instrument of the French, enemy at the time, hence legitimate booty for the King of Spain.

As prisoners, crew and passengers of the *Swan* were set ashore at the mouth of El Rio Bravo del Norte (Rio Grande) where three died of disease and malnutrition and the remainder were imprisoned a fortnight. It was not a

---

the matriculation books. As far as any printed material is concerned, we are able to unearth the first source of reference to Mr. Peyton in the biography written by his grandson, John Lewis Peyton, entitled *The Adventures of My Grandfather*, which was first published in London in 1867 and reprinted as recently as 1963 in Charlottesville, Virginia. . . .

In all candor I must add that there is a good deal of question in the minds of William and Mary historians as to the accuracy of the original book. It seems that there is a question regarding the style, punctuation and spelling that appears in the book as compared to the original letters; however, this historical criticism was never exploited fully and, therefore, I only add this as a cautionary, explanatory note. . . .

Sincerely yours,
(signed)
Dudley M. Jensen
Registrar

happy interval, nor was that which followed. Under escort of twenty guards (described by Peyton as ragged ruffians) mounted on mules, the captives chained two-by-two, Peyton to Lucas, plodded upriver with energy diminished by dysentery, a diet of mule meat and parched corn. Events in the months following (ten of them) are a credit to the will for survival of Peyton and Lucas, and to Annette Ximenez, daughter of their jailer in Santa Fe.

Lodged in a prison at the capital of the province, Peyton having recovered from five weeks of a "seasoning bilious fever," they laid plans for escape. They had the aid of rapport between Catholic Lucas and Catholic priest, and the admiration of Annette for Lucas. By necessity, plans were nebulous as the cell without chair, table, blanket and sometimes food, provided little inspiration. Victuals, without which they could not have survived, were frequently smuggled by Annette with the encouragement of the priest. Forbidden to speak with their guards who would not reply, the prisoners experienced close and oppressive confinement. Captain Jones in an adjacent cell preferred suicide.

The office of Governor of *Nuevo Mejico* has a long record of murders, tortures and abominations, and imprisonment such as Peyton's can be counted ordinary. Through intercession of Padre Lopez and of Annette, Jailer Ximenez informed Peyton that a petition to Governor Pedro de Mendinueta might result in freedom of the prison yard. According to Peyton, he wrote in Spanish, dictated by Lucas, in pencil * on the back of the Ace of Diamonds provided by the jailer. Paper was a rare commodity in Santa Fe of those years and scraps must have been very rare among jailers. Gambling in Santa Fe was a major occupation and minor vice when all industry was minor and poverty major.

The Governor gave courteous audience as the prisoner related the full account of his identity, travels, capture and

---

* In Peyton's time, a "pencil" was anything from a fine brush to a fragment of graphite. Deposits of graphite are mined in Mexico. Conceivably they were known and used in a minor way when there was no industrial use for the mineral.

imprisonment. Peyton added that dead or alive he would be avenged by his government and that the Governor had "best be prepared for that day of wrath."

Three days later, jailer Ximenez produced for Peyton's signature a paper which, translated by Lucas, acknowledged the prisoners had been taken from a French ship engaged in illegal traffic, legally imprisoned and humanely treated. For the week following rejection, the prisoners were without food save that smuggled by Annette. The short rations might have been longer had not the Priest, perhaps with the aid of Annette, persuaded Lucas to sign his employer's name and without his knowledge.

With more if not better food and freedom of the prison yard for two hours each day, Peyton was presented with a considerable bill for food, candles, attendance and kindred luxuries. Prisoners generally have no money, certainly not one of Peyton's experience, and he said so. It could not have been news to Ximenez. Peyton added that if the bill were halved, he would write a draft on Alexandria which could be cashed in Havana. He made the offer as he could think of no other way by which his family could be informed of his fate. The offer was refused but bargaining continued. In but few days Ximenez agreed to a reduction and to accept additional payment of 500 Mexican dollars for clothes and other items if that amount was included in the draft. A local merchant was to supply the luxuries.

Through Annette, Peyton offered a bribe of 500 pounds to the merchant who would be obligated to furnish horses, a pair of pistols and assorted tools. With the tools, Peyton and Lucas cut through the adobe walls and a four-inch oak plank, leaving a thin veneer of mortared stone untouched. This took time, and no doubt there was the problem of disposal of the debris, presumably in the prison yard during the daily two hours of freedom.

With horses, pistols, compass, old French map and other equipment awaiting them somewhere in Santa Fe, plans for escape became definite. From Annette they learned that on a night a few days hence, there would be a wedding and a *fandango* which her parents would attend, leaving only her two young brothers and the sentinels. Poison in coffee for the guards was suggested by Annette but Peyton urged laudanum be used instead. Laudanum, a tincture of opium, was known a hundred years before Peyton. It was sovereign remedy for every ailment. Although it cured none it narcotized the symptoms of all. Santa Fe in 1773 was a frontier town but slightly less primitive than most. It could not have contained many remedies for ills and ailments but if it had any, it is reasonable surmise that laudanum, efficacious for all, was one among the few. As a tincture, laudanum is alcoholic, hence a ready substitute for rum then, as now, a fortification of coffee.

On the fateful night Annette, covertly consulting with the prisoners the penultimate moment, was seen and questioned by a guard. She admitted she was about to bring coffee to the prisoners and she offered as much to the guards, plus a glass of rum. As both coffee and rum were laced with laudanum, in minutes the guards were asleep and in moments the prisoners free. Carrying a bag of provisions supplied by Annette, they followed her through dark streets to a stable on the outskirts of the village where the merchant and horses awaited them. There the co-conspirator provided paper, quill and light from a "dark lanthorn." As Peyton sat to enscribe the draft for five hundred pounds, the merchant demanded it be for one thousand. Peyton refused. The merchant quickly stepped beyond the door and turned the key. Through a crack in the barrier he repeated the demand, adding threat to alarm the town. Through the same crack Peyton passed the draft "for One Thousand Pounds, at sight, and without grace." In few more minutes the fugitives were beyond the settlement, headed for the mountains. By dawn they had covered forty miles and there broke fast with food provided by Annette as they rested four uneasy hours.

From the map, Peyton knew St. Louis was in "latitude 36° 10′ North and longitude 90° 05′ West." It was not quite, but it was near enough and it did not matter as Peyton had only a compass. He could be certain that if they traveled long enough (about 900 miles airline) in a northeast direction, St. Louis would be somewhere within fifty miles. In three days they crossed the mountains, no mean feat in any February. "There was little snow. The air was mild but during the night was fairly cold." In camp at the east base of the Sangre de Cristo Mountains, they sheltered in a cavern for two days while rain fell and, following Annette's directions, smoke-dried the venison of two deer. "Next day we killed two more for skins and meat and meanwhile the horses found abundant grass." It is well they did, even sparse grass in February, as Peyton calculated forty days of travel at thirty miles a day separated them from civilization in Missouri.

For twenty-one days the fugitives traveled without incident, and the account receives scarcely more than that many lines. Peyton speaks of crossing a "great river," presumed the "Rio Rouge" ("Rio", Spanish and "Rouge" French, for Red River, later the Canadian) but as he mentions golden hills of sand along it and calculates distance beyond to St. Louis at 600 miles, it was probably the Arkansas. Somewhere on the Plains on March 10th, they prepared as best they could to meet a blizzard: excavated a small chamber in a hillside and covered it with skins. It was eleven days before melting of snow allowed travel and by then their horses, half-starved, were very feeble.

In crossing streams in flood, Lucas went first, Annette next and Peyton last. Under way again, at some deep stream Annette's weakened animal drowned.. With the good luck constantly with them, the girl made the shore and the two crossed on Peyton's mount. By mid-April they were following a tributary of the Missouri and by then a second horse was lost to exhaustion. At the Missouri, reached April 28, 1774, the last horse was abandoned. To then, by good fortune, they had avoided Indians, signs of which were more numerous the further east they walked. Next day they entered an Osage village and found welcome. Peyton exchanged a musket for a canoe and "provisions of hominy and bison tongue." Promising a case of rum in payment, they secured the services of an "old Osage Indian and by skillful navigation, arrived in St. Louis in a fortnight."

From St. Louis Peyton, Lucas and Annette went to

Kentucky and eastward, arriving at the Great Kanawha
River in time for Peyton to join General Andrew Lewis
in a battle with Shawnees at Point Pleasant, western Virginia
on October 10, 1774. John R. Peyton died in Virginia in 1798.
Annette and Lucas left numerous progeny and their children's
children were in service with Peyton's grandson, author of the
account, in 1867.

South of where the fugitives had crossed the Canadian
and south of where Meriwether saw the same current nearly
half a century later: a quarter-mile below El Vado de las
Piedras, the river begins a canyon cut deeply into Dakota
sandstone which stands in nearly vertical walls, higher each
mile downstream. It is the canyon-character of the river below
the ford from which evolved its modern name: Canadian from
cañadiano, a derivative of *cañada* meaning in a general way
river-in-a-canyon, and neither related to Canada.

In the very early days of the Road, before ruts were
clearly cut, one party of traders with merchandise went south
of Rabbit Ears Peak, passed the vicinity of modern Clayton,
New Mexico, to strike the canyon of the Canadian below the
Ford. Unaware of the easier crossing upstream, they unloaded, eased wagons on a tail rope down the bluff, re-
loaded to cross the floodplain, unloaded and with triple and
quadrupled yokes, lifted the empty wagons up onto the
prairie to which men carried the merchandise.

When there was a Road to Santa Fe, at El Vado de las
Piedras near its western end, the earliest among traders left
wagons with others and rode south from the crossing to arrange payment of import duties (in 1825 they were 25% of
stated value of the goods) with the Alcalde at San Miguel
del Vado on the Pecos River. In later years, at the ford of the
Canadian were stationed customs agents to examine wagons
and hamper smuggling as best they could. As about here
Indian dangers were past, at least until invasions by an Army
stirred them, caravans dispensed with the organization which
had afforded protection for so many miles. Individual merchants, with one or two wagons, drove southwest from the

ford to Las Vegas, turned south to Tecolote and San Miguel, then west and northwest to Santa Fe.

As I soaked up the unadorned scenery at El Vado de las Piedras: bright sun on a small stream in a wide valley of short grass, no shrub in sight, and turned all this over in mind, I saw the dust of a pick-up truck coming south over the tracks, and walked back to my car on them. The truck was driven by a lady accompanied by two small boys and to her I explained my presence on her land. A right formidable barrier to travelers on the Road are owners of it, once Indians, now cowmen. In town or city one may quickly locate an owner and secure permission to see this, visit that. In the country, half a day may be spent in search of the home of an owner and reward for this virtue is the vice of his absence and warm greeting from unfriendly dogs left behind for that purpose. Everywhere I knew I should ask permission to enter private land and frequently did so. When there was no house in sight, as here none was, I simply took chance that I would not be ejected with cuts and bruises, took care to close all gates as I opened them, kept a distance from livestock about, never drove off the tracks but walked instead, and hoped for the best. The best I got, although without being a psychiatrist, I could tell the lady was not pleased to find me there.

Springer, New Mexico, about eight miles west of the crossing of the Canadian and that far off the Road, is a point of supply for ranches about, shaded by huge cottonwoods, some of the largest on Main Street (Map 18). There I met the oldest man I have ever seen. Matt McAllister is a short man with a long life: one hundred and three years. If one relates age to wrinkles, he is a surprising exception to the general rule for his face, mottled as a winter leaf, is smooth. He was an early Texas transplant to New Mexico who, at ninety, retired from ranching.

"It was too tiring," he explained, and quickly added, "but I was never thrown off a horse in all those years. Not even when I broke broncs for Tom Erath in Texas."

When I ventured that he looked healthier than I felt, he

allowed his eyes were not so good as once they were. That moment, a small figure was passing on the sidewalk across a street so wide that with 20/20 bifocals I was not certain of the sex.

"Jimmy! Hey, Jim!" McAllister shouted, waving a piece of candy he had fished from a pocket.

The only centenarian I ever saw had been a rancher on Sweet Water Creek, near Rayado, once the home of Kit Carson and Lucien Maxwell. McAllister spoke staccato of minor incidents and times long ago and I learned "nineteen and two was a very hard winter." By fortunate chance, McAllister had shipped his cattle before snow fell deeply in November and he had no financial worries in months following save those shared with him by other ranchers, as an errant mass of Gulf air brought a light sprinkle of rain on the snow. Within a day, a blast of polar wind coated the land with thick ice, armour-plate which remained on the prairie until Febraury thaws. By then ranchers faced a heavy loss: ninety-five to ninety-eight per cent.

"Before the freeze-up there were thousands of antelope in this country. By spring you could see none, or perhaps an old buck barely able to stand. There weren't any antelope to speak of after 1902."

McAllister mentioned his ranch had been a part of the Beaubien-Miranda grant and I recalled that Springer was near the south margin of a grant by Governor Armijo of land to Charles Beaubien and Guadalupe Miranda who, without ever having counted them, had three times the acres of Rhode Island.[87] When the Army came to New Mexico, Miranda retained Mexican citizenship and moved south of the Rio Grande. Beaubien, born a French-Canadian in Quebec, remained and by purchase the acres became his. Partly by inheritance and partly by purchase they fell to Lucien Maxwell who had married one of the Beaubien girls. Maxwell, son of a Kaskaskia, Illinois, merchant, had been a trapper, a trader and Mountain Man. He was one of that group who, when it came time for the military to explore and make known the west, served them as hunter and guide. It was an adjunct which insured their survival, return to civilization, acclaim and promotion. Mountain Men were the ghost-riders of the time, counterpart of ghost-writers in the age of computers.

For quite some years, Maxwell was lord of all he surveyed, first from Rayado and later from Cimarron, New Mexico (both were to be stage stations on the Mountain Branch of the Road). When eventually this came to be no relaxation, Maxwell sold to a British promoter who financed the purchase by sale of stock to Dutch capitalists. They were accustomed to law and order, and assumed both.

It had been a provision of the treaty between Mexico and the United States that citizenship for New Mexicans would be a matter of choice and whatever the choice, property rights would remain inviolate. Spanish Governors and the Crown had made some 198 grants to individuals and groups, generally on condition the land be settled but sometimes for reasons of politics. The oldest in New Mexico is dated 1693 (for 43,244 acres, a little over 67 square miles). One of the smallest was for 36 acres (in 1699). The largest and among the last was that to Beaubien and Miranda (in 1841) for 1,714,764 acres (about 2,679 square miles when the U.S. Land Office in 1878 determined the allowable limits).[88]

Either for political reasons or because it was too large for comprehension, the Beaubien-Miranda Grant was declared open for settlement by the Land Office in Washington. By the time the declaration was rescinded, damage was well-nigh irreparable. There were placer and lode miners all over the mountains (there had been some during Maxwell's ownership, with whom profits were shared), small ranchers everywhere on Dutch prairies, as well as settlers by right of purchase from the Land Office on land near running water. Considerable blood was needlessly shed and there was more than one wanton killing before Dutch title to the land was cleared. Marian Russell, who lived for a time in Santa Fe, then at Fort Union in New Mexico and later in Camp Nicols in what was to be the Oklahoma Panhandle, wrote of one death, her husband's, with remarkable forebearance, just as she wrote of other incidents with sensitivity equally remarkable on a raw frontier.

In later decades, much of the Beaubien-Miranda land was

sold, some in huge chunks. One of these came to be Philmont Scout Camp. With boundaries so wide, the mountain wilderness within could lose every scout: Brownie, Cub, Boy and Girl on the continent, and has probably done so for some so far from home as Hoboken, New Jersey.

CHAPTER XIII

The Mountain Branch

IT WAS A SATURDAY afternoon when I saw
Springer, and on the map I had run into a wide gap beginning at El Vado de las Piedras and ending at Las Vegas.
As all county offices wherein I might search for data were
closed for the weekend, I drove north across Raton Pass
and down the Arkansas to the Upper Crossing where the
Mountain Branch of the Road began (Map 13).

Whatever be the way of a man with a maid, it is minor
compared with the way of cool currents of a river with sand.
At its head near Leadville, Colorado, the Arkansas is a frothy,
high-velocity stream, made so by the steep land on which it
flows and by angular fragments of igneous, metamorphic and
sedimentary rocks detached from parent masses by frost-
wedging. On land the loose debris is a blanket of irregular
fragments, small to large: a slow-moving "stream" of clastics
with very little water. By gravity and infinitely slowly it is fed
to the Arkansas: a fast flow of water with very little clastics.
In time of high water from thunderheads over the mountains
or from spring melting of deep winter snow, volume of the
Arkansas is doubled and quadrupled. With increase in

volume comes greater velocity and greater erosive force. Angular gravel, cobbles and boulders begin their slow abrasive descent from highlands onto lower plains. In every intermittent meter of movement, fragment grinds fragment, the abrasion reducing all to greater roundness and smaller diameter with each mile. In time and space, angular cobbles and boulders, moved only by floodwaters, are reduced to gravel, sand and clay. Where the Arkansas emerges from mountains to traverse High Plains, it is overloaded on lesser gradient. Forced by decrease in velocity to deposition, with excess clastics the stream builds islands on its bed. First a gravel bar with interstices later filled with sand, on the low elongated strip seeds from catkins of cottonwood and willow take root. With the aid of reeds and rushes they bind the mass yet more firmly to the river bed.

One among the myriad of such deposits in the Arkansas River parted currents about four miles southwest of modern Lakin, Kansas. The island, thickset with brush and trees, served as a fort for Chouteau and his men for a few hours of danger and for a generation or two served carefree teamsters as a landmark to a river crossing and dangers ahead. The river, now flowing in less volume but with the same vagaries of currents which made the fluvial deposit, long ago removed Chouteau Island, spreading debris of it from Kansas to the Gulf of Mexico. The Upper Crossing remains, a dim point in history of a circumstance familiar now to very few.

For a time not long after opening of the Santa Fe trade, there had been trading posts on the upper Arkansas west of Chouteau Island. Bent's Fort, five miles from modern La Junta, Colorado, was an exceptional one. From the Upper Crossing where the Road to Santa Fe left the Arkansas for the *Jornada*, a dim but easy road led upstream to Bent's Fort. When General Kearny commanded an Army of invasion, most of his troops followed that route to rendezvous at Bent's Fort and thence straggled southwest across mountains through Raton Pass. By Kearny's order caravans of that year were collected at Pawnee Rock from where, by stern command, they followed his army with difficulty and with complaint.

What influenced General Kearny's choice of route past the Upper Crossing to Bent's Fort and south across the mountains can only be surmised. An army marches on its stomach. In it, there must always be water and sometimes food. Water was at hand in the Arkansas River for much of the distance and southwest from Bent's Fort there was sparse bitter and ample sweet water in Timpas Creek and Purgatoire River. Moreover, the Arkansas River was for 160 miles an east-west boundary between the United States and Mexico. Governor Armijo by then knew its intent, but an Army on the north shore of the river was on home ground and relatively immune to attack by militia equipped mostly with bows and arrows, unsupported by artillery.

Even after Kearny, merchandise and military freight loaded at Independence and Fort Leavenworth and bound for Santa Fe, left the Arkansas at Lower, Middle or Upper Crossing. The path the Army hacked through Raton Pass was little better than that, and in trader parlance it was a hell of a road and sixty miles longer than the Road to Santa Fe. Except by a few in the two years after the Army, the route through Raton Pass lay unused until 1861 and the Civil War. By then there was a broad much-used road from Upper Crossing past Bent's Fort to La Junta, Colorado, where it turned north toward success for a few and disappointment for the majority.

However partisan, there is something to be learned from newspapers, old or new. One may read the three lines in the *Liberty* (Mo.) *Tribune:* "Washington, May 8, 1856: Mr. Herbert, representative from California, shot the Head Waiter at Willards Hotel this morning. . . ." and surmise that although time and methods have changed, that state has not. From a short note in the Kansas City *Journal of Commerce* of May 25, 1859, one may learn the why and how of a well-beaten road unrelated to commerce with Santa Fe, leading west past the Upper Crossing: "Senors Delgado and Garcia, Merchants of New Mexico, reported meeting between the crossing of the Arkansas and Council Grove, headed for Pikes Peak 5214 men, 220 women, 351 wagons, 7375 oxen, 623 horses, 321 mules, and an equal number this side of Council Grove."

"Pikes Peak or Bust" was an aphorism that year for several thousands, most of whom achieved both. Those eleven thousand hopefuls counted by Delgado and Garcia had the glint of gold in their eyes. They were headed for Cherry Creek, now the site of Denver, in sight of Pikes Peak.

In 1848, gold picked from Sutter's millrace on American River in California released a west-flowing current of tens of thousands of emigrants the following year. Some lost their lives in the mountains and in the deserts of Nevada, and reports of difficulties of both had discouraged the transcontinental venture of many. Still, there was an auriferous ferment in the east among those who remained at home. It was a leavening which made easier the rupture of restraining bonds when next opportunity called. Opportunity with cheek, complete with tongue, called in 1858.

In the decade following discovery of California gold, remote recesses of western mountains were visited by thousands of amateur prospectors searching for another Golconda. In 1858 a party out of Lawrence, Kansas, had prospected without success the vicinity of Pikes Peak. Rumor, by means unknown, reached them, of a group of Georgians who had found placer gold in the gravels on Cherry Creek. There was very little metal to be recovered but the rumor, magnified as it echoed across the plains, fell on eastern ears as thunder: GOLD AT CHERRY CREEK!

By the end of 1858 there were twenty cabins at Denver City (after James W. Denver, Governor of Kansas) and twenty more at nearby Auriria (after a Georgia mining town). The boom was on.

Several thousand wagons and ten times as many emigrants left the frontier at Independence by way of the Road to Santa Fe. They passed the Upper Crossing, westernmost point of the Road, and Bent's Fort beyond. Near La Junta, the junction of trails from east and north, they went up Fountain Creek. In a few more days they reached Cherry Creek and disappointment.

What had been a sustaining slogan: "Pikes Peak or Bust" became a deflating "Pikes Peak Hoax." Several thousand wagons turned eastward. They had scarcely done so when

John Gregory came from North Fork of Clear Creek some forty miles west into the mountains from Denver City, with word of the first discovery of a gold lode east of California. From the lode which later became Central City, Gregory mined $900 and sold for $21,000 what was to be one of the richest mines in all Colorado. Even now, with lodes long since exhausted, Central City is a mining center where skillfully the pockets of tourists are panned.

Not many laws are promulgated by those most likely to violate them and as mining laws were, they are almost unique. In the settlements which sprang up about John Gregory's lode: Central City, Black Hawk, and those more distant: Tarry All, Buckskin Joe, Fairplay and others, there evolved through common agreement, laws which still guide those who search for metals.

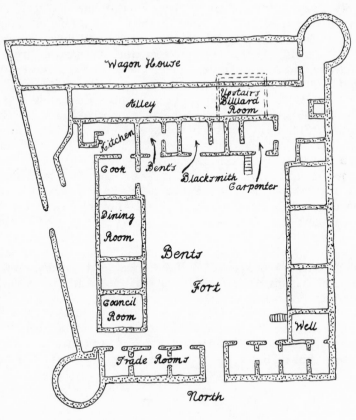

The sheriff, elected then and there if there was none, was president of a mining district and "recorder of claims." A "lode" is a vein of quartz or some other mineral with a minor per cent of gold or other desirable metal. A "lode claim" was set as an area one hundred feet long and fifty wide. A "gulch" claim could be no longer than one hundred feet and in width from bank to bank of the dry gulch. A "placer" claim was one hundred by one hundred feet of sand and gravel in a stream bed where the claimant hoped to pan gold.

None of these early mining laws was concerned with "salting." Horace Greeley, editor of the New York *Tribune* and an early enthusiastic tourist at Central City, unwittingly was. Gold is rarely seen in the rock which holds it; generally gold in rock is known from assay. For Greeley and the publicity he could give, Central City miners made it clearly and excitingly apparent. Removing the ball from a rifle cartridge, they replaced it with gold dust and very small nuggets. From a distance of twenty or thirty feet, the charge was fired at a cleaned rock surface and Greeley was allowed to see ore that would have run several thousands dollars of gold in each ton of rock, had the metal been more than skin-deep.

In 1861, Civil War placed traffic on the Road crossing M'Nees Creek within reach of raiders out of Texas and in the hands of Indians who caught Texas fever. The Mountain Branch of the Road began when, by order of the Union Army, traffic went past the Upper Crossing on a road made wide and clear by Pikes Peakers. In the last year of war, wagons rolled past Fort Aubrey and Aubrey Springs on the north bank of the Arkansas about twenty miles west of Upper Crossing (Map 19).

Francis Xavier Aubrey was an ebullient spirit among earth-bound merchants.[25, 36, 72, 83, 89] He had forded many wagons at Upper Crossing and driven south across the *Jornada*. For a time he had served the Army as a scout. That he served them well is certain for in 1865, several years after his death, the Army built and occupied for a year Fort Aubrey, west of Upper Crossing. The Fort was never a notable outpost but its name was tribute to an unusual man who won the admiration of many and a flare of enmity from an unstable mind.

Richard H. Weightman is better known for what he destroyed than for what he constructed, as commonly are those given to violence. One might guess he was a man of immaturity not evidenced by his years and the characteristic perhaps was apparent even when he was dismissed, or resigned by request, from West Point in 1838. Still, Weightman did achieve a career in the military for he served ably under Doniphan in the invasion of New Mexico and frequently in disputes with fellow officers. One quarrel was barely short of a duel when it was amicably quieted by friends of both parties. When dust of the invasion had settled, in Albuquerque Weightman practiced law and published *El Amigo del Pais* (Friend of the Country). A later dispute with Judge Houghton reached dueling heat but fortunately not to fatality.

El Amigo del Pais was no more a success than its proprietor when it printed from the borrowed original, the diary of Aubrey of a trip to California. Not long after, Aubrey located a cut-off, a better route, from Cold Spring near the Cimarron River, north across the *Jornada* to Bear Creek and on to the Upper Crossing of the Arkansas. The route was reported to encounter water more frequently than that traversed by Sibley, Brown and co-workers in 1825.

For reasons known only to Weightman, who probably knew less about the cut-off, an article in *El Amigo del Pais* questioned Aubrey's word of the feasibility of the new route. Presumably the aspersion was a business technique for in that day as in this one, editors fostered dissension, knowing that riposte even between strawmen sells newspapers.

Sometime later Weightman and Aubrey met in Mecurie's store in Santa Fe. Over glasses of brandy, Aubrey inquired of the welfare of *El Amigo del Pais*. Weightman, sourly perhaps, replied it had died for lack of friends. It was reported by some who might know, that Aubrey observed: "The lie you told about me killed it." Instantly, Weightman threw his brandy into Aubrey's face. Momentarily blinded, Aubrey drew a pistol and one chamber discharged. Unfortunately the bullet lodged in the ceiling and not in Weightman as the

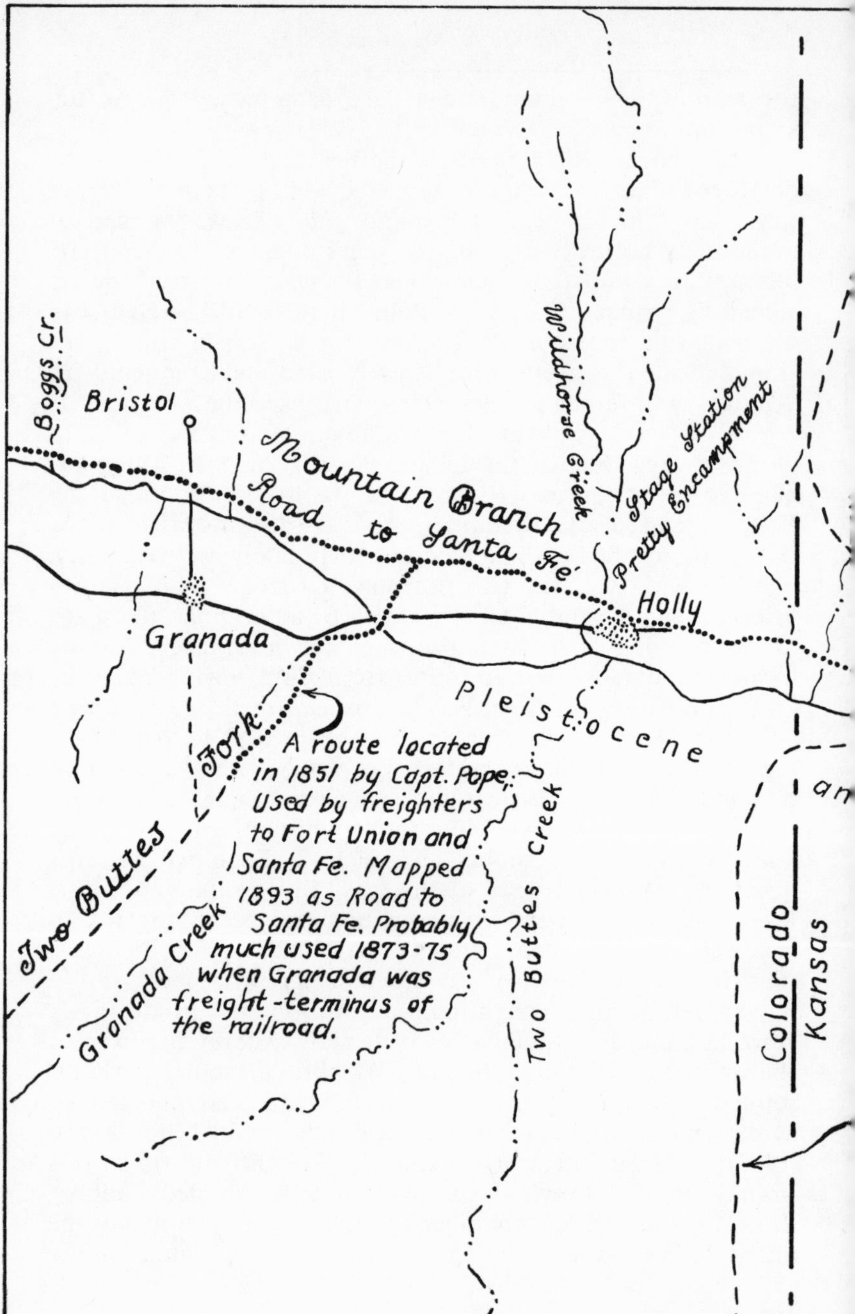

Boggs Cr.

Bristol

Mountain Branch
Road to Santa Fe

Wildhorse Creek

Stage Station
Pretty Encampment

Granada

Holly

Pleistocene

Two Buttes Fork

Granada Creek

Two Buttes Creek

Colorado
Kansas

A route located in 1851 by Capt. Pope. Used by freighters to Fort Union and Santa Fe. Mapped 1893 as Road to Santa Fe. Probably much used 1873-75 when Granada was freight-terminus of the railroad.

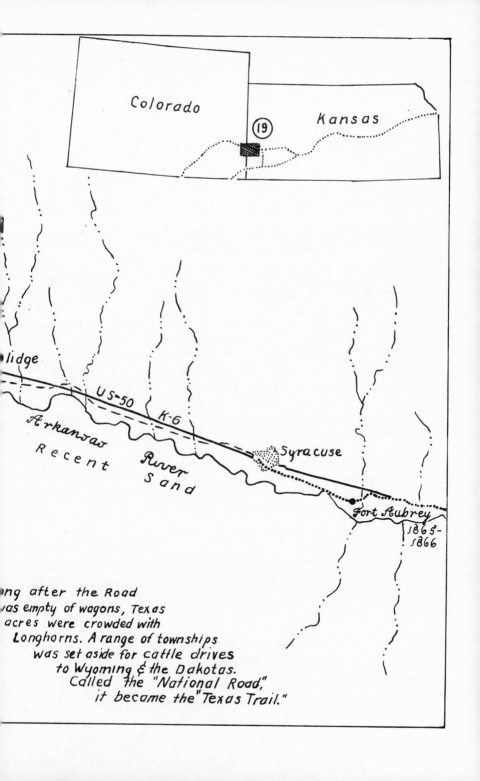

Colorado

Kansas

(19)

lidge

US-50

K-6

Arkansas

Recent

River

sand

Syracuse

Fort Aubrey

1865-
1866

ng after the Road
as empty of wagons, Texas
acres were crowded with
Longhorns. A range of townships
was set aside for cattle drives
to Wyoming & the Dakotas.
Called the "National Road,"
it became the "Texas Trail."

latter stabbed his accuser to death. A jury hearing evidence of eye-witnesses must have viewed the circumstance from a level well above that of Aubrey's blood on the floor. Weightman was judged not-guilty. Francis Xavier Aubrey and his fort have long gone to dust and Weightman to death in a Civil War of greater scope than that in which daily he lived.

Beyond the site of Fort Aubrey there are twenty miles of open valley and open road to the east margin of Colorado. Very near it, the north-south Texas cattle trail crossed the Mountain Branch where the settlement of Coolidge was to be. The intersection is now a point on pavement more remarkable for the wide space about than within it. Travelers here found the valley of the Arkansas a scattering of huge cottonwoods in a broad swale of short grass. Streams, in geological parlance, are young, mature and old. The Arkansas on the plains is no longer young in any terminology and it will not be geologically old before the millennium. But in the countless years since maturity there have been on either side of the current, marginal strips of low-level ground, depositories for excess clastics in suspension by flood-waters: a narrow floodplain framed between modest slopes of Dakota sandstone. Road and pavement, sometimes the asphalt covering the ruts, stay on higher ground north of the river. A mile or two from the highway a line of cottonwoods and willows marks the modern feeble flow. Beyond, the south margin of the valley is an easy eye-span over irrigated fields. It was so when Susan Magoffin passed in 1846 the future site of Fort Aubrey, with her husband and some 1,600 freight wagons in the rear of the Army. It was then a land watered by rare flood and infrequent summer showers. When night closed off sight beyond coals of dying fires, flashes of lightning painted in microseconds a scene more vivid than ever did the sun. In the next instant of Stygian darkness the valley filled to overflowing with a Jovian thunderbolt. It was as impressive to ears as the vivid canvas had been to eyes blinded by it. Sight and sound were without limit, overwhelming in magnitude the senses of those who saw and heard.

Four miles within Colorado is the town of Holly on Wild Horse Creek, now a region of sugar-beet culture (Map 19).

It was the site of "Pretty Encampment" when stages came this way in 1861.[47] Very few who traveled the Mountain Branch left record of poetic bent, or even knowledge. Names they gave the land were generally what one could see, and camps were a choice of utility rather than esthetics. Presumably, Pretty Encampment had both.

The Mountain Branch came to have more arms than an octopus. As very few who traversed them left record of their travel, it is difficult to know which was used when. Four miles west of Pretty Encampment and Holly is a left fork of the Mountain Branch which crossed the Arkansas and went southwest past Two Buttes (Map 19). The latter is a landmark, the congealed throat of a long extinct volcano, an outlier of igneous activity so very much more intense in the fractured and folded Rockies. Two Buttes Fork of the Mountain Branch traversed some 120 miles of the rough southeast corner of Colorado, leaving it near what now is the isolated and almost unknown settlement of Branson. The Fork appears on an 1851 military reconnaissance map as "route followed by Colonel Pope" and as an un-named trail on an 1860 map of land surveys. It was mapped in 1898 as the "Road to Santa Fe." It is a reasonable surmise that it had some use between 1851 and 1860 if by no other than military detachments. In 1853, Colonel Lowe reported the alternate, the road to Raton Pass unused, abandoned.[19] From 1873 to 1875, Granada, Colorado, was the freight terminus of the Santa Fe Railroad then building up along the Arkansas. Very likely Colonel Pope's route had much use then. Two Buttes Fork is still there, linking Mulvane, Brookfield, Atlanta and Troy: post offices born and obliterated by flick of a Washington wand about 1880 and later.

Whatever freighters used Two Buttes fork, as they entered New Mexico Territory on a route through what was to be Folsom, they passed near a spot which came to be more widely known than ever was the Road to Santa Fe, at least in the world of the archeologist. When man walked from Siberia to Alaska on the floor of the Bering seaway laid bare by transfer of water from ocean basins to continental ice sheets, his hand held the rudest of weapons: a cobble roughly but firmly bound by rawhide thong in the fork of a piece of stout branch. It was a primitive stone hammer and an effective weapon powered by a muscular arm. His children's children fashioned better, and theirs better yet.

Near Folsom, New Mexico, in 1926 was found evidence long sought by archeologists that Paleolithic man roamed North America. Beneath a layer of dark soil formed at the end of the Ice Age, among rib bones of an extinct bison lay a fluted projectile point. It was the work of "Folsom man," that very early American of such skill in Stone Age artistry as to be un-matched since. Some 15,000 years before now, a group of Stone Age hunters lived a time on the margin of a small lake near what was to be machine-age Folsom. It was debris of their village, exposed by accident of erosion, which yielded the small fragment of Paleolithic handiwork. It was the very first found on North America known to belong to a time before the melting of the last sheet of ice that lay over the central U.S. and most of Canada.

Two Buttes fork, passing near a camp of Stone Age hunters, went southwest from Folsom to join the Road a few miles north of yet older stone, that of El Vado de las Piedras in the bed of the Canadian River.

Water and time made the valley of the Arkansas. No partnership between mortals left so great an impression on it as that of the Bents: Charles, William and George and the St. Vrains: Ceran and Marcellin. They began about 1832 an adobe structure on the north bank of the river five miles below what now is La Junta. Sometime in 1833 the last adobe brick was set in the walls. Six hundred miles and about forty ox-cart days west of what civilization there was in Independence, it was a structure unequalled by any other of its kind, complete with linen on the table, a bell to call those who sat around it, the beauty of strutting peacocks to rest their eyes and a billiard table to test their skill, commonly excellent with a rifle.[89, 90, 91]

The march of the builders of Fort William, later Bent's Fort, was in step with financial success and personal tragedy.

In the Fort, William Bent lived with Owl Woman and Yellow Woman, Cheyenne sisters and the mothers of his five children, one of which became a cruel and savage renegade with a price on his head. From it, Charles Bent went to Santa Fe to become the first Governor of New Mexico Territory and the victim of Taos Indians welcoming the new American regime. En route to the Fort, Robert, youngest of the Bents, was killed by Comanches. Felix, brother of the St. Vrains, was scalped on northern prairies.

In Bent's Fort, Susan Magoffin recovered from miscarriage and loss of her first-born the day after her nineteenth birthday. Baptiste Charbonneau, son of Sacajawea who made successful explorers of Lewis and Clark by her knowledge

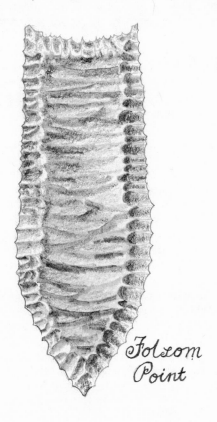

Folsom Point

of geography, worked a time at Bent's Fort. Christopher Carson was on the payroll as a hunter before fame came to him through Fremont's writings. Lucien Maxwell who was to own three times the acres of Rhode Island, managed the Fort for a brief interval. It was the rendezvous of the Army of invasion in 1846 and George Gibson, a private in it, remembered: "I heard six languages at Bent's Fort—French, Spanish, German, English, Comanche and Arapaho."

The Bent and St. Vrain trading post was a rectangle of adobe brick roughly 122 feet wide and 150 feet long, facing north. Walls were three feet thick and fourteen high. From them, at the northeast and southwest corners rose round towers, bastions, and from the towers extended adobe walls supporting a growth of cactus to discourage prowlers and to enclose an angular area for livestock and wagons. The main gate of the Fort was closed by two massive doors nearly seven feet square, sheathed in iron. Over the gates rose a watchtower with a swinging telescope and above it the belfry. Within and against the massive walls was a rectangle of twenty-five rooms for storage, council, kitchen, beds, smithy, carpenter shop and water-well around a plaza about 100 by 80 feet. The billiard room, one of the few second story enclosures, sat astride an alleyway at the south wall of the Fort. Floors of the rooms were packed mud and walls were finished with whitewash of finely crushed gypsum or red or yellow clay. Excavators a hundred years later found as many as six coats of white, red or yellow finish on eroded remnants.

For sixteen years Bent's Fort was the focus of trading ventures from Santa Fe north into Wyoming and as far east as Fort Adobe (Adobe Walls) on the Canadian River in the Texas Panhandle.[92] Movement of troops in 1846 and following years contributed much to unrest among Indians, as presumably did Mexico in retaliation for her loss. Restless Indians were not steady customers. By then Charles Bent had been scalped in Taos. William Bent's Owl Woman was dead; his brother George buried alongside Robert and Felix St. Vrain scalped in the Black Hawk war. Confident they were what they ate, his assailants ate his brave heart.

The Army in 1846 had made use of storage in Bent's Fort and later the structure was tendered for purchase by the military. What they offered is not known but it was not enough. For reasons not now of record the partnership was dissolved and the Fort became William Bent's property. In August, 1849, when trade with Indians was no longer profitable in that locality and sale of the Fort to the Army was no longer feasible, Bent removed what goods remained, rolled kegs of powder into the several rooms and set fire to tinder in each.[89]

Perhaps it was recollection of the past weighted by difficulties of the present that prompted William Bent to destruction of the monolith of mud. A gesture of such finality would suggest the end of one career and the beginning of another but it marked no change save that of geography. Downstream thirty-five miles, nearly opposite the future settlement of Prowers, Colorado, Bent construct .d three log houses in a U-shape at a locality favored as a winter camp by Indians and continued trade with Cheyennes, Arapahoes and Kiowas. Huge cottonwoods scattered about the flood-plain for some twenty miles upstream, the "Big Timbers" to those who knew them, provided fuel for fires and winter forage for Indian horses. Aside from fall-cured grass low in nourishment, there was little to sustain livestock as temperatures fell. When heavy snow blanketed the Arkansas Valley, it was the bark of cottonwood branches and twigs which enabled favored horses to survive a difficult winter.

In 1853, on a bluff rising at the north margin of the Arkansas a mile or so east of the stockade, Bent completed a stone fort and trading post about 100 feet square, enclosing twelve rooms (Map 20). As had the Old, Bent's New Fort served well as a center for trade, but it was commerce which diminished as Indian unrest increased. With a horde of easterners crossing the Plains by whatever route, conflicts between wagon trains and Indians were frequent and everywhere. Trade became as fitful as Indians and as uncertain as their temper. The latter was made erratic by deeds of land by treaty with Washington and pre-emption of that land by citizens of that Government.

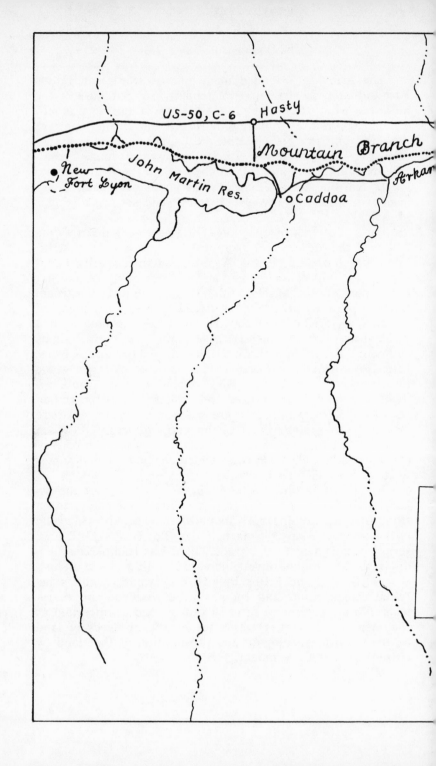

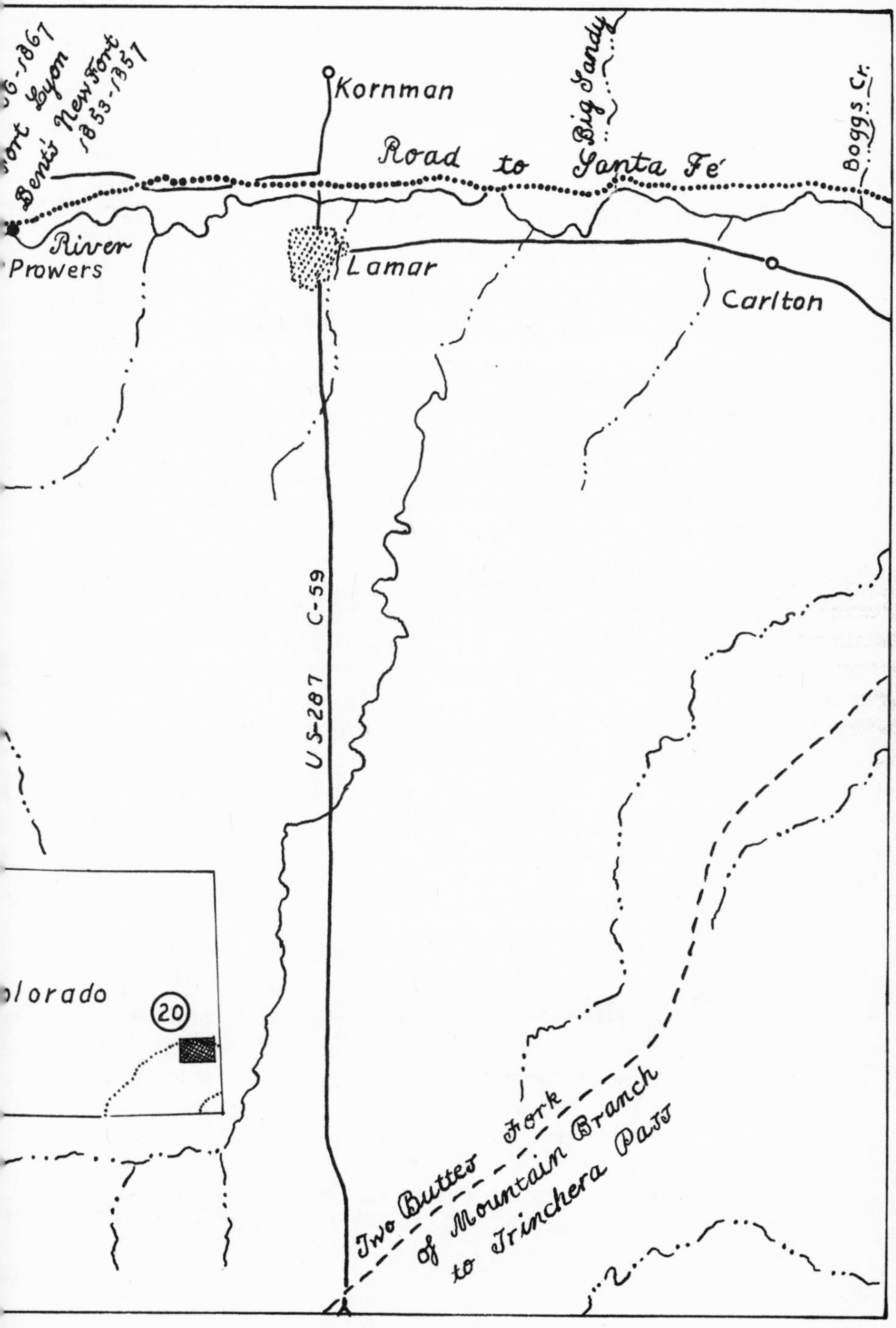

Fort Lyon 1856-1867
Bent's New Fort 1853-1857
River
Prowers
Kornman
Road to Santa Fe
Big Sandy
Boggs Cr.
Lamar
Carlton
US-287 C-59
Colorado
20
Two Butter Fork
of Mountain Branch
to Trinchera Pass

In 1857, the Army persuaded Bent to store for later dispersal, annuity trinkets distributed as pacifiers to restless Indians. With reluctance he rented the New Fort to the Army which proved it a poor business transaction. From a new home at the mouth of the Purgatoire River, Bent repeated attempts, all futile, to collect payments. When in exasperation he offered sale of the fort and title to the 160 acres about it to the Army, he reckoned without bureaucracy. Civil guardians of a government which by arms and occupancy claimed all the southwest, concluded Bent was a trespasser without fort or title to offer.

At his ranch near the confluence of the Purgatoire and Arkansas Rivers, Bent received word that one of the bloody scalps collected by soldiers raiding Cheyennes on the north plains was that of Yellow Woman, mother of three of his children. There also he learned of an unsuccessful visit on a dark night of his son Charles, disowned, a price on his head and a cocked rifle in his hands, "looking for the old man." And there, his kind unknown elsewhere any time in the west, death came to William Bent, May 19, 1869.[89]

Bent's New Fort rising on a bluff washed on two sides by waters on the sandy bed of the Arkansas, thickset now with tamarisks, was never a landmark on the Road to Santa Fe until Civil War initiated the Mountain Branch. Before then, however, it was a point familiar to thousands en route to Cherry Creek gold fields. On a June day in 1859, Charles Post (who had seen Mr. Thomas' windwagon in Kansas), hopefully in pursuit of a fortune in Colorado Territory, passed the Fort and through the limpid air of cool High Plains, saw on the horizon a dark blue cloud: the Spanish Peaks.[43] The distance was 140 miles and what Post saw had been seen by others as *Wah-to-yah*, "Breasts of the World." [93] If truly that is the translation, they were aptly named accidents of nature: two huge mammilary forms complete with nipples: pinnacles of igneous rock. The latter, remnants of erosion and circular in cross-section, are irregularly pipe-like in vertical extent from a reservoir of magma some twenty-five miles beneath. From the tubes came explosive outbursts of gas throwing tremendous splatterings of superheated liquid rock into the air, interspersed with more peaceful outpourings of lava,

to construct the cones of *Wah-to-yah*, Los Cumbres Espano-
les, The Spanish Peaks.

Some fifty miles east of where Post glimpsed the dark
blue cloud, Dr. George Willing, en route to Colorado that
same year, saw a small mound which impressed him yet
more. On a Saturday in May that same year he passed a
small mound alongside the road, a heap of soil over the body
of an infant dead the day before. For reasons unknown or
unrecorded the baby did not nurse and there was no substitute in the wilderness for the distressed mother. Two days
later the doctor, who had done as much for mother and child
as primitive circumstances allowed, was still in a reflective
mood. He thought the music of Beethoven and Mozart coming
from an adjacent camp out of place on barren plains all
around.[94]

Susan, a decade before, had traversed the road en route
to her own personal tragedy at Bent's Fort (Map 21). And the
year before the little hillock of sand marked an irreplaceable
loss, another of their sex had passed here. Julia Holmes, née
Archibald, was as feminine as her precursors, quite as gentle
and certainly a great deal more outspoken.[95] She was admired by many men, even liked some of them and one so
much that she gave to him her hand in marriage, although it
seems unlikely he ever possessed her sharp restless mind.
Marriage did not becloud sight and leave Mrs. Holmes grop-
ing in a world managed by brothers of Zeus. Julia clearly saw
men as they were: cowards, brave, strong, weak, impetuous,
diffident. She saw them plagued by indecision, ignorance and
other attributes common to the sex, all of which enabled
men, and most women by tacit agreement, to build a world
scarcely habitable by their kind.

Julia was a "feminist," a descriptive noun of opprobrium
similar to "feminine", a descriptive adjective of approval. If
tact includes submissive conformity, Julia Archibald Holmes
did not have it. "She is a regular woman's righter, wears the
bloomer, and was quite indignant when informed she was not
allowed to stand on guard. She is young, handsome and intelligent," wrote one who traveled in the same "Pikes Peak or
Bust" party.

One now would guess she was more. Julia Holmes was

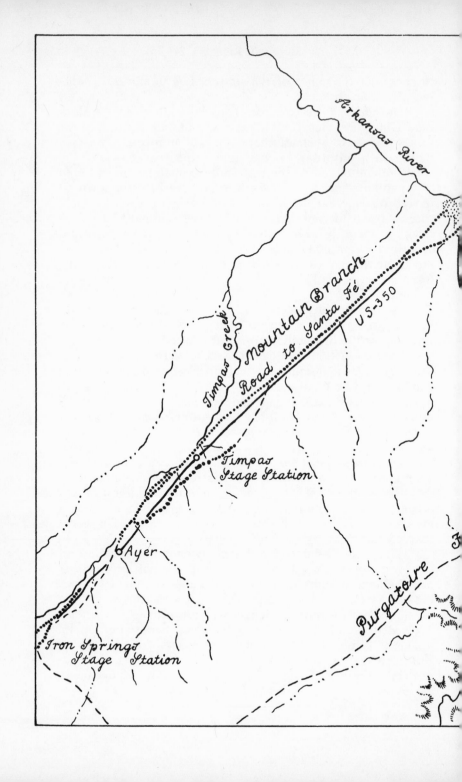

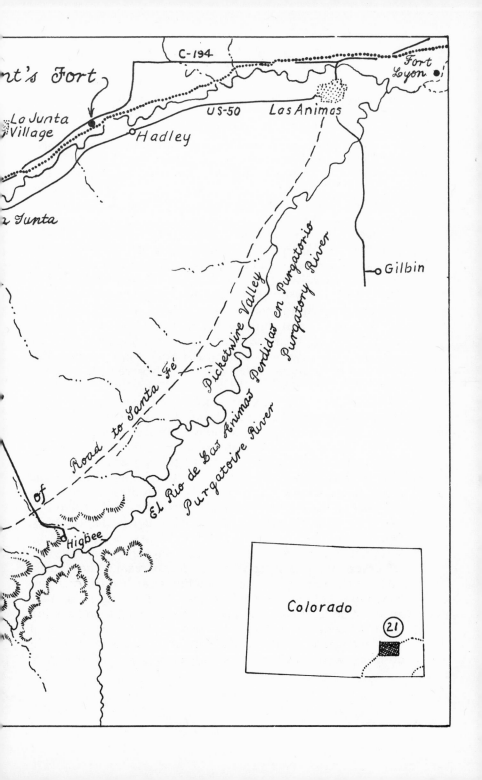

the first woman to ascend Pikes Peak (in 1858) and as Kansas acclaimed a daughter no one reminded them Julia was born a Nova Scotian. South from disappointment on Cherry Creek and the Pikes Peak Hoax, Mrs. Holmes was the able wife of an able man, James Holmes, Secretary of New Mexico Territory, and she taught well the adolescents around Barclay's Fort on the Mora where the settlement of Watrous now stands.

When Julia Holmes saw Bent's New Fort on the Arkansas, June 28, 1858, many of the men of the Kansas party ". . . were so enthusiastic in their admiration of (it) that they took the liberty of getting drunk by way of compliment. . . . Up to this time our company has been remarkably healthy. This afternoon . . . several were taken ill. Among the sufferers (were) some of the quasi-moralists who opposed my mode of dress and woman's freedom."

Two years after Julia and others admired Bent's stonework, which by then the military had preempted, the Army built another close by and named it Fort Wise to honor Virginia and its Governor (Map 20). When between Virginia and other states there was dissension and eventually war, Yankees unwilling to honor the Mother of Presidents and a rebellious son, renamed it Fort Lyon. But even with that name it was not so high as to be above caprice of the Arkansas nearby. Floodwaters inundated the Fort and another of the same name was built in 1867 about thirty-five miles upriver. New Fort Lyon saw the demise of Christopher Carson the next year, and the site now holds an impressive Veterans Hospital on the shore of the John Martin Reservoir (Map 20). The latter controls, some at least, high water in the Arkansas. Behind the dam, water has spread to cover a piece of the Mountain Branch, and through irrigation canals the reservoir refreshes miles of sugar beets downstream. The tourist through the region now may sometimes catch (strike, is perhaps more apt) an ammoniacal stench so strong as to slow an automobile. It comes in preposterous strength and solidity from the south of the highway at one or another of several feed-lots where thousands of Herefords fatten on the pulp of beets while their owners fatten on sugar of the juice squeezed from them. It seems incredible in an age of atomic fission that an odor so powerfully thick could not be sliced thin for some commercial use. John Martin Reservoir is near a "flyway," an aerial route of migrating waterfowl and a considerable number nest along water covering a segment of the Mountain Branch. Where an arm of the reservoir reaches near the highway, one may sometimes encounter two or three mallards crossing the pavement to greener grass, casually indifferent to the passing machine age and in the sky see wedges of geese frail as cobwebs wavering against infinity. As they wheel nearer, the thin strands darken and become lines of individual birds slanting down to splash water such as caravans never saw.

There had been a stage station at New Fort Lyon, now the site of a Veterans Hospital, in the later days of the Mountain Branch (Map 21). Two miles west of it the Purgatoire River joins the Arkansas and between the two, near the junction, William Bent settled on a ranch to live out his remaining time, shortened perhaps by weight of earlier tragedies.

Almost half a century before Bent, William Becknell on the first successful commercial venture into New Mexico, reached the confluence of the Purgatoire and Arkansas and

The Arkansas above Bent's New Fort

recorded (October 21, 1821): "Arrived at a fork in the River. Took left one." As a narrator of events attending an original venture, Becknell was economical if not unobservant. The next month of the same year, Colonel Hugh Glenn who operated a trading post on the Verdegris River (Oklahoma), led a party to Taos and in passing, camped on ground traversed by Becknell two miles up the Purgatoire. With Colonel Glenn was a journalist, Jacob Fowler, a great deal more observant than his predecessor on that route. Fowler was a native of New York and a resident of Covington, Kentucky, but it does not seem probable that the circumstance had much to do with his literary attainment. He was not a writer hampered by syntax when he had something to say and he was ingeniously inventive with words he needed to describe what he saw. Jacob Fowler was an artist in phonetics and semantics and his artistry is entertaining even now. Exactly as he wrote it in a camp two miles up the Purgatoire, his description of the first recorded tragedy on the route to New Mexico reads:

"13 novr 1821 tusday We found Here some grapes among the brush—While some Ware Hunting and others looking Some picking grapes a gun was fyred off and the Cry of White Bare (Grizzley bear, *Ursus horribilis*) Was Raised We Ware all armed in an Instant and Each man Run his own Cors to look for the desperet anemal—the Brush in which We Camped Contained from 10 to 20 acors Into Which the Bare Head Run for Shelter find Him Self Surrounded on all sides—threw this Conl Glann (Colonel Glenn) with four others atemted to Run but the Bar being in their Way and lay Close in the brush undiscovered till the Ware in a few feet of it—When it Sprung up and Caught Ledis doson (Lewis Dawson) and pulled Him down in an Istent Conl Glanns gun missed fyer or He Wold Have Releved the man But a large slut (dog) atacted the Bare With such fury that it left the man and persued Her a few steps in Which time the man got up and Run a few steps but Was overtaken by the bare When the Conl maid a second atempt to shoot but His (gun) missed fyer again and the Slut as before Releved the man who Run as before—but Was Son again

in the grasp of the Bare who Semed Intent on His destruction—the Conl again Run Close and as before His
gun Wold not go off the Slut makeing an other atak and
Relevening the man—the Conl now be came alarmed
lest the Bare Wold pursue Him and Run up a Stooping
tree—and after Him came the Wounded man and was
followed by the Bare and thus the Ware all three up one
tree. . . ." [96]

Lewis Dawson, the unfortunate attacked that day on the
Purgatoire at about the site of the modern Las Animas (The
Souls), Colorado, died at dawn on November 16th, his skull
having been severely fractured as the Grizzly bit into it.

Forty years after Dawson's fatal encounter, the Mountain Branch had a fork (Map 21) at the site of Las Animas
which must have passed close to Dawson's grave. By one who
drove stage on it, the route is said to have crossed the Purgatoire River five or six times in the first few miles [47] but on
old maps the Purgatoire Fork of the Mountain Branch lies
from two to ten miles northwest of that stream as it trends
toward Raton Pass and beyond. It was a road through vacant
and lonely land and even now the first seventy miles of it is
empty of settlement.

The Mountain Branch beyond Las Animas followed the
north bank of the Arkansas to the site of Bent's Old Fort.
When the Bent and St. Vrain headquarters was a thriving
outpost, detachments of the Army of the West collected there.
Their livestock, together with those of the traders, were in
number so great as to place a premium on forage adequate
for the demand. Save for that in the Arkansas, it is not well
watered country. Into even so dry a climate as southeastern
Colorado some rain must fall and a good many have in the
hundred and twenty years since abandonment of the Fort.
The debris from William Bent's destruction, and it must have
been considerable for the walls were three feet thick, has
diminished with the years. Now a National Monument, the
once considerable structure is a few segments of adobe brick
wall, none higher than three feet, enclosing an area about
120 by 150 feet. Within it, careful excavation is under way.
The Park Ranger (a school teacher in Cañon City, in winter)

courteously allowed me to see what had been found, relics housed in a temporary building near the ruins.

From what he said was the wine cellar, excavation had uncovered several brass spigots. (More likely it was for whiskey storage, for kegs of it were a very influential force in winning of the west: simultaneously exterminating Indians and promoting trade. Neolithic America was the first culti-vator of corn in the solid state. In the liquid, it made fools of unwise red men and idiots of fools.) From another spot had come two rifles as irregular rods of rust from which they hoped to exhume something recognizable. There were several trigger-guards, carefully cleaned; hands-full of small white and blue beads; buttons military and civilian; spurs and other oddments.

The Ranger spoke of Susan Magoffin's miscarriage at the Fort as a record of sorts as certainly it was, at least for her. Susan, who traveled in the luxury of a personal carriage, driver, maid and other attendants, was later to use the words of a snob when she passed through the small settle-ments of Las Vegas, Ojo de Bernal, San Miguel del Vado on the Pecos and Santa Fe. In recording her experience at Bent's Fort she spoke in prim disapproval: "There is no place on earth where man lives and gambling of some sort or another is not carried on. Here in the fort, and who would have sup-posed such a thing, they have a *regularly established billiard room*! They have a regular race track. And I hear the cackling of chickens at such a rate sometimes I shall not be surprised to hear of a cock-pit." Later, confronted with the loss of her first-born, she wrote as a realist: "Friday morning 31st of July. My pains commenced and continued until 12 o'c at night, when after much agony and severest pains, which were relieved at times by medicine given by Dctr. Mesure, *all was over*. I sunk off into a kind of lethargy. . . . Since that time I have been in bed till yesterday a little while and part of to-day. My situation is very different from that of an Indian woman in the room below me. She gave birth to a fine healthy baby, about the same time, and *in half an hour after she went to the River and bathed herself and it.*

The troops left. . . Sunday morning. . . ." [2]

CHAPTER XIV

The Road from
Fort Leavenworth

"THE TROOPS LEFT SUNDAY morning," Susan Magoffin at Bent's Fort noted in her diary. The Sunday was July 26, 1846, but it would appear that troops had been on the road to *Nuevo Mejico* for nearly half a century.

In 1805, Dearborn, Secretary for War, received from General Wilkinson in St. Louis, plans for invasion of New Mexico.[53] In recording these, Wilkinson wrote of earlier discussions of the same venture and of his adverse evaluation of it. He did not mention a reason, a provocation for war and history records none.

When in 1825, Senator Benton of Missouri secured appropriation for a survey by Sibley and Brown of a Road known and in use for four years, of which neither data of distances nor completed map was ever published by Washington, he was perhaps aware of plans for invasion. If, by chance, he was not it seems likely he was the tool of others who were. In any case, Benton later gave hand to an important strategy of the plans.

Certainly Washington knew the Road across the Cimarron Desert, the most economical in time for traders who could carry water for themselves, was not feasible for an army adequate to the task. One may guess that it was intimate knowledge of the Waterscrape which prompted planners of aggression to collect first-hand information of an alternate route for march of an army: out the Road to Santa Fe past the Upper Crossing to Bent's Fort and beyond through the difficulties of Raton Pass to easy traverse of plains in north and central New Mexico. Lieutenant Abert was selected, and sent, six months before annexation of Texas and a year before invasion, with the ostensible purpose of exploring headwaters of Red River (between Oklahoma and Texas, but then a part of the boundary between Mexico and the U.S.), that part which lay entirely within Mexican territory.[97] It had been explored long before by Major S. H. Long. When Abert returned from reconnaissance of the route through Raton Pass and of Mexican Territory without permission of owners of it, Washington had in hand a map for aggression.

Next of need was an excuse. Interference with mercantile trade and merchants of it was not a feasible provocation. Mexicans handled about half of the trade and placed no restrictions on Americans beyond legitimate taxes on imported goods, applicable to all. These, as taxes everywhere and always, were excessive to those who paid them. War is a costly extension of politics. Trade with Santa Fe involved goods considerably less in value, and yet less in profit, than cost of an army. To 1829, value of goods freighted from Missouri to New Mexico was $120,000. In the next decade it was $1,700,000 and in the following ten years $1,750,000. The total value of trade goods carried to Santa Fe in the first wagon in 1822 to the last in the year of invasion was barely more than the cost of maintenance ($3.5 million versus $3 million) for one year of an army in New Mexico.[88] As an excuse for aggression, economics was out of the question.

Nor could shedding of blood be a provocation for invasion. The only intercourse between the two nations, Mexico and the United States, was that of peaceful commerce across the prairie. Blood on the Road was shed from puncture by

Indian arrows and it flowed as frequently from Latin as from Anglo-Saxon arteries. Of *lebensraum* the United States had ample: an 1840 population of 17,069,433 on 2,936,166 square miles; 110 acres for each man, woman and child.

Politicians, if they survive in the trade, are perfect opportunists, aware that group action obviates individual conscience. When opportunity is not knocking, generally there is ample material with which the more skillful among them may compound opportunity capable of tearing the emotional public door from its individual, personal, hinges. Tools of a surgeon are those for cutting, sawing and suturing. Tools of the politician's trade are words. His art, like the actor's, is to make circumstances appear what they are not. It is no feat of semantics for a political chorus to create opportunity or engender provocation. Politics, for which so few are trained and so many practice, is more serious than surgery, as war takes lives rather than saves them.

The reader of history is sometimes left with no choice of conclusion save that history is spoken by charlatans to be revised by chauvinists. James K. Polk, most generously described as an "expansionist," a euphemism common to the euphoria of those who revise history, was one among the former. His campaign promises, tossed off with the facility of a political profligate, included promise of annexation of Texas. It was a cretinous appeal to public emotion, obviating reasoning in voters who avoided that toil and trouble. By a razor-thin margin, they outnumbered those who did not, and Polk was elected.

In 1836, a decade before Polk assumed office, if it was what it said it was, Texas was a Republic. The declaration and down-payment were simultaneous. Within the Alamo at San Antonio, 182 men, three women, their children and a boy, faced 2,400 militia under Santa Anna. Among the former were six who might claim six years of residence in Texas. The garrison included a blacksmith, a hatter, a house-painter, an ex-jockey, five doctors, representatives of other professions but no professional soldier. They came from eighteen states and five had come from the Quaker City, Philadelphia. A considerable percent of those outnumbering them thirteen-to-one were Mayan conscripts, presumably unintelligible to most of their officers, armed with smooth-bore muskets reasonably accurate up to seventy yards, but unfamiliar with the current technique of aiming a musket to preserve national honor.[98]

By the morning of March 6, 1836, Travis, Crockett, Bonham and Bowie were dead and so was the remainder of the garrison, save one. Mrs. Dickenson, Mrs. Albury, their two children, an unidentified Mexican lady and Joe, a Negro boy-servant of Travis, survived, as did Brigido Guerreo who convinced his countrymen he had been prisoner of Texans.

Even as Santa Anna closed on the Alamo, elsewhere a Convention was assembling. Before carnage was in full flower and the terrible payment made, independence of Texas was declared. But several thousand more Texans and yet more Mexicans were to contribute lives before the political hope was a political reality. Always, political change is the more precious to those who survive it if cost is paid by those who do not. And for reasons known to none on earth, follies expending blood in the past proliferate unretarded into the future.

Santa Anna, once presumed a liberal, had assumed the trappings of a dictator. He was to prove a butcher: the three hundred odd Texans captured at Goliad were shot. It was as savage a message as might be conceived in an age of slow communication, and it was received. General Sam Houston's army numbered 1,400 when others died at the Alamo. After that martyrdom, desertion reduced it to 748 by the time men, and their arms, were most needed.

The victor at the Alamo was the vanquished at San Jacinto. And it was done in "eighteen cataclysmic minutes."[98] Captured in the uniform of a private, Santa Anna, General and Dictator, faced the choice: sign or die. The public treaty bearing his signature put an end to hostilities and arranged for an exchange of prisoners. By secret treaty Santa Anna stipulated that on return to Mexico he would prepare for and hospitably receive Texas emissaries, acknowledge independence of Texas and by negotiation settle all dispute; the boundary of Texas was not to extend beyond the Rio Grande.

The month of March had not ended before Mexico published its intention to continue war.

Side by side in geography, Texas and Mexico were opponents in purpose. After San Jacinto, Texas had a President, several of them in the following decade, a loose political farmework and a constitution prohibiting importation of Africans but admitting slave-owners and their property. It had no system of taxation worthy of the name and its credit diminished to zero. Promissory notes and land-script were the basis of its fiduciary system but as Texas had no boundary and no survey of lands, its land-bank currency dropped to fifteen and ten cents on the dollar. A league and a labor of land had been given every head of a family. Enlistment for duration of war was paid for by allotment of 1,280 acres; six months service got 640 acres and three months half as much.[88] It may be these offers accounted for a mercenary per cent of the 2,000 or so citizens of the United States enlisted in the cause of the new Republic. The only flag captured at the Alamo was the blue of the New Orleans' Greys; with Santa Anna's note of victory attached it hangs now in the castle of Chapultepec.[98]

The thirty thousand or so immigrants in Texas began their fight for independence with the announced intention of seeking admission to the United States. It was more a political slogan than a political possibility for it was strictly a unilateral intent. With Santa Anna defeated and nominal independence won, the petition of Texas for admission to the Union was rejected. Texas was South and slave territory. The North would tolerate no increment of land wherein slavery was constitutional. Even recognition was opposed, for pro-tariff proponents in the United States, fearful of British trade through Texas ports, were loud in opposition. Reluctantly, independence of Texas was recognized in 1837.

With Mexico preoccupied by war with France, the Republic had an interval of relative peace as it searched for status among nations. In exchange for recognition by England, Texas assumed obligation for a million pounds sterling in Mexican bonds held in Britain. It was a luxury only a pauper could afford. When the U.S. ambassador in London learned of two warships owned by Mexico, manned by British crews and outfitting for conflict with Texas, diplomatic difficulties were immediate. The States had not been ex-colonials so long as to welcome British encroachment on their southern flank.

The French were persuaded to commercial treaty and recognition but as a result of conflicting claims of Texas pigs and French horses, diplomatic intercourse had only begun before it was interrupted. "The horses of M. Saligney, French representative in Texas, were fed on corn. Pigs belonging to Mr. Bullock, hotel-keeper, intruded into the stable to pick up corn which the horses let fall to the ground. One of M. de Saligney's servants killed one of the pigs. Bullock whipped the servant. This enraged de Saligney and Bullock was arrested. . . . Not obtaining the satisfaction he wished, the exasperated Frenchman demanded his passports and left his post." [88]

With or without M. de Saligney, Texas and Texans were in constant and serious difficulty. Austin, Archer and Wharton, having spoken before audiences in the United States for recognition, spoke for annexation. While many who heard approved their plea, union did not prevail. Immigrants from the United States, most from the South, occupied a small part of Texas claimed. All of New Mexico east of the Rio Grande was an unreasonably great deal more.

As the dripping of water on stone, the fluid fortified by the acid of national interests of the United States, Texas importunations had effect. In the summer of 1845, Abert scouted Raton Pass. By October of that year, Zachary Taylor with U.S. troops comprised a contingent unique in annals of human intercourse: a "Corps of Observation" at Corpus Christi, Texas, on land 300 years claimed by others. In December, President Tyler in a reduction of Polk's political thunder, persuaded Congress to pass a joint resolution approving annexation. Among delegates assembled in Texas only Richard Bache, grandson of Benjamin Franklin, did not concur.

As plans for invasion developed, intrigue came to be an important and logical part of them. Senator Benton introduced James Magoffin to the President and his Secretary of War. Magoffin, a convivial Kentuckian, was "Don Santiago" to Armijo, Governor of New Mexico, Juan Archuleta, second in command, Juan Vigil and all others of power in that provincial dictatorship where slavery was forbidden and peonage a way of life. Under pressure of the three, President, Secretary and Senator, Magoffin agreed to apply his considerable power of persuasion to smooth the way of the Army. He was to be eminently successful.

In February 1846, President Jones of Texas relinquished administrative authority to Henderson, the newly elected Governor, and the deed was done. Or nearly so. To now, annexation had been paper-work. To make it right, the blood of eleven thousand Americans and yet more Mexicans need be poured out.

By March 1846, the Corps of Observation was observing from Fort Brown on the Rio Grande near Matamores. As was certain when armies were so close, next month Mexican cavalry killed sixteen American dragoons on the north bank of the Rio Grande. A month later, when news of the clash reached Washington, President Polk proclaimed to all who would listen that Mexico's "army has at length crossed the Del Norte, has invaded the territory of our country and has shed American blood upon American soil." It was the expansionist expanding. Expanding also would be the conflict.

"There was . . . a claim that Texas extended south and west to the Rio Grande, by which shallow pretense the government of the northern republic managed to afford some comfort to the national conscience, on the plea that defense of this 'disputed' tract by Mexico was the first act of war. It should be remarked, however, that the first hostilities of Mexican invasion was not on the New Mexican Frontier (i.e., U.S. territory), but further southeast."

"In 1846 the United States began a war against Mexico for the acquisition of territory." [88] And in July, the Army of the West collected at Bent's Fort on the Arkansas.

CHAPTER XV

From Bent's Fort
to the Mora

EITHER AT BENT'S FORT or six miles upstream at about the site of modern La Junta, the Army forded the Arkansas, entered a very dry land and Mexican territory. Lieutenant Abert of the Army Topographic Engineers had scouted the route the year before and recommended it as better than the Road to Santa Fe from any of the crossings south across the Cimarron Desert. Despite his favorable opinion, the several hundred privates who came to know it step-by-step had scarcely printable opinions of it. They began with a very dry march of about fifteen miles across barren land southeast of Timpas Creek. As by then the men were on reduced rations, the clouds of acrid dust and the parching thirst it aggravated did little to renew strength or refurbish humor.

For a traveler better equipped, the Timpas valley even now is a very dry run and on foot, soldiers found it a great deal drier. Timpas water since the Ice Age has been sparse and commonly sour with dissolved salts. It got no praise from anyone who tested it in 1846. Although there was not nearly enough water for all in the small stagnant pools, a good many thirsty soldiers, thirstier horses, mules and oxen sampled as much as they could.

At the head of Timpas Creek is Hole-in-Rock, a natural cistern of water, sometimes sweet, which I thought to be somewhere near Thatcher, the only settlement in the seventy miles between La Junta and Trinidad in southeast Colorado (Map 22). I stopped at Thatcher for a cooling drink and information but the lady operating the only store knew nothing of Hole-in-Rock and had never heard of Hole-in-Prairie some miles beyond. Nor had a man who entered as I made inquiry.

I went outside and looked about the endless sweep of arid treeless space, wondering how a stranger might identify in a country so large, a point so small and a logistic so important in the plans of an invading army. The driver of a ranch truck stopping that moment was no help as his home was in Springer. From the store just then came a man who knew something about the place. With all these comings and goings, it might seem Thatcher was a populous place. Not so; the majority of the population was at hand. Missing was that one who could point and say: "There it is." His house was identified behind a distant blue truck and I was told Hole-in-Rock was on his land.

I went to inquire and found it so. James Hall, owner of the AU ranch accepted without comment whatever a late Sunday afternoon of a hot August might bring. He could not recall just where Hole-in-Prairie might be although he recalled his uncle having mentioned it. He could not say for certain that the considerable stone barn, now a part of his ranch, had been an equally important part of the stage station in the Sixties. He knew it had been there when livestock of the old Broom Cattle Company had cropped these arid miles and his uncle had told him it was older than 1870. Hall pointed to a nearby shallow depression as the site of the stage house and the few stones about it as all that remained. Together we walked a few hundred yards west of the stone barn, Hall limping slightly as he led a saddled horse. He explained that earlier in the day, for comfort he had re-

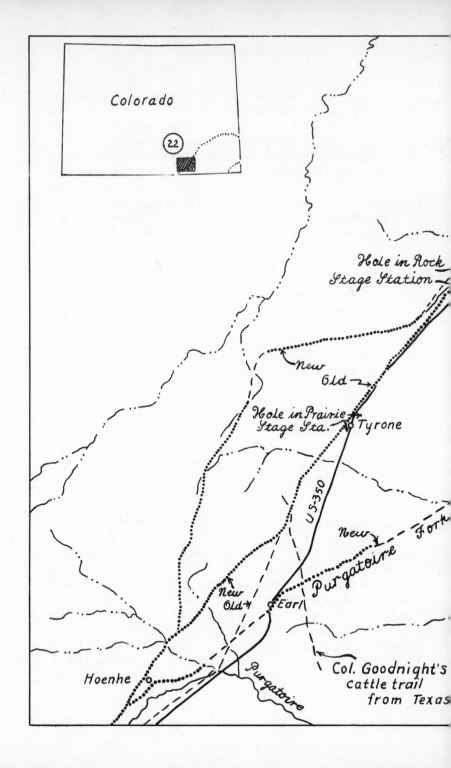

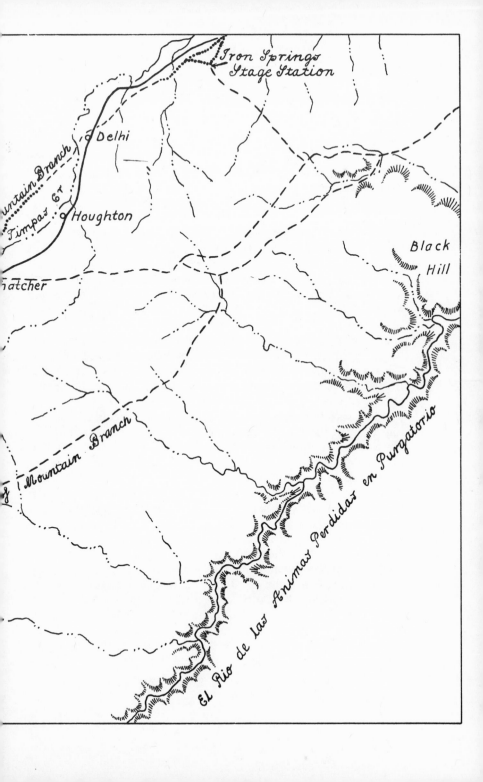

moved the binding from a sprained knee and was replacing it when his wife informed him of my inquiry.

When we came to a slight sag in the land, Hall said it was the beginning of drainage which, northeastward, became the considerable canyon of Timpas Creek. Pointing down the slight trough, he called attention to a thin line of buff color across the drain, scarcely visible between small cedars, and said it was the top of a small dam across the Timpas. Just this side of the dam was Hole-in-Rock, now filled with silt. With that, he mounted.

"Got to rope some calves," he said, and rode away.

I found the stone structure some fifteen feet high and about seventy-five long across the Timpas channel, small here. A hundred and twenty years ago, Abert camped at Hole-in-Rock and spoke of the stone cistern as a place "of water at all seasons, pure, sweet and a good change from (the) bitter" in the Timpas up to this point.[97] He wrote of the cool shade of dense cedars, a benediction every wayfarer here would appreciate. It was so dry I rustled as a field of corn. Cedars are yet dense about the Hole but all are so small that it does not seem probable that any among them now offered shade to Abert then.

For suffering in silence, one need have a peculiar psychological aptitude and Marcellus Ball Edwards did not have it. He was one among the many who on August 3, 1846 marched up the dry, parched, valley of the Timpas. In a cloud of acrid dust under a scorching sun, the next day was worse for there was no water for man or beast save in one inadequate small pool so foul with dissolved salts that one who drank need hold his breath until it was swallowed. Hole-in-rock, so Edwards thought, would be a clear fount of cool clear water ample for all. What he found was a rocky hole of filthy water stirred quickly to mud by famished livestock.[50] His companion, Abraham Johnson Robinson recorded in fewer words a similar opinion of scanty muddy water and scantier grass.[99] Lieutenant Emory was somewhat less forthright: "Hole in Rock is a large hole with plenty of pretty good stagnant water." By time Susan arrived a week later, the mud had settled in an aura not there before: "The Hole in the Rock

I found pretty much the same as described: scenery about it is quite romantic—high rocks covered with cedar trees; shelving and craggy precipices, pearly brooks and green groves, through which are seen bounding the stately antelope and timid hare; while the ear is greeted by the soft warble of feathered songsters. It is quite the place in which to build a lover's castle and plant his gardens &c." [2]

Having left Hole-in-Rock and the stagnant water at the head of Timpas Creek, the Mountain Branch and the largest group ever on it, crossed again the divide between the Timpas and the Purgatoire. At the crest of the broad gentle separation of the two streams is a depression: Hole-in-Prairie (Map 22). From rare rains it collected runoff and the shallow pond quickly became tepid, stagnant and green with algae beneath the summer sun. Even so it was both distasteful and welcome to parched man and beast. In the treeless land, the very few willows which grew about it did not last long as firewood; moreover, grass about was scanty. Hole-in-Prairie is a spot of ground somewhere near Tyrone, Colorado, a spot on the map and a flag-stop on a railroad. I had a card bearing a notation from a WPA guide which located it half a mile north from the highway on a dirt road crossing the railroad. But I could not find it, even with the aid of John Guyrman, a rancher I found working on the motor of a pump replacing a dilapidated windmill about where the landmark should be. He knew of the name and its historical import and he knew of several small depressions in the prairie about, any one of which might have been that one which held a little rainwater when troops passed here in 1846. Months later, reconstructing the scene for these paragraphs in an office several hundred miles from the locale, in a flash of mixed chagrin and retrospective insight, I knew where Hole-in-Prairie must be: about two miles east from the T-road north across the railroad at Tyrone flagstop, and half a mile south. The delayed supposition was a frustration, for I had agreed with Guyrman as he suggested that under the hooves of several generations of cattle hereabouts one small depression with occasional water might come to look much like another.

Guyrman allowed Hole-in-Prairie had historic but not

economic importance as his cattle daily got their twelve or fifteen gallons of water each from steel tanks filled by gasoline motors pumping from wells.

"Motors are a sight better than mills. Not so far to fall when you have to work on them. But the gears can chew up a finger before you feel it."

Southwest across arid sterile empty country, one may follow ruts of the Mountain Branch but in a season drier than usual they are very faint indeed. One may walk across them without recognition. About five miles southwest of Hole-in-Prairie, the shallow, almost imperceptible endless trough cut by stage coaches in the sixties and wagons before them on the gentle slope toward the Purgatoire, crosses another trail, one running northward. I was never able to find it on the ground and it was not there when the first wheels rolled on the Mountain Branch but it was well known before the last. It had been a complete surprise and a considerable pleasure to see it on an old township survey: "Colonel Goodnight's Cattle Trail from Texas." (Map 22)

The Colonel was a gruff elder of ninety-three winters (and a newly-wed) when I knew him in a small Texas town on the land he had done so much to make. He had known Christopher Carson, William Bent, Lucien Maxwell and others about whom I have since read. He had found Maxwell slow pay in purchase of cattle but he finally paid with egg-size chunks of gold smelted at one of the mines on his empire. These he had rolled from a hollow log in which he stored them. I saw the Colonel as a man old, enfeebled, with a disheveled coat and vest and a tobacco-stained white vandyke, unaware he was also a very considerable link with the past and with men who, when he knew them, lived the history of the southwest.

Since then I have learned that the Colonel himself made history but to a youngster he was only a vague but respected and important standard of some sort.[100] He had been adamant against gambling, liquor and similar pastimes when such opposition must have seemed to others a Jurassic sentiment. Goodnight had been a driver and a drover. In one period of five years he so constantly drove cattle from Texas to northern ranges in Colorado and Wyoming that the longest time he spent in one place was four days in Denver. Once, in the late Sixties, he had trailed a herd through Raton Pass where Dick Wootton had rolled aside most of the boulders to make a toll-road where the Army had eased wagons down with a tail rope. The tax of ten cents a head was an outrage to a man accustomed to loose-herding on the open prairie, and the Colonel was. Next year he found Trinchera Pass, a gap in the Ratons through which the Two Buttes Fork of the Mountain Branch passed near Folsom, New Mexico. On the old township map the small segment of "Colonel Goodnight's Cattle Trail from Texas" came from the direction of Trinchera Pass as it crossed the Mountain Branch near Hole-in-Prairie.

In later years and long after his demise I came to have a high regard for Colonel Goodnight. In his biography I learned he had organized the Panhandle Livestock Associa-

Los Ratones

tion, of which he was chief ramrod. It was that organization which brought the first doctor to the Texas Panhandle. Because the few in the 18,000 square miles were sometimes in urgent need of medical attention, the association of ranchers paid Dr. J.D. Stocking eighteen hundred dollars a year until influx of settlers provided an adequate number of patients.[100]

For the thirsty men marching in 1846 there was a gentle slope from stagnant rainwater of Hole-in-Prairie to the Purgatoire River. Just as they had been unanimous in opinion of Timpas water, so were they concerning the Purgatoire. It was a stream few failed to praise and George Gibson, one of the soldiers under Kearny, noted in his journal the welcome sight of black locusts and cottonwoods, the gooseberries, wild cherries, black currants and other conveniences and spoke of the contrast of that Eden to barren hills flanking the stream.[46] Upriver Gibson caught a mess of mountain trout, saw wild turkeys and spoke of the frequency of buffalo skulls and elk horns passed en route to Raton Pass.

The Purgatoire which these men followed to the entrance of Raton Pass, from early Spaniards had the resounding title: El Rio de las Animas Perdidas en Purgatorio, named after several of their countrymen had been cut off somewhere on its banks and scalped to the last man, dead, then, without absolution but remembered in the name: The River of Souls Lost in Purgatory. French *courriers de bois* out of Illinois, although few in number so far from home, were always about this land. Less concerned with things spiritual, they discarded all the name save "Purgatorio" and this they spoke in their own way: "Purgatoire." Mountain Men, trappers who guided the Army, could do no more with this than "Picatoire." Out of this confusion, later settlers evolved a more familiar sound: "Picketwire." The stream now flows as always it has, clear and cool from mountains, out across arid land, cutting a considerable canyon in the flanking piedmont, beyond which it joins the Arkansas River. Its name, fissioned with amoeboid frequency, is mostly preserved. At the junction of the river with the Arkansas is the town, Las Animas,

The Souls, no longer lost and there, tactfully, The Purgatoire River flows in the Picketwire Valley.

The sun was low when I drove the highway from Hole-in-Rock past an unrecognized Hole-in-Prairie, southwest toward the Ratons across the even, scarcely perceptible alluvial piedmont slope rising gently toward the heights. Low clouds shut off the sun until it touched the horizon and that moment released from it a broad shaft which tinted the sparse grass a clear bright orange, laced here and there with thin shadows of taller stems and scattered cholla cactus. Beyond the bright swath rose the deep blue of the Raton Mountains, the darker because western clouds kept them so. It was a sight to fit the sound of a Haydn symphony.

Early of a morning I found Raton Pass high, cool and crowded (Map 23). A tributary of the Purgatoire heads here

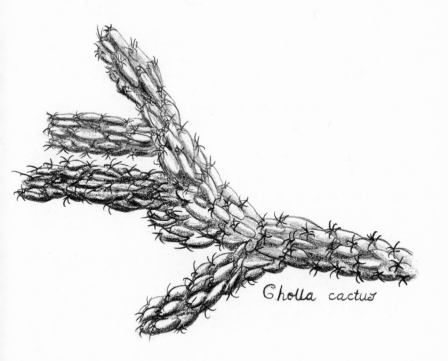

Cholla cactus

and up the valley reaches a railroad, a busy highway and the cluttered scar of an expressway leveling rock and pine. Here and there one may note the omnipresent index of American culture: the punctured beer can. Between and beneath all this debris is the old road first cut by wagons numbering 1,600, many freighting supplies for the Army.

Lieutenant Abert, who traversed the Pass the year before the Army, had not been greatly impressed with its potential difficulties for wagons, a future of which he may not have been aware, but when he came with them and again to the difficult trail he reported: "We commenced one of the rockiest roads I ever saw; no one who crossed the Raton can ever forget it." [101] It is likely few did but as not many of the 1,700 soldiers were concerned with the wagons which followed them, they remembered the Pass for other reasons. After scorching and dry August days on the Plains, the cool heights and tall pines were a welcome change as were the mountain streams, youthful and frothy on cobbles. Stronger yet were other reactions, those of men who had nothing to eat the day before and only a supper this day of half a cup of flour, beef blue and tough with age and the last of coffee and sugar.[76]

Susan Magoffin knew the difficulties of the wagons at first hand as her husband owned several among them: broken hounds, bolsters, tongues and axles and some overturned. "August 15th Saturday (they were in the Raton yesterday and today) traveling at the rate of half a mile an hour. . . . We came to camp about half an hour after dusk, having accomplished the great travel of *six or eight yards* during the day. Wednesday 18th (August 1846) Out of the Raton at last, can it be possible! We have been in it five days. . . ." [2]

Cholla Wood

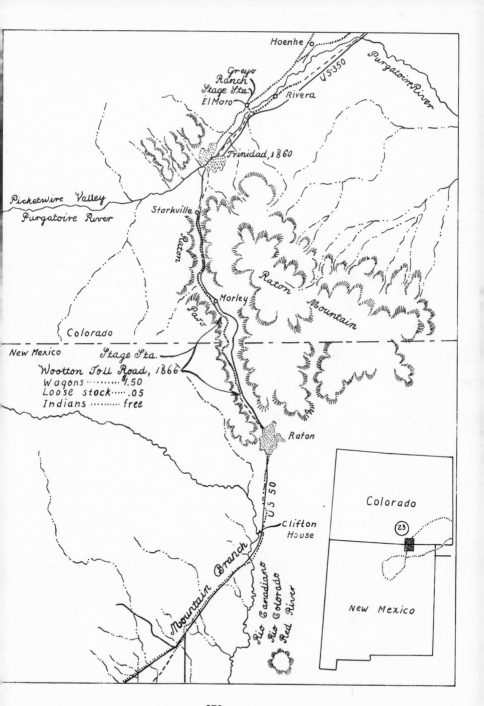

Hoenhe

US-350

Purgatoire River

Greys
Ranch
Stage Sta.
El Moro   Rivera

Trinidad, 1860

Picketwire Valley
Purgatoire River

Starkville

Raton   Mountain

Morley

Colorado

New Mexico   Stage Sta.

Wootton Toll Road, 1866
Wagons $1.50
Loose stock .... .05
Indians .... free

Raton

US 50

Clifton
House

Colorado

㉓

New Mexico

Mountain Branch

Rio Canadiano
Rio Colorado
Red River

Raton Mesa, the mountain, had its name by Spanish translation of some Indian word speaking of rodents, presumably numerous in the alpine environment. It has its origin in a thick flow of basalt from some orifice not far to the west, eastward onto an Ice Age surface of land considerably higher than now. Millennia of erosion on the north by the Purgatoire and its tributaries and on the south by the Rio Colorado (Canadian) has breached the mass of immense outpouring that flowed a cherry-red liquid onto the surface at a time when a colossal sheet of ice covered the continent northeast of the Missouri and Ohio Rivers. The breach is now Raton Pass. It was not intended, by nature at least, to be an easy road, as certainly it was not, even after the Army passed this way. It is now so only where man has made it smooth.

In Raton Pass where now wheels roll easily on pavement, where soon they will roll faster on an expressway, Richens Lacy Wootton had a rough toll-road.[81]

In 1865, the old frontiersman, with scalp illogically intact after a hair-raising career on the frontier, secured from the Colorado Territorial Legislature a franchise. It was readily granted as Colorado territorials were much more interested in gold and silver mines than in roads for immigrants or wagons freighting merchandise. Dick Wootton informed his biographer that he secured the same right from New Mexico but there is no record that he troubled New Mexico politicians, although three of the five rough miles he cleared lay in that territory.[102] A crew of workmen pushed aside the largest boulders and smoothed down rock ledges where formerly wagons were eased down with a tail-rope clutched by all hands and the wagon master. When they were done sometime in 1866, about a mile south of the present flag-stop of Morley, Wootton built a gate. South beyond it there was not much of a road; still, it was a much better one than it had been. A passing wagon paid $1.50 before Wootton opened the gate. Owners of loose stock paid five cents for each head, according to scanty records, although Colonel Goodnight's recollection raised the fee to ten cents as his indignation doubled with the years. Because Wootton knew them so very well that he could assess their reactions without ever testing them, Indians passed free.

Neither of mind nor temperament to be accountable to anyone, Wootton kept a close eye on his handiwork and no records. His partner, George C. McBride, listed receipts for a time and there is extant an accounting which shows revenue to have been $9,193 for a fifteen-month interval.[81] An income of $306 each month does not now seem plush but in 1867 dollars it would have had three or four times the purchasing power of the same sum now. When there were hundreds of beavers on every stream and a beaver hat on every head that could afford it, a trapper with little regard for dangers could do better but he worked a great deal harder for what he got. Moreover, as beavers were fewer with every year, he worked harder each season for less. And when hats came to be made of other kinds of hair, even if his own was still intact, the work of the most diligent trapper came to naught. In any case, Wootton did very well and with hair on and boots off, lived to see steel rails replace his rocky road.

South of Raton Pass, before Wootton's toll road, there was no town of Raton, nor Willow Springs, its predecessor, when wagons battered and mended emerged from the Pass and the rough trail hacked through it by the Army. But there was the welcome headwater of the Rio Colorado, the Canadian, and the open prairies across which it flowed to cut a canyon just below El Vado de las Piedras.

Six miles south of what came to be Raton, New Mexico, is a historical marker: "Clifton House, built by Tom Stockton in 1867 with materials from Dodge City (Map 23). After abandonment of the Santa Fe Trail in 1870 it fell into disuse and burned." For a few miles before and after the sign there are others less elaborate on ranch gates, bearing the names of descendants of the builder of Clifton House. It was in 1866 that the Union Pacific laid rails west of Kansas City on a route miles north of the Road to Santa Fe. As month by month rails reached toward Denver, the western terminus of rails became the eastern end of the Road to Santa Fe. After Denver was tied to Missouri by a ribbon of steel, freight and stages bound to Santa Fe left the railroad at the point nearest to New Mexico and after Wootton built his toll road, crossed Raton Pass. Much of that traffic paused at Clifton House. Year after year, the Road to Santa Fe, crossing the Arkansas and the Cimarron Desert, the Waterscrape, bore less traffic. Thirty-eight years younger than the Road, the Mountain Branch, its offspring, endured some years longer. The last few miles of it passed to limbo when rails crossing Raton Pass reached Santa Fe in 1878.

About fifteen miles south of Raton, near the fading settlement of Hoxie, is a fork in modern pavement. In that locality, the Mountain Branch had three forks. The older (?), the westernmost, ran across the toes of the mountains and although it was merely a trace, it was followed a short distance by the infantry of the Army of the West. It passed through what later was to be Cimarron, as does modern pavement and as did stage coaches in the sixties (Map 18). Lucien Maxwell lived for a time at Cimarron on a rough frontier smoothed a trifle by silver plate on linen cloth. It was at Cimarron that Colonel Goodnight delivered a herd of Texas longhorns. And later, when he came to collect payment, it was from Cimarron that he went with Maxwell into the Sangre de Cristo Mountains and the Moreno Valley. Near Old Baldy, the high altitude site of a future "E-Town" (Elizabethtown), center of gold mining in a corner of his vast holding, Maxwell up-ended his bank, a hollow log, to pour out egg-size chunks of gold in delayed payment for his cattle.

The easternmost fork of the Mountain Branch near Hoxie seems to have been the youngest. It ran due south to the vicinity of modern Springer and bent gently southwest past Gonzalito Mesa to cross Sweet Water Creek. Somewhere in that vicinity it crossed the line measured by engineer Brown from Franklin in Missouri to Taos in New Mexico.

For reasons not clear in either journal or diary, Sibley chose to run the survey direct from El Vado de las Piedras across the Sangre de Cristo Mountains to Taos on the western slope (Map 24). The alternative would have been south to Gallinas (Las Vegas), southwest to San Miguel, then west and

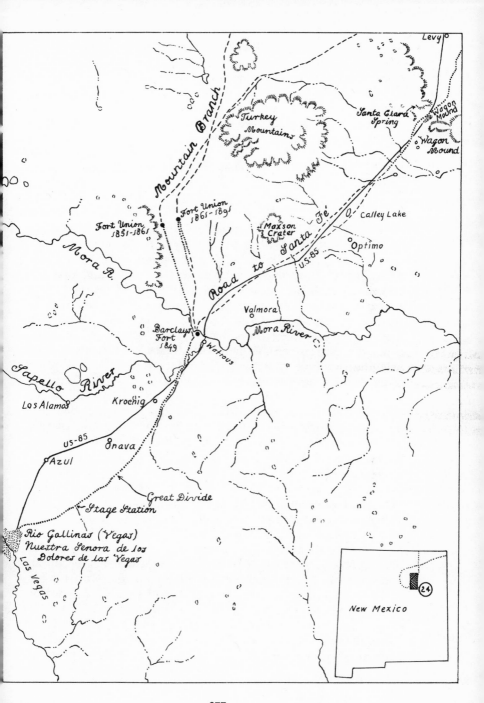

Levy

Turkey Mountains

Santa Clara Spring

Wagon Mound

Wagon Mound

Fort Union 1861-1891

Fort Union 1851-1861

Maxson Crater

Calley Lake

Mora R.

Road to Santa Fé

U.S.-85

Optimo

Valmora

Mora River

Barclays Fort 1849

Watrous

Sapello River

Los Alamos

Kroenig

U.S-85

Onava

Azul

Great Divide

Stage Station

Rio Gallinas (Vegas)
Nuestra Senora de los
Dolores de las Vegas

Las Vegas

New Mexico

24

northwest to Santa Fe—the only route feasible for wagons.

Certainly Brown did not know he was marking a path for invasion, if indeed that was the purpose of the survey. His "way-bill" map of the survey across the mountains shows two lines: the northern marked "Mule Path" and suitable only for sure-footed animals; the southern line "Wagons may travel," trending up the valley of Rio Ocate passing modern and minute settlements of Naranjos, Ocate and Black Lake, crossing the divide to the head of Rio San Fernando de Taos, down that canyon of vertical walls to debouchment of the creek at Pueblo San Fernando de Taos.

Sibley and party arrived "Sunday 30th October: Another fine morning. At daylight the Mercury stood at 17. We started after Breakfast, at 9. We kept down the Valley and Creek 8 miles, in which we found no obstruction or difficulty; and at 12, arrived at the Village of San Fernando. Our Poor Horses seemed to pluck up fresh Spirits, on sight of fields and Houses; they entered the Village merrily at a good Trot as if they meant to enjoy their *full* Share of the honour of bringing the First Wagon over the Mountains into the Valley of Taos . . . I have Said, that the distance from Ft. Osage to Taos is 740 Miles . . . we shall be able to Straighten the Road in several places as we return . . . so that the actual distance between the two places will . . . be fixed at 700 miles. Of this 700 miles, at least 680 is open Prairie. Indeed, I doubt if there be more than 15 miles of Woodland altogether, upon the whole route, as the Road goes."

"On my arrival at San Fernando, I found that a small Party of Traders had got there the day before from Franklin. They passed along upon the Mule Trace through the Mountains, while I was going around with the Wagons."

"As I shall remain at this Village or somewhere in the neighborhood, at least 'till my Horses are a little recruited, and probably all winter, I made inquiry immediately after my arrival, for a suitable House to rent, and was Shewn two, a little out of the Village, which I concluded to take. . . ."

"It was near night when I returned to the Village, where I found the Alcalde & Curate waiting for me—who it seems had called on me officially to inquire my business &c. Altho'

I suspected that these Men were acting a little arrogantly, yet I deemed it proper to treat them with proper civility. I therefore gave them to understand, as briefly as I could, why I had come here and told them that I would explain myself more fully to the Governor of the Territory, as soon as I conveniently could. After some consultation between themselves, they took leave of me very civilly, without asking any more questions. A very fine day." [32]

Four years before Sibley, the year Becknell arrived with trade goods in Santa Fe, Jacob Fowler on a trapping expedition with "Coln glann" reached Taos and thoroughly enjoyed the hospitality of it. When Carson retired from roaming mountains with Fremont, he had a home in Taos, the birthplace of his wife, Josefa Jaramillo. His house is yet there, worth the trouble of a visit. Taos was likewise the home of Charles Bent (his wife another Beaubien), appointed first Governor of New Mexico Territory by General Kearny. Taos is now the haunt of artists: some who paint, some prizewinners with their etchings, and some whose merit is impossible to find among drips and splashes. The number of artists, real and fancied, living in Taos estimated by those who count themselves natives (and time elects even a Brooklyn accent to that status) vary from 100 to 700. But a casual inquirer cannot possibly correlate the meanings given the word. The first artist in Taos was Robert Kern who accompanied Fremont on one of his more haphazard sallies for fame in the west. More dead than alive, Kern barely made Taos in 1849 through deep snow among mountains to the north. Fortunately he recovered and two years later accompanied Lieutenant Simpson in exploration of the southwest. Simpson, Kern and associates were the first Anglo-Saxons to find El Morro, a water-hole on an Indian trail through the very dry land between the Rio Grande and the ancient, now modern, pueblo of Zuni.[103] It was Robert Kern, artist, who sketched the scores of early Spanish incriptions at El Morro and it was probably Simpson who engraved in the soft sandstone the record of their visit: that unique inscription including a caret. After Simpson and Kern, one of the group with Lieutenant Beale and the camel brigade, M. H. Stacey, carved his name in the stone of El Morro, record of their camp at the water-hole.

> The leader Don Juan de Onate passed by here (on the way) to the discovery of the sea of the south on the 16th of April, 1605.

On the 25th of the month of June, year of the Faith 1709, Ramon Garcia Jurado passed by here for Suni (Zuni).

Taos, with fewer artists than art critics, is an interesting survival from another era, well worth the trouble to see. Charles Bent's house, wherein he was scalped by Taos Indians welcoming the new regime in 1846 is a museum with a clutter of junk among which is a battered trunk with a large *C B* on a flap of leather over the keyhole. As a residium of history, the house is something less than it might be, as now it is nothing Bent himself would recognize. Still, if perhaps not the same roof, it has some of the walls within which Bent lived and died. For those who have read of his fate there is a two by two foot area of wall unplastered to expose adobe bricks, presumably filling the hole cut (one was) by inmates as the mob raged about the front door. There is even hanging alongside it a long iron spoon by which it was done, perhaps.

The middle fork of the Mountain Branch near Hoxie joined the western-most branch at the crossing of Rayado Creek (Map 18). Three years after the Army (and Susan) crossed there, Christopher Carson settled on the Rayado. He had been persuaded by Maxwell as both had married and Maxwell wished to populate his vast holding. Few frontiermen had temperament requisite for sedentary farming or ranching and Carson was one of the majority. He had scarcely located a herd and built a shelter for his wife before he answered the call of Fremont and disappeared among the mountains to the north.

Rayado, the modern settlement at the junction of the western and middle forks of the Mountain Branch, rather the general store which *is* the town, has a picturesque setting between eastern foothills of the Sangre de Cristo Mountains. East and west the settlement is flanked by cuestas, narrow ridges with steep west and gentle east slopes, which are eroded upturned edges of firm layers of Cretaceous strata: hard rock bent from their original horizontal position to an eastward inclination by the super-colossal forces which, when the last arm of Cretaceous sea had been pushed from the continent, folded the Sangre de Cristo Mountains. The cuestas extending north-south, held up by strata more resistant to erosion than the average among them, mark the eastern flank of a gigantic arch, the central part of which is lost to erosion. The opposite flank is a hundred and twenty miles west, where it stands very high on North America as part of the Continental Divide. The mountains one sees now are not those uplifted by the original arch for in the sixty millions of years, more or less, since that time very slow erosion reduced all this region to a great plain only slightly above sea level. And later, during one of those slow, ponderous twitches which torment the crust of this planet, a vast segment of rock from the Aleutian Islands on the north, south through ten thousand miles to Cape Horn in the other hemisphere, was uplifted, rejuvenating streams which carved from the elevated plain the heights so impressive now, of which the Sangre de Cristo Mountains are one.

The name of the Mountains, Sangre de Cristo, means "Blood of Christ."[104] I had long thought it an odd appelation for rugged heights so green with pines. I was surprised to learn so many knew what I did not: legend has Christ's blood white. As these mountains are meters deep in snow for months of the year the name is appropriate. Or perhaps it was and now no longer is: each pristine flake brings gently to earth a quota of Strontium-90, even some of that in suspension from the very first sent heavenward by man not far south from here in the Alamogordo Valley between Mountains of the Sacrament on the east and Saint Andrew's Mountains on the west.

The Army of the West saw this country in the dry season of a dry climate. Iron tires of their baggage wagons loosened each parching day as wood of felloes shrank. The circumstance was alleviated by removing the wheels each night and soaking them in water. Swelling of the wood made tight for another day the junction of iron rims encompassing felloes.

On a Road leading due south from Rayado, the Army crossed the Ocate River, marched west of the Turkey Mountains and about twelve miles south of them, crossed the Mora (Map 25). Here they came to a small cluster of adobe houses which some thought resembled brick-kilns.[50] It was

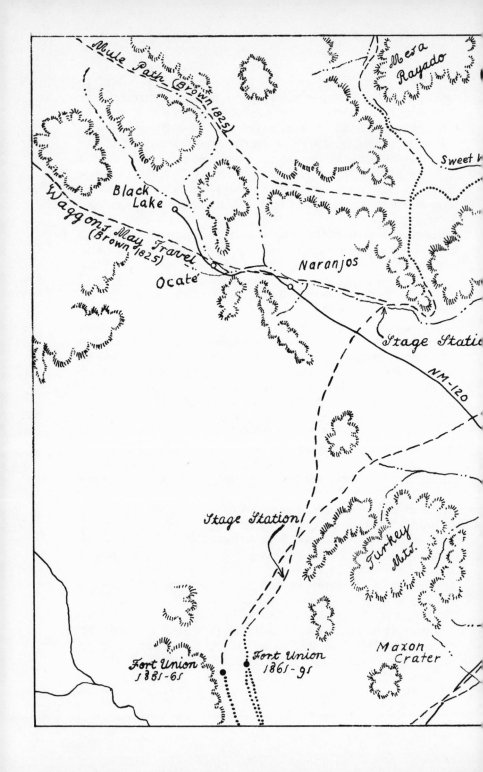

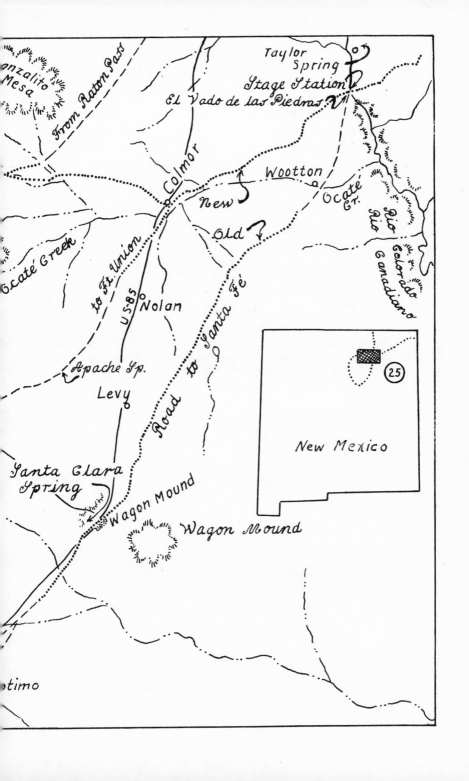

here the Road to Santa Fe, on a course southwest from El
Vado de las Piedras on the Canadian River, had crossed the
Mora River for a quarter century before the military. "Mora"
is Spanish for mulberry. Folklore suggests it was the name of
an individual, as mulberry trees are not native to the southwest and transplants find the environment inhospitable.

At Mora Creek and settlement, Susan Magoffin saw
"Here . . . a little hovel, fit to match some of the genteel
pig stys in the States—made of mud, and surrounded by a
kind of fence made of sticks; this is the *casa grande*. Its
neighbours are smaller, far inferior, and to them I have no
comparison. But they say my opinion is formed too hastily,
for within these places of apparent misery there dwells that
'peace of mind' and contentment which princes and kings
have oft desired but never found." [2]

The Road to Santa Fe, running southwest from El Vado
de las Piedras on the Canadian, to the crossing of the Mora
where it was joined by the younger Mountain Branch (route
of part of the Army), about midway passed Wagon Mound:
a huge cap of columnar basalt holding up a hill about a mile

Wagon Mound

east of the modern settlement of the same name (Map 25). A short distance west of the town is an outcrop of lava. Santa Clara Spring which issues at the base of the flow now supplies the town of Wagon Mound. In an earlier day it watered dry men, drier oxen and acres of *vega* grass. The latter refurbished gaunt stock, lean from 660 miles of Road, much of it dry.

Still long of Road but short of cash, I would have passed Wagon Mound had I been able to see in its profile a resemblance to the name. Stopping a mile or two north, I examined its silhouette from several angles but could find little resemblance to the very few Conestogas I knew. Back at the car parked on the highway berm I noted on the left front tire a knot as large as two fists. Very slowly I drove to the filling station in hope of finding a new one, depressingly aware that while the Road to Santa Fe was still long, cash was certain to be distressingly shorter.

I inquired of a highway engineer stopping for gasoline did he know in Wagon Mound a structure dating from the time of the stage line here. He could recall none but he spoke of Santa Clara Spring coming from the base of the basalt flow half a mile west, a reserve of liquid gold in a country so dry. The spring and land about it had been a grant by the Spanish to his great-great-grandfather and although it was no longer property of his family, he urged that I visit it. Later I inquired of the filling station operator.

"I live in the oldest house in Wagon Mound," he replied. It was once the stage station fronting on the Road through town. Somehow the Road became an alley and now my house fronts backward. Sure you can photograph it if you can get past the ditch for the new water-line."

His house, like most in this region, is flat-roofed and adobe. And like many older structures it has been stuccoed grey in recent years. Adobe brick are hand-made from soil: exceedingly fine-grained with an abundance of clay minerals of diverse and complex composition, all the product of weathering of bedrock in an arid climate. Mixed only with water in any receptacle handy, including a hole scooped in the prairie, the mud is shoveled to fill the four openings in a rude wooden form resting on the ground, each opening about three by twelve by nine inches. The mould is lifted from the cast and set nearby to form others. Left to dry a week or two, when the bricks are firm enough to handle they are set leaning one against the other in rows like dominoes. As they "cure" in dry air, soil colloids lose their ad- and absorbed moisture and cement firmly soil particles one to the other. In two or three months, adobe bricks have the same consistency as any hard clod of thoroughly dried mud: adequate to sustain the weight of a great many others in a wall. Mortar to bond them is the same slurry of mud and so is the plaster applied to smooth the wall. An adobe house has insulation attainable only with other material a great deal more expensive. Although a house of dried mud is so down-to-earth as to repel those who feel civilization is underwritten by mammon or the Manor, those who have lived in an adobe house know it as the coolest in summer and warmest in winter. Rain is so rare in the southwest that with only minor repairs an adobe brick house will endure almost forever. Still, as from random and rare thunderheads in every desert some rain must fall, and as sometimes a great deal falls in a very short time, the cement of stucco is welcome insurance against melting of a wall or collapse of a roof.

Immediately west of Wagon Mound is the serrate margin of an eroded basalt lava which issued from one of several long-dormant eroded vents around the Mound. In a cove between two prongs of basalt is Santa Clara Spring and in another immediately north there was once a small lake fed by the spring. No such wastage is permissible now and everything about the spring has been remade to collect water for the town.

Santa Clara Spring was once an important camp on the Road to Santa Fe. That portion of the Army which followed the Road as it was cut by wheels of commerce, camped near Wagon Mound and watered at the Spring. A diarist among them noted in a natural corral between prongs of a basalt flow just north of Santa Clara Spring, bodies and bones of some two hundred oxen stolen by Indians from traders and slaughtered for no purpose save that of triumph of victor over vanquished.[76] The "natural corral" [76] was perhaps the *rincon* in the basalt flow just north of Santa Clara Spring.

Wagon Mound and the Spring was a spot frequented by Comanches, Apaches and Utes in their wanderings and if they were bent on loot or scalps, it was a convenient one. Intervals between which one or the other were certain to be found at Santa Clara Spring were short. Letters among "Calhoun's Correspondence" tell of a time when the Santa Fe Stage, bound east, camped overnight at the Spring to be found next morning by itinerant Jicarilla Apaches and Utes bound for plunder.[84] It was about the second of May, 1850, that a party numbering ten camped near Santa Clara Spring. Messrs. Clay, Henderson (the mail carrier), Shaw, Goldstein, Brown and five unidentified companions slept soundly that night, unaware the hand of fate was closing to crush them next morning.

For reasons not clear in reconstruction of the circumstance, two men lingered a few moments at the campfire as the stage left it. In that brief interval of separation and as they mounted, Apaches and Utes charged from concealment east of a small hill near the foot of Wagon Mound. Horses of the lagging pair were killed at the campsite. The stage could not have gone far, for wounded and on foot the two men reached it, a haven for a few savage minutes. Judged from arrows scattered about, attackers were considerable in number and doubtless they pressed close as the wounded men were jerked into the wagon by their companions. Fighting then must have been hand-to-hand for eight bodies of the stage party were scattered up to seventy yards from the wagon. Looted debris and letters were everywhere about.

Whatever was gained by the Apaches and Utes, cost must have been exceedingly high. Stage drivers and their outriders were hard men, accustomed to give as they received and they were armed to give generously: one hundred and thirty-six shots without pause for reloading revolving rifles and pistols.

By time of the Wagon Mound massacre, Indians were familiar with the armouring effect of pages of paper, the Bible included, packed tight and thick between two large circles of hard, dried rawhide cut from the tough skin of the neck of buffalo bulls, the material of war-shields. Two circular layers of rawhide in a shield would impede even at close range most bullets of rifles of the day. Two layers with books between offered a great deal more protection and when they could procure the raw material, Indians had it.

One among the victors at Wagon Mound either with a wry sense of humor, a feeling for history or perhaps as a gesture of defiance, sacrificed a sheet of Army muster-roll collected there. Lieutenant Burnside dispatched with troops to track the marauders, reported to Calhoun the finding on the Road east of Rabbit Ears Creek, of a blank muster-roll on which was sketched pictorial representations of the manner the murders were done.

Calhoun, whose correspondence tells so much of early New Mexico, was soon to be appointed Governor of the Territory. It was an office he held but a short time for, en route east and in ill health, he died somewhere along the Arkansas. David Meriwether was his successor.

Others on the Road to Santa Fe found Wagon Mound and Santa Clara Spring a more peaceful locality, particularly those who saw the landmarks in the earliest days of the Road before transients became synonymous with enemies in Indian language. Major Wetmore stopped there late in July of 1828 and wrote of an attempt to "create" a wild mule.[28] Even so early in history of western commerce strayed or abandoned livestock might be found along the Road. What Wetmore attempted was to "crease" the mule. Back of the neck of quadrupeds is a cable of powerful muscle which encloses cervical vertebrae. The latter is armour of the spinal cord and locus of attachment of muscle. A hard blow on the aggregate of muscle and bone will stun man or beast. Rifles of Wetmore's time probably dealt a blow of two or three hundred foot-pounds at a range of a hundred yards (modern arms are ten to twelve times more powerful). If a ball carried with requisite and exquisite accuracy to barely notch the neck muscles enfolding the vertebrae, the animal dropped instantly. By time of recovery from the stunning blow a few minutes later it would have been firmly bound, secured practically unharmed. Of the thousands of frontier-men and hunters who knew and tried the methods, what would seem the very few truthful among them whose opinion was recorded, declare that neither they nor any within their acquaintance ever fired a successful creasing shot. Wetmore was no more skillful than the majority: his ball struck the mule in the hip and it galloped away. Still at the Spring next day, Wetmore helped to cook a mixture of tar and tallow, lubricant for creaking wheels, in quantity adequate to fill all empty buckets which customarily hung beneath a wagon at its rear. Also, he killed "two rattlesnakes five feet four inches long, the last of which had swallowed an adult prairie-dog." Next day he recorded that Mexicans of the party spent spare moments weaving strong rope from the long foretop hair of buffalo.

Wislizenus, a German physician who as a tourist ac-companied Albert Speyer, trader, over the Road three weeks ahead of the Army, attempted to climb Wagon Mound. Like so many before and after him, he was halted by the long slender vertical columns which comprise the basalt cap of the hill. In Wislizenus' day, Mexican militia met caravans at Wagon Mound and the Doctor wrote of those he saw in scraps of uniforms and rags, some mounted and some afoot, armed with lances and very few guns. "They made no formid-able appearance and had no use for such as they had friendly intentions." [38] Three hundred miles northeast, that very day and hour, a hostile militia armed with rifle and cannon, con-temptuous of spears, moved up the Arkansas. With evil intent they strode through acres of wildflowers, yellow, white and purple, en route to slay those who, this minute, regarded them as friends.

As had been Wetmore before him, so was Wislizenus headed southwest to the crossing of the Mora River (Map 25). He thought it a "fine mountain stream in a charming valley" with excellent grass and water. There had been no settlement on the Mora when Wetmore reached the crossing but Wislizenus wrote of an adobe house belonging to Messrs. Smith and Wells who offered "delicious milk, butter and pie which was not refused."

When three weeks later the Army reached the crossing

of the Mora, refreshments were not available for so many but one spoke of a refreshing sight not so nourishing as pie but quite as agreeable: a young girl came running from an adobe hut, ostensibly to fetch water in an earthen jar but more likely to see the young men. She had put on her best white stockings to impress the strangers, and she did, for at least one diarist mentioned them, her black hair, brown eyes, small hands and pretty feet. With the pyschology of the invader, he belittled the girl and noted that although she tried to communicate, he understood nothing save badly enunciated oaths.[50]

The dusky charmer of the invaders must have lived on the Mora at a time when weapons other than dark eyes, jet hair, small hands and pretty feet would have been more effective. Three years earlier, the settlement on the Mora (now Watrous, N. Mex.) had been raided by Colonel Warfield. His commission for privateering on the Plains was like that of Colonel Sniveley's. The latter had been encountered on the Arkansas by Captain Phillip St. George Cooke. Warfield had recruited a band of riff-raff, dismal characters loafing about Bent's Fort and other frontier posts and led them in a raid on the settlement at the Mora crossing. The venture was not an unqualified success as Warfield gambled with cards no higher than ten in his hands. Swooping down on the settle-ment the raiders killed five and drove off all loose horses. New Mexicans collected more mounts and men, tracked the land-pirates to a night camp, recovered their lost stock and took those belonging to the Texans as well. The latter burned their saddles rather than leave them to the enemy. Some walked the hundred and eighty miles to Bent's Fort and others a greater distance to join Snively on the Arkansas.[89]

In later years, the Mora crossing was to be the site of a trading post and fort built by Alexander Barclay (a Britisher) and Joseph Doyle in 1849.[25] Davis, who passed there in No-vember, 1853, spoke of "Barclay's Fort" as a large adobe stucture where men and animals might find food and shelter.[26] The "outside is formidable, with loop-holes and battlements. But rooms within are damp and uncomfortable, gloomy. The establishment reminded me of some old state prison." Before Davis, and after, the Mora for a time was the collecting point for eastbound wagons which there organized to caravans, and Barclay's Fort the headquarters of Mr. Kroenig who put his camel to work packing merchandise over the Road.

The Mora crossing, very near junction of that stream with the Sapello, became an important point for emigrants headed for California over the Road to Santa Fe. A good many herds of sheep from New Mexico and a few of cattle from as far east as Missouri passed here. James G. Hamilton collected a herd of 850 cattle around Kansas City and in 1857 turned them toward California.[105] He found Barclay's Fort, at least that part occupied by Joseph Doyle, considerably improved from Davis' time. "I took dinner with Doyle . . . (he) is comfortably fixed—nice rooms, carpeted, curtained and looks neat and clean. The carpets in this country are put down loose as most houses have dirt floors. Doyle has the finest garden I have seen in many a day."

What Hamilton paid for his stock in Missouri is not known but he arrived at "Warner's Ranch, California" (about 80 miles from San Bernardino) with 700 head, later sold for an average of about $45, prime heifers bringing $65. Losses on the road numbered about 155 head strayed, stolen or drowned. "On the 1st Dec. we commenced crossing the Colorado (in Arizona) and after 5 days hard work got all over. I was never so vexed and fatigued in my life. . . . We lost 15 head in crossing."

CHAPTER XVI

The Road to
Santa Fe

SOUTHWEST OF THE MORA ten easy but sometimes dangerous miles, wagons crossed an imperceptible "Great Divide" (Map 25). As it was flat country most were unaware they had passed from drainage to the Mississippi into the basin of the Rio Grande. So long as rain was not falling, very few were interested.

At Bent's Fort on August 1st Kearny had written a letter to Armijo, Governor of New Mexico: "By annexation of Texas to the United States, the Rio Grande from its mouth to its source forms . . . the boundary between her and Mexico, and I come by orders . . . to take possession of the country, over part of which you are now presiding as Governor. . . ." [88]

Remainder of the document contained promise of acceptance to the Union and benevolent adoption if no opposition was offered and dire threat of reprisal and punishment if it was. Captain Cooke had been sent to Santa Fe as messenger and with him James Magoffin to exercise his considerable talent of persuasion on those who governed New Mexico. [50] Both had been received with courtesy and heard in patience. It was about the Great Divide that a Lieutenant and two dragoons delivered Armijo's reply to Kearny. It was as noncommittal as it was courteous.

There is, of course, no record of what James Magoffin said to Armijo and others in Santa Fe, nor of their replies. What he said to Armijo and Archuleta, second in command, seems likely to have been quite different. Armijo was later to make ineffectual gestures in defense of New Mexico. To Archuleta, Magoffin suggested that "by pronunciamiento he might secure for himself western New Mexico on which Kearny had no designs." [88]

Truth is rarely for sale; deceit always is. Among Kearny's orders was one from the Secretary for War: "Should you conquer New Mexico and take possession of New Mexico and California or considerable places in either, you will establish temporary civilian governments therein. . . ."

Long before the Army and ten miles south of the Great Divide, earliest caravans on the Road encountered the first New Mexican settlement at "Gallinas," the "Vega," now Las Vegas on the eastern flank of the Sangre de Cristo.[106] M. M. Marmaduke, later a Governor of Missouri, arrived there July 22, 1822, at the "ranche, the temporary residence of Juan Peno" where the travelers were politely received. It was a small adobe on a fine spring that contributed to the flow of Rio Gallinas and, so Marmaduke said, to 160,000 sheep grazing the wide slopes about.

The year previous, the spring and several hundred square miles around had been granted to Luis Maria Cabeza de Vaca, the parcel known as *Nuestra Senora de los Dolores de las Vegas,* Our Lady of the Sorrows of the Meadows. De Vaca with seventeen children and servants settled on Ojo de Gallinas (Spring of the Chickens) but in very few years all his livestock were stolen by Comanches and Apaches and he gave up the venture. In Pena Blanca, a small settlement less exposed to Plains Indians, de Vaca was killed by one of his countrymen in 1827. He had a great deal less luck and less endurance than his forebearer, Alvar Nunez Cabeza de Vaca who, shipwrecked on the Gulf Coast east of Louisiana, traversed on foot the hazards of the thousands or so miles to safety in Mexico City. Perhaps there he prospered; certainly he proliferated: de Vaca is as common a name among Spanish Americans as Smith among Anglo-Saxons.

The full surname: Cabeza de Vaca, translates as "Head of Cow." Some Castillians are born to a lisp which gives to a "V" the sound of "B". Modern Spanish spells "cow" with a "V": *vaca*. Modern Castillians pronounce it with a "B": *baca*.

When Dr. Adolph Wislizenus came to Las Vegas in 1846, just ahead of the Army, it had its modern name, about 100 houses and much poverty (Map 25). This settlement and the country was much in contrast to his native heath: Konigsee, Germany. Wislizenus had been a student at the Universities of Jena, Gottingen and Tubingen but as then students holding political opinions divergent from those of their elders (and German politics then were on the far right of Louis XIV) were no more admired than they are today. Wislizenus fled to Switzerland to escape imprisonment and to complete training at the University of Zurich. His profession was medicine but his hobbies included meteorology, botany and geology. Wislizenus noted that for wagons the west bank of the Gallinas was a steep and difficult ascent on strata bearing Cretaceous fossils.

Gentle Susan came with the Army, and to see the southwest in its early day through her eyes was to see it sharp and clear, margins unblurred by myopia of years or cataracts of age. But it was to see the unfamiliar, the strange, through eyes accustomed to surroundings of comfort and ease. At Las Vegas, this daughter of Kentucky arrived at " . . . 2 o'k and dinner was called for." Meanwhile Jose, her carriage driver, went to see his wife for the first time in perhaps a year and a "monkey show in the States never did better business than he could have done, if he had set me up at even *dos* or *tres reales* on sight. My veil was ingenuously drawn down . . . for the better protection of my face . . . from the constant stare of the 'natives'. . . . In the room not only the children but *mujeres* (women) and *hombres* (men) swarmed around me like bees. The women were clad in camisas and petticoats only . . . and their far-famed rebozas. . . . All took a look and a seat on the floor . . . some had their babies under their rebozas. I shant say at what business. When all that were in were seated out came the little 'cigaritas' and the general smoking commenced. The old man spread a blanket on the little table before me, on this he spread a clean white cloth . . . on top of this he put another cloth so black with dirt and grease that it resembled the more common brown than white sheeting of which it was really made. And then the dinner of half a dozen *tortillas* made of blue corn, and not a plate, but wrapped in a napkin twin brother to the last tablecloth. Oh how my heart sickened, to say nothing of my stomach, a cheese . . . and two earthen *ollas* of a mixture of meat, *chilly verde* (chili verde, green peppers) & onions boiled together. . . . We had neither knives, forks or spoons, but made as good substitutes as we could by doubling a piece of *tortilla* but . . . I could not eat a dish so strong." [2]

James Webb had been eastbound at Las Vegas the year before and was much concerned with the possibiilty of loss of profits from the trading venture just completed.[25] New Mexican authorities, always in need of funds, taxed imports as much as the traffic would bear. Much of the profits of Missouri traders by necessity were in livestock. These were portable but always there was danger of loss of them to Indians on the Prairie. Traders preferred silver coins (legal tender in Missouri) and gold bullion. The outflow of metal disturbed New Mexican authorities. In Santa Fe, Webb heard rumor of impending export tax on bullion and coin. As his profits were in precious metal, he was concerned. Webb arrived untaxed in Las Vegas but still within reach of custom officials who must have known, or at least suspected, that somewhere in his baggage was silver or gold, for Webb had livestock no greater than the minimum for transit of the Prairies.

Because an unmentioned circumstance seemed likely to delay him a few weeks, soon after arrival in Las Vegas, Webb went hunting for geese grazing in cornfields south of the village. He had a sharper eye for lay of the land than for the game he appeared to stalk. Crawling alongside an *acequia* leading toward the geese, Webb came on a deep hoof-print in the soft mud of the irrigation ditch. Without pausing, he dropped the buckskin bag into the hole. A fortunate shot a few minutes later allowed him to return to the settlement with a goose. A week later, worried for fear the extended soaking would deteriorate the buckskin, Webb went hunting again. With none the wiser, he retrieved the soaked bag and cached it in some crevice in Cretaceous rocks on the west side of the Gallinas. It rested safely and was recovered, untaxed, just as his wagons rolled eastward.

At the Soil Conservation Office in Las Vegas, a busy engineer looked up from work long enough to hear my inquiry for data on the route of the long abandoned Road. "There are three possibilities: the Arrot collection at Highlands University down the street; Henry Biesman, a civil engineer with an office on the Plaza beyond; aerial photographs in the Office in Pecos." Before I could thank him he turned back to work and when I did, he replied absently: "Don't mention it."

Early Mexican mining lamp

At Highlands University library I inquired for Mr. Wallace, librarian, and learned he was out of town. To a substitute I spoke of my hope to see the maps in the Arrot collection. He disappeared, returned in a few moments to riffle through the card file and, laying out a card, inquired would it help. I read the title: Gregg, Josiah: *Commerce of the Prairie,* and explained I was familiar with the book. When I repeated my request, he responded: "Follow me."

We passed through the stacks, down aisles and up a flight or two of stairs. While my guide hunted about the shelves, I examined books. When I looked up he had disappeared. Some fifteen minutes later another stranger appeared and inquired of my presence. I explained.

"This part of the library is not open to the public," he said, "but I can show you the collection."

Downstairs he opened a small file of cards and I noted from the index on the lid that it was a minor gold mine: a list of microfilm including a diary I had not seen and at least two maps likely to be of aid. As I assayed the ore I explained I had not much time and that later, by mail, I would make what arrangements they required for interlibrary loan of microfilm. Could I see what maps in the collection might bear segments of the Road?

"No," explained the young man with some embarrassment. "These films are not available by interlibrary loan. Mr. Wallace interprets terms of the Arrot bequest as preventing either the original documents or the microfilm from leaving the library."

I was naive enough to be astonished; moreover, I was chagrinned. I had had help for the asking from laborers, farmers, librarians, ranchers, museum curators, engineers, filling station attendants, a dentist, a doctor, even a drunk with breath so alcoholic as certain to be sterile, from all of whom I might logically have expected nothing. Here, an institution whose very *raison d'etre* was the spread of knowledge had metamorphosed to a means of preventing it: bibliomorticians content to catalog, determined to embalm.

When we came to the map collection, the young man courteously laid them out sheet by sheet, contents of some eight or ten shallow drawers. Among the high per cent of tinted National Geographic cartography was a photostat of an early map by Lieutenant Wheeler, showing on a small scale most of the territory of New Mexico and, in a general way, the early roads. I later secured a copy from the National Archives. A real treasure, so I thought, was a colored "Sectional Map of Colfax and Mora Counties" compiled in 1889 by the Maxwell Land Company showing the approximate location of the Road trending across townships and sections. I traced hastily through thin paper the Road in Mora County. It was a year before I learned that a copy could be had for the asking if only one knew where to ask. By then I had carried the Road across that area on aerial photographs.

I found in the Plaza beyond Highlands University, the office of Henry Biesman, civil engineer. The Plaza of Las Vegas is "Old Town" on the west side of Rio Gallinas, a small flow of water throttling on garbage. Biesman's office was a clutter of map cabinets, a drafting table heaped with tracings and maps, among tripods, transits, chains and a confusion of essential debris common to the office of a busy engineer whose filing system is much like my own. Working among the clutter were a boy, an attractive matron and a man in conversation with another. When I could claim Mr. Biesman's attention I explained briefly my interest in all maps bearing any part of the Road to Santa Fe. As the silence which followed grew long I inquired: "Do you have many such requests for information?"

"Oh, we get all sorts of crackpots here," replied Biesman cheerfully. "You mean something like this?" he inquired as he shoved across the drafting table a preliminary map from the U.S. Geological Survey and pointed to a fine line dashed across one corner, bearing "Santa Fe Trail (Approx.)" As a licensed engineer practicing within the area of the map, Biesman was recipient of a preliminary copy along with a request to note any errors. The Geological Survey now shows on their new maps the Road as it is visible on aerial photographs from which they transcribe on paper contours of the ground by a method near to black magic. I had made use of several such maps but I had not seen this one. Later, Mr. Biesman produced a 1906 tracing of an older map of Las Vegas and vicinity, showing the Road coming into town from the northeast.

"Mind if I use this?" I asked, reaching for a triangular scale which I used as a straight-edge.

"You know better than that," said Henry as he took it from me and offered a plastic triangle recovered from beneath the confusion of maps on the drafting table. In this upsmanship I was two down as I transferred data onto my map while the young man, Biesman's son, asked questions about my interest in antiquities. It was not a good job I had done and thinking to do better with more time, I inquired the cost of a print of the 1906 tracing. The boy asked his mother who spoke to her husband, then busy with a customer.

"Four dollars," replied Henry.

Mrs. Biesman looked pained. "For that?" she asked, holding up the yard and a half of tracing.

"Four dollars," said Henry.

"Let's see," mused Mrs. Biesman, reaching for a scale. "It is only three feet long by. . . ."

"Oh, I would need only that part holding the Trail," I interrupted.

"That would be $3.00," responded Henry firmly.

"You may have it for $1.00," said Mrs. Biesman as she inserted into the machine the tracing with print-paper beneath and began to run off a copy.

"Just keep on being a nuisance," advised Henry as he went out the door loaded with transit, tripod, chain and followed by a customer, "and they'll find some more maps, maybe."

We talked for some time, Mrs. Biesman and her son, about the southwest and the men who made it. They pointed across the Plaza to a long, one-story adobe building, now plastered and newly painted, as that one according to folklore from the roof of which Kearny read the proclamation that lifted New Mexico from hands of owners and placed it in hands of invaders. Mrs. Biesman was not positive it was *the* building but they were certain it was the oldest on the Plaza. To a stranger less skeptical, it seemed so reasonable

as to be true. I recalled from eye-witness accounts that a
ladder had been provided and that Kearny from the top of
some flat-roofed building on the Plaza had proclaimed to a
captive audience as if banishing strange fevers, frenzies,
pestilence and unwholesome airs and as a man administering
a pomade of herbs. What his audience heard must have been
all wormwood and gall.

To read now the words falling on people gathered there
nearly a century and a quarter ago is to read a capitulation
from logic to rhetoric and one is made painfully aware that
words of conquerors have changed not at all: they come as
friends, so they say, and none who hear are such fools as to
believe.

Mrs. Biesman courteously invited me to return next
morning, explaining that overnight they might recall somewhere in the files another map bearing a segment of the
Road. She inquired had I seen Fort Union and I was embarrassed to admit I had passed it by, the more so because I
could not easily spare the time (i.e. money). She urged that
I see it when I admitted that it was unlikely I would be in
these parts soon again.

Next morning I drove back north toward the Turkey
Mountains and over the highway I had come, and a few miles
south from them turned northwest. The approach to what
remains of Fort Union is through country as wide now as ever
it was when caravans came this way, for very few trees grow
in this region save by aid beyond their own efforts. Asphalt
reaching ruins of Fort Union passes a small lake on the right,

Fort Union

water filling a depression of about a quarter of a square mile in basalt flows. On the slope east of the lake one may see ruts of the Road deepened by erosion to a level lower than wagons left them en route from Fort Union to Barclay's Fort on the Mora.

Under the bright sun of a warm August morning, the sandy margin of the water is a striking anomaly: it is coated with ice and snow. It must have been a welcome sight to earlier travelers. One need almost touch it to obviate the deception. And one need only taste the white efflorescence, fine crystals of sodium sulfate, nitrate and assorted compounds leached by rain from flows of lava about, to know it must have been a disappointment to those who saw it long ago. It was then, as now, interesting but useless water for it is poison to livestock. A stout fence of barbed wire sets it apart in isolation.

Fort Union, a small area on the vast grassed southwest slope from the Turkey Mountains, is a scattered grove of tall chimneys flanked here and there by eroded segments of adobe walls divided symmetrically by firm flagstone walks little affected by time. Now some years a National Monument, it has the cleanliness of such, uncluttered by Madison Avenue balderdash. A small sign tersely recommends: "Enjoy it; leave it as you find it." I found it a fascinating relic on an 1861 vector of commerce (Map 26).

After 1846, the Army came to be the chief freighter over the Road. Before them, traders looked after themselves between appeals to Senator Benton for protection from Indians. After them, contractors to the Army got protection from the Fort and as a by-product, so did traders. A mile west of what the tourist sees now, near the foot of an unnamed mesa (a flow from some vent in the Sangre de Cristo Mountains westward), is the 1851 site of a fort of logs. For economy it was constructed by soldiers themselves from timber cut in the Turkey Mountains.[107] They were unaware of the advantages of peeled logs. In but few years, crevices beneath the bark held bedbugs so numerous that privates slept outside their barracks when weather permitted, and termites so abundant that, quite literally, they ate up the logs. Ten years later

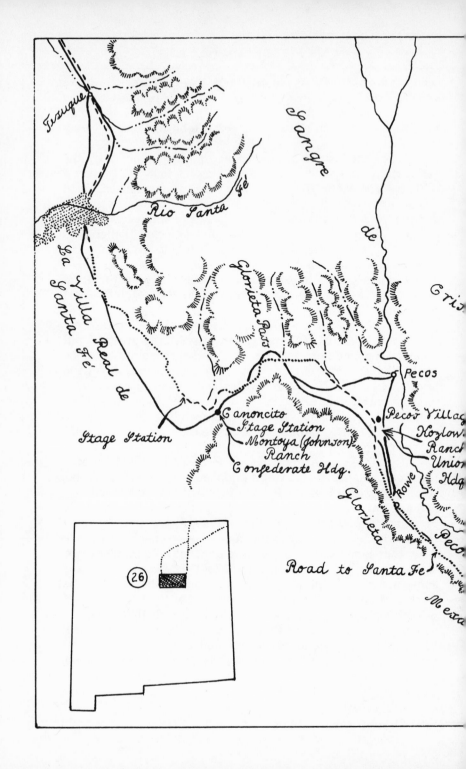

Tesuque

Rio Santa Fé

Sangre

La Villa Real de Santa Fé

de

Glorieta Pass

Cris

Pecos

Stage Station

Canoncito
Stage Station
Montoya (Johnson)
Ranch
Confederate Hdq.

Pecos Village

Kozlow
Ranch

Union
Hdq.

Rowe

Glorieta

Peco

26

Road to Santa Fe

Mesa

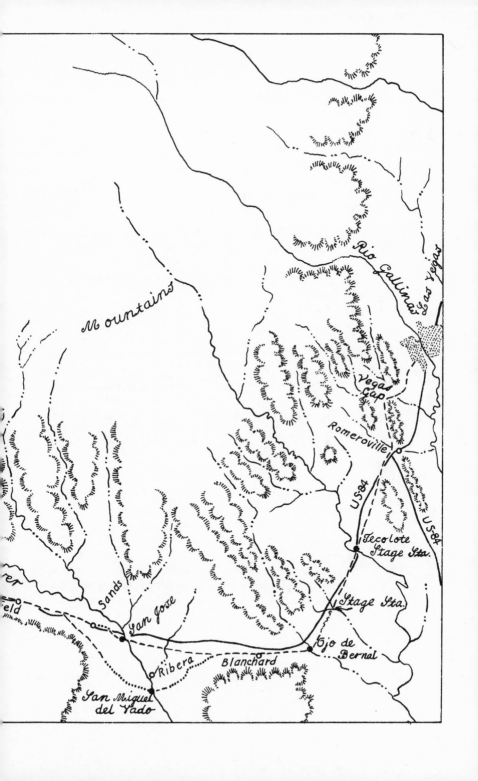

the crumbling structure was replaced by more and larger buildings of adobe brick on a site to the east. The new Fort was intended to be a point of residence and supply, rather than for defense. When, in 1862, confident Confederates came up the Rio Grande intent on capture of the Fort, Union forces hastily built a third nearby. It was a star-shaped affair of breastworks and underground embrasures. A make-do located and constructed in panic, it would have been a trap had ever the enemy reached the mesa a mile west. From higher ground a howitzer could easily (and did when tried as an experiment) drop shells into any point of the star. As virtue is always triumphant, always have lives of privates depended on such judgment of their officers who, when the contingent is wiped out and its men forgotten, are remembered as heroic leaders.

What the tourist sees of the second Fort Union—tall chimneys and sections of unroofed adobe walls—is a long row of officer quarters on the west, and east across a wide parade ground the remnants of barracks, smithy, commissary, warehouse, hospital and guardhouse. The latter is of mortared stone: half a dozen small cells strongly built, complete save for doors. They are as primitive as the punishment sometimes imposed on those within. A diet of bread and water, even to those who have not experienced it, seems more a moral censure than a physical punishment. The old English custom of drawing-and-quartering or flaying-alive had no survivors to attest to the efficacy of those correctives. But men suspended for hours by their thumbs, if they had strong hearts and stout arteries, might remember the experience for the years left them. It is not of record that recalcitrants at Fort Union were moral men after that punishment as presumably they had been immoral before.

"Officer's Row" is now a ruin of quarters which must have been quite adequate for the place, and even the time. One among them housed Colonel Christopher Carson a few months and next door lived Lieutenant Richard D. Russell and his bride, Marian.

It is not often one may read the recollections of a migrant who, as a child, traveled the Road, saw Santa Fe, lived at Fort Union, Camp Nicols and Tecolote and it is rarer yet to read the words of one who saw all five and more. Marian Russell saw them all and for her memoirs of a rugged life on the frontier, either she spoke or her daughter-in-law wrote, in words nearer to poetry than prose.[108]

Having come over the Road from West Port, one day on the dusty street of Albuquerque, Marian had been charmed as might be a girl of seven, by a baby in the arms of a matron with thick bright red hair. It was, she later learned, Adeline Wilson who had escaped slavery of the Comanches and with the help of Governor David Meriwether recovered as much as body and soul might from such a nightmare and who, that very moment, was awaiting the stage which would return her to Texas.

In Santa Fe, where her mother operated a boarding house for the military, Marian had walked the Plaza guided by the paternal arm of Colonel Carson who led her among the covered wagons crowding space there. Archbishop Jean La Tour and Father Valient, characters made known through Willa Cather's superb prose, Marian as a student at the seminary spoke to as Bishop Lamy and Father Vicario. Marian's mother, a widow, had made Bishop Lamy's robe of luxurious imported cloth and her fine stitches had formed the altar piece for the Masonic Lodge at Fort Union from a remnant of cloth from which the robe was fashioned. The altar cloth hung last in the Lodge at Wagon Mound.

Crossing the Plaza in Santa Fe late in an afternoon, Marian had seen and spoken to a prisoner behind a barred window at the west end of the Palace. He told her he had a daughter her age and for Marian's entertainment sang softly "Shoo Fly, Don't Bother I" as he had done for his own child. Next morning, with two warm cinnamon cookies as a gift, Marian returned to visit her new friend. She found him in the same chair behind the bars, sitting very still, dead with his shirt-front a large spread of brown-red clotted blood. She did not know, she only heard, he had been shot in the dusk of the afternoon he sang for her, to prevent betrayal of political secrets. Perhaps there was less blood shed in New Mexican politics this last year, but the underlying principles have changed scarcely at all.

At Fort Union, in 1864, where her mother made ends

meet with income from a boarding house, the tall slender long-haired girl learned what an unexpected sight on the frontier might do to a young and bright mind: "I was rounding a corner suddenly, my green veil streaming out behind me, the wind blowing hair in my eyes when I met him face to face. The whole world stood still."

Soon after the earth resumed rotation on its axis and orbit about the sun, Marian and her mother returned to Santa Fe. Mail service between Fort and Capital was slow and as the young girl turned from her first disappointment she was surprised when Lieutenant Richard Russell slipped his arm through hers. "I followed where he led me and soon we were at Santa Fe's great arched gateway, all alone. For one forbidden moment I stood within the circle of his arms. I saw the wide old trail flowing like a river through the gateway and far away. I heard the tinkle of distant sheep bells. I saw the little girl that had been me, the little girl of the blue pinafore and long brown braids slipping away among shadows on the trail. I knew she was gone forever. I was conscious of Richard's arms about me and his bared fair head near my own. I was a woman now, with the heart and soul of a woman."

As is inevitable when the whole world has been stopped, the fair Lieutenant and the tall slender girl were married six months later in the Chapel at Fort Union, February 1865. "I did not hear a great deal of the wedding ceremony, for a sacred and triumphant ceremony was taking place in my heart, one in which all the bells of heaven rang out."

When her Lieutenant was detailed to aid in construction of Camp Nicols in what was to be the Oklahoma Panhandle, Marian Russell invited to supper as guest of honor her Lieutenant's Colonel. Carson's eyes held humor as he promised to send for her immediately when there was a place for her to live with her husband at Camp Nichols. "Years after Colonel Carson's death I was to go and stand in the ruins of that little room and to remember the sound of his kindly voice refusing my heart's desire. I was also to remember Colonel Carson as he looked, coming across the Plaza at Santa Fe to take my arm and hold it closely as he piloted me among the covered wagons. . . . Colonel Carson piloted me surely through the troublesome days of my childhood."

More than sixty years later, Mrs. Russell recalled the days on a dappled grey and the ride of more than two hundred miles from Fort Union to Camp Nicols as something more than just memorable. On arrival at "White Creek" Carson asked her to dismount and go with him "to a pile of stones by the wayside. He said they marked the grave of Mrs. White." *

Camp Nicols for the short period May to September 1865, was the point to which caravans were escorted from Fort Union and by Carson's men guarded the long miles to Fort Larned on the Arkansas. Shortly before abandonment of the Camp "One morning the Colonel came leading his big black horse. . . . He wanted to say 'Goodby.' His last words were: 'Remember, child, the injuns will get you if you ride alone out thar.' I watched him as he rode away. I saw the great black horse enter and mingle with the dancing mirage on the horizon. I was destined never to see my friend again; but I have not forgotten him."

From Camp Nicols, Marian and her Lieutenant returned to Fort Union, and when Richard Russell was mustered from the Army the couple built at Tecolote on the Road to Santa Fe a combined trading post and home. "That second year at Tecolote news reached us of Colonel Carson's death. Strange that death should always seem so unreal and untrue. Kit Carson, the Happy Warrior of the West, could never die. Along the Old Trail even today there are chips his axe left, stone walls his hands built. . . . I cannot think of Colonel Carson as dust in a Taos cemetery. I only think of hawk wings against a western sky."

Richard and Marian Russell were confident the U.S. Land Office meant what it said when in 1874 it threw open the Beaubien and Miranda grant (Maxwell's empire) to settlement. They established a ranch at the head of Picketwire Valley on the first waters of El Rio de las Animas Perdidas en

---

* It was, perhaps, the grave of Mr. White. Mrs. White was killed, while a captive, somewhere on the Canadian River in the Texas Panhandle.

Purgatorio. In 1888 they received from the Maxwell Land Company (by then owned by Dutch capitalists) notice to "abandon the land that was ours" by right of patent. On August 24 of that year six armed deputies led by Sheriff William Hurn of Las Animas arrived at the settlement deep within the Sangre de Cristo Mountains. The settlers, about to be dispossessed, gathered and Russell, once a man of war spoke now as a man of peace as he urged the armed men to leave. Two shots interrupted a drawn breath and Marian's Lieutenant fell, mortally wounded.

"At the age of eighty-nine I made a pilgrimage into the land of yesterday . . . Among fields of corn I found the ruins of Camp Nicols where I spent my honeymoon. A little dent marked the spot where my dugout had been, the place where the shortest, sweetest summer of my life had been spent; where great wagons had gone creaking past on the long road to Santa Fe."

"At Fort Union I found the ruins of the old chapel. Here I stood a demure bride in hoop skirt and velvet cloak. In this crumbling Fort I found my little house where Colonel Carson once came to lay his hands on my head, 'Child, you must not cry.' At the ruins of Tecolote the stone walls of the little trading post still stood but the rooms behind were in ruins. An old wooden bedstead lay among the fallen stones, a bed that once had boasted valences white as snow. Rank weeds filled the doorway where my babies had played."

Mrs. Russell's narrative of a remarkable life ends with a note by her biographer that from injuries received in an automobile accident, Marian Russell, with ninety-one years, died Christmas Eve, 1936. "It was by Richard's side they laid her. As I watched the flakes of falling snow I thought of a great arched gateway where a tall young soldier stood, his arms about a slender lovely girl in a fluttering golden dress . . . the end of a long, long trail." [108]

The words Marian Russell left posterity have not changed but time has done much to the Fort that was her home for bright and happy months. Tall chimneys of burnt brick rise starkly from the prairie and high above crumbled adobe walls. From them I walked eastward across what once was the corral for mules and oxen resting from the labor of pulling heavy wagons on the long gentle slope from the Turkey Mountains. A few hundred yards east I found ruts of the Road as it came from a distant sag in the skyline. Some five or six miles in that direction there had been a stage and forage station in Marian's time. One may see such a distance through air clear as the peal of bells but nothing there interrupts the skyline now.

Returning across the prairie toward the Fort, I came on a dozen or so handwrought square nails on the sand. Remembering the sign, I resisted temptation. Fifty feet toward the Fort another scattering of several score marked the pale reddish sand. I picked up three, a felony I understand, and thus became one of the lesser among western outlaws. The nails, small slivers of corrosion, are a great deal heavier than one might think, as now no matter where they are, they rest on conscience.

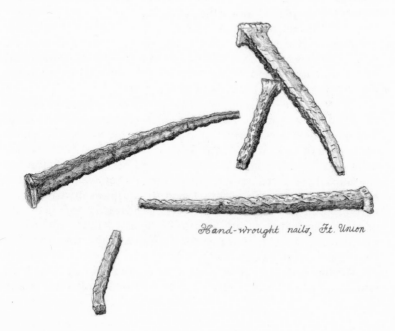

Hand-wrought nails, Ft. Union

Returning south on the highway by a short detour at Watrous—the Mora Crossing, site of Alexander Barclay's Fort and the quarters of Mr. Kroenig's camel—I found the old adobe stage station still a home for someone. Beyond, half a short mile, is the considerable corral that once held blowing mules and their fresh replacements. The mortared brown sandstone in walls five to six feet high encloses a rough square about a hundred feet on the side, amid cotton-woods and willows scattered on the floodplain of the Rio Sapello. It is a very small stream which, nearby, joins the Mora, no larger. The corral is one of the few remaining adjuncts of the Road patiently awaiting destruction which seems inevitable for such.

South two miles beyond Las Vegas, the Road to Santa Fe turned sharp west through "Vegas Gap," now El Puerto del Norte, the Door of the North, between two slender cuestas at the margin of the colossal upfold from which erosion carved the Sangre de Cristo Mountains. (Map 27). Behind the Gap, Governor of *Nuevo Mejico*, Don Manuel Armijo and his men lay in ambush for the invaders. Dissension sundered tactics at a place and time when a hundred might have stopped a thousand, and Armijo retreated westward.

Kearny had entered Las Vegas a Colonel; he left it a General. Promotion came with dispatches newly arrived from Ft. Leavenworth, delivered appropriately by a Major Swords. From the settlement the General sent cavalry in columns of fours toward the enemy reported in the Gap and ordered infantry up the gentle east slope of the cuestas to outflank Armijo's spearmen. Marcellus Edwards, one among the infantry on horseback, remembered his company had been issued cartridges in camp near Bent's Fort and before the charge on the Gap, these were passed out as far as they went: ten each. He thought it an odd circumstance to equip an invasion with neither food nor ammunition.[50] When Edwards and his companions charged the Gap, he quickly learned that shortage of provisions was the more serious, for Armijo was then in Glorieta Pass fifty miles to the west.

Tecolote is six miles beyond the Door of the North in which the old Road crossed steeply inclined strata, the roots of mountains. The settlement is now so small as scarcely to be noticed from a car speeding on the new highway which misses it by a quarter-mile. In another time vehicles made slower approach to what, for the earliest, was the first settlement west of Independence. It is probably no larger now than when Marian Russell knew it. Should you ever see Tecolote it will be a sad bit smaller. The stone trading post and home which contained the wooden bedstead with valances white as snow was being demolished when I reached it, for what better purpose than a notable landmark no one seemed to know.

At the little settlement now in its hundred and fiftieth winter, begins the long slope of Tecolote Hill. It is scarcely perceptible to a transient in an automobile, trivia to wheels of rubber impelled by horsepower on pavement. To wheels of wood shod with iron and powered by oxen, Tecolote Hill was formidable. It was sometimes the focus of the worst traffic jam between Independence and Santa Fe.

Out on the wide prairie eastward, when one caravan crept slowly up behind another, it was customary for the faster, and it was never more than slightly so, to swing out and with bullwhips popping, inch by the slower. At Tecolote Hill near to the markets most profitable for those who reached them first, for a wagon train to pass another was an affront scarcely ever offered, rarely forgiven and never forgotten. Men of the wagons toiling up the long slope, resting for intervals longer nearer the crest, were frequently dependent on each other in the miles and months of approach to Tecolote. The community of effort out there not only facilitated commerce, it was commonly a factor of survival. On Tecolote Hill, it was a very rare caravan that passed another.[25]

From the top of the slope south of Tecolote, Bernal Hill was in sight and somewhere among cedars thick about its base was Ojo de Bernal. The name is literally "Eye of Bernal," colloquial for Bernal Spring. Bernal Hill has been rechristened "Starvation Peak" by antiquarians in the New Mexico Highway Department, accustomed also to changing the landscape.

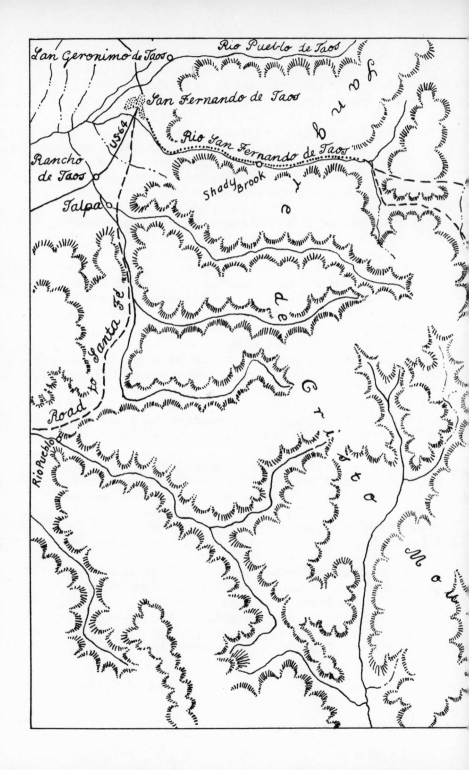

San Geronimo de Taos

Rio Pueblo de Taos

San Fernando de Taos

US64

Rio San Fernando de Taos

Shady Brook

Rancho de Taos

Talpa

Road to Santa Fe

Rio Pueblo

Sangre de Cristo Mountains

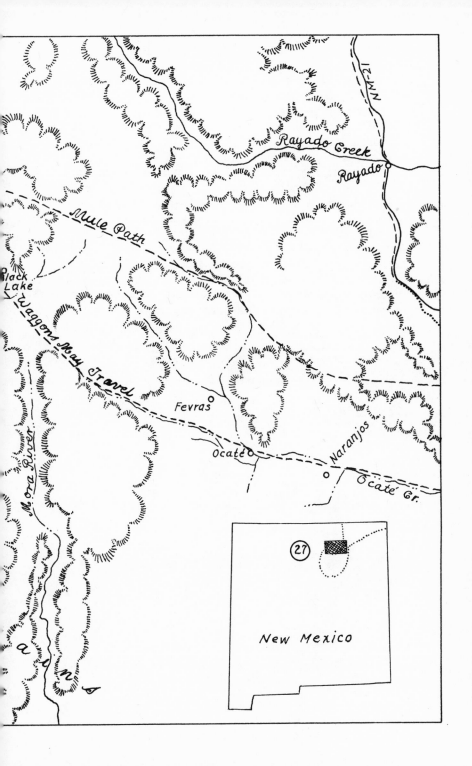

Ojo de Bernal is difficult of access by a rough track branching from the highway (Map 27). Almost forgotten since wagons passed here, the settlement has the same number if not the same scattering of houses Wislizenus saw a hundred and twenty-eight years past: about twelve. Most are maroon adobe, a hue so slightly different from the rocks around that they appear to be a part of them. By stage, Davis reached Ojo de Bernal and thought the water "strong with bicarbonate of soda, unpleasant and unhealthy to taste." [26] It is still distinctive in savor, but it is the taste of calcium sulphate, dissolved from thin beds of anhydrite in the bright vermillion and deep maroon sandstones and shales of Permian Age which make the rugged land about.

Long ago (some 250 millions of years) this region was the margin and shallow floor of an arm of a Permian sea reaching from the Gulf, beyond here and northeast into Kansas.

Bernal Hill

On the flanking lands reptiles scurried about. Small in comparison to some among their descendants, some were agile, others ponderous and all were bizarre. Among them were ancestors of dinosaurs which ruled the firmament in a later era, the genes of *Tyrannosaurus rex* in their cells. The harsh scales and cold blood of others were to evolve in another fifty millions of years to smooth feathers and warm blood of the first birds which flew in safety over the land ruled by *Tyrannosaurus*, that reptile of such gigantic menace as to appear a foible of science fiction.

In endless time, the slow gentle downward movement of the crust which allowed an arm of a Permian sea to reach far into the continent was reversed, eventually to sever the arm of the ocean. Before then a change in climate allowed very little rain to fall on this Permian land and salty sea. By evaporation, perhaps a meter or two a day, the enclosed sea became less and less. As only water evaporated and dissolved solids remained, in time the brine became so concentrated in soluble compounds common to all marine waters that first a thin layer of limestone, calcium carbonate, then a thicker one of anhydrite, calcium sulfate, was precipitated on the floor of the shrinking sea. When more than four-fifths of the water had returned to air by evaporation, salt was precipitated, thin in Kansas and up to three thousand feet in thickness in eastern New Mexico and western Texas.

Within the very arid land, in the very deepest depressions of the shallow Permian basin, now almost dry, there remained large lakes of bittern on the salt. When, in time, their waters vanished into the air, they left in the depressions layers of compounds of potassium, magnesium, bromine and other esoteric elements. Covered by wind-blown sands of what by then was the driest of deserts, the evaporites were protected from resolution. They have remained a small part of the rocks which make the crust of the earth and at no great depth, around 600 feet, they are mined in the vicinity of Carlsbad, New Mexico, for the potassium fertilizer of commerce.

Susan Magoffin had seen the bright red mountains and mesas around Ojo de Bernal soon after Wislizenus and before

Davis, and the collection of a dozen or so adobe houses in the vicinity of the Spring. From an entry in her diary, at a camp a few miles beyond Ojo de Bernal, one may learn that Kentucky mores did not match New Mexican customs: ". . . it is truly shocking to my modesty to pass through such places with gentlemen. The women slap about with their arms and necks bare, perhaps their bosoms exposed . . . if they are about to cross a little creek . . . they will pull their dresses above their knees and paddle through the water like ducks." [2]

Susan noted her disapproval in a camp two or three miles east of San Miguel del Vado on the Pecos River. Somewhere in that vicinity were wagon tracks leading from Fort Smith, Arkansas Territory, west across what now is Oklahoma, up the Canadian River across the Texas Panhandle, into New Mexico and up the Pecos River to join the Road to Santa Fe. It was a trail marked by several thousand immigrants and gold seekers and but very few traders.

San Miguel del Vado (San Miguel of the ford, on the Pecos River) was the southernmost point of the Road to Santa Fe. A visitor there now will find it a somnambulent collection of dark ocherous-red adobe houses, some eight or ten the homes of about sixty people amid the ruins of a great many more, for the population once reached three thousand. High over all stands a huge adobe church, its two square towers and massive walls coated with light tan stucco in contrast to the dark houses and ruins about. When Thomas James saw San Miguel in 1821 there were more than 100 houses, "two miserable flour mills" [109] powered by water from the Pecos, and a new and impressive church. Four years later Marmaduke was warmed by his welcome ("the natives rejoiced") as he passed through to camp at "Saint James" (San Jose) [10] three miles northwest. Davis, twenty-eight years later, spoke of San Miguel as an adobe town with a population of about 1,000 around a plaza (it has none now), at the southeast corner of which "Howland and two others were shot. Kendall was saved by intercession of Gregorio Vigil, now living there in reduced circumstances." [26]

Davis spoke of a Texas-size 1841 tragedy, a fantastic venture out of a state prone to fantasy engendered by size. It

At San Miguel del Vado

began small as all catastrophes, even in a large state. It had its beginning in hearsay falling on the ears and unfortunately filling to the exclusion of reason, the mind of General Mirabeau B. Lamar, President of Texas.

Texas had declared itself a Republic in 1836, independent of Mexico. As it had no western boundary, it promptly claimed one: the Rio Grande. Independence was not to be a matter of proclamation and boundary. Mexico, a loose political unit, accepted neither. The parent country preoccupied with other disputes, allowed the rebellious community an interval of peace, more or less.

It is the strength or weakness of newly independent states on this and other continents to impose on their neighbours the freedom they claim. Presumably it springs from the impulse of better men to impose their virtues on inferiors. Someone, somehow, convinced President Lamar that he need only offer the privilege and New Mexicans would immediately pledge allegiance to the Republic. He took recourse in obliquity: set in motion organization of an expedition ostensibly to investigate by trial the possibilities of trade between one fragment of Mexico claiming independence and half of another which remained very much a part of the whole.

The group leaving Austin numbered about 320 men. Of these, roughly 270 were military commanded by General Mc-Leod, Colonel Cooke, Major Howard, Captain Sutton, Lieutenants Hall and Lubbock, along with Surgeon Whittaker and Dr. Brenham.[88] Perhaps many of the remainder were traders for there appear to have been about nine wagons of merchandise. One among the group, George W. Kendall, was a tourist and editor of the New Orleans *Picayune*. Somewhere in the baggage were printed offers to accept as citizens of the Republic whatever New Mexicans could read and were restless under the harsh rule of Manuel Armijo, Governor of New Mexico.

Kendall, a citizen of the United States, records that the rank and file thought it a mercantile venture as did he when, in his home town he secured a visa from the Mexican Consul. Kendall's account of the expedition is that of a reporter and participant.[110] As the first, he is detailed, as the second he could not remain unbiased for he underwent cruelties lethal to the less fit. In either capacity it does not seem reasonable that he was so naive as to regard a military escort, even through Comanche-land, of 270 men a necessity for a trading venture. Most observers of that day thought it an expedition to somehow take control, with 270 soldiers, of territory east of the Rio Grande, the claimed boundary of Texas: ill-conceived, poorly planned and disastrously executed. Whatever the purpose, results verify the opinion.

Kendall's account of the miles between Austin, Texas, and Anton Chico just south of San Miguel is a narrative of thirst and hunger, troubles and tragedy. Thereafter it is an account of disaster. Confident they were only some seventy-five miles from San Miguel, "Messers. Howland, Baker and Rosenbury (were sent) to procure sugar, coffee and bread-stuffs, and to consult with the inhabitants, more particularly with some of the principal men, as to the reception the expedition would probably meet."

George Kendall was not to see Rosenbury again and he was to see across the Plaza in San Miguel only the back of Baker: kneeling, blindfolded, alone as ever few men are. Kendall was to hear the volley which left Baker writhing in agony and to hear yet one more shot which stilled his contortions.

Kendall used a great many words in his narrative and perhaps as much might have been said with half as many. None were superfluous when he spoke of meeting Howland. With Van Ness, Brenham, Fitzgerald and Howard, Kendall stood disarmed before a small adobe house in San Miguel as Samuel Howland emerged; left arm a dark clot of blood from a ragged sabre-slash, left ear and cheek cut off. Howland marched past the startled prisoners and as he turned to speak, "a placid smile of resignation lit up the other side of his face, a contrast almost unearthly." Kendall saw his companion impelled to his knees against a wall at the southeast corner of the Plaza and there saw him die: "as noble, as generous, as brave a man as ever walked the earth." [110]

From what had transpired, one may be certain Samuel Howland was.

Some days after dispatch of Howland, Baker and Rosenbury, and without news from them, on closer approach to San Miguel, Messrs. Lewis, Van Ness, Howard, Fitzgerald and Dr. Brenham were sent with letters to the alcalde of San Miguel. Kendall accompanied them. The "letters set forth that a large party of Texans (were) approaching, that their intentions were in every way pacific. . . . Several of General Lamar's proclamations were . . . to be distributed among the principal citizens, the purport of which was that the expedition was sent for the purpose of trading, and that if the inhabitants of New Mexico were not disposed to join, peacefully, the Texas standard, the expedition was to retire immediately. . . . Not a doubt existed that the liberal terms offered would be accepted by the population living within the limits of Texas and who so long had been groaning under a misrule the most tyrannical."

Near Anton Chico the party met a Mexican who told them Howland, Baker and Rosenbury were prisoners in Santa Fe, that approach of Texans was well known and that

Church at Anton Chico

Governor Armijo had informed the country the Texans intended to "burn, slay and destroy."

At Anton Chico, from the six visitors the populace scattered as frightened birds. In no great time they recovered confidence enough to sell fodder and food to the party. Although by then it was late, Kendall and his companions pushed on, intending to reach San Miguel before sleeping. In the darkness they lost their way and returned to Anton Chico to spend the night. It was not a restful one as they were crowded into a room already occupied. Shortly after midnight, disturbed by the hacking coughs of sleepers crowded close about him and hearing movement among the horses,

Kendall went to investigate. When a Mexican spoke to him, he called Captain Lewis who better understood Spanish. Together they learned all were to be taken prisoners by a party awaiting them on the road ahead and that most certainly they would be shot. For the warning, their informant asked a dollar. As the advice was judged more commercial than altruistic, it was discounted entirely and no payment made.

Next morning, fortified by a bowl of *atole* sweetened by *miel*, the six Texans moved on toward San Miguel. At the foot of a rocky descent immediately before the few adobe houses which were the settlement of Cuesta, Lewis, Van Ness, Brenham and Kendall waited for Howard and Fitzgerald ten minutes behind. As they did, they were suddenly surrounded by a hundred men roughly dressed, very well mounted, armed with a few ancient carbines, lances, bows and arrows. Dimasio Salezar, leader, addressed them with courtesy and as *amigos*. He inquired who might they be and from whence they came. When Howard and Fitzgerald arrived, the visitors mounted and, surrounded by the welcoming delegation, rode to the first house in Cuesta.

Among all peoples, including Latins, there is *cortez* and *urbano*. The first is the bland unction of superficial courtesy; the second is that sincerity which makes of the individual a valued member of any community. With *cortez*, Salezar persuaded the visitors that it was his unpleasant duty, but duty nevertheless, to require them to put their rifles and pistols in his care, each correctly labeled with name of the owner so that when their business with the authorities of New Mexico could be arranged, their effects might be returned without confusion. The visitors complied, most of them confident all would be well.

Salezar then conferred with his minions in the nearby house, having distributed the collected arms among them, and leaving the Texans outside, free and unarmed. A second time Salezar addressed the Texans: they were to form a line and as his orders from Armijo required, they must relinquish all papers and articles on their person. When their effects had been tied in bundles, Salezar suddenly ordered twelve of his men armed with decrepit muskets into a line fronting the

Texans at three yards distance. "That we were to be immediately shot was now terribly manifest. At this juncture an altercation ensued between Dimasio Salezar and a Mexican named Vigil."

It was this incident Davis mentioned in his account of San Miguel and it was Don Gregorio Vigil who saved Van Ness, Howard, Fitzgerald, Brenham and Kendall for future exhaustion, hunger and thirst which they survived and the life of Captain William P. Lewis who betrayed them, betrayed the Texans yet free on the Road to Cuesta and San Miguel, and who prospered, for a time at least, by that perfidy.

From Cuesta to San Miguel is about fifteen miles and it was nearly sundown before the small group of Texans glimpsed the church towers (it still stands) and were lodged in a cell near to it.

Next day, under guard and limping on the Road to Santa Fe, the group met Armijo and his militia. The Governor questioned them closely and with only minor abuse. He demanded that one who spoke the best Spanish. Captain William P. Lewis who had lived in Chihuahua, stepped forward and after speaking with him in Spanish which the others poorly understood, Armijo provided him with mount and rode on, having ordered the remaining prisoners back to San Miguel.

Worn to the bone, they were scarcely within a small cell with a high window opening on the Plaza before a young priest entered by permission of the guard and told them that one of their party was to be shot immediately. Van Ness, Howard, Fitzgerald, Brenham and Kendall, stricken to silence, glanced at each other, wondering how selection was made, who was to die. "The young priest raised himself on tip-toe and looking over our heads, pointed through the window. . . . We were shocked at seeing one of our men, his hands tied behind his back . . . led across . . . the plaza. . . . That he was a Texan was evident from his dress . . . six of the guard stepped back three paces and *shot the poor fellow in the back!*" It was Baker.

The prisoners were marched past the body, cloth on it burning from the last close shot, to stand in front of another adobe house three or four blocks away. There Armijo demanded of them their names, one by one, and repeated them through the small window to someone concealed within. They could not hear a reply but when he was done, Armijo informed the Texans that the answers they had given him earlier in the day concerning their names, and their relations to the expedition, had been confirmed by "Don Samuel." As they told the truth their lives would be spared; Don Samuel was to be shot immediately. Bewildered for the moment, they were startled when guards opened the cell and from it escorted the battered and bloody Howland past them. He gave them a grotesque smile and turned his head to speak: "Goodby, boys; I've got to suffer. You must. . . ." and his words faded as distance increased. Ten yards behind they marched to the Plaza where guards threw Howland to his knees alongside Baker, dead and smouldering. Six of the guard took aim and shot him in the back.

The men now dead, and Rosenbury, had arrived three weeks before in Santa Fe. Armijo had word of some sort, enough for suspicion and they had been imprisoned. The three men had escaped but Armijo threw searching parties, who knew the country, across every route in the direction of the three-hundred-odd Texans still on the plains. By pursuers Rosenbury was killed, Baker and Howland captured just before Kendall and his companions were taken. Howland, who spoke Spanish, had been offered booty, life and liberty to enjoy it, the same terms Captain Lewis accepted, if he would betray his comrades. Samuel Howland had refused.[110]

Armijo remained in Cuesta as Captain Lewis went with the Mexicans to meet the Texans. On sight of the militia, the visitors from Texas moved to positions of defense but reassured by sight of Lewis at the head of the advancing group, they relaxed. Lewis told his companions that he had seen 600 armed troops, that 4,000 were to arrive in a few hours, and that 5,000 more were en route from Chihuahua. If they would now give up their arms, in eight days these would be returned. Lewis declared he *knew* this to be the custom of traders out of Missouri and that no harm would come of it. On this, Captain William P. Lewis pledged his honor.

Some days later, after a second segment of the expedition was taken by the same tactics, Kendall and others in the small cell facing the Plaza were to see the arrival of more prisoners and eventually the wagons of merchandise. As these were unloaded (it occupied most of the day; there must have been considerable loot) they saw Lewis, by wave of arm, lay claim to whatever he chose, the remainder going to the merchants of San Miguel.

In perhaps a month the Texans went past Pecos Village north a ways on the Road, and beyond Glorieta Pass turned south for the very long march down the Rio Grande and on to Chihuahua. Not all received the same brutal treatment as did Kendall's unfortunate group. In command of his detachment was their original captor, Demasio Salezar. He informed them any man who lagged behind would be shot and his ears cut off for proof to Armijo that he had not escaped. Although several steers were driven with the prisoners, intended for food, most of what they ate north of El Paso was roasted pumpkin and ears of corn handed, with tears, from the women of the villages through which they passed. It was not enough and three of the group, exhausted at various stages of the march downstream, were shot when they could not rise from the bedground. Ears were severed from the bodies and strung on cord later to be shown to Armijo.

Once in El Paso their treatment was a great deal better. Even so, it was not a picnic and several died from disease, aided by exhaustion. Those who survived the march to Chihuahua, and the reasonably mild detention there, eventually were set free. Kendall's account of the treachery, tortures and abominations, published in 1844, was the southwest forerunner of a later "Uncle Tom's Cabin."

San Miguel where Kendall's imprisonment began, is today scarcely less of a ruin than Pecos Village was when distraught and haggard Texans passed it, having completed the first twenty of the fifteen hundred miles to Chihuahua. The decrepitude of Pecos was the abrasion of age, the vicissitudes of weather and abandonment.

Those peoples now living in pueblos along and near the Rio Grande are a distinct branch of the tree of sociological evolution. Long, long ago their forebears had been cliff-dwellers, living beneath the overhang of thick massive sandstones outcropping along canyons. It is probable the first to seek shelter had no other, but in time some genius among them devised yet a better of thin sandstone slabs, broken to convenient size and laid without mortar in walls beneath an overhanging ledge. Somewhere in the vicinity of every such collection of peoples in stone houses were crudely cultivated fields. Out on the Plains, distant cousins of cliff-dwellers lived on floodplains along creeks and rivers in more temporary shelters. When they exhausted the fertility of the rich alluvium with crops of melons and corn, they moved to a virgin site.

In the southwest, as populations increased and as cliff-dwellers became more expert in stonemasonry, they moved from cliffs to flatter lands near water. They constructed apartment houses of stone, two and three stories high, adequate for a thousand or two people. Pecos Village was one such. When climatic change in the southwest reduced the nearest water to a trickle inadequate for so many, villages moved to larger springs or to the nearest permanent stream. By then some among them had become technicians adequate to construct shelters of puddled mud or perhaps adobe brick. Some still held to the ancient ways, building houses of stone. They did not all speak the same dialect and some of those who did, came to a parting of ways. Pecos Village was of stone, an apartment house of three stories located on two good springs. Pecos villagers had cousins speaking the same dialect living in adobe houses in what now is Jemez Pueblo on Rio Jemez, about fifty miles due west.

When in 1541 Coronado left the Rio Grande to explore the plains eastward, he visited Pecos Village, one of the larger among stone-age settlements.[3] He found it a thriving settlement, beset on occasion by raiders from the Plains. Although there was easy access to Pecos for war parties from the prairies, the villagers had the protection of stone walls of their apartments which they entered by ladder to the roof. From that height, they were able to give as they received. By the time horses had become a part of the economy of Plains Indians, stone walls were no longer the protection they had been as the mounted raiders were very fast in sudden assault. There must have been many raids and raiders, for by the time the first wagons passed, the population of Pecos either by epidemics of plainsmen or of bacteria had been reduced to a tenth of the original. By then there was a huge maroon adobe church at the south end of the stone pueblo on the low hill, but its massive high mud walls offered no more protection than stone to those who failed to reach it in time.

In the worship of villagers in Pecos was a tenet older by far than the church. As father passed it to son and priest to supplicant, they spoke of a sacred fire given by Montezuma, with admonition never to let it die. The donor would return from out of the east some day and, presumably by light of the perpetual flame, deliver them from all menace. Some among those out of Missouri may have embellished the lore, for traders mentioned that at dawn every morning from the height of the stone apartment house on the hill, a group peered eastward in hopes of sight of Montezuma. Quite as probably they were hoping for no sight of Comanche, Apache or Ute.

Susan Magoffin's husband had slept in a crumbling room at Pecos Village and told Susan of the ten or fifteen remaining of the thousand or two, still faithful attendants of the fire. Two years later, when Susan visited the room her husband knew, the last of the villagers had taken their sacred flame and joined their cousins on Jemez River fifty miles west. Among the hundred or so adobe houses which are now Jemez Pueblo in a cove of the Nacimiento Mountains, a minor part of the Sangre de Cristo range, there must be a residual spark of the sacred fire, either on a hearth or in gene and chromosome. At any rate, Jemez Pueblo has survived unto the present. For a brief interval, it even had a part in the atomic age. It is pleasing to believe that some descendant of a Pecos villager had an active part, although only random chance would let it be so.

After World War II, in the 1950's, "Element S" emerged

from top secret reports and became uranium, the object of a desperate and intense search. All over the southwest small two-passenger planes flew a hundred feet or so above the rough ground, in each a cautious pilot, a geologist-observer and a scintillometer. They flew over selected areas and they followed the imaginary lines of a regular grid. When one passed over the lands of Jemez Pueblo, the needle of the scintillometer jumped far to the right: index to the impact of gamma radiation from disintegrating uranium atoms in the sandstones below.

Immediately the geologist-observer tapped the pilot's shoulder. The plane banked to circle over the spot as the geologist traced their route on a photograph of the ground above which they flew. As the needle jumped again, he looked quickly overside for some landmark on the photograph: an arroyo, a cliff, a cedar tree. By the time several such "passes" had been flown, the geologist with confidence could mark with X on the photograph the spot on the ground.

The hazards of flying so very low were many and they were fewest in the two hours after sunrise and before sunset. Between those times, convection in the warming air produced up-an-down drafts that might lift a small plane two hundred feet or dash it against rocks below. In the hours unsafe for flight, the geologist visited by jeep, the X on the aerial photograph and the uranium prospect on the ground owned by Jemez Pueblo. When he had done so, he reported to the Atomic Energy Commission office in Grand Junction, Colorado, what he had found and where.

There is a great deal of empty space in the southwest. Most of it is public domain, open and free to entry of any claimant of a mineral deposit within it. Smaller but equally vacant areas surround the Pueblo villages of which Jemez is one. It is land closed to everyone save with permission of the Jemez Tribal Council and its Chief. A casual transient across their lands suffers no abuse, but no one, least of all the AEC, explored for a deposit of uranium on Indian lands without their permission.

When word of the find on the Jemez reservation filtered down from upstairs, I called the Agent of the Pueblo Tribes.

To him, in Albuquerque, I explained the circumstances and what we wished to do. He listened to the long explanation and replied that it would take some talking. We agreed on a day convenient to him and in Albuquerque I explained again, adding every detail of operation we might need to perform in order to make certain of the size of the deposit and tenor of the ore. He agreed to arrange a pow-wow.

A week or two later, in company with the District Geologist, we picked up the Agent in Albuquerque and drove to Jemez Village. It was a warm spring day, bright as always they are in that region where the sun makes of shadows, masses of substance almost as solid as the objects which cast them. The agent cautioned me to drive very slowly and with absolute care as we moved among the small two and three room adobe houses irregularly distributed. When we arrived at a space slightly larger than most we had traversed, he directed me to stop. We sat in the warming car for a few minutes, with none in sight save ourselves. The Agent unfolded a generous six feet of height and the seventh of a tall Stetson and high-heeled boots, walked to the door undistinguished among the many about, and knocked. In the long silence that followed I imagined residents behind the door awakening from a nap. The door opened, there were a few moments of inaudible conversation; then the Agent beckoned. We entered in order: Chief Jemez, Chief Agent, Chief Geologist, Chief District Geologist. Coming from bright sunlight to the dark cool interior, I did not see the seven chairs arranged in a circle but by the time the Agent folded into one, I caught the gesture of his hand and took another. They must have been waiting nearby, for immediately three men entered the bright open doorway to fill the remaining chairs. To the left of the agent sat a dark-skinned middle-aged man, dressed in khaki and blue shirt, open at the collar. He was later to interpret with a facility I had never witnessed before. To his left sat the Chief, older by considerable, with a serape about his shoulders. Between Jemez Chief and Chief Geologist were three ex-chiefs, life members of the Tribal Council they once headed. To my left was the District Geologist and beyond him the Agent.

As we sat in silence, a council member removed from a buckskin bag a handful of pieces of corn husks and a small sack of tobacco. These he placed in the center of the circle of chairs and on the buckskin bag. The silence lengthened, nor was it interrupted as the Chief rolled a cigarette from the makings on the floor, as did his counselors. I had not given thought to what one might see within a Jemez home. In the interminable quiet (but no more than fifteen minutes) I glanced about, wishing to learn what the Jemez thought a necessity on what must have been one of the lowest incomes in the nation. It was not much. Bright sunlight from the open door modeled another closed to a room westward, to my right. Against the wall of a corner in that direction was a Grand Rapids dresser with a mirror. On the wood stood an ordinary kerosene lamp. Adjacent was another dresser without a mirror and on it a second lamp. Behind was the adobe wall plastered smoothly with the same limonite-brown mud as the bricks it covered. To the left at the far end of the room were two iron bedsteads with brass knobs on the posts. The beds were arranged with heads against the north and south walls with the space of a foot or so between their opposite ends. The beds and space between them were a measure of width of a room perhaps twice as long. When eyes were accustomed to the semi-twilight in corners distant from the open door I could see hanging from nails in the wall above each bed a walking stick with a silver head. These two items were the only furnishings not reasonably counted necessities on a low income.

The Chief broke the silence with a few words of Jemez. His counselors replied with yet fewer. After a long moment of quiet, the Chief nodded to the Agent.

For about five minutes the Agent spoke. He told what uranium was, that it was to be found in several compounds and he mentioned the color of some of them. He spoke of radiation and its detection by scintillometer from the air. His words were directed to the Chief, and when he paused he looked at the man to his left. The interpreter spoke as long to the Chief and without hesitation. I listened with interest to what I could not understand: a language not direct from the stone age but certainly heir to inflections, perhaps even words from it. When he was done, the interpreter turned from the Chief to face the Agent. The latter took up where he had left off.

He sometimes used technical terms as he explained our request for permission to map the geology of the radiation anomaly, to make a jeep trail to reach it, perhaps to cut a road for a core-drilling rig, to drill holes in the rock and extract cores of stone from them, perhaps later to mine the ore. He was better coached than I thought and he had a better memory than I knew. As the interpreter took over, I could not help but wonder how "scintillometer, drilling truck, rock cores, dynamite, mining, frame-of-reference" might translate into Jemez, but not once did he hesitate or grope for a word.

When all was said, alternately by Agent and interpreter, the silence which followed was quite as long as that before the beginning. One after another and each several times, the counselors spoke to their Chief who either nodded, meditated long moments or spoke a word of reply, sometimes all three.

When at last he addressed the interpreter, I learned we had permission. There were certain places on the reservation we could not go, not even for uranium ore, and these would be pointed out for us. There were certain days we would not be welcome. We were not to use water from the springs nor the creek as these were barely adequate for the village, and we were not to interrupt village life or agriculture nor molest village flocks. If by accident we damaged crops or injured livestock we were to pay. We agreed. We sat in silence long after the last word and when the Chief rose, the pow-wow was done.

As the district geologist showed the Chief and his Counselors a geiger counter and tested the few specimens of ore they produced from pockets, I thanked the interpreter for his help and included a casual comment on the handsome canes on the wall. He spoke to the Chief who nodded, lifted them from the wall and held them out to me. They were straight tapered ebony sticks and the thick silver head of the first was worn completely smooth. As I examined it with curiosity, the interpreter explained that the stick was the symbol of Authority, given by the Spaniards to their appointed Jemez Chief (they had removed the first, as he had not been malleable), sometimes in the early sixteen hundreds. From hand to hand, Chief to Chief, it came through three hundred years to that one who this day brought his tribe into the atomic age. I looked at the second with equal interest. It was, the interpreter said, likewise a symbol of Authority but from another source and more recent. In the flowing curves of Spencerian script both were clear to be read: "A Lincoln 1863." Among mice and men are no sadder words than: It might have been. Had circumstances been but slightly different, the script might have read: "Jefferson Davis 1862." Circumstances were very nearly so where the Road to Santa Fe crosses Glorieta Pass.

A mile south of Pecos Pueblo, one Kozlowski had a ranch in the latter days of the Road. He had been a Dragoon in the Army of the West and when the tumult and shouting of invasion had died, along with a considerable number of Mexicans and Americans, Kozlowski turned to pursuit of peace when not pursuing rustlers and Indians. Not much remains now of his place save the land. Even that is less. It has been reduced by erosion for country here stands some 6,000 feet above the sea. No matter how far from it, it is the fate of all lands standing higher to be reduced in geological time to that level. What once Kozlowski claimed is now in the hands of Hollywood characters, like their predecessor, retired to a less hectic life.

From a point not far from Kozlowski's old place, one may glimpse segments of adobe walls standing high and anomalously in a region sparsely settled. They are the remains of the massive adobe chapel at the south margin of Pecos Pueblo. Untenanted and untended a hundred and twenty-five years, Pueblo and church have been reduced to ruins. The Pueblo is scarcely more than a heap of stone a hundred yards long by half as wide, a few of which still mark the limits of small rooms. The massive walls of the adobe church are a great deal less than when Susan and her husband walked here. When next you see them they inevitably will be yet less for they lose to each rare passing shower a part of their stature.

From the vicinity of Kozlowski's ranch and Pecos Pueblo, the Road curves west to pass the springs which supplied both, and heads toward Glorieta Pass through a prong of the Sangre de Cristo Mountains. Drainage eastward to the Pecos River and westward to the Rio Grande has cut so deep a notch in Permian rocks as to expose older strata of Pennsylvanian age which underlie them. The notch is Glorieta Pass.

Before the prevailing mania for expressways laid waste to home and hovel, piñon and pine, Glorieta Pass was a quiet segment of rough tree-studded land. It was a great deal quieter in covered-wagon days. Even so, it was not so quiet as one might think. In March, 1862, the acrid smoke and the thunder of Civil War rose from this land just as it had from Fort Sumter in Carolina the year before. Had it not been for one Chivington, the symbol of Jemez authority, that silver-headed walking stick in Jemez Pueblo might have been engraved with another name and date.

Church at
Pecos Village

General H. H. Sibley had been an officer at Fort Union.[107] When guns fired on Fort Sumter in Carolina, he resigned from the Army. From Texas, and with troops, he returned to the Rio Grande, for centuries the route of invaders. On it he captured Fort Craig and other outposts in south and central New Mexico. With no serious opposition and with determination to make New Mexico safe for the Confederacy he marched north. It was his aim to take Fort Union and had he done so, New Mexico Territory and perhaps all the land to the west coast and the gold of California would have been in Southern hands. In frantic haste a militia was collected in Colorado. To nearly the point of exhaustion they marched southward all the days and as far into the nights as endurance allowed. At Fort Union they barely paused to rest and to collect what men and arms were available. Bone-tired, they went south on the Road past Las Vegas, through El Puerto del Norte, up Tecolote Hill, by a short-cut went north of San Miguel and up the Pecos River to Kozlowski's ranch. West six miles from headquarters at the ranch was Glorieta Pass. Three miles farther west was Montoya's ranch, now the tiny settlement of Cañoncito. It was the headquarters of the Confederates, and in ordered groups about were their wagons containing supplies brought nearly a thousand miles from central Texas.

There must have been skirmishes between scouting parties before the armies joined at a point just west of Glorieta Pass on March 26, 1862. But none of these were decisive, including the first battle, and Confederates had still the upper hand. Two days later they carried the Pass and pressed hard on Union forces at Pigeon's Ranch, a couple of miles east of the Pass. It was a point known to some traders out of Missouri, for Old Man Valle raised and sometimes sold corn there and somehow acquired the nickname of "Pigeon."

Glorieta Mesa is a high table of land immediately south of Glorieta Pass. The mesa spreads to several miles width no great distance south. While Confederates and Union forces maneuvered around Old Man Valle's place, each seeking a disadvantage for the other, Colonel John M. Chivington, a fire-breathing elder of the Methodist Church in Denver,

marched a detachment of Colorado militia due west from
Union headquarters at Kozlowski ranch, up the steep east
escarpment of Glorieta Mesa and across the ten or twelve
miles of tableland. At the west margin, Chivington looked
down upon a rare prize, Confederate supply wagons filled
with spare rations, spare arms, spare ammunition. Chivington spread fire, death and destruction among supplies essential to Confederate survival. Few Colonels and yet fewer
Elders of the Church have acquitted themselves so well. It
was a decisive feat of arms: it won the battle of Glorieta
Pass for the Union; it impelled retreat of Confederates from
northern New Mexico and it won acclaim for Chivington.

Either the feat or the acclaim stirred Chivington's political ambitions as unfortunately such have stirred so many
of his kind since. Two years later he was to be soundly
defeated for the office of Territorial delegate to Congress.
Having expended in political loss the prestige accrued at
Glorieta Pass, Chivington, Colonel and Elder of the Church,
sought another circumstance from which he might wring
a dividend of political stature. With the connivance of John
Evans, Governor of Colorado Territory, he was to find one
in perfidy unequalled since Caesar's time.

Black Kettle, Chief among Cheyennes and a personage
among their relatives, the Arapahoe, was a leader when an
1851 treaty with Washington legally defined the domain of
Cheyenne and Arapahoe as that land between the South
Platte and the Arkansas. Very few citizens living now would
think such an agreement more or less than absurd and but
few less would think it ridiculous not to have taken the land
from them. By treaty with Washington in 1861, Black Kettle
and his Cheyennes and the Arapahoes were allotted much
smaller reservations in southeast Colorado, the north and
east boundaries of which were marked by Sand Creek.[111]

Black Kettle and his tribe were hungry. There were few
buffalo on their reservation and they had no other source
of meat. Moreover, they were convinced every year there
would be fewer yet anywhere on the plains as whites collected tens of thousands of hides, leaving meat to rot on the
prairies. Cheyennes did not hesitate to rob, raid and scalp

Glorieta
fro

as a way of life and as a way to food. Convinced eventually that they could not possibly compete with the hordes of whites laying waste to the buffalo range, Black Kettle and the destitute Cheyennes petitioned Major Edward W. Wynkoop at Fort Lyon for food and for peace with whites. The Major gave them food and took Black Kettle, White Antelope, Neva, Bosse, Heaps-of-Buffalo and No-ta-nee to Denver for parley with John Evans, Governor. In cold November weather, Wynkoop pushed ahead of the party to advise Evans of their arrival.

John Evans had achieved that prominence which is an adjunct to the office he held and he was ambitious for greater distinction. Although it was not true, Evans had convinced Washington that Cheyennes were on the verge of ravaging frontier settlements. To counter the conjured threat, he had been authorized to organize, recruit, equip and arm a Third Colorado Regiment, and he had just done so with enthusiasm. John Evans refused Wynkoop's request to treat with the Cheyennes. When Wynkoop pressed hard in argument, the Governor demanded in the chill of callous ambition: What would he do with the Third Regiment if now he made peace? But Wynkoop prevailed.

In parley the Cheyenne leaders spoke for armistice and Black Kettle pleaded: "All we ask is that we may have peace with the whites." He was instructed to place himself and his people in care of the military. He did so. Back at Fort Lyon, Wynkoop advised him and the Arapahoe to locate their villages near the post where he could prevent difficulties with other whites and he provided them with prisoner-allowance of rations for ten days. Black Kettle made camp on Sand Creek and within the reservation a few miles north of the Mountain Branch of the Road in southeast Colorado.

There was talk in Denver that Black Kettle was "running Fort Lyon." On November 5, 1864, Major Scott J. Anthony, a man rich in turpitude and little else, arrived from Fort Leavenworth with orders signed by General Curtis. The orders relieved Wynkoop of responsibility and placed Anthony in command of Fort Lyon. Black Kettle was disturbed as well he might be, for experience had taught him that whites

he might trust were rare; they were very few and times between them were long. Wynkoop explained the circumstance
and Anthony agreed he would follow the same course of
action. He issued rations and ordered the Indians to give up
their arms and all horses and mules belonging to the government or to white citizens. The Indians agreed: they gave up
three rifles, one pistol, about sixty bows, four horses and
ten mules.

On November 14, Chivington put in motion the Colorado
Third, parts of the First and whatever other troops he could
collect. In deep snow they headed toward the Arkansas
River. As they passed Bent's ranch at the mouth of the
Purgatoire, Chivington threw about it a cordon of guards
and took Robert, son of William Bent, as a guide. Bent's
other two sons, George and Charles, and their sister were
in Black Kettle's camp on Sand Creek.

At Fort Lyon, Chivington set a line of pickets about the
post from which no one might leave. Anthony, in complete
agreement, not only permitted the curious arrangement by
an officer to whom he was not subordinate, but collected
arms and men and joined Chivington. When Lieutenant
Silas S. Soule protested, Chivington replied that he believed
it right and honorable "to use any means under God's heaven
to kill Indians who would kill women and children" and
"damn any man in sympathy with Indians." He declared that
such men as Soule and Wynkoop had better get out of the
United States service.

There is no comparison between what is lost by not suc-
ceeding and what is lost by not trying. Lieutenants Minton,
Colly and Crosset made a last attempt to dissuade Chivington but the burly, thick-necked, fire-breathing Old Testament
Preacher, livid with anger at opposition, was a man of few
words and those repetitious. With another "Damn any man
who is in sympathy with an Indian!" he ended the meeting.
At 8 P.M. November 28, 1864, the Colonel and righteous
Elder marched north toward Sand Creek with 700 militia.

At dawn next morning firing commenced. Black Kettle
tied a large American flag to a lodge-pole, added a large white
flag beneath it and hoisted it above his tipi. White Antelope,

an Arapaho, ran from the village toward the troops, holding his hands high in the air. One of the bravest of the brave,
he stopped in the bed of Sand Creek and folded his arms
over his chest in a gesture of peace. His appeal was the lodge-
ment of a score of bullets. His scalp, his nose, his ears and
his testicles were cut off, the latter for a tobacco pouch.
Shortly after, a three year old child wandered onto the bed
of Sand Creek. One after another, three brave men of the
Third Colorado bent on defeat of any Indian who would kill
women and children, took aim. At the third shot, the child
fell dead. Chivington and his men found easy vent for armed
fury in slaughter of redskin, male and female, in tipi, in bed,
in cradle. When victory was won and two hundred were
dead, two-thirds women and children, the famed Third
Colorado Regiment consolidated their gains by cutting off
the breasts of the women, cutting out their labia to hang
over saddle-horns and tearing off their scalps. They were
trophies that should hang with the regimental flag of the
Third Colorado forever.

John Evans' career is clear proof that crime pays and
very well indeed. Evanston, Illinois, is the namesake of a
scoundrel. But blood is not the best of foundations for a
political career and from it Chivington did not rise. One
needs a clear understanding of the religio-politico-military
mind to appreciate Chivington's public statement many years
later: he had done rightly. It was a statement so astounding
as to have raised the dead. Unfortunately it did not and
Chivington died with scalp intact.[111]

The road from Glorieta Mesa for Chivington was long
and bloody. The asphalt from Glorieta Pass to Santa Fe is
short to where it passes the Chapel of Our Lady of Guadalupe, crosses the feeble Rio de Santa Fe and a block further
enters the southeast corner of the Plaza, crowded now with
vehicles circling counter-clockwise in congestion greater each
year.

While Franklin for a time and Independence for years
was the beginning of the Road, Santa Fe was not always the
end. From it the Royal Road, older by two hundred years,
led south to other markets. But for all who left Missouri,

Santa Fe was a destination and an occasion. Bullwhackers and muleskinners had seen no place so large (it had 5,790 people in 1827) or so safe for relaxation in the nearly 800 miles and sixty days, and they prepared for it. On the Road they had little practice with water as a libation but they generally used some the evening before they arrived at the capital. Perhaps they shaved; certainly they combed their hair for the typical teamster wore it long, as now do others with less reason. No doubt teamsters changed their shirts if they had a spare, and those with or without, generally affixed a new cracker to their bullwhip. A mile or so from the village, they fired their guns and from there to the Plaza the buckskin cracker repeated the sound much more frequently than necessary. Men who had crossed the prairies did not think of arrival in Santa Fe in terms of modesty; rather, they thought in terms of a job if not well, then safely done.

Most merchants had left their wagons in care of others, a hundred or so miles eastward, at El Vado de las Piedras or even at Lower Cimarron Spring which they left at night in order to avoid Comanches, Apaches and Utes.[25] In Santa Fe they employed clerks to translate their manifests. With these in hand they met their wagons at the Governor's Palace, where cargos were off-loaded and examined. Every merchant was anxious to retrieve his goods for the earliest, most profitable sale, and equally reluctant to pay duty on them. What they paid depended much on whim: in different years from $500 to $950 for each wagon.

The Governor's Palace, of which the custom house was a part, had no baroque facade nor dimpled statuary about its entrance. It was mud. And it differed from other structures of Santa Fe in that it was palatial in size.[33] Its plus-three-hundred feet width still occupies the whole of the north side of the Plaza. When traders saw it, an eight-foot adobe wall behind enclosed about ten acres and other structures belonging to the establishment. Not many Missourians who had business within recognized what they saw: the oldest government building on North America. Occupied first in 1610, or perhaps the year before, by Governor Pedro de

Peralta, for an even three centuries it was the seat of governors, good, bad and indifferent. Its first seventy years were as peaceful as the time and place. An index to both: beneath the portal of the Palace which extended the width of the Plaza, hanging here and there were cords threaded with ears of Indians, where tourists now see ears of Indian corn. They won less attention than did the narrow windows of glass, as the Palace was the only structure that had them.

In 1680, the adobe Palace was the fort of Spaniards resisting siege by Pueblos determined to conquer their conquerors.[112] In front of the Palace in August of that year, forty-nine Pueblo prisoners were faced to the wall and shot. It was small revenge and great loss when later Indians had driven all Spaniards from New Mexico, they burned the

Governor's Palace

archives of their oppressors. It was to the Palace that Don Diego de Vargas returned twelve years later. Within it, in 1844, Governor Martinez, with a single blow of his chair, brained a Ute chieftain. For two hundred and twelve years there was a Spanish flag over the Palace, replaced in 1822 by the green and white banner of Mexico. In another twenty-four, that one was replaced by yet another. Kearny slept here, while in Congress Abraham Lincoln demanded the Administration point to any spot where, before invasion, Mexican rifles had take a single American life, but they were unable to do so.

The southwest corner room of the Governor's Palace was the *calabozo*, prison, for David Meriwether, and when he returned as Governor of the Territory, the southeast corner room was the post office. Neither room is a part of the Palace now. Within the mud walls, Governor Wallace, preoccupied with artistic attainment and indifferent to blood shed by guilty and innocent alike, wrote "Ben Hur" and ignored Billy the Kid and the Lincoln County War. Few government buildings have witnessed so much and none for so long.

When merchants from Courthouse Square in Missouri reached the Plaza in New Mexico, they were more than eight hundred miles from home. They were within a culture older than that to which they were born, in a foreign land older than the nation of which they were citizens. As it was different, most easterners thought it less. Their most frequent description of Santa Fe was that it resembled a collection of brick kilns. Houses of the New Mexican capital were one-story, flat-roofed and either puddled mud or adobe brick, delivered at $8 a thousand. It was building material adapted to the land, so much so that it is still the most common in use. Within and without, homes of *Santafeanos* were white-washed by finely crushed, soft white gypsum, spread on smoothed mud walls by mops of sheepskin, and generally by women.

Very few houses of Santa Fe held furniture of any sort. In place of cabinets and closets were leather trunks and wooden chests. In place of chairs and couches were *col-*

chones, bedding neatly rolled and covered with Navajo blankets, as colorful then as now. Floors were packed mud, carpeted by those who could afford it with *gerga*, a weaving of coarse wool. Ceilings were sometimes strips of unbleached muslin secured to massive *vigas*. More commonly they were small sticks laid from beam to beam in a herringbone pattern and stained blue, yellow or red. In some rooms in most homes however poor, on walls above *colchones* which served as seats by day and beds by night, were santos: pictures or carved figures of saints. The houses of the poor, and a great many were, had few of these luxuries. As do the poor everywhere, they existed, preoccupied by the effort involved, whether they lived in a colony, a province, a territory, or a state.

La Villa Real de Santa Fe, the Royal Village of Holy Faith, in the days before traders was scarcely three blocks long by half as wide on Rio Santa Fe, a small flow. Scattered about at random on radii up to a mile or two were two hundred or so adobe houses amid small fields irrigated by the convenient water. As the climate was arid, "streets" were rarely as deep in mud as commonly they were in dust. Most homes were built around a patio with but a single outside entrance and no windows, save those opening by shutters within the enclosure. It was a design perhaps born of caution, fixed by custom and continued by habit, for it is a modern design throughout the land four thousand miles south of the Rio Grande. Around the Plaza, in its earliest days, on three sides two-story structures housed Taos Indians, an important part of the economy: an unwilling source of unpaid labor. Few of these houses survived to the time of traders and none to the present. Structures about the Plaza then, and later, were shops of traders close-set, each a part of the next. From each projected a *portal*, a roof supported by stout logs, offering shade during the day and unneeded shelter for the promenade which began daily near sunset.

The Plaza itself, the goal of wagons unloaded at the custom house in the Governor's Palace was, between caravans, the market place. One who saw it in 1837, recalled it a litter of garbage, barren of trees such as shade it now. On the south side, opposite the Palace was Capillo de los Soldados, the military chapel (gone now) and a block east was the Parochial Church.[26] There was a third church two blocks south of the Plaza, passed by wagons en route to the

custom house: Chapel of Our Lady of Guadalupe, constructed by slave labor. Adjacent was a house, now described as the oldest structure on the continent. More truthfully, it is old walls on a much older foundation of mud, relic of **Pueblo Analco** inhabited in 1200 A.D., on the site of which Spaniards built La Villa Real de Santa Fe, four hundred and ten years later.

Casa Analco
Santa Fe'

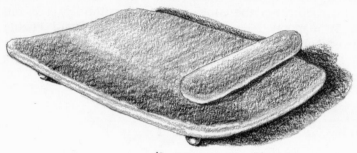

Metate and Mano

Santafeanos were a pastoral people rather than agri-culturalists as few plantings matured without aid of irriga-tion. What did, grew in quantity not quite adequate to meet demand and made of Santa Fe the most expensive habitation in the United States when New Mexico was a Territory. Corn, beans, peas, red peppers and peach trees were common. No writer with a returning caravan mentioned Mexican beans as sustenance of traders, but they must have had them. Even now a heaping plate of Mexican beans well-cooked with salt pork, and well seasoned with chili, is fortifying. In that time two of them each day would have obviated every hazard on the return trip, save perhaps scalping. Corn got mention as it was frequent in Mexican homes. Boiled in lime-water to soften the hard shell, the stew was ground to a paste on a *metate* with a *mano*. Spread thin on a sheet of copper or tin by those who had them and on hot stones by those who did not, the paste cooked to a *tortilla* in a very few minutes. The *tortilla*, a thin crust, was rolled to serve as a spoon and both spoon and beans eaten.

In Santa Fe a good many drank wine, and most made what they drank.[50] Those who did, sewed a bull-hide or buffalo skin to a roughly cylindrical form open at one end and while still green, filled it with sand as a mould. When completely dry, the rawhide cask was supported by four stout stakes and across the opening was secured a sieve of the same material. On this a barefooted peon tramped out the vintage, the juice trickling into the bull-hide cask as the sieve held most of the stems and part of the skins and seeds. From time to time the debris was added to the juice and when all was done, the cask was closed by a plug of mud on thin sticks or hewn planks and set aside to ferment for sixty days. Wine bottles were leather flasks, as glass was unknown save in the windows of the Palace. At El Paso, where grapes flourished in warmer climate at lower elevation, by 1853 the annual wine harvest was around 200,000 gallons, each at $2. If it was not a wine to mitigate a poor meal or glorify a good one, it was cheap. As by then in the Territory there were fewer than 500 Americans, exclusive of soldiers, most consumers must have been born to the region. Still, as one reporter described Santa Fe as the place recruits whose term had expired departed drunk and those with time to serve remained drunk, there must have been some consumption by the invaders. Some, no doubt, drank "Taos Lightning," a brandy, the effects of which were instantaneous and apt to be spectacular.

Although few of the newcomers were much concerned with their own foibles, with one exception they decried those of Mexicans. George Brewerton, en route from Taos to Santa Fe, noted on the trail the occasional crosses marking the site of a murder and stopped for the night in Valdito (?). He later recalled the warm hospitality met there as he wrote: "I like these daughters of New Mexico. They are women unstayed and unpadded who have grown in blissful ignorance of a milliner's mode." Susan Magoffin, who reached Santa Fe two years before and from Raton Pass, was not so approving.

Most men caught a whiff of the same Mephitic vapors as did Susan and some were momentarily unhinged when the odor proved to be smoke of a *cigarillo* in the hand of an unstayed, unpadded daughter of New Mexico. Man and woman, boy and girl, they smoked: fine-cut tobacco carried in a *gague*, rolled in a *hoja* (corn husk) and lighted by flint and steel. And they gambled, too, at any age. Still, the long-haired Puritans from the East were not deeply offended with welcome by a wine-bibbing, smoking gambler wearing a bright colored serape if he was a customer, and they were flattered if the customer wore a *rebozo*, as did most of the ladies. Nor were they violently repelled if their customer sensibly raised her skirt to cross the Rio Santa Fe or an *acequia.*

Next to the Governor and one or two others of his sex, the most prominent personage in Santa Fe for years was Doña Gertrudes Barcelo. "A woman of loose habits," she had come as "La Tules" from poverty in Taos to Santa Fe where all domestics were slaves and a considerable number of the women who were neither were mistresses. By stroke of good luck at *roulette* or *monte*, she won capital adequate to become herself a banker at gambling and a respected guest in any house, including the Governor's. Doña Gertrudes never drove a wagon across the plains but her cash filled several

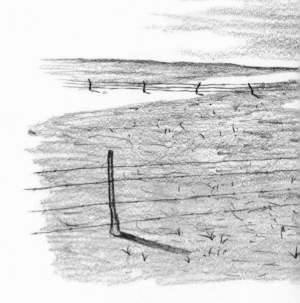

with merchandise driven by others. In 1846, when Colonel Price ordered Colonel Mitchell to lead the advance of troops downriver into Chihuahua, he offered no money for purchase of food to a subordinate who had neither funds nor bank from which to draw them. It might have been recourse of desperation but more probably it was one of pleasure when Colonel Mitchell escorted Doña Gertrudes to a *baile* and later drew on her for funds with which to feed an invasion. Few indeed are the prostitutes who served the Army in that capacity, and no banker has served his country so well.

Doña Gertrudes is long gone to dust, as have the men, mules and oxen who engraved in sod the thin line, fainter each year, from Courthouse Square in Missouri, 780 miles southwest to the Plaza in Santa Fe.

Requiescent in pace.

The Road to Santa Fe

CHRONOLOGY

1541: Coronado and associates from the Rio Grande traversed the Plains and reached Quivira on what later was to be Cow Creek (Kansas), very near its crossing by the Road to Santa Fe.

1598: Don Juan de Onate with 130 soldier-colonists, plus servants and Indians, 83 wagons of supplies and 7,000 head of cattle went north from the Rio Concho to settle New Mexico.

1610: La Villa Real de Santa Fe established.

1630: Since Neolithic time, Indians had been agriculturalists in small settlements on fertile river-bottom lands. About this decade, most southwestern tribes had become horsemen, their livestock captured as strays and booty from Spanish settlements.

1750: New Mexico population: 3,779 Spaniards, 12,140 Pueblo Indians.

1762: All Louisiana west of Mississippi ceded by France to Spain.

1800: Louisiana returned by Spain to France.
Last buffalo killed in Pennsylvania.

1803: Louisiana Purchase: about 752,912 square miles, roughly 481,863,680 acres at five cents an acre.

1804: William Morrison, merchant of Kaskaskia, Illinois, sent Baptiste LeLande, Laurent Durocher and Jeanot Metoyer with trade goods to Santa Fe. They were detained.

1805: General James Wilkinson, Governor of Louisiana Territory, from St. Louis dispatched to the Secretary of War a plan for invasion of New Mexico. Lt. Zebulon Pike left Belle Fontaine on the Missouri River for the west.

1806: New Mexico sent to the plains 100 dragoons, 500 militia with about 2,000 horses to intercept Pike. They did not find him.

1807: Lt. Pike escorted by Spanish troops to Natcetoches, Louisiana.

1808: Fort Osage completed on the Missouri River as the westernmost outpost.

1809: McLanahan, Smith and Patterson of St. Genevieve, Missouri, arrived with trade-goods in Santa Fe. They were imprisoned two years.

1810: Publication of Pike's report on New Mexico stimulated interest in trade with the southwest.

1812: McKnight and others left Missouri with trade goods for Santa Fe. They were imprisoned nine years.
Cooper's Fort opposite modern Arrow Rock on the Missouri River.

354

1815: Arrow Rock, Missouri, settled.

1816: Franklin, Missouri laid out.

Auguste Chouteau and twenty trappers besieged by Indians on an island in the upper Arkansas. As "Chouteau Island" it later became a landmark of the Upper Crossing of the Arkansas River for wagons en route to Santa Fe.

1819: Treaty with Spain vaguely described the common boundary between New Spain and the Louisiana Purchase.

Steamboat "Independence" first to reach Franklin, Missouri, seven days out of St. Louis.

Major S. H. Long left the frontier to scout the southwest.

1820: Daniel Boone died at Charette Village, Missouri, in his 90th year.

1821: Mexican independence from Spain.

William Becknell and four (?) unnamed left Franklin, Missouri, with trade-goods on pack animals and found profitable market in Santa Fe. Outbound they went up the Arkansas River and over Raton Pass. Returned, presumably on advice from *Santafeanos*, by a route suitable for wagons, about where the Road to Santa Fe was to be.

Col. Cooper and party went to Taos, New Mexico.

Houses at what was to be Independence, Missouri.

1822: Becknell and small party went to Santa Fe with some trade goods in the first wagon on the Road. Cooper and Baird parties went also. Factories (Government trading posts for Indians) discontinued.

1823: Traders return to Franklin, Missouri, with about 400 mules, jacks and jennies received in exchange for merchandise.

1824: Traders from Franklin, Missouri, and points east rendezvous on Missionary Ridge, ten miles southwest of Fort Osage, to organize for protection in travel to Santa Fe.

Settlement of Tecolote (New Mexico).

1825: Sibley, Brown and party began at Fort Osage a survey of the Road to Santa Fe. Traders rendezvous at Fort Osage. Party of about 40 with trade goods on pack animals, left Jackson, Tenn., and another with about $80,000 in trade goods left Huntsville, Alabama, for Santa Fe. Traders returned to Franklin with about 600 mules, jacks and jennies.

1826: Christopher Carson, apprentice to a saddlery in Franklin, ran away.

Senor Escudero of New Mexico left Franklin with six or seven wagons of trade goods, the first of his countrymen to engage in the Santa Fe trade.

1827: Traders of Franklin and points east rendezvous at Blue Springs near Independence, Missouri.

Population of Santa Fe about 5,790; of San Miguel del Vado, about 2,900.

Fort Leavenworth, Kansas, begun.

Traders return to Franklin with about 800 mules, jacks and jennies.

1828: A returning wagon train lost 1,000 mules to Indians.

New Franklin, Missouri, laid out.

1829: Major Wetmore recommended use of oxen as draft animals on the Road. Military escort of annual caravan to the Upper Crossing of the Arkansas River.

1830: Traders rendezvous at Blue Springs, Missouri.

1831: Jedediah Smith killed by Comanches at Lower Cimarron Spring (Kansas).

Traders rendezvous at Council Grove (Kansas).

Gallinas (Las Vegas, New Mexico) has one house.

1832: Washington Irving began "A Tour of the Prairies."

Cholera everywhere.

Traders return with about 1,350 mules, jacks and jennies.

1833: Bent's Fort on the upper Arkansas completed. Traders rendezvous at Lone Elm (Kansas).

About 100 traders return to Franklin, Missouri, with estimated $80,000 in species and a large number of mules and bales of furs.

West Port, Missouri, now a settlement.

1834: About 125 wagons of trade goods left Franklin for Santa Fe. Some returned loaded with wool.

First printing press to New Mexico for "La Crepusculo."

1835: Asiatic cholera everywhere. Traders return to Franklin with estimated $200,000 in specie and about as much in mules, furs and other goods.

1836: John A. Sutter (later of Sutter's Mill, California) engaged in trade at West Port, Missouri.

Texas declared itself a Republic, independent of Mexico.

Blue Mill on Little Blue River, Missouri.

1837: Texas independence recognized by the United States.

1838: St. Louis, Mo. *Argosy:* "There arrived here yesterday a wagon from Chihuahua, via Santa Fe, with $50,000 in bullion and $30,000 in specie."

1839: Thomas J. Farnum and party of 15 left Independence, Missouri, for Oregon. New placer mines opened in the Ortiz Mountains south of Santa Fe.

1840: Beaver skins sell for $4.00 a pound (about $10.00 a skin), with 80 skins to the hundred-pound bale.

1841: Expedition of 320 Texans from Austin to Santa Fe ended in disaster.

1843: Col. Snively from Texas raided commerce on the Road to Santa Fe.

Capt. Cooke commanded a military escort of wagons to the frontier and disarmed Snively.

1844: June 13-16 terrific rainfall; Missouri River five to six miles wide.

A yoke of oxen sell for about $45 in Kansas City.

1845: During the summer, Lt. J. W. Abert scouted a route beyond the Upper Crossing of the Arkansas and across Raton Pass in

Mexican Territory. October: President Polk ordered the "Army of Observation" to Corpus Christi, Texas.

December: Polk announced annexation of Texas.

Fort Mann, near Dodge City.

1846: May: James Buchanan declared state of war between Mexico and United States. Army of the West organized by Capt. Kearney at Ft. Leavenworth. August 12: Army of the West (about 3,000 men) reached Santa Fe. Mexican militia, armed with bows, arrows, and a few muskets, offered no opposition.

At Council Grove (Kansas) a Government blacksmith shop.

Estimated 100,000 buffalo hides reached eastern markets.

At Wayne City Landing, Missouri, Francis Parkman began "The Oregon Trail."

1847: Charles Bent, first Governor of New Mexico Territory, scalped at Taos.

Boon & Hamilton trading post at Council Grove.

1848: Gold discovered at Sutter's Mill, California.

Population of Kansas City about 700.

During the summer, 12,000 persons and 50,000 head of livestock passed Fort Mann (Dodge City, Kansas) on the Road to Santa Fe.

Treaty of Guadalupe-Hidalgo.

1849: From Independence, Missouri, about 20,000 left for California gold fields, some via the Road to Santa Fe.

Military pony-express from Ft. Leavenworth to Santa Fe, 16-20 days one way. Barclay and Doyle Fort at Mora-Sapello River junction.

About 110,000 buffalo hides sold in St. Louis.

Independence, Missouri population about 1,600.

1850: Waldo, Hall & Company establish monthly stage and mail line, Kansas City to Santa Fe. Massacre of mail stage at Wagon Mound, New Mexico. Fort Atkinson completed at future Dodge City. Fort Mann abandoned.

1851: Cholera epidemic. Kansas City population reduced from 700 to 300.

Fort Union, New Mexico completed.

1852: William Bent destroyed Bent's Fort on the upper Arkansas River.

1853: California produced estimated $70 million in gold. David Merriwether appointed Governor and W. H. H. Davis Attorney General of New Mexico Territory.

Monthly stage from Santa Fe to San Antonio, Texas.

Exclusive of soldiers, not more than 500 Americans in all New Mexico Territory.

Bent's New Fort completed opposite modern Prowers, Colorado, on Arkansas River.

Fort Atkinson (Dodge City) abandoned.

More than 100,000 sheep driven from New Mexico to California markets.

Estimated 400,000 buffalo killed for hides on the upper Missouri River.

1854: Smallpox and Indians are the hazards of the Road this year. Col. P. G. Lowe reported route over Raton Pass abandoned. Fort Atkinson (Dodge City) reoccupied for four months.

1855: Kansas Territory in turmoil; many caravans attacked by abolitionists. Allison & Booth trading post at Walnut Creek Crossing (Kansas).

1856: First steam engine freighted over the Road to Placer (Ortiz) Mountains, N. Mex.

1857: Semi-monthly stage from Kansas City to Santa Fe.

1858: Gold at Cherry Creek (Denver), Colorado Territory. This season, for Santa Fe via Council Grove, Kansas, 1872 wagons, 67 carriages, 15,714 oxen, 5,316 mules, 429 horses.

1859: Twenty-five wagons of wool from Santa Fe arrived at Kansas City this season. Yoke of oxen sell for $50 to $75. Fort Larned completed on Pawnee Fork in Kansas.

1860: About 25 wagons leave Kansas City each week bound for Cherry Creek (Denver) gold fields. Fort Fauntleroy (=Ft. Wise = Ft. Lyon) completed on Arkansas River opposite modern Prowers, Colorado.

1861: From Council Grove, Kansas during week ending May 4th: For California: 16 wagons, 93 oxen, 12 horses, one mule, 75 men, women and children. For Santa Fe: 20 wagons, 106 oxen, 9 mules, 38 men. Ruins of Bent's Old Fort converted to stage station on route over Raton Pass by Overland Mail and Express Company.

1862: Gen. Sibley, out of Texas, captured Santa Fe. Confederates defeated at Glorieta Pass (N. Mex.); by this the gold of California was preserved for the Union.

1863: Three camels sold at St. Louis for $545. Archduke Maximilian of Austria made ruler of Mexico, by Napoleon III of France.

1864: C. E. & W. J. Musick passed Council Grove with 20 head of Brahma cattle for Chihuahua. Fort Zarah completed near future Dodge City. By end of year UPRR opened to Lawrence, Kansas. Fort Larned abandoned.

1865: Fort Aubrey completed on Arkansas River, above Upper Crossing on the Mountain Branch. Henry M. Stanley at Walnut Creek Post. Camp Nicols, (Oklahoma Panhandle). Ft. Dodge near Dodge City.

1866: Toll gate opened in Raton Pass on the Mountain Branch. RR at Topeka and Junction City. All wagons from here now. Ft. Aubrey abandoned.

1867: New Fort Lyon at Junction of Purgatoire with Arkansas River. Ft. Fauntleroy (= Ft. Wise = Ft. Lyon) abandoned.
1868: Collection of buffalo bones for fertilizer begun. Estimated that by 1881, bones of 31 million buffalo freighted to Kansas City.
Christopher Carson died at New Fort Lyon.
By treaty of Medicine Lodge (Kansas) Indians would remain south of the Arkansas River and no whites would be allowed in that region.
1869: Ft. Zarah abandoned; Ft. Lyon abandoned.
William Bent died at his ranch at confluence of the Purgatoire and Arkansas Rivers.
1870: Ceran St. Vrain died, Mora, New Mexico.
1871: More than 250,000 buffalo hides sold in St. Louis.
1872: By the end of the year, AT&SF RR five yards into Colorado along the Arkansas River.
1877: This winter more than 100,000 buffalo hides taken in December-January on the Texas range, the area from which whites were prohibited.
This is the last winter of the "Big Hunt."
1878: By the end of the year AT&SF RR at New Mexico line.
1880: February 9: First train of AT&SF RR reached Santa Fe—59 years after Becknell.
1884: Buffalo hides sell for $5-$10.
1885: Buffalo hides sell for $25-$75.
1886: Few straggling buffalo killed. Since 1849 an estimated sixty million slaughtered for hide and tongue.

SOURCES

1 Collinson, Frank: *Life in the Saddle*, Univ. Okla. Press, Norman, 1963.

2 Drumm, Stella M.: *Down the Santa Fe Trail and into Mexico: Diary of Susan Shelby Magoffin*, Yale Univ. Press, New Haven, Conn., 1962.

3 Barry, Louise: *Kansas before 1857*, Kan. Hist. Quart. V. 27, 1961, p. 61.

4 Folmer, Henri: *The Mallet Expedition . . .* , Colo. Mag., V. 16, 1939, pp. 161-173.

5 Cox, Isaac J.: *Opening of the Santa Fe Trail*, Mo. Hist. Rev., V. 25, 1930-1931, pp. 30-66.

6 Pike, Zebulon M.: *Journals, Letters . . .* (Jackson, Donald, ed.), Univ. Okla. Press, Norman, 1966.

7 Duffus, R. L.: *The Santa Fe Trail*, Longman, Green & Co., N.Y., 1930.

8 Broadhead, G. C.: *The Santa Fe Trail*, Mo. Hist. Rev., V. 4, 1910, pp. 309-319.

9 Gregg, Kate L.: *The History of Fort Osage*, Mo. Hist. Rev., V. 34, 1939-1940, pp. 439-488.

10 Missouri Intelligencer and Boon's Lick Advertiser, Franklin, Fayette, Columbia, Mo.,

April 23, 1823	(Becknell Journal)
Sept. 29, 1832	(Washington Irving)
April 29, 1826	(losses, payments)
Sept. 2, 1825	(Marmaduke Diary)
Sept. 17, 1822	(no rain)
Oct. 24, 1828	(Capt. John Means)
Sept. 12, 1828	(Capt. Monro)

11 *Missouri*, p. 353, Amer. Guide Ser., Duell, Sloan & Pearce, N.Y., 1941.

12 Thwaites, R. G. (ed),: S. H. Long Expedition, *Early Western Travels*, V. 14, 1905, Arthur H. Clark Co., Cleveland, Ohio.

13 Prucha, Francis P.: *A Guide to Military Posts of the United States*, State Hist. Soc. Wis., Madison, 1964.

14 Frazier, Francis P.: *Forts of the West*, Univ. Okla. Press, Norman, 1965.

15 Wood, D. E.: *The Old Santa Fe Trail from the Missouri River*, E. L. Mendenhall, Kansas City, 1955.

16 Morgan, Dale: *Overland in 1846*, (Pringle diary), V. I, Talisman Press, Georgetown, Calif. 1963.

17 Adams, Franklin G.: *Reminiscences of Frederick Chouteau*, Kan. Hist. Soc. Coll., V. 8, 1903-1904, p. 423.

18 Shumway, George; Durrell, Edward; Frey, Howard C.: *Conestoga Wagon 1750-1850*, George Shumway and Early American Industries Assoc., York, Penn., 1966.

19 Lowe, P. G.: *Five Years a Dragoon*, Univ. Okla. Press, Norman, 1965.

20 Wyman, Walker D.: *Bullwhacking, a Prosaic Profession*, New Mexico, Hist. Rev., V. 7, 1932, p. 297.

21 Custer, Elizabeth B.: *Tenting on the Plains*, Webster & Co., N.Y., 1889.

22 Gregg, Josiah: *Commerce of the Prairie* (Morehead, Max, ed.), Univ. Okla. Press, Norman, 1954.

23 Niles Register, Baltimore, Md., V. 45, November 23, 1833, p. 200.

24 Pritchard, J. A.: *Diary of a Journey from Kentucky to California* Mo. Hist. Rev., V. 18, 1923-1924, pp. 535-545.

25. Webb, James Josiah (Bieber, R. P. ed.): *Adventurers in the Santa Fe Trade*, Arthur H. Clark Co., Glendale, Calif., 1931.

26 Davis, W. W. H.: *El Gringo or New Mexico and her People*, Harper & Bros., New York, 1857.

27 Garretson, Martin S.: *The American Bison*, N.Y. Zoological Soc., 1938.

28 Stephens, F. F. (ed.): *Major Alphonso Wetmore's Diary*, Mo. Hist. Rev., V. 8, pp. 177-197, 1914.

29 Webb, W. L.: *Independence, Missouri, a Century Old*, Mo. Hist. Rev., V. 22, pp. 30-50, 1927-1928.

30 Favor, A. F.: *Old Bill Williams*, Univ. Okla. Press, Norman, 1962.

31 Sibley, George C.: *Route to Santa Fe, Council Grove, &c.*, The Western Journal of Agriculture . . . and General Literature, V. 5, 1850.

32 Gregg, Kate L.: *The Road to Santa Fe*, Univ. New Mexico Press, Albuquerque, 1952.

33 Brewerton, G. Douglas: *Incidents of Travel in New Mexico*, Harper's New Monthly Magazine, Vol. 8, April 1854.

34 Wyman, W. E.: *Kansas City, a Famous Freighter Capital*, Kan. Hist. Quart., V. 6, pp. 3-13, 1937.

35 Brown, Theodore A.: *A Frontier Community, Kansas City to 1870*, Univ. Mo. Press, Columbia, 1963.

36 Bernard, Wm. R.: *Westport and the Santa Fe Trade*, Kan. Hist. Coll., V. 9, pp. 552-565, 1905-1906.

37 Lane, Wm. C.: *Diary* . . . , Hist. Soc. New Mexico, Pub. 20, 1917.

38 Wislizenus, Adolph: *Memoir of a Tour to Northern Mexico*, 30th Cong, 1st Sess. Sen. Misc. Doc. 26, Washington, D.C., 1848.

39 Thwaites, R. G.: *Early Western Travels*, V. 28, 1906, A. H. Clark Co., Cleveland, Ohio.

40 Connelley, Wm. E.: *History of Kansas*, Amer. Hist. Soc., Chicago, 1928.

41 Morgan, Lewis H. (White, L. A., ed.): *The Indian Journals*, Univ. Michigan Press, Ann Arbor, 1959.

42 Haffen, LeRoy R. (ed.): *Windwagon*, Southwest Hist. Ser., V. 10, p. 297, Arthur H. Clark Co., Glendale, California, 1941.

43 Haffen, LeRoy R. (ed.): *Diary of Charles C. Post*, Southwest Hist. Ser. V. 11, pp. 17-55, Arthur H. Clark Co., Glendale, California, 1936.

44 *Kansas*, p. 482, Amer. Guide Ser., Viking Press, N.Y., 1939.

45 Stocking, Hobart E.: *The Camel Brigade*, Nat. Hist. V. 53, p. 396, 1944, Amer. Mus. Nat. Hist., N.Y.

46 Bieber, Ralph P. (ed.): *Journal of a Soldier . . .* (George Rutledge Gibson), Southwest Hist. Ser., V. 3, Arthur H. Clark Co., Glendale, Calif. 1935.

47 Ryus, W. H.: *The Second William Penn*, Riley Pub. Co., Kansas City, Mo., 1913.

48 Bergum, Edwin G.: *The Concord Coach*, Col. Mag., V. 16, p. 173, 1939.

49 Anon.: *Historic Sites and Structures*, Kan. Hist. Quart., V. 23, p. 164, 1957.

50 Bieber, Ralph P. (ed.): *Journal of Marcellus Ball Edwards*, Southwest Hist. Ser., V. 4, 1936, Arthur H. Clark Co., Glendale, California.

51 Spear, Joseph J.: *Reminiscences of the Early Settlement of Dragoon Creek, Waubansee County*, Kan. Hist. Coll., V. p. 345, 1913-1914.

52 Wetmore, Alphonso: *Gazetteer of the State of Missouri*, St. Louis, 1837.

53 Letter, General Wilkinson to Secretary of War, September 8, 1805, Durrett Papers Ms., University of Chicago.

54 Anon., Kan. Hist. Coll., V. 19, p. 565, 1905-1906.

55 Cooke, Phillip St. George: *Journal . . .* , Miss. Valley Hist. Rev., V. 12, pp. 72-98; 227-255.

56 Richardson, Wm. H.: *Journal of a Private Soldier . . .* , Mo. Hist. Rev., V. 22, p. 206, 1927-1928.

57 Shields, Clara M.: *The Lyon Creek Settlement*, Kan. Hist. Coll., V. 64, pp. 143-170, 1915-1918.

58 Marcy, Randolph B.,: *Border Reminiscences*, Harper & Bros., N.Y., 1872.

59 Mead, James R.: *The Little Arkansas*, Kan. Hist. Coll., pp. 7-14, V. 10, 1907-1908.

60 McDermott, J. F. (edit): *Audubon in the Far West*, p. 80. Univ. Okla. Press, Norman, 1965.

61 Denhardt, Robert: *The Beginnings of American Horses*, N. Mex. Hist. Rev., V. 13, p. 255, 1938.

62 Worcester, D. E.: *The Spread of Spanish Horses in the Southwest*, N. Mex. Hist. Rev., p. 255, V. 19, 1944.

63 Houck, Louis: *The Spanish Regime in Missouri*, p. 350-358, V. 1, 1909, Chicago, Ill.

64 Anon. Kan Hist. Quart., V. 23, p. 164, 1957.

65 Peters, D. C.: *Life and Adventures of Kit Carson*, Estes & Lauriat, Boston, 1887.

66 Estergreen, M. M.: *Kit Carson*, Univ. Okla. Press, Norman, 1962.
67 Birch, James H.: *The Battle of Coon Creek*, Kan. Hist. Soc. Coll., V. 10, p. 409, 1907-1908.
68 Unrau, Wm. E.: *The Story of Fort Larned*, Kan. Hist. Quart., V. 13, pp. 257-280, 1957.
69 Walker, Joel P.: *Narrative of Joel P. Walker*, Bancroft Library, Ms. 170, California.
70 Beckwith, E. G.: *Report of Exploration of a Route for the Pacific Railroad . . .* , 33rd Cong., V. 5, Pt. 2, Exec. Docs., 1853-1854, Washington, D.C.
71 Sampson, F. A. (ed.): *The Santa Fe Trail: M. M. Marmaduke Journal*, Mo. Hist. Rev., V. 7, pp. 1-10, 1911.
72 Meriwether, David: *My life in the Mountains and on the Plains*, Univ. Okla. Press, Norman, 1965.
73 Missouri Argus, March 24, 1827, St. Louis, Mo.
74 Sullivan, M. S.: *The Life of Jedediah Smith*, The Pioneer Press, New York, 1937.
75 Odessa Democrat, February 23, 1917, Odessa, Missouri.
76 Bieber, Ralph P. (ed.): *Diary of Phillip Gooch Ferguson*, Southwest Hist. Ser. V. 4, pp. 238-361, Arthur H. Clark Co., Glendale, Calif., 1936.
77 Stocking, Hobart E.: *Roads North*, The Cattleman, V. 38, p. 18, Ft. Worth, Texas, 1952.
78 Tyler, Sergeant Daniel: *A Concise History of the Mormon Battalion . . .* , Rio Grande Press, 1964.
79 Waldo, Wm.: *Recollections of a Septuagenarian*, Mo. Hist. Soc. Pub. 12, St. Louis, Mo., 1880.
80 Emory, Wm. H.: *Notes on a Military Reconnaissance . . .* , 30th Cong., 1st Sess., Sen. Ex. Doc., V. 3, No. 7, Washington, D.C., 1847.
81 McKinnan, Bess: *The Toll Road over Raton Pass*, N. Mex. Hist. Rev., V. 2, p. 83, 1927.
82 Rainey, George: *No Man's Land*, Enid, Okla., 1937.
83 Twitchell, Ralph E.: *Leading Facts of New Mexico History*, V. 1, Cedar Rapids, Iowa, 1911.
84 Abel, Annie H., (ed.): *Official Correspondence of James S. Calhoun*, U.S. Office of Indian Affairs, Washington, D.C., 1915.
85 Seton, E. T.: *Wild Animals I have Known*, Grosset & Dunlap, N.Y., 1898. *Trail of an Artist-Naturalist*, Scribner's Sons, N. Y., 1940.
86 Hodge, F. W.: *A Virginian in New Mexico*, N. Mex. Hist. Rev., V. 4, p. 239, 1929.
87 Pearson, Jim B.: *The Maxwell Land Grant*, Univ. Okla. Press, Norman, 1961.
88 Bancroft, Hubert Howe: *Works: Arizona and New Mexico*, V. 12, San Francisco, 1890.
89 Lavander, David: *Bent's Fort*, Doubleday, Garden City, N.Y., 1954.
90 Grinnell, George B.: *Bent's Old Fort and its Builders*, Kan. Hist. Coll., V. 15, p. 28, 1919-1922.
91 Dick, Herbert W.: *Excavation of Bent's Old Fort*, Col. Mag., V. 33, p. 276, 1956.

92 Anon.: *Soldier and Brave;* Nat. Park Service, p. 22, Harper & Row, 1963.

93 Gerrard, L. H.: *Wa-To-Yah and the Taos Trail,* Univ. Okla. Press, Norman, 1955.

94 Bieber, Ralph P. (ed.): *Diary of a Journey to Pikes Peak Gold Mines in 1859,* Miss. Valley Hist. Rev., V. 14, pp. 360-378, 1927.

95 Spring, Agnes W.: *A Bloomer Girl on Pikes Peak by Julia Archibald Holmes,* Denver Public Library, 1949.

96 Coues, Elliot (ed): *The Journal of Jacob Fowler,* F. P. Harper, New York, 1898.

97 Abert, J. W.: *Journal* . . . , 29th Cong., 1st Sess., Sen. Doc. 48, 1844-1846, Washington, D.C.

98 Lord, Walter: *Myths and Realities of the Alamo,* American West, May 1968, V. 5, No. 3, p. 18, 1968.

99 Bieber, Ralph P. (edit.): *Journal of Abraham Robinson Johnston,* Southwest Hist. Ser., V. 4, pp. 73-106, Arthur H. Clark Co., Glendale, Calif., 1936.

100 Haley, J. Evetts: *Charles Goodnight,* Houghton Mifflin Co., N.Y., 1936.

101 Abert, J. W.: *Report* . . . , 30th Cong., 1st Sess., House Exec. Doc. 31, 1846-1847, Washington, D.C.

102 Conrad, H. L.: *Uncle Dick Wootten,* E. E. Dibble & Co., Chicago, 1890.

103 Simpson, J. H.: *Journal of a Military Reconnaissance from Santa Fe to the Navajo Country,* Univ. Okla. Press, Norman, 1964.

104 Grant, Blanche C.: *When Old Trails were New,* Press of the Pioneers, New York, 1934.

105 *My Dear Cornelia:* Letters by James G. Hamilton, Aug. 26, 1857-April 15, 1858, during an overland trip from West Port, Mo., to California. Compiled and copyrighted 1951 by his granddaughter, Katharine Jones Moore (Mrs. M. G. Moore) of Long Beach, Calif.

106 Laumbach, Verna: *Las Vegas before 1850,* N. Mex. Hist. Rev., V. 8, p. 241, 1933.

107 Utley, Robert M.: *Fort Union National Monument, New Mexico,* Nat. Park Service, Handbook Series No. 35, Washington, D.C.
 : *Fort Union and the Santa Fe Trail,* N. Mex. Hist. Rev., V. 36, pp. 36-48, 1961.

108 Russell, Mrs. Hal: *Memoirs of Marian Russell,* Col. Mag., V. 20, 1943; V. 21, 1944.

109 James, Thomas: *Three Years among Indians and Mexicans* (1846), Lippincott, Philadelphia, 1962.

110 Kendall, George W.: *Narrative of the Texan Santa Fe Expedition,* Lakeside Press, Chicago, 1929.

111 Hoig, Stan: *The Sand Creek Massacre,* Univ. Okla. Press, Norman, 1961.

112 Twitchell, Ralph E.: *Old Santa Fe,* Santa Fe Republican Pub. Co., Santa Fe, New Mexico, 1925.

INDEX

M-1, M-2 etc. indicate map numbers. Map list to be found on p. viii

Abert, Lt. J. W., 256, 260, 262, 272
Abiquiu, N. Mex., 207
Adobe brick, 287
Alamo (Tex.), 257
Albert (slave), 214
Allen, Alfred (Baird, et al.), 10
Alvarez, Don Manuel, 99
Anthony, Maj. Scott J., 340
Anton Chico, N. Mex., 320
Archuleta, Juan, 261, 295
Argus (St. Louis, Mo.), 40
Armijo, Gov. Manuel, 137, 180, 226, 231, 261, 294, 312
Army of the West, 73, 253, 261, 276
Arrow Rock, Mo. (M-1), 10, 13
Atahualpa, 112
Atomic Energy Commission, 329
Aubrey, Francis X., 165, 205, 234
Aull, James, Robt., John, 16, 27
Auriria, Ga., 232

Bache, Richard, 260
Baird, James, 143
Baker, (Tex. Exped.), 320, 324
Baldwin City, Kan. (M-4), 64, 72
Barklay, Alexander, 206, 292
Barcelo, Doña Gertrudes, 352
Barnum, Vail & Vickery, 75
Beale, Lt., 68, 280
Beaubien, Don Carlos, 226
Beaubien-Miranda grant, 309
Becknell, Wm., 5, 6, 10, 25, 31, 195, 251
Beckwith, Lt., 143
Beckwourth, James, 53

Bent, Charles, 112, 204, 240, 282, 341
Bent, George, 240, 341
Bent, Robert, 241, 341
Bent, William, 40, 240, 246, 251
Benton, Senator, 17, 83, 86, 255
Bernal Hill (M-26), 313
Biesman, Henry, 300
Big Blue Camp, Kan.-Mo. (M-3, 4), 61
Big Elk, 214
Big Timers, 243
Black Jack, Kan. (M-4), 64, 72
Black Kettle, 337, 341
Blanco Canyon, Tex., 197
Blue Mills, Mo. (M-3), 56
Boise City, Okla. (M-15), 180, 186
Bois de vache, 98
Boon & Hamilton, 88
Boons Lick, Mo., 6
Boonville, Mo. (M-1), 6
Branson, Colo., 239
Brewerton, George, 54, 142, 351
Broadus, Andrew, 122
Brown, John, 64
Brown, Joseph C., 17, 74, 83
Buffalo, 48, 105, 123
Bullwhacker, 37
Bullwhip, 38
Burlingame, Kan. (M-5), 79
Burnside, Lt. A. E., 290
Burr, Aaron, 23

Caches (M-11), 143, 168
Calhoun, James S., 201, 289

Camels, 67, 69
Camp Nichols, Okla. (M-15), 188, 308
Camp Osage, Kan., 116
Camp Verde, Tex., 68
Cañoncito (M-27), 336
Carson, Christopher, 11, 121, 142, 188, 206, 250, 306
Carson, Nemiah, 125
Cather, Willa, 307
Central City, Colo., 233
Cement, 30
Chacon, Apache Chief, 207
Charbonneau, Jean B., 241
Charleston, Kan. (M-11), 134
Chavez, Don Antonio, 110
Cherry Creek (Denver, Colo.), 232
Chert, 13
Chihuahua, Mex., 37, 154, 326
Chivington, Col. John M., 335
Cholera, 12, 57
Chouteau, August, 87
Chouteau, Francis, 57
Chouteau Island (M-12), 136, 145, 160, 182, 230
Ciboleros, 26, 195, 198
Cicuique, N. Mex., 215
Cienequilla del Barro (M-16), 194
Cimarron Desert (M-12, 13), 134, 145
Cimarron, Kan. (M-11), 134, 146
Cimarron, N. Mex. (M-18), 227, 276
Clayton, N. Mex. (M-16), 190, 207
Clifton House (M-23), 275
Collinson, Frank, 2, 196
Colonel Goodnight Trail (M-22), 268
Colorado Third Regiment, 341
Commissioners, the, 101
Conestoga wagon, 32
Cooke, Capt. Phillip St. George, 90, 136, 292
Coolidge, Kan. (M-19), 176, 238
Cooper, Benjamin, 13, 83, 134, 151
Coronado, Francisco Vasquez de, 111, 327
Council Bluff, Iowa, 214

Council Grove, Kan. (M-6), 75, 88, 151
Council Oak, 88
Cortez, Hernando, 112
Costello, Jack, 95
Creek
    Ash (M-9), 125
    Bear (M-13), 161
    Big John, 90
    Bridge (M-5), 75
    Cherry, 232, 246
    Cold Spring (M-15), 186
    Coon (M-9, 10), 125, 130
    Corrumpa (M-16), 190
    Cottonwood, 45
    Cow (M-8), 51, 67, 111, 115
    Don Carlos (M-17), 113
    Dragoon (M-5), 79
    Dry Turkey (M-7), 101, 104
    Fountain, 232
    Jarvis (Chavez) (M-8), 110
    Louse, 190
    Lyon (M-7), 95
    Marias des Cygnes (M-4, 5), 172
    M'Nees (M-16), 190
    Mulberry (M-10, 11), 133, 150
    One Hundred Ten Mile (M-5), 75
    One Hundred Forty-two Mile (M-5), 82
    Onion (M-5), 82
    Prairie Chicken (M-5), 82
    Rabbit Ears (M-16), 290
    Rock, Kan. (M-6), 74, 82
    Running Turkey (M-7), 101
    Sand, Colo., 341
    Sand, Kan. (M-12, 13), 148, 337
    Soldier (M-5), 79
    Sora Kansa (M-7), 101
    Sweet Water (M-26), 226
    Terrebeau, Gros, Petit (M-2), 16
    Timpas (M-21, 22), 231, 262
    Turkey (M-17), 51, 101
    Ute (M-17), 201
    Wakarusa (M-4), 72
    Walnut (M-9), 45, 104, 120

Whetstone (M-17), 200
Wildhorse (M-19), 238
Crossman, Maj. G. C., 67
Cuesta, N. Mex., 323
Curtis, Gen., 340
Cuzco, Peru, 113

Dakota sandstone, 122, 146, 168, 172, 180, 212, 238
Davis, W. W. H., 61, 90, 125, 196, 316
Dawson, Lewis, 253
Dearborn, Sec. War, 255
Delassus, Carlos D., 24
Denver, Colo., 79
Denver, James W., 232
Dodge City, Kan. (M-11), 137
Dodge, Gen., 120
Don Carlos, 201
Don Carlos Hills (M-17), 195, 208
Doniphan's Brigade, 184, 235
Doyle, Joseph, 292
Dry route (M-10), 125
Dundee, Kan. (M-9), 125
Dunn, Isaac, 206
Durham, Kan. (M-7), 45, 98
Durocher, Laurent, 7

Easton, Col., 130
Edwards, M. B., 266, 312
El Amigo del Pais, 235
Element "S", 328
Elkhart, Kan. (M-14), 169
Ellenwood, Kan. (M-9), 116
El Morro, N. Mex., 280
El Vado de las Piedras (M-18), 100, 168, 212, 343
Emory, Lt., 266
Ensign, Kan. (M-11), 133
Espinosa, Vincente, 113
Evans, John, 337, 340, 342

Factory (trading post), 17
Farnham, Thomas J., 63

Ferguson, Phillip G., 172
Fitzpatrick, Maj., 142
Folsom, N. Mex., 239, 269
Ford, Kan. (M-10), 133
Fort
  Adobe Walls, Tex., 242
  Atkinson (M-11), 142
  Barclay's (M-25), 67, 250
  Bent's (M-20), 58, 136, 184
  Bent's New (M-20), 243, 250
  Cooper's (M-1), 12
  Dodge (M-11), 139, 189
  Larned (M-9), 125, 130
  Leavenworth (M-3), 17, 37, 82, 126, 340
  Lyon (M-20, 21), 250, 340
  Mann (M-11), 126, 142
  Osage (M-2), 6, 10, 12, 15, 26
  Sumpter, Car., 335
  Sutter's, Calif., 142
  Tejon, Calif., 69
  Union (M-25, 26), 189, 302, 336
  Wise, 250
  Zarah (M-9), 104, 120
Fowler, Jacob, 252, 279
Franklin, Mo. (M-1), 6, 11, 26, 342
Fremont, Gen., 280

Gallinas (M-24), 276, 295
Garden City, Kan. (M-12), 151
Gardner, Kan. (M-4), 63
Gibson, George, 105, 242
Gladstone, N. Mex. (M-17), 208
Glenn, Col. Hugh, 252
Globe, Kan. (M-4, 5), 74
Glorieta Mesa (M-27), 336, 342
Glorieta Pass (M-27), 312, 326, 342
Gonzalito Mesa (M-18), 276
Goodnight, Col. Charles, 268, 276
Governor's Palace, 216, 343
Granada, Colo. (M-19), 239
Grand Pass, Mo. (M-1), 15
Great Divide (M-25), 294
Greeley, Horace, 234
Gregg, Josiah J., 87, 191
Gregg, Kate L., 17, 87, 93

Gregory, John, 233
Grier, Major, 206
Guyamo, Cuba, 113
Guymon, Okla., 182
Guyrman, John, 267

Hadji Ali, 71
Hall, James G., 263
Hamilton, Alexander, 23
Hamilton, James G., 293
Harper's Ferry, Md., 64
Harrisburg, Penna., 31
Hay's Tavern, 89
Hearn, Sheriff William, 310
Hickory Point (M-4), 73
Highlands Univ., Las Vegas, 299
Hole-in-Prairie (M-22), 263, 267
Hole-in-Rock (M-22), 263, 266
Holly, Colo. (M-19), 238
Holmes, James, 250
Holmes, Julia Archibald, 247
Horses, 112
Houston, Gen. Sam, 258
Howland, Samuel, 318, 320, 325
Hoxie, N. Mex., 276
Hugoton, Kan., 163
Hundredth Meridian (M-11), 83, 137

Ice Age (Pleistocene), 146, 240
Independence, Mo. (M-3), 5, 14, 27, 56, 342
Indians
  Apache, 128, 142, 205, 289
  Arapaho, 204, 337
  Cheyenne, 204, 337
  Comanche, 7, 103, 113, 128, 142, 154, 181, 204
  Kaw (Kansa, Konza), 82, 101, 102
  Kiowa, 103, 142, 154
  Navajo, 177, 204
  Osage, 82
  Pawnee, 7, 82, 130
  Pueblo, 157, 204

Ute (Utah), 207
Wichita, 112
Ingalls, Kan. (M-11), 144
Irving, Washington, 58

James, Thomas, 318
Jefferson City, Mo., 5
Jemez Pueblo, N. Mex., 327
Jerk-line, 35
Jockey-stick, 35
John Martin Reservoir (M-20), 250
Journal of Commerce, Kan. City., 231

Kansas City, Kan.-Mo. (M-3), 5, 33
Kansas-on-the-River (M-3), 58
Kansas Press (Council Grove), 66, 73
Kearny, Gen. Philip, 230, 294, 312
Keelboat, 30
Kendall, George W., 318
Kern, Robert, 280
Keyes, Okla. (M-15), 188
Kinsley, Kan. (M-10), 126, 133
Kozlowski ranch (M-27), 333
Kroenig, Wm., 67, 293

La Jornada (M-13), 148, 150
La Junta, Colo. (M-21), 230, 232, 240, 263
Lakin, Kan. (M-12, 13), 158, 230
Lamar, Mirabeau B., 319
Lamy, Bishop, 307
Larned, Kan. (M-9), 125
Las Animas, Colo. (M-21), 253, 270
Last Chance store, 89
Las Vegas (M-25, 27), 5, 216, 225, 254, 296
La Lour, Archbishop Jean, 307
Lawrence, Kan. (M-4), 64
Leadville, Colo., 115
LeLande, Jean B., 7, 10, 24

Lewis and Clark, 7, 24
Lewis, Capt. Wm. P., 323
Lexington, Mo. (M-2), 15
Liberty (Mo.) *Tribune*, 231
Lincoln, Abraham, 346
Lone Elm (M-4), 62
Long, Major S. H., 15, 256
Lorenzen, Henry, 212
Louisiana, Kan. (M-4), 73
Love, Lt., 131
Lowe, Col. P. G., 94, 142, 239
Lower Crossing (M-10), 133
Lucas, Charles, 218
Luston, Mary Jane, 102
Lyons, Kan. (M-20), 105, 111

Magoffin, James W., 61, 261, 294
Magoffin, Susan, 3, 48, 78, 88, 123,
    254, 266, 272, 286, 296, 318, 328,
    351
Manna, 169
Maps (see list p. viii)
Marmaduke, M. M., 15, 160, 212,
    295, 318
Martinez, Governor, 346
Mather, 87, 88
Maxwell, Lucien, 226, 242, 276, 300
McAllister, Matt, 225
McLanahan, 10
McPherson, Kan. (M-7), 49, 51,
    101, 105
Means, Capt. John, 181
Melgares, Don Facundo, 7, 215
Mendinueta, Pedro de, 220
Merchandise, trade goods, 46
Meriwether, David, 151, 166, 214,
    216, 290, 307, 346
Meteors, 41
Metoyer, Jeannot, 7
Middle Crossing (M-11), 134, 138,
    144, 146, 165
Miranda, Guadalupe, 226
Missionary Ridge, 44
Missionary Road, 56
Missions (M-3), 56, 90
Missouri Batallion, 184

Missouri Intelligencer, 6, 31, 40,
    110, 191
Mitchell, Colonel, 353
Monro, Capt. Daniel, 191
Montezuma, 328
Montoya ranch (M-27), 336
Mora plains, 26
Morley, Colo., (M-23), 274
Mormon Batallion, 180
Morrison, William, 7, 24
Mountain Branch (M-12, 22-25),
    176, 229, 234, 246, 253, 268, 276,
    282, 286
Mountain men, 51, 63, 227
Muleskinner, 37

Nacimiento Mts., 328
Narrows, the (M-4), 72
National Road (M-14, 19), 176, 185
New Santa Fe, Mo., Kan. (M-3,
    4), 61, 75
Nine Mile Ridge (M-11), 146
No Man's Land, 182, 185
North Bend (M-9), 45, 112, 120,
    134

Oaxaca, Mex., 113
Oklahoma, Panhandle, 5, 176, 182,
    308
Olathe, Kan., 66
Onate, Don Juan de, 195
Oregon Trail (M-3), 58
Osage Trace (M-1, 2), 6, 10, 15, 56
Osnaburg, 34
Overbrook, Kan. (M-5), 74
Owens Landing (M-3), 27
Owens, Samuel C., 27
Owl Woman, 241

Padilla, Padre Juan de, 111
Paleolithic man, 240
Palmyra, Kan., 64
Pappan's ferry, 82
Parkman, Francis, 58, 74

Pate, Henry, 64
Patton, Nathaniel, 50
Pawnee Rock (M-9), 122, 126, 168, 230
Pease, Governor, Tex., 154
Pecos Village (M-27), 215, 326, 333
Peppard, Samuel, 66
Peralta, Gov. Pedro de, 344
Peyton, John R., 218, 224
Picketwire Valley (M-21), 270
Pigeon's ranch, 336
Pike, Lt. Zebulon, 7, 24
Pikes Peak, 79, 232, 250
Pikes Peak Hoax, 232
Pizarro, Francisco, 112
Plum Buttes, 51, 115
Point-of-Rock (M-17), 201, 207
Polk, James K., 257
Pope, Colonel, 239
Porter, Lt. D. D., 67
Post, Charles, 66, 246
Post Office Oak, 88
Prairie flies, 48, 60, 64
Pretty Encampment (M-19), 239
Price, Colonel, 353
Prowers, Colo. (M-20), 243
Pueblo Analco, 349

Quartz, Arizona, 71
Quivera (M-8), 112, 115

Rabbit Ears Mt. (M-16), 194
Raton Mesa (M-23), 274
Raton Mt. (M-23), 26
Raton Pass (M-23), 26, 184, 231, 269
Rayado, N. Mex. (M-18), 226, 283
Reeves, 87
Rendezvous, of caravans, 41, 44
Rhyolite (Nev.) *Journal*, 70
Richardson, William H., 125
Riley, Maj. Bennet, 37, 182
River
    American, Calif., 59, 142, 232
    Arkansas (M-9, 20), 25, 100, 116, 146, 238

Big Blue (M-3, 4), 60
Brazos, Tex., 103
Cañadiano (Canadian) (M-17, 23), 100, 103, 224
Canadian, N. Fork (M-16), 114, 161
Cimarron (M-13), 54, 114, 137, 174
Colorado (Tex.), 102, 113
Cottonwood (M-7), 98, 100
El Rio de Las Animas Perdidas en Purgatorio (M-21, 22), 26, 184, 231, 270
Rio Jemez, 327
Kansas, 82
Little Arkansas (M-8), 48, 105
Little Blue (M-2, 3), 27
Missouri (M-1, 2), 6, 10
Mora (M-25), 291, 293
Neosho (M-6), 51, 83, 98, 131
Nepestle, 111
Pawnee Fork (M-9), 54, 100, 125, 130
Pecos (M-27), 224, 334
Red (Tex.), 103, 137, 356
Rio Colorado (Canadian) (M-18), 213
Rio Conejos, 10, 24
Rio Gallinas (M-25, 27), 295
Rio Grande, 10, 219, 327
Rio Ocate, 278
Rio San Fernando de Taos (M-24), 278
Rio de Santa Fe (M-27), 342
Rio Sapello (M-25), 312
Snibar, Big, Little (M-2), 16
Cheval aux Heber, Gros, Petit (M-2), 16
St. Peter and St. Paul, 111
Verdegris, 252
Wichita, 103
Robinson, Abraham J., 266
Robinson, Dr. John H., 24
Rolla, Kan. (M-14), 163
Rosenbury, of Tex. Expedit., 320, 325
Round Mound (M-16), 113, 194

Royall, Lt., 126
Russell, Lt. Richard D., 189, 306
Russell (Majors & Waddell), 16
Russell, Marian, 189, 227, 306

Sacajawea, 241
Salezar, Demasio, 323, 326
Saligney, M. de, 260
San Fernando de Taos (M-24), 84
Sangre de Cristo Mts. (M-24), 84, 216, 276, 282
San Miguel del Vado (M-27), 224, 254
Santa Anna, Gen. of Mex., 257
Santa Fe, N. Mex. (M-27), 343, 347
Santa Fe Republican, 59, 67
Santa Fe *Weekly Gazette*, 207
Sargo, Francisco, 135
Seton, Ernest T., 208
Short-grass country, 48, 115
Sibley, George C., 17, 74, 82, 101, 158, 194, 278
Sibley, Gen. H. H., 336
Sibley, Mo. (M-2), 21
Sierra Grande, 190, 194
Simpson, Lt. J. H., 280
Smith, Jedediah, 161, 165
Snively, Colonel, 137, 292
Soule, Lt. Silas S., 341
South Bend (M-10), 125, 133
South Park, Colo., 116
South Pass, Wyo., 63
Spanish Peaks, 246
Speyer, Albert, 177
Spring
  Aubry, 234
  Big John (M-6), 87, 90
  Cedar, 168, 188
  Cold (M-15), 168, 184
  Diamond (M-6), 51, 87, 92
  Emigrant, 59
  Fremont, 90
  Hickory, 73
  Lost (M-7), 95
  Lower Cimarron (M-13), 136, 148, 161, 165, 343

  Middle Cimarron (M-14), 172
  Ojo de Bernal (M-27), 254, 313
  Ojo de Gallinas, 295
  Santa Clara (M-25), 287
  Upper Cimarron (M-15), 180
  Wagonbed, 165
  Willow (M-4), 73
Springer, N. Mex. (M-18), 225, 276
Stacey, M. H., 280
Stage, Concord, 76
Stage Station, 75, 105, 212, 227, 251, 263, 287, 312
St. Andrews Mountains, 283
Sterling, Kan., 109
Stillwater, Okla., 182
St. Vrain, Ceran, 136, 240
St. Vrain, Felix, 242
St. Vrain, Marcellin, 240
Sumner, Col. E. V., 142
Sutter, John, 57
Switzler, John, 79

Taos, Pueblo (M-27), 276
Taylor, Zachary, 260
Tecolote, N. Mex. (M-27), 225, 309
Tenochtitlan, Mex., 113
Texas, Panhandle, 183, 196, 206
Texas, Republic of, 257, 259
Texas Trail (M-14, 19), 176, 238
Thatcher, Colo. (M-22), 263
Tlaltizapan, Guatamala, 113
Topeka, Kan., 82
Trail City, Colo., 176
Trinchera Pass (M-17, 20), 269
Trinidad, Colo., 263
Turkey Mts. (M-25, 26), 283, 302
Turnpike, 31
Two Buttes Fork (M-19), 239, 269
Tyrannosaurus rex, 123, 317
Tyrone, Colo., 267

Ulysses, Kan. (M-12, 13), 161
Upper Crossing (M-12), 58, 136, 150, 160

Vaca, Alvar Nunez Cabeza de, 295
Vaca, Luis Maria Cabeza de, 295
Vargas, Don Diego de, 346
Vegas Gap (M-27), 312
Vial, Pierre, 113, 201
Vicario, Father, 307
Vigil, Gregorio, 318, 324
Villanueva, Josef, 113

Wagon Mound, N. Mex. (M-25),
 286
Wakarusa war, 73
Waldo, Hall & Co., 61, 75, 88
Walker, Big John, 59, 90
Walker, Capt. Joe, 135
Walker, Joel, 134
Wallace, Gov. N. Mex., 346
Waner, Bob, 93
Ward-Starkey ranch (M-17), 208
Warfield, Colonel, 292
Warner's ranch, Calif., 293
Waterscrape (M-12), 134, 148, 167,
 256
Watrous, N. Mex. (M-25), 69, 292
Wayne, Lt. H. C., 67, 71
Wayne City landing (M-3), 30
Webb, James, 50, 173, 180, 297
Weston, Samuel, 56
West Port Inn, 59
West Port Landing (M-3), 33, 57

West Port, Mo. (M-3), 56
Wetmore, Maj. Alphonso, 37, 51,
 60, 74, 87, 191, 290
Wet route, 139
White Antelope, Arapaho, 341
White, Mr. & Mrs. J. M., 205
Whitman, Marcus, 63
Wichita, Kan., 25
Wightman, Richard H., 235
Wilkinson, Gen. James, 23, 87
Williams, Old Bill, 101˙
Willing, Dr. George, 247
Willock, David, 184
Willow Bar (M-15), 177, 181
Wilmington, Kan. (M-5), 82
Wilson, Adeline, 154, 307
Windwagon, 66
Wislizenus, Dr. Adolph, 91, 182,
 296
Withington, Mr., 88
Wootton, Dick, 269, 274
Wynkoop, Maj. Edward W., 340

Ximinez, Annette, 218

Yellow Woman, 241, 246

Zuni Pueblo, 280